Ranganathan Series in Library Science, 4

Madras Library Association Publication Series, 26

COLON CLASSIFICATION

Some other books by the author

Anuvarga-suchi-kalpa
Classification and communication
Classified catalogue code
Depth classification
Education for leisure
Elements of library classification
Five laws of library Science
Grantha-adhyayanartha-hai
Granthalaya-prakriya
Heading and canons
Library development plan
Library legislation
Literature for neoliterates
Organisation of libraries
Philosophy of library classification
Prolegomena to library classification
Public library provision and documentation problems
Rural adult education
Social bibliography
Social education literature
Union catalogue of learned periodical publication in South Asia

Ranganathan Series in Library Science

1 *Library movement in India, a symposium*, ed by P N Kalu
2 *Classified catalogue code with additional rules for dictionary catalogue code*, by S R Ranganathan
3 *Library administration*, by S R Ranganathan
4 *Colon classification*, by S R Ranganathan
5 *Social science research and libraries*, ed by S R Ranganathan and Girja Kumar
6 *Library manual*, by S R Ranganathan

COLON CLASSIFICATION

BY

S R RANGANATHAN

BASIC CLASSIFICATION

SARADA RANGANATHAN ENDOWMENT
FOR LIBRARY SCIENCE
Bangalore-560 078

Shiyali Ramamrita Ranganathan

Sixth Edition	1960	Twenty Sixth Reprint	2005
Twenty Fifth Reprint	1999	Twenty Seventh Reprint	2006
Twenty Sixth Reprint	1999	Twenty Eighth Reprint	2007
Twenty Seventh Reprint	1999	Twenty Ninth Reprint	2008
Twenty Eighth Reprint	1999	Thirtieth Reprint Thirty	2010
Twenty Ninth Reprint	2000	First Reprint Thirty	2012
Thirtieth Reprint	2000	Second Reprint Thirty	2014
Fifteenth Reprint	2001	Third Reprint	2015
Sixteenth Reprint	2001	Thirty Fourth Reprint	2016
Seventeenth Reprint	2001	Thirty Fifth Reprint	2017
Eighteenth Reprint	2002	Thirty Sixth Reprint	2018
Nineteenth Reprint	2002	Thirty Seventh Reprint	2019
Twenty First Reprint	2003	Thirty Eighth Reprint	2020
Twenty Second Reprint	2004	Thirty Ninth Reprint	2021
Twenty Third Reprint	2004	Fortieth Reprint	2022
Twenty Fourth Reprint	2005	Forty First Reprint	2023
Twenty Fifth Reprint	2005	Forty Second Reprint	2024

Forty Third Reprint 2025

2:51 N3

qN60

ISBN: 978-81-7000-423-3
Price: Rs.395/-

Published by:
Ess Ess Publications
4831/24, Ansari Road, Darya Ganj,
New Delhi-110 002
Tel. : ***+91 63993 73993***
E-mail: info@essess.net.in
www.essess.net.in
For:
Sarada Ranganathan Endowment for Library Science
#1198, 2nd Main Road, Srirampura 2nd Stage
Mysore-570 023

Printed and Bound in India

To

My Beloved Professor

EDWARD B ROSS

CONTENTS

PREFACE TO EDITION 6

The following are the substantial changes introduced in ed 5, and in this edition. Changes 6 to 8 have been made in this edition. The chapters of the Part "Rules" have been re-arranged and partly re-written in this edition.

1 In view of the re-organisation of the constituent states, a brief alternative schedule of divisions of India is given in chapter 4 of the Schedules. It will take some years for the formation of the districts to be finalised by the new states. Therefore, the details of the old schedule are retained. The new brief schedule is given at the end of the old.

2 Chapter 6 of the Schedules is new. It gives the schedules for Phase, Intra-Facet, and Intra-Array Relations. The two latter concepts lead to some economy in the length of certain kinds of class numbers.

3 The canonical divisions of "N Fine Arts" have been revised. Capitals are used to denote them in the place of numerals. The reason for this revision has been explained in the *Annals of library science*, 2, 1955, 102-103.

4 The schedules for Management and Labour in "X Economics" have been revised. In recent years, a considerable literature has grown on these subjects. Their proliferation continues to be incessant. To meet their pressure, a more versatile scheme has become necessary. A detailed draft has been published in the *Annals of library science*, 3, 1956, 33-64, to elicit suggestions. The brief version of it included in this volume belongs to a relatively stable level.

5 Some substantial additions have been made in the schedules for "Z Law". These have been suggested by the work of classification in progress in the Library of the Ministry of Law of the Government of India.

6 This edition gives a selection from the schedules for second levels of time and space facets, and common energy isolates. For, books appear needing their use.

7 In the light of experience, the subject facet has been brought over from the second to the first level in the second round of the main class Education.

71 A short energy schedule has been added to Nuclear Physics and Nuclear Engineering.

73 To meet existing literary warrant the partially comprehensive main class "NZ Language and Literature" has been formed.

8 To avoid the use of Greek letters in main classes with much literary warrant, η (etah) representing Mining has been replaced by HZ and λ (lamda) representing Animal Husbandry has been replaced by KZ. This change in notation does not disturb the position of the main classes.

Another change is the omission of the details in the schedules for "J Agriculture". It has been found from experience that these details are seldom needed in the classification of books.

The omission of these details is a part of the contemplated re-organisation of this and the future editions of the *Colon classification*. It is proposed to have two stages for it.

The version at stage 1 will contain only such isolates as are sufficient for the classification of Macro Thought embodied in books, taken in general libraries such as pubic libraries and libraries of schools, colleges, and universities. To make demonstration of application to specialised monographs possible, all the isolates appearing in the earlier editions, except those of Agriculture, have been retained.

The version at stage 2 is intended to give the more elaborate schedules necessary for the Depth Classification of Micro Thought embodied in articles in learned periodicals. Minute or depth classification of such articles is necessary to enable the library profession to play its role in the development of research. The profession should do intensive Documentation Service to specialist readers. Documentation service is really exhaustive, expeditious, pinpointed, bibliographical service to specialists, with emphasis on nascent micro thought. Such a service needs as its basis the use of depth classification in international abstracting periodicals, in national documentation lists, and in special bibliographies prepared, from time to time, by research libraries.

To fit any scheme for documentation service, continuous work is necessary, both in the theory and in the application of classification. It is not practicable to work out all at once full schedules for all the classes. To keep pace with the dynamic development of the universe of knowledge, the schedules will have to be ever-growing. Nor will the development be equal in intensity in all classes. Therefore version 2 will have to be issued in separate fascicules for different classes.

In the work being done since 1951 as rapporteur-general to the Committee on the General Theory of Classification of the International Federation for Documentation, considerable experience is being gained in the requirements of Depth Classification. But there are still many unsolved problems, both in the idea plane and in the notational plane. The schedules will have to be worked out jointly by expert classificationists and experts in the classes concerned.

To give an omnibus single volume, embodying all the details for all classes, will be to scare away, from classification, the majority of librarians working in general libraries. It is proposed to publish the depth schedules as separate fascicules of version 2, for the use of librarians specialising as documentalists in particular classes of knowledge.

Version 1 will be basic for all such fascicules. At its relatively smaller depth, its schedules will be sufficiently stable in spite of the turbulance in the universe of knowledge.

Bangalore S R RANGANATHAN
Vijayadasami, 11 Oct 1959

CHAPTER 00

INTRODUCTION

001 Purpose of the Book

The purpose of this book is not to expound the philosophy of classification, or discuss its theory, or provide a practice-book, or furnish a primer. These purposes are served by the author's 1 *Philosophy of library classification*; 2 *Classification and communication*; 3 *Prolegomena to library classification* hereinafter referred to as *Prolegomena*; 4 *Library classification: Fundamentals and procedure*, hereinafter referred to as *Fundamentals*; 5 *Elements of library classification*, hereinafter referred to as *Elements*; 6 K M Sivaraman's *Colon system and its working*; and 7 Palmer and Wells' *Fundamentals of library classification*; 8 Another new book *Practical classification by postulational approach*, hereinafter referred to as *Practical classification*, is in preparation. The aim of the present book is to furnish the schedules of the Colon Classification, and the Rules for constructing the Colon Number for any subject.

002 Enumerative Classification

The Colon Classification differs from the Decimal Classification and the Congress Classification in some fundamental respects. It is their manifest aim to provide ready-made Class Numbers for most subjects. Hence, such manuals consist, for the most part, of the Schedules of Classification. And their Schedules are, by several times, larger than that of the Colon Classification. Each such scheme is called an Enumerative Classification. Colon Classification is not an enumerative scheme.

003 Analytico-Synthetic Classification

0031 Meccano Analogy

In the Colon Classification, ready-made Class Numbers are not assigned to subjects. The schedule in the Colon Classification may be said to consist of certain standard unit-schedules. These correspond to the standard pieces in a meccano apparatus. By combining these standard pieces in different ways, many different objects can be constructed. Even a child knows this. So also, by combining the numbers in the different unit-schedules in assigned permutations and combinations, the Class Numbers for all possible subjects can be constructed. In this scheme, the function of the Colon (:) and other connecting symbols is like that of the bolts and nuts in a meccano set. It is therefore an Analytico-Synthetic Classification.

0032 Mnemonic Quality

One natural result of the method of giving certain standard unit-schedules, rather than ready-made Class Numbers for subjects, is the mnemonic quality inherent in the scheme. After a little experience, the need for looking into the Schedule becomes increasingly small—smaller than in the case of the other Schemes; and this is so even for a specialised monograph requiring a long-drawn-out Class Number. This has become more so in classifying articles or micro thought. This is due to its scheduled and seminal mnemonics.

0033 Rules

The Meccano feature makes it necessary to give, in addition to the unit-schedules, a set of Rules for constructing Class Numbers with the aid of the unit-schedules. The spirit of standardisation has greatly simplified the Rules themselves. The first eight chapters, occupying a major portion of Part 1, bring together many of the general Rules and Devices, and discuss them once for all; with the result that the chapters devoted to the classification of specific subjects gain considerably in brevity and clarity.

004 Minuteness

Another feature of this scheme is the very great minuteness of classification in most of the subjects. Even extremely specialised monographs get individualised in this scheme more easily than in others. Such a detailed classification is quite necessary to provide for all the resources of a library on every subject, however great its intension, being disclosed to readers with the least expenditure of time.

005 Hospitality

In addition to the great minuteness of its classes, this scheme is much more hospitable than any other, owing chiefly to the Devices explained in Chapters 05, 6, and 7 of Part 1. This can be experienced in the schedule of almost every subject.

006 Notation

Further, the notation is completely decimal-fractional. Therefore its elasticity is quite commensurate with the hospitality of the schedules. The length of notation is proportionate to the intention. Thus the Call Number of a common text-book sought by common people will be short—even shorter than in many other schemes.

007 Terminology

The terminology of Focus, Facet, and Phase, first developed in the *Fundamentals*, has been adopted. The canons given in the *Prolegomena* and the principles leading to helpful sequence and given in the *Elements* and the *Prolegomena* and also in Chap 07 and 08 of Part 1 are freely used without any attempt to define them. A full glossary is given in the *Annals of library science*, 5, 1958, 65-112.

008 Parts and Chapters

0081 Part 1: Rules

Chapters 01-04 deal respectively with Call-Number, Class-Number, Book-Number, and Collection Number.

Chapter 05 introduces the concept of Facet and shows the part played by the connecting symbols Colon and other symbols in the construction of Facet Formulae and Class Numbers. It also introduces the concept of Focus and gives the devices by which Foci may be formed in the Facets of Class Numbers.

Chapter 06 gives a list of the contractions used.

Chapters 07 and 08 give the Canons of Classification and the Principles for securing helpful sequence.

Chapter 1 is on Main Classes; and Chapter 2 is on Common Isolates.

Chapters 3 to 5 deal with Time, Space, and Language Isolates. These will be needed in the construction of the Call Numbers of many books. The two former also are Common Isolates.

Chapter 6 introduces the concepts of Phase, Intra-Facet, and Intra-Array Relation. These concepts add greatly to the hospitality of the Scheme.

Chapter 7 deals with Classic Device. This is a special feature of the Colon Classification. It is of great help in organising the classics in Indology and other fields.

The rest of the Chapters are devoted one to each of some of the Main Classes. The rules in these chapters deal only with the peculiarities in the classification of the Main Classes concerned.

0082 Part 2: Schedules

Part 2 gives the schedules of classification. It is also divided into Chapters. Its Chapter 03 gives the schedule of Form Divisions for Book Number. Chapters 1 to 5 give respectively the preliminary schedules of the Main Classes, the Common, the Time, the Space, and the Language Isolates. Chapter 6 gives the schedules for the Phase, the Intra-Facet and the Intra-Array Relations. The schedules for the several Facets of the several Main Classes are given in the remaining Chapters.

The Alphabetical Index to the schedules of Space Isolates and of the Personality Isolates in Botany and Zoology are given in Part 2 immediately after the respective schedules themselves. For, these schedules are long and relatively unfamiliar. Indeed, experience has shown that the index is often consulted for the isolates in these schedules only. Therefore, it is a help to have these schedules and their indexes in juxtaposition. The Alphabetical Index to all the other isolates is given in one Alphabetical Sequence at the end of Part 2.

0083 Part 3: Classics and Sacred Books

Part 3 gives classes and classics in Indology worked out in far greater detail than in other schemes. Books on Indology are numerous, not only in Indian libraries, but also in many foreign ones The Indological schedules will also be of use in classifying Manuscript Libraries. It includes schedules of Sacred Books with special names.

0084 Examples

Part 4 of the second edition gave about 3,000 examples in the form of a classified catalogue without an alphabetical index, in response to requests for illustrations of Colon Numbers. It has now been omitted. Those examples are no longer necessary, since several books containing Colon Numbers have now come out. For example, the *Fundamentals* gives 1,008 graded examples and exercises.

Many examples are also found in the following books of the author:—

1 *Bibliography of reference books and bibliographies;*
2 *School and college libraries;*
3 *Organisation of libraries in India;*
4 *Classification of Hindi literature;*
5 *Classification of Marathi literature;*
6 *Classification of Telugu literature;* and
7 *Library manual.*

Lastly, the printed catalogues and bibliographies, of the Library of the Ministry of Labour and of the Ministry of Law of the Government of India, and of the Madras University Library, are available for those wishing to have ready-made class numbers of different depths.

ANNEXURE

ANNEXURE

To meet the pressing demand for copies of the *Colon Classification,* this reprint of Edition 6 of 1960 is being produced with this Annexure inserted at the end of the preliminary pages, but before the title page of Part 1.

The major change brought into use after 1960 is the changing of the Connecting Symbol for [T] from a 'dot' to a 'single Inverted Comma'. This change is the result of an investigation published in the article *Connecting symbols for space and time in CC* published in *An lib sc.* 8; 1961; 169-112 Users of Colon Classification are requested to note this change. This Annexure contains also corrections of mis-prints and a few minor changes as shown below:

PART I

Page 1.5, Rule 0214: for **Octavising Digit** read **Sectorising Digit;** for **Octave Device** read **Sector Device.**

Note: This change should be made in all the places where these terms occur.

Page 1.8, Rule 0261 (last section): for **Elements ed 2, 1959 chap 8** read **Elements ed 3, 1962, Chap N.**

Page 1.32: At the end of **Rule 05833,** add the following new Rule:

05834 When the evaluation of a class is in respect of some other class, the evaluation digit *g* may be sharpened by (SD).

Page 1.40: At the end of **Rule 086** add the following line: The latest version is in the **Elements** ed 3, Chap N.

Page 1.43, Rule 20: for **V44:255t** read **V44:55'N5t;**

for **X44:9.44t** read **X:9.44'N5t;**
for **Z56:9511t** read **Z56,9511'N5t.**

Page 1.48, Rule 271: Add at the end, "The (CD) number should be preceded by "9". The [P] should be preceded by a comma".

Page 1.48, Rule 272: for **B9.44g2,Kr** read **B9.44,f2,Kr;**
for **D.44,t4,R,13:3:N5** read **D.44,t4,R,12:3'N5;**
and for **B.44f,N.N5** read **B.44, g, 9N'N5.**

Page 1.51, Rule 40: Replace this Rule by the following Rules:

40 The Space Isolates (SI) and the numbers representing them are given in chap 4 of the schedules.

401 The schedule admits of four blocks:

1 Physiographical features;
2 Political divisions;
3 Population clusters; and
4 Orientation divisions.

402 These four blocks can be put in the form of a single telescoped schedule.

403 The often-used political divisions form block 2. They are to be assigned to Zone 2. In other words, the initial digit as well as the first significant digit of each of its (IN) is an Indo-Arabic numeral. They form pages 2.8 to 2.17 of Part 2.

404 Individual localities or population clusters form block 3. They are to be assigned to the Last Sector of Zone 3. In other words, the initial digit of each of its (IN) is a Roman Capital. In fact, the (IN) is got by (AD).

405 The orientation divisions form block 3. They are to be assigned to the Penultimate Sector of Zone 3. In other words, the initial digit of each of its (IN) is the Empty Digit 9 and the second digit is a Roman Capital. The Orientation Divisions are indicated for '1 World'. In this case, they do not form a new level. But when applied to any other political division, they will form a new level.

406 The divisions based on physical features form block 1. They are to be assigned to Zone 1. In other words, the

initial digit of each of its (IN) is a Roman Small.

407 It should be specially noted that in the schedule of (SI), block 2 forms an earlier level in relation to the other blocks. Further, blocks 3 and 4 form earlier levels in relation to block 1. Again, block 3 forms an earlier level than block 4.

Page 1.53, Rules 491 to 494: Replace these Rules by the following Rules:

4A Physical Feature

4A1 Some (SI) forming physical features or Featured Space are given in Zone 1 in page 2.17 of Part 2.

A more detailed schedule of them will be given in a fascicule of the version for Depth Classification. A discussion of the problem and a provisional schedule are given in the *Review of documentation* 24; 1957; 18-28, in the article *Space isolate* secs. 5 to 56. That schedule did not admit of telescoping. This was due to the same connecting symbol " . " having been then used as (CS) for both [S] and [T]. But in 1961 this anomaly was removed by prescribing a single inverted comma as the (CS) for [T]. This is described in the article *Connecting symbols for space and time in CC*, in *An lib sc.* 8; 1961; 69-112. As a result of this, all the four zones of the first array can accommodate (IN) of [S]. In view of this freedom, the initial digit of the (IN) for any physical feature has been made any Roman Small. A discussion of this problem will soon appear in the *An lib sc.*

4A2 A dot is to be inserted as the (CS) before the (IN) of a physical feature if it follows the (IN) of a political division or of a locality of an Orientation Division.

4A21 The geographical area isolate preceding a physical feature isolate is to be the one of the least extension containing the whole of the physical feature being classified.

4A3 A physical feature is to be individualised, when warranted, by (AD).

Examples:-

J.44.*g*1G'N5 Agriculture in the Gangetic Valley in 195-
J.441.*g*1K'N5 Agriculture in the Kaveri Valley in 195-
K:12.44.*g*7V Fauna of the Vindhya Mountains
U8.4*g*7H'N5 Himalayan expeditions brought up to 195-
Y:1.*g*1 River valley civilisation

4A4 It may be repeated that a document dealing with a physical feature in general terms will get only the (IN) of the physical feature without being preceded by the (IN) of a geographical area.

Examples:

U11.*g*7 Cartography of mountains
U4.*d* Anthropo-geography of desert areas
U8.*g*7 Mountaineering

4B Population Cluster

4B1 The (IN) for a population cluster or a Locality is to be got by (AD).

4B2 A dot is to be inserted as (CS) before the (IN) of a population cluster.

4B3 The isolate of the geographical area preceding the isolate of a population cluster is to be that of a country, constituent state, district (county), taluk, etc., depending on the size of the population cluster.

For a village it may have to be a taluk. For a town it may have to be a district or county. For a super-city, it may be sufficient to make it the country. All this will depend further on the subject-context.

Examples:

D88.594.Z'*r*	Street cleaning in Zurich during snow period
D885.594 Z'N5	Street cleaning in Zurich in 195-
T.4411.M'N5	Education in Madras City in 195-
T.4411.MA'N5	Education in Madurai City in 195-
T.44114.S'N5	Education in the town Sirkali in 195-

ANNEXURE

4C Orientation Division

4C1 The (IN) for the orientation divisions are given in the penultimate sector of Zone 3.

4C2 A dot is to be inserted as a connecting symbol before the (IN) of Orientation division, unless it immediately follows the digit "1" for world.

4C3 An orientation division should not ordinarily be subdivided so as to reach any political division or population cluster within it.

4C4 An orientation division may have to follow the population cluster number when warranted.

19E	Far Eastern Countries
44.9W	North Eastern Zone of India
4413.B.9S	Northern Zone of Bangalore.

Page 1.64, Rule 924 (Examples):
for 2:51N3,(2) read 2:51N3,9(2)
for 2;45:6 read 2;44:6
for 234:45:81 read 234;44:81

Page 1.69, Example 5: for **B9.56,g2Gr** read **B9.56,f2,Gr.**

Page 1.104, Example 4: Replace the last digit in the class number by "3".

Page 1.113, Rule T3: Replace this Rule and the examples by the following:

T3 [2p] after Problem Facet

T32 In the case of a book dealing with "2 Curriculum", "3 Teaching technique", "4 Student's work", and "5 Educational measurement"—which are all isolates in [E]—the [2P] schedule is a telescoped one.

T321 In the schedule for[2P] under each of the above

[E] Isolates in chap T of the Schedules, only the first block is given.

T322 The second block belongs to Earlier Level. The isolates in it should be got by (SD).

T322P In the application of (SD) to [2P], the modification in "P Linguistics" given at the end of Chap T of the Schedules should be borne in mind.

Examples:

T: 31	Audio-visual method
T:3(B2)	Method of teaching Algebra
T:3(B2),1	Audio-visual method of teaching Algebra
T15:3(B2),1	Audio-visual method of teaching Algebra in elementary school.
T2:5(C),55	Marking in Physics in secondary schools
T45:4(B),6	Competition in Mathematics among post-graduate students
TN3.44'N5	Basic schools in India brought up to 195-
TN3,15:2(B2)	Curriculum in Algebra for basie elementary schools.

Page 1.115, Rule V319 and **V3191**: Replace these Rules by the following:

V31 In the case of a book dealing with any policy of a State, the amplification of the policy number should be on the analogy of Rule V319 and its sub-divisions.

V319 In the case of foreign policy, the Isolate whose number ends with "19" shall be deemed a Host Class.

ANNEXURE

Host Class V:19
V:190 Facets

Facet	*Term*	(IN) *by*
[P]	Community	(GD)
[P2]	Subject	Enumeration and (SD)

The above two give a schedule of telescoped facets.

V3191 The Isolate in [P] should be the community to which the foreign policy is turned.

V3192 The Isolate in [P2] should be the subject of the foreign policy.

V3193 It can be seen that the schedule of the Isolates by (GD), and by Enumeration, and by (SD) respectively can be deemed to form a single schedule of telescoped facets.

Page 1.116, Rule V9Y7 and Examples: Replace by the following:

V9*y*7 The (CN) for the biography of a person whose importance is due to the part played by him in the development of the history of a geographical area (country, constituent state, locality, etc.) should be got by adding the (ACIN) "*y*7" after the Community (IN) and by sharpening it by (CD), the epoch used being his year of birth.

Examples:

(India is taken as the Mother Country and Great Britain as the Favoured Country).

V1-3,1:3'N3	The functions of the head of the British Empire brought upto 193-
V1N4,2'N5	The executive of the United Nations brought up to 195-
V2:19 (*z*T)'N5	India's disarmament policy brought up to 195-

V2,6: 2'N5	Constitution of Local Bodies in India brought up to 195-
V211: 16 (2) 'N5	Relation, in respect of libraries, of the State Government to the Local Bodies in the Madras State brought up to 195-
V211,M,1: 3'N5	Functions of the Mayor of the Madras City brought up to 195-
V3: 195'N5	Britain's European policy brought up to 195-
V3: 195, (X) 'N5	Britain's European economic policy brought up to 195-
V3: 2: (Z) 'N5	British constitutional law brought up to 195-
V41: 710bQ4	Buddhist archaeology of China
V53*y*7L49	Life of Mirabeau
V53*y*7L69	Life of Napolean
V5 (W4) ,3: 3'N5	Functions of legislature in the European monarchies brought up to 195-
V6-52'N3	History of the Italian possessions in Africa brought up to 193-
V73*y*7N17	Life of Kennedy

PART 2

Page 2.17: Replace **Section 42** by the following:

Physical Features

a	Geosphere	*g*7	Mountain
*e*5	Delta	*j*	Hydrosphere
*e*6	Island	*p*1	River
f	Forest	*p*6	Lake
*g*1	Valley	*r*	Ocean

Telescoping Point
Political Divisions
Earlier Level

ANNEXURE

Page 2.88, From M3 to end of column 1: Replace by the following:

M2 Carpentry
M3 Smithy
M5 Glass industry
M7 Textiles

M7 [P]; [M]: [E] [2P]

Foci in [P]

1 Yarn
2 Rope
3 Cloth
4 Knit fabric
5 Carpet

Foci in [M]

1 Cotton
2 Wool
3 Silk
4 Flax
5 Coir
6 Hemp
7 Jute
8 Sisal
9 Other similar fibres
998 Metal

Foci in [E]
if no [P]

1 Sorting
2 Ginning
3 Baling
4 Scouring
5 Carding
6 Oiling
7 Washing

Foci in [E]
if there is [P]

1 Spinning
2 Twisting
3 Weaving
4 Knitting
5 Bleaching
6 Sizing
7 Printing
8 Dyeing

M8 Dress-making
M92 Masonry
M95 Photography
M97 Leather industry
M98 Packaging
MA Home and hotel science

Foci in [P]

2 Maintenance
3 Cooking
4 Serving
7 Beauty culture

Page 2.96, Column 2: Omit the last 3 lines

In page 2.108, replace the seven entries "191 Diplomacy" to "1954 Disarmament" by the following:

Host Class
V:19 Foreign Policy

Foci in **(P)** by **(SD)** and the following:

Additional Foci

(zA) World affairs
(zB) Diplomacy
(zD) Espionage
(zE) Cold war
(zF) Clash
(zG) Aggression
(zJ) Neutrality
(zK) Non-alignment

(zL) War and peace
(zM) War
(zN) Offence
(zP) Defence
(zQ) Peace
(zR) Armament and disarmament
(zS) Armament
(zT) Disarmament

COLON CLASSIFICATION

BY

S R RANGANATHAN

PART I

RULES

SARADA RANGANATHAN ENDOWMENT
FOR LIBRARY SCIENCE
Bangalore 560 078

The Five Laws of Library Science

1. Books are for use.
2. Books are for all; or Every reader his book.
3. Every book its reader.
4. Save the time of the reader.
5. A library is a growing organism.

ग्रन्थालय-शास्त्र-पञ्च-सूत्राणि

ग्रन्थालयी सदा-सेवी पञ्च-सूत्री परायणः ।

ग्रन्था अध्येतुम्-एते च सर्वेभ्यः स्वं स्वम्-आप्नुयुः ॥

अध्येतुः समयं शेषेत्-आलयो नित्यमेव च ।

वर्धिष्णुरेष चिन्मूर्तिः पञ्च-सूत्री चिरं जयेत् ॥

CHAPTER 01

CALL NUMBER

01 The **Call Number** of a book unit is the symbol used to fix its position relatively to other books.

The most helpful arrangement of books in a library is the classified arrangement on a subject-basis. This has been shown in the *Five laws of library science*. Subject-approach is the most common approach to books among readers. Literature may look an exception. But it is not really so. For an author becomes a class or subject in Literature. In Literature even a work becomes a class or subject. A sacred book in Religion also becomes a class or a subject. So also any classic in any subject whatever can be made into a class or a subject. This is shown in Chapter 7 of the Rules. This is also discussed in Chapter 62 of the *Prolegomena*, ed 2. Classes of this kind are called Quasi Classes. A classified arrangement on a subject-basis will facilitate the finding of his book by every reader, increase the chance of every book getting its reader, and also save the time of the reader. Thus all the Five Laws of Library Science will be fulfilled.

In some libraries books are placed permanently in particular shelves; and their positions are indicated by Press-Marks. In such a rigid arrangement it will not be easy to bring together all the books on the same subject, as the library adds new books and grows. Fixing the position of a book relative to the other books rather than in relation to the shelves is the only helpful method.

010 The **Call Number** of a book individualises it.

In some schemes and even in some libraries the Call Number does not actually individualise a book; that is, more than one book may have the same Call Number. It is desirable to remove this ambiguity and satisfy the Canon of Book Number; and it is not difficult to do so.

It is not enough if the subject of a book or its position is indicated in ordinary words. Then the daily arrangement of books will require the services of persons who know the relative sequence of all the subjects and their subdivisions. It is impracticable and uneconomical to get the services of such persons. Hence the name of the specific subject of each book should be translated into a distinctive ordinal number so that the arrangement of specific subjects becomes mechanical; and there should be an additional ordinal number by which all the books in the same specific subject can also be arranged among themselves in a mechanical way.

011 The **Call Number** may be used by readers in calling for a book.

In libraries not adopting 'open access' system, the Call Number is used to "call" for the book.

012 The **Call Number** consists of three parts—**Class Number, Book Number,** and **Collection Number**.

013 A double space should separate the Book Number from the Class Number, except in the cases provided for by Rule 0131.

Examples:—B43 N26 C56 113N29 L3 *p*7N52

0131 On the spine of the book and on the back of the title-page, the Book Number may be written below the Class Number.

Examples:—	B43	C56	L3
	N26	113N29	*p*7N52

014 Collection Number may be written above the Class Number wherever necessary.

CHAPTER 02

CLASS NUMBER

02 The **Class Number** of a book is a translation of the name of its specific subject into the artificial language of ordinal numbers specified and elaborated in the rest of this book.

Part 1 of the *Fundamentals* discusses the need for an artificial language of ordinal numbers. It also lays down the essential qualities which such a language should have. It uses the term Classificatory Language to denote such an artificial language and the term Colon Language to denote the artificial language made up of the Class Numbers of the Colon Classification.

020 The **Class Number** of a book thus becomes the symbol used to fix the position of its specific subject relatively to other subjects.

021 A **Class Number** consists of an intelligible concatenation of one or more of the following symbols:—the ten Indo-Arabic numerals; the twenty-six capital letters of the Roman alphabet; the twenty-three small letters of the Roman alphabet got by omitting *i*, *l* and *o*; some Greek letters, the punctuation marks, circular brackets, and horizontal arrows.

Intelligible concatenation means intelligible in the light of and in accordance with the schedules and the rules framed for the purpose and given hereinafter.

0211 The digit "0", the punctuation marks, and the arrows will occur only as connectives or conjunctions in the Colon Language. They are called **Connecting Symbols.**

0212 The brackets serve a special purpose. This is explained in section 0583 of the Rules. The first bracket " (" is called **Starter**. The second bracket ") " is called **Arrester**.

0213 The numerals 1 to 9 and the letters of the alphabet are called **Substantives** in the Colon Language.

0214 The digit 9 is called an **Octavising Digit.**

The result of this is that the following numbers are co-ordinate though they have a different number of digits in them.

1	2	3	...7	8	91	92	93...	97	98
991	...	992	993	...	997	998	9991	992	...

This method provides for an infinity of co-ordinate numbers in an array or great hospitality in array. It is denoted by the term "Octave Device". In 1948, I recommended the adoption of this in UDC. It has now been adopted. The Octave Notation gives satisfaction to the Canons of Hospitality in Array. The hospitality is really infinite.

0215 *z* and Z also may be used as octavising digits.

0216 The other substantives are called **Significant Digits.**

022 Each one of the symbols in a Class Number will be called a **Digit**.

023 The Digits are written from left to right.

024 The place-value of a Digit is as in a decimal-fraction.

The decimal-fraction notation invests the notation with great hospitality in chain. In other words, any number of numbers can be interpolated between two consecutive numbers. For example, if 22 and 23 are read as integers, we cannot interpolate another integer between them. But if they are read as decimal fractions, 221, 222............229 lie between them. Again 2211, 2212..... also lie in that interval. In fact an infinity of numbers lie in that interval and they can all be interpolated as and when required.

The addition of a digit on the right does not in any way affect the place value of the digits existing already. On the other hand, if the numbers are used as integers, it would completely change their place-values.

The Decimal-Fraction Notation gives satisfaction to the Canon of Hospitality in Chain. The hospitality is really infinite. It also secures conformity to the Canon of Relativity.

025 The **Substantive Digits** used in constructing Class Numbers shall be taken to fall in the following sequence when arranged in the ascending sequence of absolute value:

a b c d e f g h j k l m n p q r s t u v w x y z 1 2 3 4 5 6 7 8 9 A β B Γ C D E F G H I J K L M μ Δ ν N O P Q R S Σ T U V W X Y Z.

In this book, Roman smalls are printed in italics to make them stand out clearly. This is not essential. In particular, they need not be underlined if the call number is written by hand or type-written.

0251 Any number followed by a Roman small or an arrow shall have precedence over the original number.

This rule endows small letters and arrows with **anteriorising value.**

Examples:—B63*a* has precedence over B63. L23:45*a* has precedence over L23:45. N ← M has precedence over N.

0252 The **Connecting Symbols** shall be taken to fall in the following sequence when arranged in the ascending sequence of absolute value.

← → 0 . : ; , –

0253 The absolute value of any **Connecting Symbol** is less than that of any Substantive Digit. In other words it is less than that of *a*.

0254 The absolute value of the **Starter** is greater than that of Z.

0255 The absolute value of the **Arrester** is less than that of ←.

0256 The arrows may have to be used only in Depth Classification in Documentation Work for specialist readers.

0257 Notwithstanding the rules 0252 and 0253, the ordinal value of a 0 occurring in a year, or decade, or century number lies between those of *z* and 1.

026 The process of assigning the Class Number to a document is Classifying or Classification. It is equivalent to translating the name of the subject of the document from a natural language to the artificial language of ordinal numbers, forming Classificatory language.

0261 **Classifying** a document consists of the following steps in succession.

Step 0 Raw Title (=Title as found in the document).

Step 1 Full Title (=Title expressing each of the relevant basic and isolate ideas in the subject of the document, got by filling up all the ellipses in the Raw Title).

Step 2 Kernel Title (=Full Title minus all the auxiliary or apparatus words and with each composite term denoting a composite idea replaced by the fundamental constituent terms denoting its fundamental constituent ideas).

Step 3 Analysed Title (=Kernel Title with each kernel term marked by a symbol, denoting the fundamental category of which the idea denoted by the term is a manifestation and also the round and the level to which it is assigned in conformity to the Postulates of Classification).

Step 4 Transformed Title (=Analytical Title with the kernel terms re-arranged according to the symbols of analysis attached to them).

Step 5 Title in Standard Terms (=Transformed Title with the kernel terms replaced, wherever necessary, by their respective equivalents as given in the appropriate schedules).

Step 6 Title in Facet Numbers (=Title in Standard Terms with the kernel terms replaced by their equivalent numbers).

Step 7 Class Number (got by removing the symbols of analysis and inserting the appropriate Connecting Symbols between the facet numbers in accordance with the Rules).

Step 8 may be added to translate the synthesised class number into natural language by way of verification.

Parts 2 and 3 of the *Fundamentals* give detailed instructions to do the translation in a systematic way, and it also provides 1,008 graded examples and exercises.

The forthcoming *Practical classification* gives detailed instructions to classify (or to translate from natural language to classificatory or ordinal language) as set forth in Rule 0261. It gives 1,008 graded examples and exercises.

For the time being, examples can be found in

1 *Prolegomena*, ed 2, 1957, chap 7;
2 *Elements*, ed 2, 1959, chap 8; and
3 *Annals of library science*, 5, 1958 and 6, 1959.

027 The **Ultimate Class** of a book is the class of the smallest extension admitted by the scheme of classification, into which it can be placed.

CHAPTER 03

BOOK NUMBER

03 The **Book Number** of a book is a symbol used to fix its position relatively to the other books having the same **Ultimate Class.**

030 The **Book Number** of a book individualises it among the books sharing the same class number.

03011 The **Book Number** of a book is the translation of the names of certain of its specified features into the artificial language of ordinal numbers, specified and elaborated in the rest of this chapter.

03012 The **Book Number** consists of an intelligible concatenation of one or more of the following symbols: the twenty-four Roman Capitals got by omitting I and O; the twenty-three Roman smalls got by omitting *i*, *l* and *o*; the punctuation marks dot, hyphen, semicolon and colon; and the ten Indo-Arabic numerals.

03013 Each one of the symbols in a Book Number will be called a **Digit.**

03014 The digits are written from left to right.

03015 The place-value of a digit is as in a decimal-fraction except in the cases covered by the Rules 0331, 03412, 0353, 0372, and 0382.

03016 When arranged in the ascending sequence of their absolute values, the symbols used in constructing Book Numbers shall be taken to fall in the sequence in which they are mentioned in Rule 03012.

0302 The **Book Number** may consist of one or more of the following successive **Facets:** Language Number; Form Number; Year Number; Accession Part of Book Number; Volume Number; Supplement Number; Copy Number; Criticism Number; and Accession Part of Criticism Number.

Of these, the Copy Number will be needed only in libraries and library catalogues, but not in any other form of bibliography and particularly not in National and International Bibliographies.

The need for an individualising Book Number is fully discussed in the *Prolegomena*, chapter 66.

Many of the schemes of classification do not provide for Book Numbers. It therefore happens that some independent schemes have been devised for

Book Numbers. In the Colon Classification, however, the Book Number has been designed in organic relation to the Class Number.

In many of the schemes of Book Numbers the name of the author is used to individualise a book. In the Colon Classification the Year of Publication, and some other characteristics also in some cases, are used for the purpose. For except in Literature and in the case of the classics in any subject, where the author is made into a class in the Colon Classification, it is felt that the Year of Publication will be a more relevant and helpful characteristic than the name of the author for individualising a book. If we remember that a library is a growing organism, it is more often the year of publication that determines the value of a book in all cases except the ones excluded above. The majority of readers are interested in the latest books in an ultimate class, while antiquarians may be interested in the oldest books. Most pedestrian works cease to have value to an ordinary reader at the expiry of ten to twenty years after publication. Any work with long-persisting value is likely to come out again in a new edition.

Hence the chronological arrangement of the books in an ultimate class saves the time of many of the readers and gives them greater satisfaction.

It is felt further that it may be convenient for most of the readers if the books with the same ultimate class but written in different languages are separated into different language groups and arranged among themselves by their Years of Publication. Hence the Language of the book is also made an essential part of the Book Number in the Colon Classification.

So also, it will be convenient if books in an unusual form of exposition such as alphabetical, or pictorial, or dialogue are brought together. Hence the form of exposition is also made an essential part of the Book Number. See volume 1 of the *Abgila* for a discussion of this question. See also *Prolegomena*, chapter 66.

031 The Language Number

031 The **Language Number** is got by translating the name of the language in which the book is written into appropriate symbols in accordance with the language schedule given in chapter 5 of the Schedules.

It will be convenient at this stage to introduce two definitions.

0311 The **Favoured Language** of a library is the language in which the majority of the books of the library are found written.

Normally the language of the country is likely to be the Favoured Language. But under the peculiar conditions of India at present, it is likely to be English for some time.

0312 Each library should have a descending scale of popularity for the languages, the Favoured Language being given the first place. Among a given set of languages the **Most Popular Language** is the language which occurs earliest in the scale of popularity.

It is not easy to give a definite and unique sequence of popularity for arranging the languages. But each library may be able to decide from experience some working scale. All that is wanted is that this should be a fixed one. For example, in the University Library at Madras, English was used as the Favoured Language. The scale of languages was as follows: English, Tamil, Malayalam, Telugu, Kanarese, Sanskrit, Hindi, Urdu, French, German, etc.

If a book is written in more than one language, three important cases may arise. Either the book may consist of the same matter in more than one language; or it may consist of a classic with commentaries in one or more languages or simply of commentaries of a classic in more than one language. Practically these are the only types of polyglot books which will have to be considered. If any other type occurs, it may be dealt with in an analogous manner.

The three following Rules deal with the three types mentioned above.

0313 In the case of a book consisting of the same matter in more than one language, the Most Popular of the Languages in which the matter occurs should be used to construct the Language Number.

0314 In the case of a book consisting of a classic with commentaries, in one or more languages,

1 if the classic is of greater importance than the commentaries, the language in which the classic is given should be used to construct the Language Number; and

2 if the classic is of less importance than the commentaries, the Most Popular of the Languages in which a commentary occurs should be used to construct the Language Number.

0315 In the case of a book consisting of two or more commentaries of a classic but not containing the classic itself, the Most Popular of the Languages in which a commentary occurs should be used to construct the Language Number.

0316 In the case of a book belonging to a Main Class other than 'Literature', if it is in the Favoured Language or if the Language to be used to construct the Language Number is the Favoured one, the Language Number need not be written.

This rule is intended to effect economy in notation. By definition, the majority of the books in a library should be in the Favoured Language. Therefore this rule results, really, in saving a large amount of labour and time. It reduces the Book Number to two or three digits only, in the case of a majority of books in a library. Incidentally, this rule leads to another desirable effect. According to this rule, among the books in any ultimate class, the group of those in the Favoured Language will have precedence over the groups in the other languages. For by Rule 03016, a Roman capital has precedence over all other kinds of digits in a Book Number and the Book Number of a book in prose in the Favoured Language will begin with a Roman Capital, whereas that of a book in any other language will begin with a numeral.

0317 In the case of a book belonging to the Main Class 'Literature', if the language of the book is the same as the language of the literature, the Language Number need not be written.

This rule also is intended to effect economy in notation. Normally the majority of the books falling in the Main Class 'Literature' are likely to be in the language of that literature. Hence it is an advantage to suppress the language number if the language of the book is the same as the language of the literature. A few books such as translations, biographies, and criticisms, may be in languages other than the language of the literature. In such cases, the Language Number ought to be written. It may be explicitly stated here that even if the language of the book or the language to be used to construct the Language Number is the Favoured Language, the Language Number ought to be written.

0318 In the case of a periodical publication, the language number need not be written.

Normally the language of a periodical publication is likely to be the language of the country where it is published; and this country is represented in the class number of the publication. If the publication is the *Proceedings* of an international conference, it is likely to be in several languages and it may be treated as if it were in the Favoured Language of the library. No doubt some anomalies may arise. But they will be so few that they may be ignored. This problem is fully discussed in the *Prolegomena*, section 627.

032 Form Number

032 The **Form Number** is got by translating the name of the form of exposition into appropriate symbols in accordance with the Form Schedule given in Chapter 03 of the Schedules.

It may be stated that the Form Number need not be written if the book is in the conventional prose form. Thus, the majority of books in a library will not need the Form Facet in their Book Numbers.

0320 Form number beginning with *w* is not applicable to a book in the Main Class "Literature"

033 Year Number

033 The **Year Number** is got by translating the number of the year of publication into appropriate symbols in accordance with the Time Schedule given in Chapter 3 of the Schedules and the Rules of Chapter 3 of this Part.

0331 If preferred, libraries, whose books are mostly recent ones, may use the following special chronological schedule for the Book Number.

Chronological Table for Book Number

A	Before 1880	K	1960 to 1969	U	2050 to 2059
B	1880 to 1889	L	1970 to 1979	V	2060 to 2069
C	1890 to 1899	M	1980 to 1989	W	2070 to 2079
D	1900 to 1909	N	1990 to 1999	X	2080 to 2089
E	1910 to 1919	P	2000 to 2009	Y	2090 to 2099
F	1920 to 1929	Q	2010 to 2019	ZA	2100 to 2109
G	1930 to 1939	R	2020 to 2029	ZB	2110 to 2119
H	1940 to 1949	S	2030 to 2039	ZC	2120 to 2129
J	1950 to 1959	T	2040 to 2049	ZD	2130 to 2139 etc.

This will save one digit in all Book Numbers.

0332 In the case of a periodical publication the year, covered by the volume, should be used for the Year Number.

03321 If the volume of a periodical publication covers two or more years, the earliest of them should be used.

03322 If the issues of a periodical publication, covering a year, form two or more volumes or parts, such volumes or parts should be regarded as an indivisible set; and Rule 034 and its parts are to be applied.

03323 If the volumes of a periodical publication cannot be related to definite years, they may be deemed to constitute a multi-volumed book; and Rule 034 and its parts may be applied.

Refractory cases, such as the *Epigraphica carnatica*, call for this desperate Rule to be used as the last recourse.

034 Accession Part of the Book Number

034 When the above Rules give the same Book Number to two or more books having the same class number, these should be arranged in the sequence of accession, or otherwise in any arbitrary sequence. In the case of the first of such books, the Book Number should end with the Year Number. In the case of the second, the digit 1 should be added after the Year Number; in the case of the third, the digit 2 should be added; the digit 3, in the case of the fourth; and so on, the digit *n*-1 being added in the case of the *n*th.

0341 If the Accession Part of the Book Number consists of more than one digit, it should be read as an integer and not as a decimal fraction.

035 Volume Number

It may happen that a work is in more than one volume. In such a case it would be desirable to design the Book Numbers of the volumes in such a way that they are all brought together. The device that is employed for this purpose is given in Rule 0351. But before going to that Rule, it will be convenient to formulate a test for deciding when the volumes of a set are to be kept together. The following Rule gives a set of sufficient tests.

035 A set of volumes is to be deemed to be indivisible and to form a **Multi-Volumed** Book if one or more of the following conditions hold good:

1 The set possesses a common index.

2 The same sequence of pagination is continued throughout all the volumes of the set.

3 The subject matter is so distributed among the volumes of the set that it is not helpful to treat each volume as a separate book.

The tendency should be to separate the volumes of a set except in very rare circumstances. Then only the volumes will get placed along with the other volumes in cognate classes. Hence the tests have been so framed that a set will be deemed indivisible only in rare and exceptional circumstances.

0351 In the case of an indivisible set of volumes, the volumes of the set are to be individualised by putting a dot after the Year Number or the Accession Part of the Book Number, as the case may be, and putting the number of the volume in Indo-Arabic numerals after the dot.

03511 The digit or digits thus added after the dot may be termed the **Volume Number.**

03512 If the Volume Number consists of more than one digit, it should be read as an integer and not as a decimal fraction.

The device given in these Rules secures in a very natural way that the volumes of the set are kept in their proper sequence.

If the volumes of an indivisible set are not published in the same year, the year to be used for the Year Number is indeterminate. The following Rule is enunciated to remove the indeterminateness.

0352 The Year of Publication of an indivisible set is the year in which the earliest published volume of the set is published.

One might ask why the year of publication of the first volume of the set is not to be used for the Year Number. Not infrequently it happens that the volumes of an indivisible set are not published in a normal sequence. Exigencies may lead to the publication of a later volume before the first.

Hence, if the labour of changing the numbers is to be avoided, it is obvious that the most convenient year that can be used for the Year Number of the set is the year in which the first published volume of the set appears.

036 Supplement Number

036 In the case of a volume with supplementary volume(s), the Book Number(s) of the supplementary volume(s) should consist of the Book Number of the corresponding main volume followed by a dash which is itself followed by the number of the supplement in Indo-Arabic numerals.

0361 If a supplementary volume relates to more than one volume of an indivisible set of volumes, the number of the supplement should be attached to the Book Number of the last of such volumes in the set.

The result of this rule is to attach the supplementary volume to the last of the volumes to which it relates.

0362 The digit or digits thus added after the dash may be called the **Supplement Number.**

0363 If Supplement Number consists of more than one digit, it should be read as an integer and not as a decimal fraction.

037 Copy Number

The Rules given so far will be sufficient for arrangement of books in national, international, and all other forms of bibliography except Library Catalogues. But they may not be sufficient for arranging the books on the shelves or their main cards in the catalogue-cabinets of a library. In libraries, the complicating factor is the presence of two or more copies of the same book. The Rules given so far will give the same Book Number to all the copies of a Book. We have therefore to design a Copy Number for individualising the copies and yet keeping them together.

037 The Book Number of the second, third, etc copies of a book should consist of that of the first copy followed by a semi-colon and thereafter by the digits, 1, 2, etc respectively.

Examples: If the Book Number of the first copy is N49, those of the other copies will be as follows:

1	Second copy	N49;1	Hundredth copy	N49;99
	Third copy	N49;2	Hundred and first copy	N49;100
	Fourth copy	N49;3	*n*th copy	N49;*n*-1

2 If the book number of the first copy is N491, those of the other copies will be as follows:

Second copy	N491;1	Third copy	N491;2

3 If the book number of the first copy is N491.7-2, those of the other copies will be as follows:

Second copy	N491.7-2;1	Third copy	N491.7-2;2

0371 The number added after the digit " ;" in accordance with Rule 037, may be called the **Copy Number.**

0372 If the Copy Number is in more than one digit, it should be read as an integer and not as a decimal fraction.

0373 Facsimile reproductions, reprints, and even the successive non-distinctive editions of an ordinary book, without any substantial or distinctive changes, should be treated as copies of the book.

This means that the Year Number of such an edition will be that of the original and that the Copy Number should be added thereafter, ignoring the year of publication of the facsimile, reprint, or non-distinctive edition.

0375 A distinctive edition of a Work in Literature or a Sacred Book in Religion or a Classic in any other subject, with a class number of its own, should not be treated as a copy; but it should be individualised by using its own year of publication to construct Year Number.

03751 Re-issues and renewed editions of one and the same Distinctive Edition of a Work in Literature or a Sacred Book in Religion or a Classic in any other subject should be treated as copies of the earliest issue of the Distinctive Edition in question.

Arden *Tempest* and Warwick *Tempest* will not be treated as copies. But the successive Arden editions of the *Tempest* will be treated as copies. The Nirnaya Sagara and the Vani Vilas editions of Sankara's *Brahmasutrabhashya* will not be treated as copies. But the successive re-editions of the Vani Vilas edition will be treated as copies. The editions of Aristotle's *Rhetoric* in the Heinemann and the Loeb Classical Series will not be treated as copies. But the successive editions in the Loeb Classical Series will be treated as copies.

0376 If a library finds it helpful to bring together successive editions of one and the same ordinary book, though there are changes from edition to edition, and at the same time disclose the year of publication of each of the successive editions, they may all be treated as copies with the modification that the Copy Numbers may be made of the translations of the years of publication of the different editions instead of serial integers as provided in Rule 038.

This device will be of use particularly in the text-book collections in academic libraries.

Examples: N49;N52 N49;N57 N49;N60

038 Criticism Number

038 When a book is not deemed a classic and is therefore not made a class by itself by the Classic Device prescribed in chapter 7 of the Rules and if another book is written on it, say as a criticism or a reply or for any other reason, and is best kept with it, the former is called a **Host Book** and the latter an **Associated Book.**

0381 The Book Number of an Associated Book should consist of that of its Host Book followed by " :*g* "

0382 The number thus added may be called the **Criticism Number.**

A full discussion of the need for this device and of its usefulness will be found in the article on *Pseudo-Classics* by P K Garde published in the *Annals* of the Indian Library Association (1, 1949, 15-19) forming part of the *Abgila*.

0383 Accession Part of the Criticism Number

0383 The Book Number of the second, third, etc Associated Book of the same Host Book should consist of that of the first followed by the digits, 1, 2, etc respectively.

03831 The number so added after the Criticism number may be called the **Accession Part of the Criticism Number.**

03832 If the Accession Part of the Criticism Number consists of two or more digits, it should be read as an integer and not as a decimal fraction.

CHAPTER 04

COLLECTION NUMBER

04 It may not be helpful to arrange all the books of a library in a single sequence, strictly according to their class numbers. For example, pamphlets or under-sized books should be separated out from books of normal size. This will give a Pamphlet collection. The pamphlets will of course be arranged among themselves by their class numbers. Similarly separate collections should be formed for over-sized books, for books of abnormal or poor physique, and for worn-out books. Again, it may be necessary to form a separate collection for the reference books in the reading room, for the periodicals, for the less-used books (secondary collection), and for the still-less-used books (tertiary collection). Separate collections will have to be formed also according to the Departments of location in academic and business libraries.

It is necessary to indicate the collection both in the book itself and in the library catalogue and other records.

The need for forming different collections is fully discussed in chapter 8 of my *Library administration*, ed 2, 1960.

041 The **Collection Number** of a book denotes the collection to which it belongs.

042 **A Collection Number** is a suitable symbol to be improvised by each library according to its needs.

043 The following scheme may be of use for collections likely to occur in most libraries:

Collection	Collection Number
Under-sized	Underline Book Number
Over-sized	Overline Book Number
Abnormal	Underline and Overline Book Number
Worn-out	Encircle Book Number

Here are some other examples:

Collection	Collection Number
Reading Room	RR
Secondary	SC
Tertiary	TC
Periodicals	PC
Physics Department	CD
Law Department	ZD

044 In a university, college, school, or other institutional library, a particular professor, teacher, or other member may desire to have in his own special collection or in the collection of his department an assortment of books taken from different classes. Such an assortment is seldom permanent. It is not proper to force the class numbers of the books in such a special collection to represent the interest of the person desiring it, instead of the true thought contents of the respective books. The correct method of keeping the assortment together as a collection is to use the device of Collection Number.

045 A fuller discussion of this will be found in the *Prolegomena*, chapter 67.

CHAPTER 05

FOCUS AND FACET

050 Basic Focus

0501 Some of the (MC)—viz. B Mathematics, C Physics, H Geology, M Useful Arts, N Fine Arts and R Philosophy—are divided in the first instance into **Canonical Classes** (CC).

0502 In certain subjects the canonical mode of division may be repeated more than once. For example in B23 Algebraic Equation, it is done twice.

0503 A (MC) or (CC) is said to be a **Basic Class** (BC).

0504 The term **Basic Focus** or **Basic Facet** (BF) is applicable equally in the Plane of (1) Idea, (2) Language, and (3) Notation.

0505 In the Plane of Idea, (BC) is the equivalent of (BF).

0506 In the Plane of Language, **Basic Subject** (BS) is the equivalent of (BF).

0507 In the Plane of Notation, **Basic Class Number,** (BCN) is the equivalent of (BF).

051 Facet

051 Each (BC) may be divided on the basis of one or more Trains of Characteristics.

The above can be put in the following terms:—

Each (BF) may be sharpened by division on the basis of one or more Trains of Characteristics.

05111 For example the (BC) 'Literature' admits of the four trains of characteristics: Language, Form, Author, and Work Characteristics.

This may be put in the following form:

In the (BC) Literature, we may recognise four facets: The Language, The Form, The Author, and the Work. This is in the idea plane. In the verbal plane, this is equivalent to saying that the name of a subject in literature may include the names of a Language, a Form, an Author, and a Work; in other words, the name of the subject may present these four facets. In the notational plane, it is equivalent to saying that a Class Number in Literature may have four parts corresponding to the four facets; in other words the Class Number may present these four facets.

These four facets are indicated by the symbols [P], [P2], [P3], and [P4] respectively. The Facet Formula given at the head of Chapter O of the Schedules is accordingly.

O [P], [P2] [P3], [P4]

To use colourful words, we may write the above facet formula in the form:—

O [Language], [Form] [Author], [Work]

This Facet Formula prescribes the sequence in which the four facets should be arranged in Class Number. A simple calculation will show that there are twenty-four ways of arranging four facets. The problem is to decide which of these twenty-four possible sequences will be the most helpful to those using books. It is only the experience of libraries that can give the necessary information about it.

The sequence suggested by the facet formula has been found to be the most helpful.

The result of this sequence may be put as follows: We shall imagine all the 'Literature' books divided according to their languages; and we shall imagine a separate building for the literature of each Language. A reader interested, say, in English literature will have to go into the 'English' building, so to speak. On entering the building he will find that all Poetry is put in one room, that all Drama is put in another room, all Fiction is put in a third room, and so on. Let us assume that the reader is interested in Drama and that he enters the 'Drama' room. There we may imagine that he will find several cupboards each devoted to one Dramatist. If the cupboard, pertaining to any Dramatist, is opened, he will find that each shelf is devoted to one work of the Dramatist. In that shelf all the editions of that work and all the criticisms of that work will be found arranged in a helpful sequence. Roughly speaking, this is the result of taking the four facets in the sequence given by the facet formula. One can easily construct a similar picture for the other possible sequences of the facets and satisfy oneself about the greater helpfulness of the particular sequence prescribed by the facet formula.

05112 Here is a second example:

The (BC) History admits of the four trains of characteristics: Community, Constituent, Problem, and Chronological. This may be put in the following form. In a subject of the (BC) History, we may recognise four facets, Community, Constituent, Problem and Chronological. This is in the idea plane. In the verbal plane, it is equivalent to saying that the name of a subject in History may include the names of a Community, a Constituent, a Problem, and a Period. In other words, the name of the subject may present any or all of those four facets. At the notational level, it is equivalent to saying that a Class Number in History may have four parts corresponding to the four Facets; in other words, a Class Number may present any or all of those four facets.

These four facets are indicated by the symbols [P], [P2], [E], and [T] respectively. The Facet Formula given at the head of Chapter V of the Schedules is accordingly.

V [P], [P2]: [E]. [T]

To use colourful words, we may write the above facet formula in the form:

V [Community], [Constituent]: [Problem]. [Period]

This Facet Formula prescribes the sequence in which the four facets should be arranged in Class Number. A simple calculation will show that there are twenty-four ways of arranging four facets. The problem is to decide which of these twenty-four possible sequences will be most helpful to those who use books. It is only the experience of libraries that can give the necessary information about it.

The sequence suggested by the facet formula has been found to be helpful in the majority of cases.

The result of the sequence may be put as follows: We shall imagine all the history books divided according to the country about which they treat; and we shall imagine a separate building for the history of each country. A reader interested, say, in Indian History will have to go to the 'India Building' so to speak. On entering the building, he will find that all the books on the Cabinet of India are put in one room, all the books on the Legislature of India are put in another room, and so on. Let us assume that the reader is interested in the Legislature and that he enters the 'Legislature' room. There he will find several cupboards, each devoted to a particular problem such as Constitution, Function, Archives, etc. Let us assume that he is interested in Constitution. Then he will open the cupboard marked 'Constitution'. There he will find that each shelf is reserved for a different period. Roughly speaking, this is the result of taking the four facets in the sequence given by the facet formula. One can easily construct a similar picture for other possible sequences of the facets and satisfy oneself about the appropriateness of the particular sequence prescribed by the facet formula.

05113 Other examples of facet analysis will be found in section 221 of the *Fundamentals*, in Chapters 7 and 8 of the *Elements*, and in the forthcoming *Practical classification*.

05114 Facet Formulae will also be found in the Schedules for some Canonical Classes. Some examples are,

B22 Equation, B33 Differential Equation, B6 Geometry,
C3 Sound, C5 Radiation, H1 Mineralogy,
M7 Textile, MJ7 Rope-making,
R3 Metaphysics, R4 Ethics.

0512 In each Facet Formula, each square bracket represents a Single Train of Characteristics.

05121 The totality of the divisions of a (BC) based on a Single Train of Characteristics is said to constitute one of its **Facets.**

05122 In a Class Number, the part of it, corresponding to a Single Train of Characteristics, is said to be one of its **Facets.**

In the (MC) Literature: Language, Form, Author, and Work are Facets.
In the Class Number:

O111, 2J64, 55

111, 2, J64, and 55 are its Facets.

The term "Train of Characteristics" is, for the time being, an assumed or undefined term. The characteristics in it are often those yielding subclasses formed of whole entities forming the universe classified. This will get a better explanation in section 055 and its subdivisions. An account will be found in the *Prolegomena*, ed 2, chap 35.

05123 The totality of the divisions on the basis of a Single Characteristic is said to constitute an **Array.**

052 Isolate

0521 Each division in a Facet is said to be an **Isolate Focus** (IF) or simply an **Isolate** (I).

0522 The term Isolate is applicable equally in the Plane of (1) Idea, (2) Language, and (3) Notation.

0523 In the Plane of Idea, **Isolate** is the equivalent of Isolate Focus.

0524 In the Plane of Language, **Isolate Term** (IT) is the equivalent of Isolate Focus.

0525 In the Plane of Notation, **Isolate Number** (IN) is the equivalent of Isolate Focus.

053 Compound Focus

0531 A Subject made of a (BC) and one or more Isolates is said to be a **Compound Class** (CdC).

0532 The term **Compound Focus** (CdF) is applicable equally in the Plane of (1) Idea, (2) Language, and (3) Notation.

0533 In the Plane of Idea, **Compound Class** (CdC) is the equivalent of Compound Focus.

0534 In the Plane of Language, **Compound Term** (CdT) is the equivalent of Compound Focus.

0535 In the Plane of Notation, **Compound Class Number** (CdCN) is the equivalent of Compound Focus.

0536 A (CdF) with one facet is said to be of the **First Order**, one with two facets is said to be of the **Second Order**, and so on.

Examples: Here are examples of (CdF):

Compound Class Number (CdCN)	Compound Term (CdT)	Order
L185	Ophthalmology	First
L185:4	Disease of the eye	Second
L185:4:6	Treatment of disease of the eye	Third
L:4	Disease	First
L:4:6	Treatment of disease	Second

where

Number	Term	Nature
L	Medicine	(BF)
185	Eye	(IF)
4	Disease	(IF)
6	Treatment	(IF)

It may be remarked here that an (IF) cannot by itself constitute a Subject. On the other hand, a (BC) can by itself constitute a Subject.

An (IF) should be attached to an appropriate (BC) to form a Subject. These statements bring out the significance of the epithets " Basic " and " Isolate ".

In the above table, the (BC) " L Medicine " is a subject by itself. But the (I) " 185 Eye " is not a subject by itself. It must be attached to " Medicine " or to " Zoology " or to " Animal husbandry " or to " Sociology " or to some other basic class to yield a subject.

054 Amplified Basic Class

0541 Kind 1

0541 If a Subject is expounded according to a particular System of Thought, its (BC) must be fitted with an **Amplifying Facet of Kind 1**. We may call it also **System Facet** (SmF).

05411 The (SmF) should precede all the other facets of the Subject.

05412 The Focus in the (SmF) should be got by the Chronological Device, using the Date of Origin of the System as the epoch.

05413 The Focus in the (SmF) should be omitted, if the exposition is according to the currently **Favoured System**—that is the system in which the majority of the books are expounded.

05414 If a book gives or deals with two or more systems, the Focus in the (SmF) should be represented by the digit A.

0542 Kind 2

0542 If the exposition of a (BS) is restricted to a limited range only of any of its facets, its (BC) must be fitted with **an Amplifying Facet of Kind 2.** We may call it also **Specials Facet** (SpF).

05421 The (SpF) should succeed the (SmF) but precede all the other facets.

05422 The Focus in the (SpF) should be got by Enumeration. Its number begins with the digit 9 followed by a Roman capital.

Examples of Foci in (SpF) will be found at the ends of chapters C and L of the Schedules. A full discussion of this will be found in the *Annals of library science*, 2, 1955.

A result of the Rules 0541 to 05422 is the following sequence of books:

1 Books giving an exposition in the Favoured System without any special restriction in the range of any facet;

2 Books giving an exposition in the Favoured system of the different Specials; and

3 Books giving an exposition according to particular Systems.

To take the particular example of Medicine, we shall begin with books in Allopathy, then will come specials such as Child Medicine, Female Medicine, Industrial Medicine, and according to allopathy; and lastly will come books on particular Systems such as Ayurveda, Unani, and Homoeopathy.

A result of these Rules is that books which give the favoured exposition will come first, of course, classified in all possible ways. Then the books which expound according to particular Systems of Thought will follow in the chronological sequence of the systems. The books of each system will stand classified among themselves in all possible ways.

See the ends of Chapters C, L, S, T, and X of the Schedules for examples.

A full discussion with examples and exercises will be found in sections 263C, 264C, 265C and 266C, of the *Fundamentals*. This is also discussed in the *Annals of library science*, 2, 1955.

0543 A (CN) with a focus in the (SmF) or in the (SpF) is called an **Amplified Class Number.**

0544 The term **Amplified Focus** is applicable equally in the Plane of (1) Idea, (2) Language and (3) Notation.

0545 In the Plane of Idea, **Amplified Class** is the equivalent of Amplified Focus.

0546 In the Plane of Language, **Amplified Subject** is the equivalent of Amplified Focus.

0547 In the Plane of Notation, **Amplified Class Number** is the equivalent of Amplified Focus.

055 Fundamental Categories

0550 Each facet of any subject as well as each focus in it is regarded as a manifestation of one of five **Fundamental Categories** (FC).

05501 The five Fundamental Categories are given below in the increasing sequence of concreteness with their respective **Connecting Symbols** (CS).

Fundamental Category (FC)	Connecting Symbol (CS)	Symbol for the Facet
Time	'. (Dot)	[T]
Space	. (Dot)	[S]
Energy	: (Colon)	[E]
Matter	; (Semicolon)	[M]
Personality	, (Comma)	[P]

05502 Each (IN) in a (CdCN) should be preceded by its prescribed (CS) unless its omission is indicated by the Facet Formula or by Rule.

05503 Unless an Amplifying Facet precedes it, the first Personality (IN) of any (BC) need not be preceded by a comma.

Examples

015,2D40,3 Sakuntala of Kalidasa.

In this, the first [P] (IN) is 15. It is not preceded by comma. The third [P] (IN) is D40. It is not preceded by comma as its omission is indicated by the facet formula at the head of chapter O of the Schedules.

X62:8.44.N5 Management of banks in India brought upto 1950's.

In this, the first [P] (IN) is 62. It is not preceded by comma.

XM,62:8.44.N5 Management of co-operative banks in India brought up to 1950's.

In this, M is a focus in (SmF). This is an Amplifying Facet. Therefore, the first [P] (IN) 62 is preceded by a comma.

05504 If both (SmF) and (SpF) occur in a Class Number, these two facets should be separated by a comma.

Examples

LL,9C,185 Children's ophthalmology according to Homoeopathy.

Here the second L is the focus in (SmF); 9C is the focus in (SpF); and 185 is the first [P] (IN).

0551 The facet formula of a class which is a **Local Description** or **History** of any subject will have [S] and [T] at the end.

05511 This is equivalent to saying that the class Number of a Local Description or History will end with [S] and [T] (IN), in other words, with [S] and [T].

Examples

X.44.N5. Economic condition of India brought upto 1950's.

X:9.44.N5. Labour in India brought upto 1950's.

T2.44.N5. Secondary education in India brought upto 1950's.

0552 It may be emphasized here that when Time or Space is not a manifestation of Time or Space *qua* Time or Space, but is a manifestation of Energy, Matter or Personality whose number is constructed by Chronological or Geographical Device, the (CS) should be the one appropriate to the fundamental category of which it is a manifestation.

0553 [E] usually consists of problem, action, etc.

05531 It is not yet possible to give an exact criterion to recognise the manifestation of Energy as a Facet or a Focus. However, the difficulty is got over provisionally by actual enumeration in the various schedules. What is enumerated will prove sufficient for ordinary library collections. It is hoped that when sufficient experience is gained a more precise definition of the manifestation of Energy will be possible. Generally speaking, Energy manifests itself either as action, inter-action, or mutual action of some kind or as one of the isolates postulated to be energy—such as those denoted by the terms Morphology,

Physiology, Disease, Ecology, Phylogeny, Ontogeny, and their equivalents in other class-contexts.

05532 Generally speaking, [E] (IN)s are characterised by seminal mnemonics (See Rule 05861 and also *Prolegomena*, section 261, for definition of seminal mnemonics).

05533 In Geography what looks like Energy Category—the Geography Facet—is regarded as a manifestation of Personality.

0554 [M] usually consists of materials used for construction, consumption, etc.

05541 Standard schedules of [M] will have to be constructed to meet the needs of diverse subjects. These will be given in version 2. The few given in this volume will be sufficient for classifying books in a general library.

05542 When more experience is gained in documentation and depth classification, it is hoped to provide further Matter Schedules needed for that kind of work. These schedules will be characterised by scheduled mnemonics to a large extent and perhaps also by seminal mnemonics to some extent.

05543 In some subjects ranging from C Physics to M Useful Arts, it will be seen that Matter manifests itself as Personality.

0555 From what has been already stated, the isolate in a [P] may be got by enumeration or by (CD) or by (GD) or may be indicated by terms which look like Energy terms or Matter terms. The same material will have to be taken as manifestation of the (FC) Matter in some class-contexts and as manifestation of the (FC) Personality in others. For example, 'Timber' is [M] in Carpentry but [P] in Forestry. Steel is [M] in Machine Building but is [P] in Metallurgy. Reference Book is [P] in Bibliography and [M] in Library Science.

0556 It is not yet possible to give strict criteria in this matter. It is hoped that greater experience in documentation and depth classification will lead to the formulation of strict criteria.

056 Rounds of Manifestation

0561 Energy may manifest itself in one and the same subject more than once.

0562 The Second, Third, etc. Manifestations of Energy in one and the same subject are respectively called **Second Round Energy** [2E], **Third Round Energy** [3E], etc.

The first manifestation may be called the **First Round Energy.** For brevity it is represented simply by [E] instead of [IE].

0563 It is possible for manifestation of Personality and Matter to occur after First Round Energy. These manifestations are respectively called **Second Round Personality** [2P] and **Second Round Matter** [2M].

0564 It is possible for manifestation of Personality and Matter to occur after Second Round Energy. These manifestations are respectively called **Third Round Personality** [3P] and **Third Round Matter** [3M]. And so on.

Examples

In L:4:6 Cure of Disease, the isolate '6 Cure' is [2E]. In the isolate L:4:616;41171 Saline Injection '616 Injection' is [2E] *cum* [2P]. And the isolate '41171 Salt' is [3M].

0565 The possible omission of the (CS) prescribed for [2P], [3P] etc. will be indicated by the facet formula or by rule.

0566 Generally speaking if the [E] (IN), initiating a round, will always consist of the same number of significant digits, **the connecting symbol of the Personality (IN) following it may be omitted.**

0567 It can be seen that [P] is used for First Round Personality instead of [1P] just for brevity. Similarly is the use of [M] for [1M], and [E] for [1E].

057 Levels of Manifestation

0571 In each round there may occur more than one manifestation of the (FC) Personality and Matter. The second, third, etc., manifestations of Personality and Matter in one and the same round are respectively called **Second Level Personality, Third Level Personality,** etc ; and **Second Level Matter,** etc.

05710 Symbols like the following may be used:

[P2]=Second Level Personality Facet; [P3]=Third Level Personality Facet; [M2]=Second Level Matter Facet, etc. So also [2P2], [2P3] . . . [2M2], etc.

The first manifestation may be spoken of as the First Level. For brevity, we write [P] instead of [P1] for First Level Personality Facet.

Examples

In " O15,2D40,3 Sakuntala of Kalidasa,

" 15 Sanskrit " is [P]. It represents the Language of the work.

" 2 Drama " is [P2]. It represents the Form of the work.

" D40 Kalidasa " is [P3]. It represents the Author of the work.

" 3 Sakuntala " is [P4]. It represents the Work.

0572 To be truly expressive, the symbols for the facets in the above examples should be [1P1], [1P2], [1P3], and [1P4].

0573 In the first three editions, Colon was the only (CS) used. It is this symbol which gave the Classification Scheme its distinctive analytico-synthetic character. The scheme was therefore called Colon Classification. The requirements of the depth-classification, needed in documentation work and service, have led to the use of some more (CS). These were introduced in edition 4; and they have come to stay. They cannot however challenge the right of " Colon " to give the name to the scheme. For, the " Colon " still plays a unique part in the scheme. It derives this quality by being the (CS) for Energy whose manifestation alone can initiate Rounds of Manifestation. For this reason, apart from the historical one, the scheme can still be appropriately called Colon Classification.

058 Formation and Sharpening of Isolate

058 One or more of the following Devices may be employed to form or sharpen the Focus in any Facet:

1 Chronological Device;

2 Geographical Device;
3 Subject Device;
4 Mnemonic Device;
5 Alphabetical Device; and
6 Superimposition Device.

These devices have been used in the formation of the isolates found already in the Schedules. These schedules may, therefore, be used as illustrations of the use of these principles and devices.

When new subjects come into existence and call for the formation of new isolates or the sharpening of existing ones and the forging of numbers co-extensive with them, these devices will enable the Classifier to meet the situation without waiting for guidance from the Classificationist. Correct employment of these devices will, generally, lead to the same (II) and the same (IN) whoever is the classifier. This is a measure of the addition to the autonomy to the classifier, going with the analytico-synthetic nature of Colon Classification.

A preliminary account of these principles and devices is given here to secure clarity and brevity in the enunciation of the Rules of Classification and the enumeration of the isolates in the Schedules.

0581 Chronological Device

0581 The **Chronological Device** (CD) consists in using the appropriate Chronological Characteristic for the formation or the subdivision of an isolate, capable of chronological formation or subdivision, or when the individualisation of the isolates or sub-isolates may be made to depend conveniently on the period of origin or birth or on the year of first investigation or on the year of discovery or on the year of initiation or commencement or on the year of occurrence or on the year that may be definitely associated with the respective isolates in any other manner or for any other reason. Some of the cases where this device may be employed are generally indicated either in the Schedules or in the Rules. Similar cases, where it may be employed, will suggest themselves in the course of actual classification.

05811 The epoch to be used to construct the Chronological Number will be that which is specified in the concerned Rules or Schedules or, if it is not so specified, that which may be most appropriate.

05812 The Chronological Number should be worked out to the first, or the first two, or the first three digits of the year forming the epoch as specified in the respective Rules or, if there are no specific rules on the point, according to the following convention.

05813 For the first isolate in an array, whose epoch falls within a century (or millennium), the first digit alone should be used.

05814 Among the other isolates calling for the same first digit, for the first isolate, whose epoch falls within the same decade (or century), the first two digits should be used.

05815 Among the other isolates calling for the same first two digits, for the first isolate, whose epoch falls within the same year (or decade), the first three digits should be used.

05816 For each of the other isolates calling for the same first three digits, some vacant neighbouring years are to be used.

05817 If no neighbouring year is vacant to make the application of the above convenient, the digits, 1, 2 etc. respectively may be added after the three-digited number obtained by Rule 05835. These added digits should be read as integers and not as decimals.

05818 In many cases of (CD), (LED) is prescribed. Then Rules 311 and 312 should be followed.

See *Elements*, p 31-32, and *Prolegomena*, section 1432.

The Schedules contain many examples in which this device is usefully employed. The great hospitality which this scheme gets by this device is illustrated in the individualisation of special forms and functions in 'Mathematics', in fixing the Author Numbers in 'Literature', in the classification of artificial languages in the schedule of language classes given in Schedule 5, in the classification of religious sects, and of the different Systems in Physics, Medicine, Psychology, Education, Economics, and in many other instances which it would be unnecessary to list here exhaustively.

The (CD) automatically secures conformity to the Canons of Consistent Sequence, Helpful Sequence, Hospitality in Array, Hospitality in Chain, and Mnemonics.

0582 Geographical Device

0582 The **Geographical Device** (GD) consists in using the appropriate Geographical Characteristic (that is, continent, country, state, district etc., as the case may be) for the formation or the subdivision of an isolate which is capable of such formation or subdivision, or when the individualisation of the isolates, or sub-isolates, may be made to depend conveniently on the place of origin or prevalence or habitation or one that may be definitely associated with the respective foci in any other manner or for any other reason. The cases where this device may be applied are generally indicated either in the Schedules or in the Rules.

See *Elements*, p 32-33, and *Prolegomena*, section 1434.

In the language table given in Chapter 5 of the Schedules, it will be seen that the languages not belonging to the Indo-European, the Semitic, or the Dravidian families are to be individualised by the (GD).

Again Rules P101 and P105 of Chapter P of the Rules utilise the (GD) for the individualising of dialects and jargons. The (GD) is also employed to individualise certain religions as can be seen from Chapter Q of the Schedules. It is needless to multiply examples at this stage.

The (GD) automatically secures conformity to the Canons of Consistent Sequence, Helpful Sequence, Local Variation, Hospitality in Array, Hospitality in Chain, and Mnemonics.

0583 Subject Device

0583 The **Subject Device** (SD) consists in using the appropriate Class Characteristic for the formation or the subdivision of an isolate which is capable of such formation or subdivision, or when the individualisation of the isolates, or sub-isolates, may be made to depend conveniently on a Class that may be definitely associated with the respective foci in any manner or for any reason. The cases where this Device may be applied are generally indicated either in the Schedules or in the Rules.

05831 The part of an Isolate Number contributed by (SD) may be called the **Subject Device Number** (SDN). The corresponding part of the Isolate Idea may be denoted by (SDP). If the whole Isolate Idea is got by (SD), it may be denoted by (SDI).

05832 (SDN) should be enclosed within circular brackets.

The (SD) secures automatic conformity to the Canons of Consistent Sequence, Helpful Sequence, Hospitality in Array, Hospitality in Chain, and Mnemonics. This Device is employed at different stages in certain subjects. Many illustrative divisions by the (SD) are given in the Schedules. Special reference may be made here, to the Ethics part of Schedule R, and to the functions in [E] for V Schedule. In some cases, it will be found that the number used for the (SD) has been modified slightly. But such modifications should not be freely indulged in by individual classifiers.

05833 In particular, (SD) may be used, whenever warranted, to extend the schedule in any [E]. The (SDI) should be more abstract than the (BC) in such a case.

(1) D646:(C:47) is the class number for Harry R Ricardo, *Engines of high output: Thermodynamical considerations*, C:47 being the number for Thermodynamics;

(2) G:(C) is the class number for George Chile's *Phenomena of life; A radio-electric interpretation* which deals with the physics of living organisms;

(3) J:(E:3) is the class number for C Harold Wright's *Agricultural analysis*;

(4) J:1:(G91) is the class number for Selman A Waksman's *Principles of soil microbiology*, where J:1 stands for soil and G91 for bacteriology or microbiology;

(5) Δ:(R) is the class number for Thomas Hywel Hughes' *Philosophic basis of mysticism*;

(6) Y:(X76).56 is the class number for report of the British Treasury entitled *Public social services; total expenditure under certain Acts of Parliament during the financial years etc.*; and

(7) Y:(Z56) is the class number for John J Clarke's *Social administration including the poor laws* which deals with the statutory and executive laws and regulations of Great Britain for the working of Social Service.

0584 Mnemonic Device

0584 The **Mnemonic Device** (MD) consists in choosing the digit for the further division oı a class, i e the formation or the sharpening of a focus, in accordance with a convention in regard to the different possible significances of the digits available for use.

05841 These mnemonics have been called **Seminal Mnemonics** in the *Prolegomena*, section 271. This term was suggested in the *Fundamentals of library classification* of Palmer and Wells. This is apart from the **Scheduled Mnemonics.**

The digit 1 is used as mnemonic for unity, God, world, the first in evolution or time, one dimension or line, solid state, and all other entities, existential or conceptual, which may be viewed as correlates to the above.

The digit 2 is used as mnemonic for two dimensions, plane, conics, form, structure, anatomy, morphology, sources of knowledge, physiography, constitution, physical anthropology, and all other entities, existential or conceptual, which may be viewed as correlates to the above.

The digit 3 is used as mnemonic for three dimensions, space, cubics, analysis, function, physiology, syntax, method, social anthropology, and all other correlates to the above.

The digit 4 is used as mnemonic for heat, pathology, disease, transport, interlinking, synthesis, hybrid, salt, and all other entities, existential or conceptual, which may be viewed as correlates to the above.

The digit 5 is used as mnemonic for energy, light, radiation, organic, liquid, water, ocean, foreign land, alien, external, environment, ecology, public controlled plan, emotion, foliage, aesthetics, woman, sex, crime, and all other correlates to the above.

The digit 6 is used as mnemonic for dimensions, subtle, mysticism, money, finance, abnormal, phylogeny, evolution, and all other entities, existential or conceptual, which may be viewed as correlates to the above.

The digit 7 is used as mnemonic for personality, ontogeny, integrated, holism, value, public finance, and all other correlates to the above.

The digit 8 is used as mnemonic for travel, organisation, fitness.

05842 This is a powerful device which secures a high degree of autonomy for individual classifiers. For this reason it can be handled only by classifiers who are highly attuned to the insight—I would even say spiritual insight into the indentity of patterns at seminal depths—or intuition which enables one to perceive directly—i e unassisted by the ordinary senses—the very depths of entities, the depths at which are disclosed the indentity of patterns in spite of the differences in their manifestations at the level of sensual perception. It is, for the same reason, desirable that all the foci formed by this device should be brought up for discussion at periodical conferences before they are finalised.

This device fulfils the Canon of Mnemonics in its deepest implications.

05843 It has not yet been possible to find similar seminal mnemonic significance in the case of the letters of an alphabet. There is an Indian tradition about it. But I have not yet succeeded in getting access to it.

0585 Alphabetical Device

0585 The **Alphabetical Device** (AD) consists in using the first or the first two, or the first three, etc., initial letters (all in caps) of the name of an entity, existential or conceptual, for the formation or the subdivision of an isolate.

The following convention is suggested in dealing with names having the same initial letter. The first letter alone may be used for the most favoured entity, *i.e.*, the entity which has the greatest literary warrant or which is the first on which literature arrives. The first two letters are to be used for the second favoured entity with the same initial letter, using 'favoured' in the above sense and so on. The use of the first three letters may be invoked if the name of another entity has the same two initial letters as the one already selected for two-letter-representation. The number of letters used may be further increased to the necessary extent.

This device is to be used only in cases where no other method of subdivision gives a more helpful sequence. The Schedules and the Rules indicate the places where this Device has to be used.

05851 The (AD) can be applied only in respect of proper names, trade names, and certain technical nomenclature which are internationally current.

05852 There are some unsolved difficulties in the application of this device. Certain combinations of letters occur frequently at the beginning of names. Then, several letters have to be brought into use to secure individualisation.

0586 Superimposition Device

0586 When an isolate is not scheduled in a facet but can be regarded as the mutual denudation of two of the scheduled isolates, it is called a **Superimposed Isolate** (SII).

05861 The Number of an (SII) is got by the **Superimposition Device** (SID).

05862 The (SID) consists in connecting the numbers of the constituent Isolates by " - "..

05863 The constituent isolate which occurs earlier in the schedule should normally form the first nember of a (SII).

05864 If the number got by Rule 05863 is unintelligible and the using of the constituent isolate, which occurs later in the schedule as the first member, will yield an intelligible and a more helpful isolate number, it must be made the first member.

05865 If both the sequences of the constituent isolates give intelligible isolate numbers and yield different meanings, the sequence should be determined by the meaning sought to be represented.

These Rules provide a solution to what was described as the fourth unsolved problem in section 4224 of the *Fundamentals*.

Examples: (1) In the Organ Facet of L Medicine, 163 is Arms, 36 is Veins and the Veins of Arms is not scheduled. The number for the last may therefore be fixed as 163-36 or 36-163. Both are intelligible and also specify the same thing. We therefore prefer the former.

(2) In the Geographical Divisions, 44 is India and 56 is England. 44-56 will mean British Territory in India. 56-44 will similarly mean Indian Territory in Great Britain. Here both the combinations are intelligible. But they specify totally different things. The number to be used will therefore depend on what we wish to represent.

A full discussion and more examples will be found in section 351 and its subdivisions in the *Fundamentals*. See also *Prolegomena*, section 237.

0591 Favoured Focus

0591 Any focus, simple or compound, which represents the subject of specialisation of a library or the isolate in which its collection is more numerous than in other co-ordinate sub-classes, may be called its Favoured Focus.

05911 The Favoured Focus of a library, other than Mother Country, and Favoured Country, and any other focus for which there is no special provision in the Schedule of Classification or in the Rules, may be represented by " — " if the number prescribed for it by the schedule is of two or more digits.

For example, in a library which is stronger in English Literature when compared with the literature in other languages, the focus " English " in the Language-facet of the (MC) Literature may be represented by "—". Thus English Poetry may be represented by O—, 1 instead of by O111,1 and English Drama by O—, 2 instead of by O111, 2. Again in a library which specialises in Railway Economics, X415 may be replaced by "—". Thus Railway Labour may be represented by—:9 instead of by X415:9. Similarly the library of a dairy may replace KZ311:71 by "—" and thus effect considerable economy in notation. As the ordinal value of "—" is less than that of 1, the number for the favoured focus of a library will automatically secure for it precedence over every other one. This is a convenience.

CHAPTER 06

CONTRACTIONS

(*The number within brackets is that of the section in this book*)

(ACI) Anteriorising Common Isolate (201)
(AD) Alphabetical Device (0585)
(BC) Basic Class (0503)
(BCN) Basic Class Number (0507)
(BF) Basic Focus (0504)
(CD) Chronological Device (0581)
(CI) Common Isolate (20)
(CxC) Complex Class (620)
(CdC) Compound Class (0531)
(CdCN) Compound Class Number (0535)
(CdF) Compound Focus (0532)
(CLD) Classics Device (72)
(CS) Connecting Symbol (05501)
(FC) Fundamental Categories (0550)
(GD) Geographical Device (0582)
(I) Isolate (0521)
(IAR) Intra-Array Relation (642)
(IFR) Intra-Facet Relation (63)
(II) Isolate Idea
(IN) Isolate Number (0521)
(IT) Isolate Term (0524)
(LED) Last Effective Decade (3120)
(MC) Main Class (11)
(MD) Mnemonic Device (0584)
(PCI) Personality Common Isolate (27)
(PCL) Posteriorising Common Isolate (202)
(PR) Phase Relation (6204)
(SD) Subject Device (0583)
(SDN) Subject Device Number (05831)
(SmF) System Facet (0541)
(SpF) Specials Facet (0542)
(SID) Superimposition Device (0586)
(SII) Superimposed Isolate (05861)

[E]	Energy Facet (05501)
[2E]	Second Round Energy Facet (0562)
[M]	Matter Facet (05501)
[2M]	Second Round Matter Facet (0563)
[P]	Personality Facet (05501)
[P2]	Second Level Personality Facet (05710)
[P3]	Third Level Personality Facet (05710)
[2P]	Second Round Personality Facet (0563)
[2P2]	Second Round Second Level Personality Facet (05710)
[S]	Space Facet (05501)
[S2]	Second Level Space Facet (05710)
[T]	Time Facet (05501)
[T2]	Second Level Time Facet (05710)

And other similar contractions.

CHAPTER 07

CANONS OF CLASSIFICATION

as developed in edition 2 of the *Prolegomena*

(*The number of the section in the* Prolegomena *is given in brackets*)

071 Canons for Characteristics

1 Canon of Differentiation (131)
2 Canon of Concomitance (132)
3 Canon of Relevance (133)
4 Canon of Ascertainability (134)
5 Canon of Permanence (135)
6 Canon of Relevant Sequence (136)
7 Canon of Consistency (137)

2 Canons for Array

8 Canon of Exhaustiveness (141)
9 Canon of Exclusiveness (142)
10 Canon on Helpful Sequence (143)
11 Canon of Consistent Sequence (144)

3 Canons for Chain

12 Canon of Decreasing Extension (151)
13 Canon of Modulation (152)

4 Canons for Filiatory Sequence

14 Canon of Subordinate Classes (161)
15 Canon of Co-ordinate Classes (162)

5 Canons for Terminology

16 Canon of Currency (171)
17 Canon of Reticence (172)
18 Canon of Enumeration (173)
19 Canon of Context (174)

6 Canons for Notation

20 Canon of Relativity (1881)
21 Canon of Expressiveness (1882)
22 Canon of Mixed Notation (1883)

7 Canons for Knowledge Classification

23 Canon of Hospitality in Array (221)
24 Canon of Hospitality in Chain (231)
25 Canon of Mnemonics (241)
26 Canon of Verbal Mnemonics (253)
27 Canon of Scheduled Mnemonics (261)
28 Canon of Seminal Mnemonics (271)

8 Canons for Book Classification

29 Canon of Classics (621)
30 Canon of Local Variation (631)
31 Canon of Book Number (662)
32 Canon of Collection Number (678)
33 Canon of Distinctiveness (685)

CHAPTER 08

PRINCIPLES AND POSTULATES FOR HELPFUL SEQUENCE

080 The work in the seven steps of classification, enumerated in Rule 0261, requires some guiding principles and postulates.

0801 Step 1 calls for the filling up of ellipsis. It is only familiarity with the schedules of classification and experience that can be of help in this step.

0802 Step 2 calls for the break-down of composite ideas into fundamental, constituent ideas. No principle has yet been discovered to determine the depth of the level up to which the break-down should be carried out. At present, one has to be guided only by the facets of isolates scheduled in the scheme of classification. This amounts to transferring the burden to the classificationist. He himself has generally done it under the guidance of intuition or unexpressed flair.

0803 Step 3 is the critical step in the work of classifying. It involves the sensing of the fundamental category of which each kernel idea is a manifestation. This has to be learned only by practice, at first under guidance, and later by trial and error. The assignment of each kernel or facet to the appropriate round and level is the vital task. A few principles have been found to be helpful. The arrangement of the facets within a round is another problem. This can be based on some postulates, resulting in helpful classification or arrangement of subjects. But more principles will have to be discovered to meet the requirements of the depth classification of the micro subjects needed in documentation. However, the principles and postulates now available prove sufficient for book classification or the classification of macro thought.

0806 Step 6 is the next essential step in the completion of the classifying work. Occasionally in book classification, and quite often in depth classification, isolate numbers, not found in the schedule, will have to be designed. Some guiding principles are now available for this work.

0807 The chief principles and postulates now available are listed in the rest of this chapter. For those developed before ed 2 of the *Prolegomena*, the number of the section in that book is given within brackets or in parallel column. In these sections, an exposition and illustration will be found. Those formulated later will be without section numbers against them. An exposition and illustration of them will be given in the forthcoming book *Practical classification by postulational approach*. Some account of them will also be found in the demonstration given in ed 2 of the *Elements* and in the articles in the *Annals of library science*, 5 and 6, 1958 and 1959.

0808 Section 081 to 084 and 086 contain only Principles. Section 085 contains only postulates.

Numb	Principle or Postulate	Desc in Sec	Numb	Principle or Postulate	Desc in Sec
		081 General			
1	Increasing Concreteness	3581	2	Increasing Artificiality	3582
		082 For Helpfulness among Isolates in an Array			
3	Zone Analysis	36211			
		083 For Helpfulness among Enumerated Common Isolates			
4	Quasi Subject Device				
		084 For Helpfulness among Enumerated Special Isolates			
5	Increasing Quantity	1431	11	Away-from-Position	
6	Later-in-Time	1432	12	Clock-wise	
7	Later-in-Evolution	1433	13	Increasing Complexity	1435
8	Spacial Contiguity	1434	14	Canonical Sequence	1456
9	Bottom-Upwards		15	Literary Warrant	1417
10	Left-to-Right		16	Alphabetical Sequence	1458

085 Postulates for Sequence among Fundamental Categories

17 PME Postulate (= within a round, [P], [M], [E] should be arranged in this sequence) (3561).

18 ST Postulate (= [S] and [T] should be put in the last round) (3561).

086 For Helpfulness of Sequence among Facets

19 Basic Facet Principle (= the basic facet should be put as the first facet) (3561).

20 Cow-Calf Principle (= inseparable facets should be put together in the same round).

21 Act-and-Action-Actor Principle (4611).

22 Wall-Picture Principle (= a facet depending on another facet for its very existence should come after that other facet).

23 Whole-Organ Principle (= within a round the organ should be at a later level than the whole).

CHAPTER 1

MAIN CLASS

11 The Main Classes (MC) are enumerated and the digits representing them are given in Chap 1 of the Schedules.

1101 All the (MC) are not co-ordinate. Some of them are partially comprehensive of others.

The classes B to M are all subdivisions of class A Natural Sciences.

The classes C to F constitute the generic class called " physical sciences ". This is represented by the Greek letter Γ (gamma).

The classes G to L constitute the generic class called " bio-sciences ". This class may be represented by G itself.

Δ " Spiritual Experience and Mysticism " forms a class by itself.

The classes T to Z constitute the generic class called " social sciences ". This class is represented by the Greek letter Σ (sigma).

The classes N to S constitute the generic class called " humanities ". This class is represented by the Greek letter ν (Nu).

The Greek letter μ (Mu) is used to represent " humanities and social sciences " taken together. For there are books and periodicals of a general nature falling within this partially comprehensive class.

We have also books and periodicals comprehending O Literature and P Linguistics. This partially comprehensive main class is represented by NZ.

Any book, dealing with more than one of the classes H to L, is to be placed in class G.

Any book, dealing with more than one of the natural sciences, ie with more than one of the classes B to M, but one at least of which falls outside and one at least inside the group of classes G to L, is to be placed in class A.

Any book, dealing with more than one of the classes T to Z, is to be placed in class Σ.

Finally, any book, dealing with more than one subject, one at least of which falls outside and one at least inside the group of natural sciences, is to be put in the class ' Generalia '.

1102 There is some kind of helpful sequence among the classes of each generic class and among the generic classes themselves. This is shown in the *Prolegomena*, section 717. The appropriateness of placing Δ between the natural sciences on the one side and the humanities and the social sciences on the other. is shown in chapter Δ of the Rules and in the *Memoirs* of the Madras Library Association for 1939.

1103 There are periodicals and reference books covering the generic classes enumerated. The generic classes are included in the schedule of (MC) in order to provide a proper host class for such periodicals and reference books.

1104 The classes, represented by Indo-Arabic numerals and enumerated at the beginning of the schedule under consideration, fall outside these partially generic and the other main classes.

1105 Generally speaking, a (MC) cannot be represented either as a subclass of another or as a combination of two or more of the (MC)s. New (MC)s emerge occasionally.

1106 The task of making the (MC)s, other than the generic ones, mutually exclusive is by no means easy. For the terms used to name these classes are not definite in their denotation. The boundary lines between the different (MC)s are never either clear or definite. Subjects usually shade into one another; and the boundary line gets shifted from time to time. Hence, the only practical way to make the terms definite is to define each term by successive subdivisions. *See* Canon of Enumeration explained in the *Prolegomena* ed 2, Section 173. This will be done in the later chapters of the schedules. The mutual exclusiveness of the classes will be secured by taking care to see that the subdivisions are so constructed as to avoid overlapping. Further, once a subdivision gets itself attached to a particular (MC), due care should be taken to see that it is not disturbed from its position. In other words, the library should be absolutely consistent in the use of the subdivisions. Again, the same isolate may occur in different host classes. Its significance is not the same in all cases. The correct significance is to be determined by the Canon of Context given in the *Prolegomena*, ed 2, Section 17. For example, "Gold" in the class-context of Chemistry is different from the same in the class-context of Economics.

1107 New (MC)s emerge from time to time. Some of them are methodologies, such as those for compiling bibliography, encyclopaedia, and directory. These have been distilled out, as independent disciplines, so to speak, from long-continued rule-of-thumb methods. These disciplines were first embodied in articles only. But some of them have now been cultivated with sufficient elaboration and have been embodied in whole books. Other similar new disciplines are Communication Theory, Planning Technique, Standardisation Technique, and so on. None of these new disciplines can be expressed conveniently in terms of the traditional (MC). Therefore these also have to be treated as (MC)s. Some samples of them are given in Chapter 1 of the Schedules. More will be given in the volumes for depth classification.

12 Each subject will belong to one and only one (MC).

The (MC) of a subject will have to be determined by the Method of Trial and Error. The procedure to be followed has been elaborated, described, and illustrated in the *Fundamentals*. It will be similarly elaborated, described, and illustrated in the forthcoming *Practical classification and postulational approach*.

13 As determined by its main subjects, each book will belong to one and only one (MC).

A book may comprehend two or more subjects. The determination of one of them as its main subject is a matter of judgement and convention. This will be illustrated in the forthcoming *Practical classification and postulational approach*.

CHAPTER 2

COMMON ISOLATE

20 The **Common Isolates** (CI), attachable to many classes of many (MC), are enumerated and the digits representing them are given in chap 2 of the Schedules.

It is not maintained that every one of the Common Isolates can be attached to every possible class. All that is meant is that they may be applicable to many classes irrespective of the degree of their extension or intention, or of their (MC). For example,

P*v* is History of Linguistics;

P111*v* is History of English Linguistics; and

P111:J1*v* is History of Modern English Phonology. Similarly,

C*v* is History of Physics;

C5*v* is History of the Physics of Radiation; and

C53*v* is History of the Physics of X-Rays. So also,

V44:255*t* is an Indian Franchise Committee;

X44:9·44*t* is an Indian Labour Committee; and

Z56:9511*t* is a British Committee on Death Sentence.

Chap 3 to 5 of the Rules should be read to understand the rest of the Rules of this Chapter.

201 A (CI), attachable to host class number directly without a connecting symbol, is an **Anteriorising** (CI) or (ACI).

202 A (CI), needing a connecting symbol for attachment to host class number, is a **Posteriorising** (CI) or (PCI).

203 Unless otherwise specified, the Class Number is to be worked out on the basis of the facet-formula prescribed in chapters 9*z* to Z of the Schedules to the fullest extent admitted by the book before a (CI) digit is attached to it.

2031 In the case of biographies and some types of collected works, the Class Numbers are to be worked out to the least extent possible.

The exact extent has to be left to the flair of the classifier.

2032 Whenever warranted, two or more (ACI) may be attached in succession.

"History of bibliography" will warrant successive amplification by *a* and *v*. *Bav*44.N5 is "History of bibliography of Mathematics, in India brought up to 1950's".

204 Most of the (ACI) are to be fitted with one or two Personality Facets, as prescribed in chap 2 of the Schedules and mentioned in sec 21 of this chapter and its subdivisions.

See sec 61 of chapter 05 of the "Preliminaries" for an explanation of the term Facet.

205 The isolates of the two Personality Facets are to be got by (GD) and (CD) respectively.

206 When both the facets are prescribed, the facet by the (GD) is to be put first. And the two facets are to be separated by a comma, as prescribed in Rule 05501.

207 The following is the key to the terms used in the specification of the isolate in the Personality Facet, to be got by (GD).

'Country' means either Country, or State in the case of a large polyglot country such as India and Russia.

'Locality' means the geographical area of smaller extension than country, which is relevant to the context.

'Region' means any geographical area other than country or locality, which is relevant to the context.

'Location' means the country, locality, or region in which the entity concerned is located.

'Origin' means the country, locality, or region in which the entity concerned had its origin.

'Purview' means the country, locality, or region falling within the purview of the entity concerned.

208 The following is the key to the terms used to indicate the focus in the Personality Facet, to be got by (CD).

'Origin' means the year of foundation, birth, or origin of the entity concerned.

'Covered' means the effective decade which is the end of the period covered by or falling within the purview of the entity concerned or the effective decade of the year of foundation, birth, or origin of the entity concerned, as may be appropriate.

See Rules 311 and 312 for the use of the term **Effective Decade.**

21 Anteriorising Common Isolate

21 The following is the table of facets for (ACI).

(ACI)	[P] by (GD)	[P] by (CD)
k	Geographical Area of Purview	Epoch of Origin.
m Periodical	Country or Locality of Origin of Parent-Body, if sponsored by it.	do
	Country or Locality of Origin if not sponsored by a Corporate Body.	do
n Serial	Geographical Area of Purview	do
p Conference	Geographical Area of Purview	Year (worked to three digits) if an isolated one
		Epoch of Origin, if periodically held.
w Biography		Origin of Biographee. Three digits, if single. Latest Effective Decade covered if collected
x Works		Origin of Author. Three digits, if single. Latest Effective Decade covered, if many.

21*a* The digit *a* may be fitted either with [T] worked to the Latest Effective Decade covered, or with facets as in Generalia Bibliography (*See* Rule 9*z*8) if the nature of the book warrants it.

21*a*2 The following few lines will illustrate the advantages of the [T] only, when fitting of facets as per Rule 9*z*8 is not warranted. Let us take the class " Principles of Literary Criticism " as an example. It is possible to have many bibliographies of this subject brought up to one of several periods, like the Aristotelian period, the Augustan period, the Elizabethan period, the Victorian period, the Georgian period, and so on. If the digit *a*, coming after the Class Number of the class " Principles of Literary Criticism," is not fitted with [T], all these bibliographies will get arranged only by their years of publication. As a result, the bibliographies on the different periods get intermingled. On the other hand, if the digit *a* is fitted with [T] as laid down in Rule 21, the bibliographies will be grouped by the latest periods covered by them and the groups will themselves fall in chronological sequence. It is helpful to have them grouped in this way.

21*f* The digit *f* may, if warranted, be fitted with [T] worked to the Latest Effective Decade covered.

21*m* As a result of the facet-formula, all the volumes of a specific periodical will get the same Class Number. They will be brought together as their Class Number will be unique. They will be individualised by their Book Numbers.

21*m*1 To represent a Cumulative Index, the digit *b* should be added after the facets attached to *m*.

21*m*2 If a volume of a set is in more than one part, the parts should be regarded as an indivisible set in constructing the Book Number. Rule 0351 should be applied.

21*m*3 If a corporate body or any other agency sponsors two or more associated periodical publications on the same class of knowledge, the class number for the first should be constructed as provided in Rule 21; and the class numbers for the second, third etc., should be got from that of the first by adding to it a comma and thereafter the digit 1, 2 etc., respectively. If the number thus added be in two or more digits, it should be read as an integer and not as a decimal.

As a result of this rule, all the periodicals, sponsored by the same corporate body or agency and treating of the same class of knowledge, will come together. *Examples*:

A*m*56,K	Philosophical transactions, Royal Society of London.
A*m*56,K,1	Proceedings, Royal Society of London.
A*m*56,K,2	Yearbook, Royal Society of London.

21*n* Similar to 21*m* and its subdivisions.

21*v* The digit *v* is to be fitted with [S] and [T] in succession.

21*v*1 The [S] and [T] are to be connected by a dot.

21*v*2 The isolate in [S] is to be the Geographical Area coming within purview.

21*v*3 The isolate in [T] is to be the Latest Effective Decade covered.

Example: B*v*44.N5 History of Mathematics in India brought up to 1950's.

21*w* The host class of a biographical book is to be the class with which the name of the biographee is primarily associated.

For example, the biography of a mathematician is to be placed in Class B; the biography of an astronomer in class B9.

21*w*1 On the other hand, the biography of a person whose name cannot be definitely associated with some subject or another is to be placed in 'Generalia'. Similarly, if a book gives the biography of a number of persons, whose names are associated with more than one subject, one at least of which falls among the group of (MC) △ to Z, and one at least in the group of (MC) A to M, it is to be placed in 'Generalia'.

21*w*2 The letters and correspondence of a person are to be treated as part of his biography for the purpose of this Rule.

21*w*3 In many of the Social Sciences and in the divisions of the Main Class △, it is possible for the case-study or observation-study mode of exposition to take the form of a biography. In such a case, the (CI) Number is to be *y*7 and not *w*.

Examples: Purohit Swami's *An Indian monk; his life and adventures* is to be given the Class Number △2*y*7M82 and not △2*w*M82.

2 E Allison Peer's *Ramon Lull: a biography* is to be given the Class Number △6*y*7G32 and not △6*w*G32.

3 But, a biography of Rom Landau or of Paul Brunton is to be amplified only by *w* though its Main Class may be △, since their biographies are of interest not as case-studies but only as lives of persons who have made a special study of the Main Class △.

21*w*4 The biography of a person, whose importance is due mainly to his association with some other person of importance, either as a relative or as a friend, or in any other manner, is to be given the Class Number of the biography of that person of importance.

The biography of such a relative or friend is of interest to readers, only because of the light it throws on the life of the person of importance. For example, the biography of Jane Welsh Carlyle is of interest because it throws light on the life of Thomas Carlyle. Hence the book will have a greater chance to find a reader if it is placed with the biographies of Thomas Caryle. It is just this result that is sought to be secured by this Rule.

21*w*5 In the case of a collective biography of persons of a specific Geographical Area, the digit *w* is to be fitted with Two Personality Facets. The isolate in the first is to the Geographical Area concerned. The isolate in the second is to be got by (CD). It is to be the Latest Effective Decade covered.

21*y*7 See rule 21*w*2. *y*7 is to be fitted with facets as for *w*.

22 Anteriorising (CI)

Applicable only after [*S*]

22*s* The digit *s* is to be fitted with Personality Facet, got by Chronological Device as for *m*.

27 Personality Posteriorising (CI)

27 A personality common Isolate (PCI) should generally be added after [S].

271 A (PCI) is to be fitted with [P]. The isolate in the [P] is to be got by (AD) if a localised body or by (CD) if a non-localised body.

272 A (PCI) may be fitted, when warranted, with [P2], [E], and [T] as the (MC) " V History ".

Examples:

B9.44g2,Kr Report of the Kodaikanal Observatory.

D.44,e4,R,13:3.N5 Functions of the Vice-Chancellor of the Roorkee Engineering University in the 1950's.

B.44f,N.N5 History of the Indian Mathematical Society brought up to the 1950's. (This was the first of the Mathematical Societies founded in India in the twentieth century).

CHAPTER 3

TIME ISOLATE

30 **The Time Isolates** (TI) and the numbers representing them are given in sec 31 of chap 3 of the Schedules.

In the (MC) 'History', [T] will be essential. Many of the (CI) have to be fitted with [T] or with [P] got by (CD). Formation or sharpening of isolate by (CD) is found helpful in many classes. This variety of the uses of (TI) invests the Colon Classification with a great measure of hospitality.

31 In the case of each isolate from E onwards, a letter stands for a century. The decade is to be indicated, whenever necessary, by adding the digit of the decade — 0, 1,... or 9, as the case may be — after the century digit. The year is to be indicated, whenever necessary, by adding the digit of the year — 0, 1,...or 9 as the case may be — after the decade digit.

Examples:—E55=1055 AD M00=1800 AD P01=2101 AD

311 The digits for an **Effective Decade** (ED) are 1, 3, 5, 7 and 9

312 Whenever the focus in a [T] is prescribed to be the (ED) the Decade Number is to end

with 1 when the natural decade number ends with 0 or 1;
with 3 when the natural decade number ends with 2 or 3;
with 5 when the natural decade number ends with 4 or 5;
with 7 when the natural decade number ends with 6 or 7; and
with 9, when the natural decade number ends with 8 or 9.

Grouping by intervals of about one generation is helpful and also sufficient in the arrangement of subjects. For, a generation is a natural and significant unit in the progress of human affairs and thought. A decade is only arbitrary and arithmetical. (ED) also makes the work of the classifier less arduous than a decade or a year.

3120 We shall denote "Latest Effective Decade covered by a Book" by the symbol (LED).

32 D represents the first millennium AD. A century in it is to be indicated, if necessary, by adding the digit of the century — 0, 1,...or 9 as the case may be — after D. A decade is to be indicated, if necessary, by adding the digit of the decade — 0, 1,...or 9, as the case may be — after the century digit. And so on.

Examples:—D001 = 1 A D D010 = 10 A D D541 = 541 A D

33 C represents the first millennium BC; a century digit, a decade digit, or a year digit is to be arrived at as follows:—

Write the year in ordinary Indo-Arabic numerals.

The excess of nine over the number representing the century is to be used for the century digit;

The excess of nine over the number representing the decade is to be used for the decade digit; and

The excess of nine over the number representing the year is to be used for the year digit.

Examples:—3 B C = C996. 10 B C = C989. 500 B C = C499.

330 This method of determining the digits of a BC Number may be called the **Method of Complements.**

34 B represents the second to the tenth millennium BC. The digits succeeding it are to be got by the Method of Complements.

351 Whenever a Rule prescribes a decade as the focus, the number of digits of a (TI) Number beginning with B, C or D is to be two.

352 Whenever a Rule prescribes a year as the focus, the number of digits of a (TI) Number beginning with B, C or D is to be three.

391 Some (T1) of [T 2] are given in see 32 of chap 3 of the Schedules.

A more detailed schedule for [T2] will be given in a volume for depth classification. A discussion of the problem and a provisional schedule are given in the *Review of documentation*, 23, 1956, 70-79, in the article on *Time isolate*, sec 5.

392 A dot is to be inserted as the connecting symbol between [T] and [T 2].

Example:—U2855·56·N59·*n*7 Rainfall in Great Britain in the winter of 1959.

CHAPTER 4

SPACE ISOLATE

40 The **Space Isolates (SI)** and the numbers representing them are given in sec 41 of chap 4 of the Schedules.

41 When "World" is used in the integral, unifocal sense, it is to be represented by 1.

41-1 When "World" is used in a disjunctive, multifocal sense, it is to be represented by 1-1.

41-2 The (IN) of an empire having territories in two or more continents is to be derived from 1 by (SID) (see Rule 688), using the (IN) of the Ruling Country as the Super-Imposed Number.

Examples:

1-52 Roman Empire
1-53 French Empire
1-56 British Empire

411 The (IN) of an area made of countries, surrounding a water-formation and falling in two or more continents is to be derived from 1 by the addition of the (IN) for the water-formation *sans* the initial digit 9.

Examples are given in Chapter 4 of the Schedules.

412 The (IN) of an area made of countries, falling in two or more continents and coming together under an organisation with near-sovereign powers, is to be derived from 1 by (CD) (see Rule 683 and its subdivisions).

Examples are given in Chapter 4 of the Schedules.

413 The (IN) of an area made of countries, falling in two or more continents but deemed as a unit focus on the basis of a Subject Characteristic, is to be derived from 1 by (SD) (see Rule 685 and its subdivisions).

Examples:

1(H7118) Countries with gold-mines
1(P111) English-speaking countries
1(Q7) Muslim countries

42 The digit 2 may be used to represent the country of the library — The **Mother Country.**

It is likely that a library will have a more extensive collection of books pertaining to its country. Hence the number for that area will have to be inserted very frequently. Further it will have to be subdivided much more profusely than those of other countries. As the number it gets in its natural place in the Space Schedule will contain at least two digits and may contain many more, it would add to economy of notation if it can be indicated by a single digit. Hence, it is suggested, that the normal number it gets in its natural place may be left unused and the digit 2 be used to represent it. Incidentally, this rule gives precedence to Mother Country over all other countries. This rule secures satisfaction to the Canon of Local Variation.

43 The digit 3 may be used to represent the **Favoured Country.**

Here, the term "favoured" means the country about which the library has a much larger collection than about other countries barring its own country. All the remarks made under Rule 42 are applicable to this rule also.

44 If any ultimate area mentioned in the schedule requires further subdivision, the subdivision may be effected in accordance with the following plan:—Let the area be divided into eight convenient sectors and the sectors be numbered as hereunder:

1. East	3. South	5. West	7. North
2. South-east	4. South-West	6. North-west	8. North-east

If only one sub-area falls in a sector, the number of the sector may be given to the sub-area. If more than one sub-area falls in a sector, it may be further subdivided in a similar manner. The digit '9' may be reserved for indicating the islands in the neighbourhood of the area.

A strict adherence to this principle is not demanded; nor is it possible in all cases. All that is intended is that the rule may be used as a rough guiding principle. It will be found that sec 41 of chap 4 of the Schedules gives subdivisions of certain countries only.

In the case of India and Pakistan, the schedule for undivided India (before 1947) is retained in this edition also.

An additional short schedule is added showing the newly formed States in India and Pakistan, after partition. It is too early for the districts to be finalised in the newly formed States.

45 In the local collection of a library, " — " (dash) may be used to denote the locality.

46 The (IN) of an area made of subdivisions of any geographical division in a disjunctive, multifocal manner, is to be got from the number of the geographical division by the addition of the Disjunctive Symbol " - 1 ".

47 The (IN) of an area made of non-contiguous subdivisions of any geographical division or is an orientation division of it,

is to be derived from the number of that geographical division on the analogy of the Rules and the schedule for the world.

Examples:

44-542	Portuguese India
44L	India under Mahratta Power
44 (P152)	Hindi-speaking States of India
49M	West Asia
4N	Seato

491 **Some (SI) of [S 2] are given in sec 42 of chap 4 of the Schedules.**

The isolates in [S2] are all physical features. A more detailed schedule for [S2] will be given in a volume for depth classification. A discussion of the problem and a provisional schedule are given in the *Review of documentation*, 24, 1957, 18-28, in the article *Space isolate*, sec 5 to 56.

492 **A dot is to be inserted as the connecting symbol between [S] and [S 2].**

493 **The isolate in [S] is to be the one of the least extension, containing the whole of the isolate in [S2].**

494 **An isolate in [S 2] is to be individualised, when warranted, by (AD).**

Examples

D885.594.3Z.p8	Street cleaning in Zurich during snow period.
D885.594.3Z.N5	Street cleaning in Zurich in the 1950's.
D885.594.37.N5.p8	Street cleaning in Zurich in the snow period of the 1950's.
J.44.16G.N5	Agriculture in the Gangetic valley in the 1950's.
J.441.16C.N5	Agriculture in the Cauvery valley in the 1950's.
K:12.44.2V	Fauna of the Vindhya Mountains.
Q2:38.44.3V	Varanasi sthala purana.
U8.4.2H.N5	Himalayan travels in the 1950's.
Y:1.1.16	River valley civilisation.

CHAPTER 5

LANGUAGE ISOLATE

50 The **Language Isolates** (LI) and the numbers representing them are given in Chapter 5 of the Schedules.

51 To represent a language, definitely known to belong to one of the three families represented by the digit '1', '2' or '3' but not indicated in the schedule, the digit 9 should be added after the number of the ultimate division into which it will fall and the digit 9 should be further divided by (GD). The (GI) in which it first became current, should be used in the (GD).

54 A language comprised by the classes 4....9 should be individualised by (GD). The (GI), in which it became first current, should be used in the (GD).

55 The (IN) for an Artificial Language should be got by (CD), using the year, in which it was coined, as the epoch.

56 The digit "—" (dash) may be used for the Favoured Language of the library in the Language Facet of a Class Number.

The Language Facet occurs in the (MC) Literature and Linguistics. A library will have a more extensive collection of books in the Literature and the Linguistics of the Favoured Language than of the other ones. Hence the number for that Language will have to be inserted frequently. It will, therefore, add to economy of notation if it can be represented by a single digit.

Moreover, it will be helpful if the group of books belonging to the Favoured Language comes prior to those belonging to the other ones. This requirement, coupled with the fact that the numbers of all Languages begin with 1, 2 . . . or 9 indicates that the digit to be used for the Favoured Language should have an ordinal value anterior to 1. Thus the digit "—" (dash) is prescribed.

This Rule secures satisfaction of the Canon of Local Variation.

CHAPTER 6

PHASE AND INTRA-FACET RELATION

61 A subject is **One-Phased** if it consists of only a single (MC) or any of its subclasses, ie if it is a (BC) or a (CdC).

62 A subject is **Two-Phased** if it brings into relation two (BC) or two (CdC) or a (BC) and a (CdC).

620 The Class formed by a Two-Phased subject is called a **Complex Class** (CxC).

6201 The constituent of a Two-Phased subject, which is the primary subject of exposition or is otherwise deemed to be primary, is called its **First Phase.**

6202 The constituent of a Two-Phased specific subject, which is merely affecting the exposition of the First Phase, is called its **Second Phase**.

6203 The Class Number of a Two-Phased specific subject is got by inserting, between the Class Numbers of the First and the Second Phases, the Connecting Symbol 0 and an appropriate digit to represent the phase-relation.

6204 Sec 61 of chap 6 of the Schedules gives the schedule of **Phase-Relation** (PR).

Each phase-relation digit is a Roman small.

6205 The Second-Phase of a (CxC) is named after the Phase-Relation.

Examples: Bias Phase; Comparison Phase; Influencing Phase.

62a General Relation Phase

62*a* **"General Relation"** denotes a more or less all-comprehensive relation—that is, not merely any one of the other relations listed in the Schedule.

62*a*1 The constituent, whose Class Number is of smaller ordinal value than that of the other, is to be used as the First Phase.

62*a*2 The Second Phase is called Relation Phase in this case.

Example: W0*a*X Relation between Political Science and Economics.

62b Bias Phase

62*b* **Bias Relation** indicates that the exposition of the First Phase is biased towards the Second Phase, that is, the exposition is specially attuned either by selection or arrangement of topics or emphasis or standard or examples or other means to the needs of a specialist in the subject forming the Second Phase.

62*b*1 The Second Phase is called **Bias Phase** in this case.

A few examples may be given here to illustrate Bias Relation.

The general text-books of Mathematics will have the Class Number B. But it is likely that some of these books are written especially for the use of physicists, engineers, biologists, economists, etc. In the case of such books, the Class Number B may be added to so as to read B0*b*C B0*b*D B0*b*G B0*b*X etc., respectively. If such books are not differentiated by the Bias Device, they will get intermingled with the ordinary text-books in Mathematics. When an engineer comes and asks for a mathematical text-book, the library cannot readily find out the books suited to him.

Take another example. The general books on Statistics have the Class Number B28. But some of them are written for the use of engineers, some for the use of psychologists, and so on. It will be convenient if such books can be differentiated by adding to their Class Numbers so as to read B280*b*D, B280*b*S, etc.

Similarly, we have

L0*b*Z Medical jurisprudence

S0*b*L Psychology for doctors

X:90*b*YZ Labour economics for social workers

A further discussion and plenty of examples and exercises will be found in section 301 and chapter 31 of the *Fundamentals*.

62c Comparison Phase

62*c* When a **Comparison** is made between two subjects, the one whose class number is the earlier ordinal number is to be treated as the First Phase.

62*c*1 The Second Phase is called **Comparison Phase** in this case.

Example: C0*c*E = Physics compared to Chemistry. E0*c*C also will virtually mean the same thing. In other words, two synonymous class numbers are possible. But a Classificatory Language should have no synonyms, as prescribed in section 1934 of the *Fundamentals*. It is to eliminate synonymous class numbers and to secure consistency that Rule 82*c* is prescribed.

62d Difference Phase

62*d* When the **difference** between two subjects is expounded, the one whose class number is the earlier ordinal number is to be treated as the First Phase.

62*d*1 The Second Phase is called **Difference Phase** in this case.

Example: B850*d*CN2 = Difference between Wave Function and Wave Mechanics.

62g Influencing Phase

62*g* When the Influence of one subject on another subject is expounded, the latter should be treated as the First Phase.

62*g*1 The Second Phase is called **Influencing Phase** in this case.

Example: W0*g*U = Geopolitics = Political Science as influenced by Geography. A reference may be made to T N Koranne's *Phase-relation and special vs general principles* published in pages 37 to 39 of Volume 1 of the *Annals* of the Indian Library Association forming the first part of *Abgila*. The connecting symbol he has used is slightly different. That is because we were still experimenting on connecting symbols at the time he wrote the article.

63 The above Rules go some way in solving what was described as the Sixth Unsolved Problem in section 4226 of the *Fundamentals*. As and when new Phase Relations come to be distinguished, the solution of the problem will improve further.

63 Intra-Facet Relation

63 It is possible to have books expounding the relation between two isolates in one and the same facet of a class. We shall call it **Intra-Facet Relation** (IFR).

631 An isolate formed by thus bringing into relation two isolates in the same facet shall be called a **Complex Isolate** (CxI).

632 A (CxI) belongs to the same Facet as its constituents.

633 The (IN) of a (CxI) is got by inserting, between the (IN) of the Constituent Isolates, the connecting symbol 0 and an appropriate digit to represent the Intra-Facet Relation.

634 Sec 62 of chap 6 of the Schedules gives the Schedule of Intra-Facet Relation.

635 Rules analogous to Rules 82*a* to 82*g* hold good for Intra-Facet Relation.

636 Intra-facet relation is different from mutual denudation or superimposition.

64 Intra-Array Relation

64 It is possible to have books expounding the relation of two Array-Isolates in one and the same array.

641 An array isolate formed by thus bringing into relation two array isolates in the same array may be called a Complex Array Isolate.

642 Rules analogous to Rules for Phase and Intra-Facet Relations hold good for Intra-Array Isolates (IAR).

Examples

X:5.440*j*56	Commercial relation between India and Great Britain.
Z,40*j*5	Relation between torts and crimes.
L:20*k*3	Physiological anatomy.
X5.440*k*1N48	Commonwealth preference in India's commerce.
B910*m*43:63	Comparison of the constitution of earth and mars.
CN10*m*:N2	Comparison of Quantum Physics and Wave Mechanics.
E:30*n*5	Difference between analytical chemistry and extractive chemistry.
O111,2M560*r*J64	Influence of Shakespeare on Bernard Shaw.
Q60*r*4	Influence of Buddhism on Christianity.
Y310*w*5	Difference between rural folk and city folk

CHAPTER 7

CLASSIC

7 A book stimulating other books and literature on itself is a **Classic.**

This is strictly a classifier's definition. It naturally uses that quality of Classics which challenges a classificatory language to deal with it properly. It wants that a Classic and its associated literature should be arranged like a continuous spectrum, with nothing outside itself intervening. The different editions of the Classic itself and its several translations should occupy the centre — the umbra, as it were. The literature on it should be spread on either side — the penumbra — in correct filiatory sequence — bibliographies, catalogues, and accounts of exhibitions, transactions of learned bodies, periodicals, yearbooks, reports, of conferences, histories, biographies, commentaries, sub-commentaries adaptations, parodies and criticisms bearing on the Classic.

The inherent qualities of a Classic stimulating such auxiliary literature are that:

1 It has elements of permanent value;

2 It is saturated with the personality of the author—which in itself was very powerful and highly organised; and

3 It is a seminal book cutting new ground, blazing new trail, stimulating new thought, and so on.

The basic sacred books of a religion are of such a nature. Any scheme of classification generally makes each sacred book a class by itself. Works of poets, dramatists, novelists, and other literary artists are generally of such a nature. Some schemes of classification make each such work a class by itself and also make each such author a class by himself. But classics are not peculiar to the main classes 'Religion' and 'Literature'. Any other (MC) may have classics of their own. Even a subclass, such as 'Greek Philosophy,' 'Sanskrit Linguistics' and 'International Law', has several classics.

71 An author, one at least of whose works is a classic, is a **Classical Author.**

72 The **Classic Device** (ClD) is employed for bringing together the different editions of a classic in a class, the different editions of each of its commentaries, the different editions of each of the sub-commentaries of each of its commentaries, and so on, and of securing that the group of sub-commentaries of a commentary is in juxtaposition to the commentary, that the group of commentaries of a classic is in juxtaposition to the classic, and that the group formed of each classic and its associated commentaries is in juxtaposition to the groups of the other classics of the same class.

73 The (ClD) consists in putting the digit *x* after the number representing the ultimate class to which the classic should

be otherwise assigned and adding after it an Author Facet and also a Work Facet, if we cannot be certain that the Author wrote only one work, provided the classic is not a sacred book or a work belonging to the (MC) O Literature, as these are individualised otherwise.

731 Author and Work Facets are [P]. But "," need not be put between *x* and Author Number.

732 The isolate in the Author Facet of the Class Number may be determined by the Favoured Category Principle for not more than 16 Classical Authors, and by the (CD), as in the (MC) O Literature, for the others.

733 The isolate in the Work Facet is to be determined as in the Work Facet of the (MC) O Literature.

74 A Commentary Facet may be added after the Work Facet. The isolate in it may be determined by the Favoured Category Device for not more than 16 Commentaries and by the (CD) for the others.

75 Second Order Commentary, Third Order Commentary, etc Facets may be added successively after the Commentary Facet. The isolates in them may be determined as in the latter.

751 All Commentary Facets are [P].

An implication of all the above-mentioned facets being declared to be [P] is that the Connecting Symbol for each of them is a comma.

761 Part 3 of this volume gives a list of Indian Classics with their Class Numbers constructed by the (ClD).

762 The (ClD) secures conformity to the Canon of Classics.

763 The problem that the (ClD) seeks to tackle is frequent in the case of classical works written in Sanskrit. A reference to the illustrative divisions by the (ClD) given in Part 3 will show how wide-spread this problem is. There are also some cases of occidental classics—such as the Classics of International Law and the Greek and the Latin Classics—which may more conveniently be grouped by the (ClD).

764 One result of the application of the (ClD) is that the classic becomes a class by itself. Hence its different editions come together, with the book number differentiating them. In the case of a classic, several editions are likely to appear even at distant dates. But for this device, they will get scattered and intermingled with ordinary books in the same class. Such an intermingling is bound to be revolting to the mind of readers. It is certainly not desirable that Aristotle's *Poetics* or Dandin's *Kavyadarsa* should be indiscriminately clubbed with the ordinary modern books on literary criticism. Nor will it be happy to mix Sankaracharya's works on Indian Philosophy with the modern text-books on this subject.

765 It frequently happens, particularly in works in the Sanskrit language, that the classic gets many commentaries which themselves become classic and get many editions and many sub-commentaries. All the Laws of Library Science

will be best served if and only if the whole family of commentaries and sub-commentaries are grouped together and placed next to the different editions of the classic itself. Usually the commentaries and the sub-commentaries carry forward the theories contained in the classic. This carrying forward is done step by step, in the hierarchy of commentaries and sub-commentaries. Hence the happy grouping of a classic with its commentaries and sub-commentaries brought about by the (ClD) incidentally arranges the books in the proper evolutionary sequence. This adds greatly to the convenience of readers — nay, it is even educative.

766 It may be stated here that the use of the digit *x* in the (ClD) is not in any way in conflict with the use of the same to indicate collected works. As a matter of fact the one use is but a natural and consistent extension of the other.

77 In reality the (ClD) converts a work into a class. Therefore the class so formed is called **Quasi Class**. See *Prolegomena*, chapter 62. This term was originally coined by me in the *Heading and canons: Comparative study of five catalogue codes* (1955), section 2191.

CHAPTER 9*z*

GENERALIA

9*z* By 'Generalia' is meant a class into which should go any publication which deals with several subjects which cannot go into any other single main class enumerated in Chapter 1 of the Schedules.

9*z*1 The bare digit *z* is to hold only ordinary exposition of Generalia.

9*z*2 If the exposition is confined only to generalia materials on a specific geographical area, the digit *z* should be divided by (GD), using the area concerned for the purpose.

Examples

*z*4	Orientalia	*z*44	Indology
*z*41	Sinology	*z*5	Occidentalia
*z*42	Nipponology	*z*7	Americana

9*z*3 If the exposition is confined only to generalia materials by and on a specific person, the digit *z* should be amplified by (AD) using the name of the person concerned for the purpose.

Example:—*z*G Gandhiana

This Rule is applicable only to a person of truly "generalia" activity or output, and not to one who is dominantly assignable to a subject lying within any other main class. Indeed, this Rule will be applicable only to a few persons.

9*z*4 Whenever the bare digit *z* (ie not amplified by (GD) or by (AD) calls for (ACI), the digit *z* may be omitted and it is sufficient if the (CN) begins with the (ACI) digit.

Examples

*k*56,L	Encyclopaedia Brittannica
*m*44,N37	Hindu herald
	(For definiteness the chronological number is worked out to three digits.)
*n*56,M	Statesman's year book.
*m*1N48,M	Who's who in the Commonwealth.
*z*44*m*56,M	Journal, Royal Asiatic Society of Great Britain and Ireland.

9*z*8 In the case of Generalia Bibliography the facet formula and schedules given in Chapter 9*z* of the Schedule should be fitted to the digit *a*.

9z80 Facet

Facet	Term	(IN) *by*
[P]	Material	Enumeration
[P2]	Kind	Enumeration

9z81 Further Facet

1 When (IN) in [P2] is 1

[P3]	Area	(GD)
[T]	Period	(LED)

2 When (IN) in [P2] is 2

[P3]	Country	(GD)
[P4]	Origin	(CD)

21 When (IN) is Union Catalogue

[P3]	Geographical Area Covered	(GD)

3 When (IN) in [P2] is 3 or 4

[P3]	Publisher or Book-seller	(AD)

5 When (IN) in [P2] is 5

[P3]	Country	(GD)
[P4]	Origin	(CD)

CHAPTER 92

LIBRARY SCIENCE

920 Facet

Facet	*Term*	(IN) *by*
[P]	Library	Enumeration
[M]	Material	Enumeration
[E] [2P]	Problem	Enumeration

923 Problem Facet

92351 A specific scheme of classification should be individualised by (CD).

Examples

2:51M	Decimal	2:51N	Congress
2:51M9	Expansive	2:51N3	Colon
2:51M96	Universal Decimal	2:51N34	Bibliographic

92355 A specific cataloguing code should be individualised by (CD).

924 When the focus in the [E] is Classification, [2P] may be the subject classified and its number should be got by (SD).

Examples of Class Numbers

2:51N3,(2)	Colon Classification of library science
2;45:6	Circulation of newspapers
234:81	Book selection in university library
234:45:81	Newspaper selection in university library
268:88	Maintenance work in libraries for the blind
Aem55,M	Zeitschrift fur Instrumentenkunde.

CHAPTER B

MATHEMATICS

B It is not possible to enunciate any relevant characteristics which may be made the basis for the classification of Mathematics as a whole. In fact we have to divide Mathematics, in the first instance, along canonical lines. Even some of the (CC) of Mathematics have to be further subdivided only on canonical lines. But certain (CC) and subclasses admit of classification on the basis of definite and appropriate trains of characteristics, as can be seen from Schedule B.

The terms used to denote the classes of Mathematics cannot be said to be quite definite. Even the Oxford Dictionary does not help us in fixing their denotation. Their denotation is to be fixed only by the enumeration of their subdivisions.

There are several Special Forms in Mathematics about each of which literature has accumulated and is accumulating. Such Special Forms appear in all subdivisions of Mathematics. For example we have Special Arithmetic Functions, Special Algebraic Equations, Special Algebraic Transformations, Special Groups, Special Series, Special Integrals, Special Differential Equations, Special Differential Operators, Special Functions, and so on.

The method employed in Mathematics as well as in all other subjects to represent such Special Forms, Topics, Theories etc., is that of working out the Class Number as far as it is possible on the basis of the characteristics of classification and further subdividing the (CN) thus arrived at, by (CD). The year of the first publication of an authentic exposition or investigation of the Topic or Theory or Form, as the case may be, is to be used as the epoch. The volumes of *Encyklopadie der mathematischen Wissenshaften* will be of help in fixing the Chronological Number in most of the cases. Other books on the History of Mathematics will also be of help.

B1 Arithmetic

B1 It may be stated here that books on Cardinal Numbers, Ordinal Numbers, Transfinite Numbers, and similar topics are not to be placed in this division. Their appropriate place is ' Foundations of Analysis '.

B11 Lower Arithmetic

B11 By ' Lower Arithmetic ' is meant arithmetic as it is popularly understood. Some of its subdivisions are indicated in Chapter B of the Schedules. It is unlikely that there will be books on topics which are more specialised than the subdivisions given in the Schedule. If there be any, each subdivision may be further subdivided in any suitable manner.

B12 Concept of Numbers

B12 The division ' Concept of Numbers ' should be used only for books which do not deal either with the special psychology of numbers on the one hand or with the foundations of Analysis on the other. The division is intended to hold popular accounts of the ' Concept of the Numbers ' such as Conant's *Concepts of numbers*.

B13 Theory of Numbers

B13 The term ' Theory of Numbers ' is traditionally used to denote the study of the properties of Integers. Its use is also nowadays extended to the study of certain other classes of numbers such as Ideal Numbers and higher Complex Numbers which are given as further divisions of B1. In this extended sense, ' Theory of Numbers ' is also denoted by the term ' Higher Arithmetic '.

B130 Facets

Facet	Term	(IN) *by*
[P]	Number	Enumeration
[P2]	Theory	Enumeration
[E]	Method	Enumeration

B131 The foci in the Number Facet are not intended to be mutually exclusive in the sense that the same number should not occur in more than one class. It is only the aspect studied that will be different in the different classes. The evolution of the ' Theory of Numbers ' indicates that the centre of attention is not on the numbers as such but on the aspect of numbers indicated in the Schedule. Further aspects, which may appear in future, can be accommodated either as subdivisions of the classes already given or as additional classes.

B133 It can be seen that the foci in the Method Facets are mnemonically derived from the (CC) of the (MC) ' B Mathematics ' and their subclasses. Whenever necesary, they may be further sharpened in the same way as the (CC) of Mathematics are.

B2 Algebra

B2 The subdivision of Algebra is not based on any characteristic. The subclasses are merely canonical ones.

B21 Elementary Algebra

B21 By ' Elementary Algebra ' is meant Algebra which does not involve infinite processes. The subclasses of ' Elementary Algebra ' are also on canonical lines.

B23 Algebraic Equation

B230 Facets

Facet	Term	(IN) *by*
[P]	Equation	Enumeration
[E]	Problem	Enumeration

B25 Higher Algebra

B25 The facet formula and the foci given in the Schedules indicate the connotation of the term ' Higher Algebra '.

B250 Facets

Facet	*Term*	(IN) *by*
[P]	Form	Enumeration
[P2]	Degree	Enumeration
[E] [2P]	Transformation	Enumeration

B3 Analysis

B3 The subdivision of Analysis is not based on any characteristic. The subclasses are merely (CC).

B33 Differential Equation

B330 Facets

Facet	*Term*	(IN) *by*
[P]	Equation	Enumeration
[P2]	Degree	Enumeration
[P3]	Order	Enumeration
[E] [2P]	Problem	Enumeration

B37 Real Variable and

B38 Complex Variable

Facet	*Term*	(IN) *by*
[P]	Variable	Enumeration
[E] [2P]	Problem	Enumeration

B39 Special Functions

B39 Each Special Function may be fitted with the same facets as ' B38 Complex Variable '.

B4 Other Methods

B4 The subdivisions of B4 by the Favoured Category Principle are given in Chapter B of the Schedules. If more methods of Analysis are discovered than can be accommodated by this Principle, the (CD) will have to be employed. The divisions representing each method may have to be further subdivided on the basis of appropriate characteristics. This is left for V2.

B6 Geometry

B6 The first focus in the Space Facet is anomalous. It is devoted to books on the 'Foundations of Geometry'. Each of the other foci has been further subdivided on the basis of the Degree of the Curve or Surface studied in the book. As usual, Special Curves and Special Surfaces should be individualised by (CD). The Favoured system of Geometry to-day is Euclidean Geometry. Therefore, the other systems go by the name of Non-Euclidean Geometry. Each of them is to be individualised by the (CD).

B60 Facets

Facet	*Term*	(IN) *by*
[P]	Space	Enumeration
[E] [P2]	Method	Enumeration

B7 Mechanics

B70 Facets

Facet	*Term*	(IN) *by*
[P]	Matter	Enumeration
[E]	Problem	Enumeration

B9 Astronomy

B90 Facets

Facet	*Term*	(IN) *by*
[P]	Body	Enumeration
[E]	Problem	Enumeration

Examples of Class Numbers

βm677,N	Proceedings, Math and Physical Soc. Egypt. 1937—
B13:5K	Fermat's last theorem
B23:1	Numerical solution of algebraic equations
B252,7:1	Linear transformatjons of *n*th degree binaries

B331,1,2:1	Numerical solution of ordinary linear differential second order equations
B37:1N	Lebesgue integral
B62:3	Differential plane geometry
B622:23	Analytical conics
B9.56,g2Gr	Report of the Astronomer Royal, Royal observatory, Greenwich
B9:513	Right ascension
B952:72	Orbits of comets
Γm541,N	Annales, Sociedad Espanola de Fiscia y Quimica 1903—

CHAPTER C

PHYSICS

C Physics is one of the subjects in which the rules for subdivision cannot be begun with the enumeration of some trains of characteristics to be used as the basis of their classification. On the other hand, we have to divide Physics, in the first instance, on canonical lines. Some of these (CC) admit of further subdivision on the basis of certain trains of characteristics.

C2 Properties of Matter

C20 Facets

Facet	*Term*	(IN) *by*
[P]	State	Enumeration
[E] [2P]	Problem	Enumeration

C3 Sound

C30 Facets

Facet	*Term*	(IN) *by*
[P]	Wave length	Enumeration
[E] [2P]	Problem	Enumeration

C4 Heat

C40 Facets

Facet	*Term*	(IN) *by*
[P]	State	Enumeration
[E] [2P]	Problem	Enumeration

C5 Radiation

C50 Facets

Facet	*Term*	(IN) *by*
[P]	Wave Length	Enumeration
[E] [2P]	Problem	Enumeration

C6 Electricity

C60 Facets

Facet	Term	(IN) *by*
[P]	Electricity	Enumeration
[E] [2P]	Problem	Enumeration

C7 Magnetism

C70 Facets

Facet	Term	(IN) *by*
[P]	Magnetism	Enumeration
[E] [2P]	Problem	Enumeration

Examples of Class Numbers

C*am*56,M	Science abstracts. A Physics.
C*um*56,N	Reports on progress in physics. (Physical Society, London) 1934 ——.
C25:53	Compressibility of liquid.
C3:11;5	Velocity of sound in water.
C53:3	X-ray spectra.
C9B7:58	Scattering of cosmic rays.
CN2,5:33	Band spectra according to wave mechanics.

CHAPTER D

ENGINEERING

D The traditional divisions of Engineering are Civil Engineering and Mechanical Engineering. But the term Civil Engineering is too vague. Foci 2, 3 and 4 in the Work Facet will come in the category of Civil Engineering. Municipal and Sanitary Engineering is an additional division which it has been found convenient to introduce.

D0 Facet

Facet	*Term*	(IN) *by*
[P]	Work	Enumeration
[P2]	(1) Part (For all but D6)	Enumeration; differentiated
	(6) Field of Application for D6	Enumeration; differentiated
[P3]	Part for D6	Enumeration; differentiated
[M]	Material	Enumeration; differentiated
[E] [2P]	Problem	Enumeration

D2 Part Facet

D2 The Foci in the Part Facet would naturally depend upon the Work Division and would be different for different types of work. Hence the Foci in the Part Facet of certain Work Divisions only have been given in the Schedule by way of illustration. For the other Work Divisions, the parts will be given in a volume of depth classification.

D26 The Foci in the Part Facet become very specialised in each branch of Mechanical Engineering. In a specialised Engineering library it would be necessary to work out the parts for each one of the Work Divisions given as subdivisions of Mechanical Engineering. But they may not be necessary in a general library. Lionel S. MARK's *Mechanical engineer's handbook* may be of much use in working out such details.

D5 Problem Facet

D515 The focus '15 Hydraulics' in the Problem Facet should hold books dealing with general Hydraulics, topics such as flow of water, etc. Books dealing with irrigation should be put in the Work Division '2'.

D8 Common Isolates

D8*e* The way in which the Common Isolate Digit '*e*' should be subdivided when applied to the Work Number '66' is indicated in Chapter D of the Schedules, as there are likely to be monographs on particular electrical instruments. A more comprehensive schedule will be given in a volume of depth classification.

Examples of Class Numbers

D27,3:4	Designing of surplus weir for tank
D41531,5	Narrow gauge railway curves
D5153,8:5	Specification for the brake of railway carriage
D65,45	Television
D65,8(2:55)	Electronic searcher
D65,8(B)	Electronic computer
D65,8(P:795)	Translating machine
D66,2	Transmission of electricity
D66,21:7	Construction of over-head transmission wires
D66,71:4	Design of electric lifts
D665,47	Telegraphy
D85:(G)	Biology of water supply

CHAPTER E

CHEMISTRY

E0 Facets

Facet	*Term*	(IN) *by*
[P]	Substance	Enumeration
[P2]	Combination	Enumeration
[E] [2P]	Problem	Enumeration

E1 Substance Facet

E11 The Substance Division '1' should accommodate books on the chemistry of specific elements. The Classification of Elements has been based on the Periodic Table. In fact, the second digit in the numbers of the sub-divisions of the Substance Division represents the group to which the Element belongs and the third digit ordinarily represents its period. It may be recollected that the vertical and horizontal rulings in the Periodic Table give rise to 90 cells.

Each cell ordinarily accommodates one element. When there are two elements in a cell the number corresponding to the cell is assigned to one of the two elements and for the other this number is amplified by the digit '9'. In three cells of Group 8, however, there are three elements. In these the third element has been, for convenience, assigned to the next later period, which happens to be vacant in all the three cases.

The reason for assigning the digit '9' for the second element, if any, in a cell and for transferring the third element to the next cell will become clear in the remarks under Rule E1203.

Ammonia has been treated as an element for the purposes of classification.

E111 The group of digits following the initial digit '1' may be termed the Element Number.

Thus every element has an Element Number consisting of either two digits or three digits. It may be repeated that if the Element Number runs to three digits or more, the third digit will be '9'.

E119 The Substance Focus '19' is introduced to accommodate special groupings of Elements which are common.

E120 If a book deals primarily with a hydroxyl or a basic oxide of an Element, its Substance Number should consist of digit '2' followed successively by the number of the constituent element ie the element whose hydroxyl or basic oxide forms the primary subject-matter of the book, and the Valency Number ie the Arabic numeral representing the valency of the element in the oxide.

E1201 An amphoteric oxide should be treated as a basic oxide in constructing its Substance Number.

E1202 The Element Number followed by the Valency Number may be termed the Full Element Number.

E1203 If there be more than one basic oxide with a given valency for the element, the number got by Rule E120 should be used for one of them and the numbers 1, 2, etc., are to be added to the number got by Rule E120 in the case of the second, third, etc., respectively of the basic oxides.

It is known that the valency of no element is higher than 8. Hence, the Valency Number amplifying an Element Number will always be a number not exceeding 8. It is on account of this fact that the digit '9' was used to represent the second element, if any, in a cell, with a view to avoiding a connecting symbol between the Element Number and the Valency Number.

E129 The Substance Number 29 is used, as is indicated in Chapter E of the Schedules, for binaries other than water which are neither hydroxyls nor acids nor salts. Water is regarded as the hydroxyl of hydrogen in the construction of its Substance Number.

E1290 If a book deals primarily with a binary, its Substance Number should consist of the number '29' followed by the Full Element Number of the first constituent element and then by that second constituent element.

E1290 If there be more than one binary with the same two Full Element Numbers, they should be numbered in a manner analogous to that given in rule E1203.

E130 If a book deals with an acid or acidic oxide of an element, its Substance Number schould consist of the digit '3' followed by the Full Element Number of the constituent element, ie the element whose acid or acidic oxide forms the primary subject matter of the book.

E1301 Neutral oxides should be treated as acidic oxides in constructing their Substance Number.

E1303 If there be more than one acidic oxide with a given Full Element Number, they should be numbered in a manner analogous to that given in Rule E1203.

E140 If a book deals primarily with a salt, its Substance Number should consist of the digit '4' followed by the Full Element Number of the constituent basic element and then by that of the constituent acidic element.

E1403 If there be more than one salt with the same two Full Element Numbers, they should be numbered in a manner analogous to that given in Rule E1203.

E142 In the case of a double salt the Substance Number should consist of the Full Element Number of the first basic element, then that of the second basic element, and then that of the acidic element.

E1423 If there be more than one double salt with the same Full Element Numbers, they should be numbered in a manner analogous to that given in Rule E1203.

E18 In the case of analytical chemistry, an Inter-facet Bias Isolate may be added in [P] using as its focus the number of the substance whose presence in the original substance is being investigated by analysis.

E2 Combination Facet

E28 The Combination Number '8' may be amplified by the Full Element Number of the constituent element or elements, as the case may be.

Examples of Class Numbers

E:2	Physical chemistry
E:(C)	Chemical physics
E1:34,C3	Volumetric inorganic analysis
E111:14	Atomic weight of sodium
E194:3	Analysis of alloy
E1940*k*13:34	Estimating the presence of copper in an alloy
E210:3	Composition of water
E3616:4	Synthesis of sulphuric acid
E41871:4	Synthesis of gold chloride
E5:3,6	Commercial organic analysis
E5:33	Qualitative organic analysis
E9G,92:3	Biochemical analysis of alkaloids

CHAPTER F

TECHNOLOGY

F1 Substance Facet

F0 Facets

Facet	Term	(IN) by
[P]	Substance	Enumeration
[E] [2P]	Problem and Process	Enumeration and Alphabetical Device

F1 The Foci in [P] are the same as for 'E' Chemistry' and, in addition, those given in Chapter F of the Schedules.

If there is more than one industrial form for any substance, the different forms should be indicated by the Favoured Category Principle.

Here are some examples worked out for the substance Iron:

182	Iron	1823	Steel
1821	Cast iron or Pig iron	1824	Steel alloy
1822	Wrought iron		

F2 Process and Problem Facet

F2 The foci in the Process Facet will depend upon the substance. As far as possible, they should be determined by the (AD).

F21 Each Process Number may have to be further subdivided according to the nature of its technique.

No attempt has been made in this volume to give illustrative schedules of the processes for the techniques of different substances and their subdivisions. A volume of depth classification will give them.

F22 In the case of a book not dealing with a particular substance or with a particular process corresponding to the focus in the Substance Facet but giving an account of some aspects of the problems of Technology in general, the second digit onwards in the subdivisions of the Problem Division '8 Manipulation' of the (MC) E Chemistry may be used to represent the corresponding problem.

F23 If a book presents Process Isolates as well as Problem Isolates, the Process Isolate should be added first and the Problem Isolate thereafter. The two Isolate Numbers should be separated by a Colon.

Examples

F:6	Industrial electro-chemistry
F:8	Catalysis in industry
F:(G91)	Industrial micro-biology
F191:6	Electro-metallurgy
F551:2	Hydrogenation of coal

CHAPTER G

BIOLOGY

G0 Facets

Facet	*Term*	(IN) *by*
[P]	Organ and special grouping	Enumeration
[E] [2P]	Problem	Enumeration

G1 Organ Facet

G1 A general account of life as a biological phenomenon should be given the Organ Number ' 1 '.

G2 Problem Facet

G233, When the focus in the Problem Facet is ' 33 Metabolism ' or 341 or 345 or 346 or any of their subdivisions, [2M] should be added. It may be called Substance Facet. The foci in it are the same as for ' E Chemistry '. This array may be augmented by (SD).

G25 When the focus in [E] is 12 to 18 or 5 or any of its subdivisions, [S] may have to be added.

Examples

G:12.575*m*M	Acta, Societas pro Fauna et Flora Fennica. 1875—
G:13.44	Plants and animals of India for everybody
G:54*p*1,N	Proceedings, International (Technical) Conference for the Protection of Nature, 1946—
G:(C):(B)	Mathematical biophysics
G11:2	Microscopical anatomy

CHAPTER H

GEOLOGY

H Geology is one of the subjects which has to be divided, in the first instance, on canonical lines. Some of these (CC) admit of further subdivision on the basis of certain facets.

H1 Mineralogy, H2 Petrology, and H7 Economic Geology

Facet	*Term*	(IN) *by*
[P]	Substance	As per rule, and enumeration
[E] [2P]	Problem	Enumeration

H11 The foci in [P] are the same as for ' E Chemistry ', except that amplification by the Valency Number may not be necessary.

H111 If there is more than one mineral with the same chemical composition but differentiated from one another either isomerically or by the presence of impurities, they should be individualised by enumeration.

" DANA (Edward Salisbury): *A system of mineralogy* " will be of help in constructing the Substance Number in Mineralogy.

H119 The focus ' 9 Precious stones ' in the Substance Facet has been specially formed since precious stones form an important class of substances in Geology. If they are given the Substance Number according to the Rule H11, the books on the different precious stones will be scattered. Hence it is suggested that all books on precious stones may be brought under the class H19 and its subdivisions.

H6 Palaeontology

H6 The canonical class ' Palaeontology ' should be used only for ' Palaeozoology '. Books on Palaeobotany are accommodated in the Main Class ' I Botany '. The Palaeontology Focus ' H6 ' should be sharpened by the ' Natural Group Number ' of Zoology.

H68*u* In the case of descriptive palaeontology and palaeontological surveys, whenever warranted the focus in [T] should be the one for the appropriate stratigraphical age, given as subdivisions of ' H5 Stratigraphy ' and not one taken from the Chronological Schedule. ' A ' should replace H5.

H7 Economic Geology

H7 The class ' H7 Economic Geology ' should accommodate books on ore deposits, underground water, and non-metallic and organic deposits. It

may be stated that an ore is defined as " the natural mineral containing a precious or useful metal in such quantities and such chemical composition as to make its extraction profitable ". Thus the denotation of the term ' ore deposit ' is likely to vary from time to time. However, from the point of view of the user, on account of the great economic importance of ore deposits, it is recommended that they may be grouped together in the division ' H7 '.

H711 Same as H11 and H111.

The substance, which forms the essential constituent of the ore ie the substance whose presence makes the ore economically valuable, should be used as the focus in the Substance Facet.

H72 The foci in [E] are the same as for ' H1 Mineralogy.'

H8 Cosmic Hypotheses

H3 Specific hypotheses should be individualised by (CD). The date of the first publication of an authentic exposition of the hypothesis should be used as the epoch.

Examples

H1:82:(B)	Mathematical crystallography
H191:16	Genesis of diamond
H4115.53	Volcanos of France
H4132.42	Earthquakes of Japan
H53.A76	Mesozoic stratigraphy of Alaska
H667.1.A34	Cretaceous Bryozoa of the world
H7.438	Mineral resources of Burma
H7113:16.8	Origins of the copper deposits of Australia
H71879.63	Platinum ores of South Africa
H7210.677	Underground water in Egypt

CHAPTER HZ

MINING

HZ0 Facets

Facet	*Term*	(IN) *by* ,
[P]	Substance	Enumeration
[P2]	Work	Enumeration
[E] [2P]	Problem	Enumeration

HZ1 Substance Facet

HZ1 Similar to Rule H711.

CHAPTER I

BOTANY

I0 Facets

Facet	*Term*	(IN) *by*
[P]	Natural group	Enumeration
[P2]	Organ	Enumeration
[P]	Problem	Enumeration

I1 Natural Group Facet

I1 It may be noticed that the divisions '2 Thallophyta', '3 Bryophyta' and '4 Pteridophyta' in [P] are subdivisions of the division '1 Cryptogamia'. Similarly, the divisions '6 Gymnosperms', '7 Monocotyledons', and '8 Dicotyledons' are subdivisions of the division '5 Phanerogamia'.

I3 Problem Facet

Same rules as for Problem Facet in Chapter G.

Examples

I*w*M17	Life of J D Hooker
IxM17	Hooker's works
I:12.692	Botany of Socotra
I22:12.42	Japanese algæ
I5,15:3	Physiology of leaves
I5,16:2	Morphology of flowers

CHAPTER J

AGRICULTURE

J0 Facets

Facet	*Term*	(IN) *by*
[P]	Plant	Enumeration and (AD)
[P] (Array 1)	Utility	Enumeration
[P] (Array 2)	Part	Enumeration
[P2]	Organ	Enumeration
[E]	Problem	Enumeration
[2P]	(1) Nature for 1 Soil of [E]	Enumeration
	(2) Substance for 2 Manure of [E]	Enumeration
	(3) Substance for 3 Propagation of [E]	Enumeration
	(4) Cause for 4 Disease of [E]	Enumeration
	(7) Material for 7 Harvesting of [E]	Enumeration
[2E] [3P]	Operation	Enumeration

J1 Plant Number

J1 The first significant digit of a Plant Number is **Utility Number**, the second is **Part Number;** the third is either **Genus Number** or **Species Number,** representing the botanical genus or species to which the plant belongs. If the third significant digit represents Genus, the fourth represents Species. The later digits of a Plant Number represent a Cultivar, which is the technical term for Cultivated Variety. These digits may be together called **Cultivar Number.**

J11 Utility Number

J11 The Utility Number is devised so as to give a favoured treatment to certain plants. It is true that a plant may be utilised for several purposes. But it is the primary purpose that should decide the Utility Number of a given plant. To take an example, in the case of rice, the seed is used as human food. The straw is used as animal food and as roofing material. Perhaps, it may also be used for some textile purposes. But it will be easily conceded that the primary use of rice is as human food.

J12 Part Number

J12 If more than one part of a substance is likely to be put to the primary use made of it, that part which is more commonly used should be used to construct the Part Number.

J13 Genus or Species Number

J13 The Genus and Species Numbers are enumerated on the basis c the Favoured Category Principle.

J14 Cultivar Number

J14 The Cultivar Number is got by (AD).

The fuller schedule of Cultivar Numbers will be given in a volume of depth classification.

J471 When the focus in the Farming Facet is '7 Harvesting' the focus in the Material Facet should be the Part of the plant which is the dominant part in the Material. If two or more materials call for the same part number, the most widely used material should have the bare part number, and for the 2nd, 3rd, etc. materials, (IN) should be got by adding the digit 1, 2, etc. respectively to the part number. If the added number is in two or more digits, it should be read as an integer and not as a decimal.

CHAPTER K

ZOOLOGY

K0 Facets

K0 Same table as in Rule I0

K1 Natural Group Facet

K1 It will be noticed that the divisions '2' to '8' in the Natural Group of Animals Facet are really subdivisions of the division '1 Invertebrates'.

K12 In Chapter K of the Schedules, the divisions in the Natural Group Facet are worked out only up to the Sub-Order Stage. This subdivision may be carried still further up to the Family Stage, whenever necessary, in an analogous manner. The tables given at the beginning of the volumes of *Cambridge natural history* may be used in constructing the Family Numbers.

K3 Problem Facet

K3 Same rules as for Problem Facet in Chapter G.

CHAPTER KZ

ANIMAL HUSBANDRY

KZ0 Facets

Facet formula and formation of foci are similar to those in J Agriculture.

Examples of Class Numbers

KZ311	**Cow farming**
KZ311:7	**Dairying**
KZ311:73:8	**Preservation of butter**
KZ351	**Fowl farming**
KZ351:4	**Disease of poultry**
K7351:421:5	**Prevention of tuberculosis in poultry**

CHAPTER L

MEDICINE

L0 Facets

Facet	*Term*	(IN) *by*
[P]	Organ	Enumeration
[E]	Problem	Enumeration
[2P]	(4) Cause (for 4 Disease) of [E]	Enumeration (Comma need not precede [2P])
[2E] [3P]	(4) Handling, (for 4 Disease) of [E]	Enumeration

L1 Organ Facet

L111 If a book deals with the special properties of the Cells or the Tissues of a particular organ, the Number for 'Cells' or 'Tissues', as the case may be, may be added to by the Auto-Bias Device, the appropriate Organ Focus being used as the Biasing Focus.

L112 Most of the subdivisions of the Organ Number '1' are devoted to the regional divisions of the human body, whereas the Organ Numbers '2' to '8' are devoted to the functional divisions.

L113 The parts of the functional organs within a regional organ may be indicated by adding to the Regional Organ Number by the Auto-Bias Device, the appropriate Functional Focus being used as the Biasing Focus.

For example, the bones of the thorax will have the Number L15-81. The arteries of the arm will have the number L16-337. Again the pigment of the face will have the number L181-875.

L2 Problem Facet

L24 An illustrative list of specific diseases with their (CN) is given at the end of the subdivisions of the [2P] for '4 Diseases.' It can be seen from the list that the (CN) of any disease has, for its organ part, the Number of the organ which is the seat of primary affection or the focus of infection. The (CN) for other diseases should be constructed along similar lines.

L241 " STEADMAN (Thomas Lathrop): *Practical medical dictionary* " and " OSLER (William): *Systems of medicine* " will be of use in constructing the (CN) for diseases.

L246 It can be seen that the subdivisions of ' 62 Physicotherapy ' are analogous to the subdivisions of the (MC) C Physics. Similarly, ' 63 Pharmacotherapy ' may be subdivided on the analogy of the Substance Facet in the (MC) E Chemistry.

L3 Third Facet

L3523 When the focus in the Problem Facet is '523 State Control of Food ', ' 524 State Control of Poisons ', ' 526 State Control of Medicine ', and ' 573 Food ' and its subdivisions, the third Facet may have to be Substance. Its foci should be the same as for ' E Chemistry ' and ' F Technology '.

L3577 When the focus in the Problem Facet is ' 577 Clothing ', the third Facet may have to be Material. Its Foci should be the same as for ' M7 Textiles '.

L9 Specials and Systems

L9 The numbers ' L9A ' onwards are set apart for books dealing with groups of persons, as can be seen from the subdivisions of ' L9 ' given in Chapter L of the Schedules. As a result of this, all the books dealing with Medicine in general will have precedence over the books which specialise in special groups such as ' Children ', ' Old people,' and ' Inhabitants of tropics.'

L91 It should be remembered that, if an Organ Number is attached to a " Specials Number " or " System Number," it should be preceded by a comma. Also, if a " Specials Number " is attached to a " System Number," the former should be preceded by a comma.

Examples

L:4	Diseases
L:4:3	Diagnosis of disease
L18511:415	Inflammation of eyelids
L27219:415:7	Appendicitis operation
L9F:3	Obstetrics
L9F:4	Gynaecology
LB:4:6	Ayurvedic cure
LB,27219:415:6	Ayurvedic cure for appendicitis
LC,9F:4	Gynaecology according to Siddha System

CHAPTER LZ

PHARMACOGNOSY

LZ Pharmacognosy is first divided on canonical lines. Some of these (CC) admit of further subdivision on the basis of certain trains of characteristics.

LZ3 Pharmacology

LZ30 Facets

Facet	*Term*	(IN) *by*
[P]	Substance	Enumeration
[E]	Action	Enumeration
[2P]	Organ	(SD)

LZ5 Pharmacopoeia

LZ50 Facets

Facet	*Term*	(IN) *by*
[P]	Nation	(GD)
[P2]	Kind	Enumeration

CHAPTER M

USEFUL ARTS

M0 The (MC) M Useful Arts is a miscellaneous class. Indeed it may be called a hold-all class. It should accommodate all the arts and crafts; in fact all the applications of sciences, not provided for in the other (MC).

M01 From these remarks it will be obvious that the division of the (MC) M can only be canonical. Chapter M of the Schedules is only brief and illustrative. The fascicules on Depth Classification will contain more detailed schedules.

M02 Facet formulae should be constructed for each of these divisions. By way of illustration, the schedules for ' M7 Textiles ' and ' MJ7 Rope-making ' are given. In the case of other subjects, similar schedules should be constructed. The number of subjects is infinite. Further, it is only in recent years that any appreciable literature has begun to grow in these subjects.

M7 Textiles, MJ7 Rope-making

M70, MJ70 Facets

Facet	*Term*	(IN) *by*
[P]	Material	Enumeration
[E] [2P]	Work	Enumeration

Examples of Class Numbers

M71:2	Cotton spinning
M73:7	Silk weaving
MJ75:13	Jute carding

CHAPTER △

SPIRITUAL EXPERIENCE AND MYSTICISM

As the (MC) △ Spiritual Experience and Mysticism occurs here for the first time in any printed scheme of classification, its connotation may first be indicated.

Since the Arabic numerals and the Roman alphabet had already been exhausted, a new symbol had to be found for this new Main Class. The △ of age-long mystical significance naturally suggested itself. Its standing outside the formal series of the other symbols fittingly represents the irresoluble nature of all it stands for.

It is possible for any class of knowledge to be presented from an occult or mystical point of view.

To call such an exposition 'irrational' will violate the Canon of Reticence. The terms 'rational' and 'irrational' refer to the plane of intellection; whereas mystic, occult, and spiritual experiences do not belong to the sphere of intellectual apprehension at all. They are said to involve direct (trans-intellectual) insight.

Little, no doubt, is generally known about the nature or modes of such mystical apprehension; and its validity and even existence are often questioned. But it is not for the classifier to take sides in a controversy. He is simply concerned to separate literature based on sense-experience and intellection from that presuming or using trans-intellectual apprehension. In India such a distinction is traditionally recognised. Exposition based on intellection is called *Kartrtantra* (experimental, analytical study of things in their phenomenal modes); and *Vastutantra* (global, holistic study of thing-in-itself) an exposition based on illumination.

The (MC) △ is to hold the latter. All ordinary (non-mystical) expositions are accommodated in the (MC) 1 to 9 and A to Z. A mystical, occult or spiritual exposition of any subject—say E Chemistry—is referred to the (MC) △ — and individualised as △(E). In other words, △ should be added to by (SD) to accommodate mystical expositions of particular subjects.

Examples:

Friend's *Monograph on the chemistry of gold* belongs to the class E118

But Kolisko's *Gold and the sun* is to be classed in △(E118).

Jone's *Problems of civilisation* (American soeial science series) treats of civilisation on the ordinary intellectual basis and belongs to the Class Y:1.

But Earnest Wood's *Seven rays* which expounds the same subject from an occult point of view belongs to the Class △(Y:1).

The Creation of the (MC) △ thus implies the division of the whole library into two parallel sequences to which, however, N Fine Arts, O Literature and Q Religion are common. This overlapping corresponds with facts; for fine arts, literature, and religion represent the cross-roads or point of fusion between direct (mystical, spiritual) and meditated (sensory, intellectual) modes of experience and expression. It is by no means easy to separate the books of these overlapping classes into △ and non-△ without infringement of the Canon of Consistency. We shall therefore adopt the following convention.

1 No book with a claim to be classed as N or O or Q should ever be classed as △; and hence

2 Numbers like Δ(N), Δ(O), Δ(Q) are inadmissible.

Rule 025 has defined the ordinal value of Δ as lying between those of M and *v*. Thus Δ stands between the sciences and their applications (A to M) on the one side, and the humanities and the social science (*v* to Z) on the other.

The words used by General Smuts to define the position of a new discipline which he calls Personalogy will with a slight modification apply with equal force to the position assigned to the (MC) Δ.

Its province falls within a large debatable territory between science and philosophy; between theory and practice, which has been very little explored and is still *terra incognita* to all intents and purposes. Its difficulties are immense; from that wide and wild No Man's Land between sciences and humanities it rises like some forbidding mountain peak into the heavens; and no daring spirit, except the Mystics, the Seers, and the Rishis, has yet ventured to approach it, let alone to scale its dizzy heights. But beyond a doubt, it is going to occupy a foremost place in the attention of even the ordinary inquirers in future. And the time may come when the (MC) Δ may be the very keystone of the arch, and serve to complete the full growing circle of organised human knowledge. It will then synthesise all sciences and humanities and become the basis of a truer spiritual outlook than we can possibly have in the ignorance and confusions of our present state of knowledge.

That time is not yet; but it may be ventured to hope that the assignment of a proper place to the (MC) Δ in the map of knowledge such as has been attempted here will help to direct attention to what is undoubtedly one of the greatest and most potential fields for cultivation.

A fuller account will be found in my *Spiritual experience and mysticism: A problem in classification* forming pages 121-146 of the *Memoirs* of the Madras Library Association for 1940.

Δ0 Facets

Facet	*Term*	(IN) *by*
[P]	Religion	Enumeration
[P2]	Entity	Enumeration
[E] [2P]	Problem	Enumeration

Δ1 Religion Facet

Δ1 It may be observed that the foci in the Religion Facet are mnemonic with those for 'Q Religion'.

While religious distinctions cease to exist after illumination, religious traditions are believed to be a source of stimulus up to illumination. Further any writing on the subject has to be only about the pre-illumination stage, when religious bearings would not have completely vanished. Hence the prescription of the Religion Facet. Perhaps readers also would find helpful the resulting grouping of mystic literature on a religious basis.

Δ2 Entity Facet

Δ2 The foci enumerated in Entity Facet are those figuring most in books on mysticism and occultism. As an illustration of a class, written upon fairly often, mention may be made of "Δ,16:8 Psychical research and spiritualism".

△3 Problem Facet

△3 Most of the classes grouped under the label 'S8 Metapsychology' in the first edition of this book, following the prevailing practice, are now placed in the Problem Facet '8 Occultism,' of △ along with the other occult practices like Astrology and Palmistry.

△86 Devices

△86 △ should be amplified by [SD] to represent mystical or occult expositions of subjects except Fine Arts, Literature and Religion.

See introduction to this chapter for explanation and examples.

△9 Common Isolates

△9*y*7 The [ACI] Number for the lives of mystics and realised persons is *y*7 and not *w*. [See Rule 2*w*12].

Examples

△:8	Occultism
△:864	Astrology
△,16:5	Vision of disembodied souls
△2y7M79	Life of Ramana Rishi
△(E118)	Occult chemistry of gold
△(J:6)	Occult plant-breeding

CHAPTER N

FINE ARTS

N0 Style

Most of the (CC) of the (MC) N Fine Arts will admit of being divided by **Style.**

Style is individualised by the country and the century of its origin. This means that style is a joint manifestation of Personality in two levels. Accordingly the following table may be applied to any (CC) of the (MC) N.

Facet	*Term*	(IN) *by*
[P]	Region	(GD)
[P2]	Epoch	(CD)
[P], [P2]	Style	

The *Encyclopaedia Britannica* or any good book on the history of the Fine Arts concerned will be of help in fixing the Style Focus. In the case of non-descript styles, which are not at all localised, naturally there will be no Style Focus and the appropriate (CS) should be put before any other facet is added to the (CC) Number. In the case of non-descript styles peculiar to a definite country, the Style Focus will consist only of the focus in [P]. [P2] will not occur.

It may be remarked here that as a result of this arrangement and of the fact that the first digit of the focus in the Personality Facet after the Style Focus is invariably an Arabic numeral in the case of each Fine Art, the general non-descript styles will come first. In the case of localised styles, with any given Geographical Number, the non-descript styles will come first and the specific styles originated in different periods will come thereafter in the proper chronological sequence.

N09*x* The Common Isolate Digit *x* should hold illustrations of the Fine Arts concerned.

N09*x*1 The digit *x* should be amplified by (AD) using the name of the Artist. It may be followed by Work Facet, as in " O Literature ", if warranted. If the name of the Artist is not known, the conventional name of the Work of Art may be used for the (AD).

NA Architecture

NA0 Facets

Facet	*Term*	(IN) *by*
[P], [P2]	Style	(GD) and (CD)
[P3]	Utility	Enumeration
[P4]	Part	Enumeration
[E], [2P]	Technique	Enumeration

NA1 Some Style Foci are given as illustrations.

NA2 The Utility Numbers are first worked out by the Favoured Category Principle. Other buildings, that is those not represented by the Favoured Category Principle, should be represented by 9 followed by (SD).

Any number got by the Favoured Category Principle represents a special class of buildings; and it may be further subdivided in a suitable manner. Such further subdivision has been illustrated in Chapter N of the Schedules, in the case of the numbers '2', '3' and '4.' The divisions of 9 by (SD) make the Schedule of Utility Numbers highly hospitable.

ND Sculpture

ND0 Facets

Facet	*Term*	(IN) *by*
[P], [P2]	Style	(GD) and (CD)
[P3]	Figure	Enumeration
[M]	Material	Enumeration
[E], [2P]	Technique	Enumeration

NN Engraving

The Schedule gives only the (CC) of 'Engraving'. Each of the (CC) will have to be fitted with appropriate Facet Formula.

NQ Painting

NQ0 Facets

Facet	*Term*	(IN) *by*
[P], [P2]	Style	(GD) and (CD)
[P3]	Figure	Enumeration
[M]	Material	Enumeration
[E], [2P]	Technique	Enumeration

NR Music

NR0 Facets

Facet	*Term*	(IN) *by*
[P], [P2]	Style	(GD) and (CD)
[P3]	Music	Enumeration
[M]	Instrument	Enumeration
[E], [2P]	Technique	(To be worked out)

Examples of Class Numbers

ND44,C Buddhist sculpture
ND44,C8(Q4) Buddhist iconography
NQ44,3;3:6 Indian distemper fresco painting of landscape

CHAPTER O

LITERATURE

O0 Facets

Facet	*Term*	(IN) *by*
[P]	Language	Enumeration
[P2]	Form	Enumeration
[P3]	Author	(CD) (Minimum of three digits)
[P4]	Work	Enumeration

O1 Language Facet

O1 The language, to the literature of which the book belongs, or about the literature of which the book treats, should be taken as the focus in the Language Facet.

For example, Kalidasa's *Sakuntala*, which belongs to Sanskrit literature, should be given the language number of Sanskrit. S M Natesa Sastri's *A review of Sakuntala*, though it is in English, should be given the language number of Sanskrit and not English; because it treats about *Sakuntala* which belongs to Sanskrit literature.

Language of Work *is not equal to* **Language of Book**

This may be called **Language Inequality.**

O164 In the case of the literature in the Favoured Language, the Language Number may be replaced by " — ".

O2 Form Facet

O2 The Form of literature which the book contains or about which the book treats should be taken as the focus in the Form Facet.

The terms used for the foci in the Form Facet are by no means definite. Nor can we say that the term ' Literature ' itself is quite definite. Overlooking for the time being, the general meaning of the word ' Literature,' *viz.*, the body of writings produced in a particular country or period or in a particular subject, the restricted meaning that the big Oxford Dictionary gives is as follows: " Writing which has claim to consideration on the ground of beauty of form or emotional effect."

Taking the term ' Poetry ', the definition which the Oxford Dictionary gives is as follows:—" Composition in verse or metrical language, or in some equivalent patterned arrangement of language, usually also with choice of elevated words and figurative uses, and option of a syntactical order, differing more or less from those of ordinary speech or prose-writing." The Dictionary adds under this a note to the following effect:—In this sense, poetry in its simplest or lowest form has been identified with versification or verse. This raises the question whether we should classify under 'Poetry' everything in verse. We find that even scientific treatises of medieval India such as treatises in Mathematics, Natural Science, and so on, are in Sanskrit verse. Certainly such books are not to be classified as Poetry'.

Evidently to exclude such versifications whose primary interest is the exposition of technical matter, the Dictionary adds another meaning to 'Poetry' in the following words:—"With special reference to its functions: The expression or embodiment of beautiful or elevated thought, imagination or feeling, language adapted to stir the imagination and emotions, both immediately and also through the harmonic suggestions latent in or implied by the words and connections of words actually used, such language containing a rhythmical element and having usually a metrical form." As if to render such a definition still more indefinite the Dictionary adds, "The term is sometimes extended to include expression in non-metrical language having similar harmonic and emotional qualities (Prose-Poetry)."

The definition of the term 'Drama' is equally difficult.

As for the term 'Fiction' the Oxford Dictionary defines it as, "The species of literature which is concerned with the narration of imaginary events and the portraiture of imaginary characters . . . now usually prose novels and stories collectively."

From these authoritative definitions, it can be seen that, in the case of many border-line books, it will be difficult, even for experts in the field, to assert whether they should be put in the class 'Literature' and if so in what Form Division of literature. In such border-line cases the classi is to be guided by the consensus of public opinion among students of literature. But in the majority of cases, the appropriate Form Division can be decided without much difficulty.

With regard to the Form Isolate 'Letters', special attention should be paid to the notes attached to that class. The private correspondence of authors is not to be put under this form Class but should really be put with the biography of the author. It is only works like 'Chesterfield's *Letters to his son*' that should come under the Form Class '4'.

The Isolate '6' is not to include literary criticism. It must include only prose as a species of literature, as opposed to poetry, fiction, and drama. A book containing the biography or a criticism of, say, a poet will be given the Form Number for Poetry, as it treats about poetry. Similarly a book containing the biography or criticism of a dramatist will be given the Form Number for Drama as it treats about drama, and so on. Here also we must remember what may be called **Form Inequality,** *viz.*

Form of Work *is not equal to* **Form of Book.**

O3 Author Facet

O31 The author of the literary piece or work which the book contains or about which the book treats or of the literary author about whom the book treats should be taken as the focus in the Author Facet.

If the book is a biography or a criticism of, say, a poet, it is the poet who will determine the Author Number and not the author of the biography or criticism. For example in the case of 'G K Chesterton's *Innocence of Father Brown*' Chesterton will determine the Author Number; but in the case of the book 'G K Chesterton's *Charles Dickens*' it is Dickens and not Chesterton that will determine the Author Number. In other words we must recognise what may be termed **Author Inequality,** *viz.*

Author of Work *is not equal to* **Author of Book.**

O32 The author (IN) should be constructed by (CD). The Chronological Number should be worked out at least to three digits. The year of birth of the author should be used as the epoch.

The arrangement of the authors, belonging to a particular Form Isolate, may be made either alphabetically by the name of the author or chronologically; in other words, the name of the author and the date of the author are two alternative characteristics which can be used for classifying the books in any given Form Isolate. But it can be easily seen that the name of the author is, in a sense, an accidental characteristic. On the other hand, the needs of students of literature will be better met if the chronological sequence of the authors is made the basis of classification.

Assuming that the authors should be classified on a chronological basis, there are three main epochs which can be made the characteristics of classification:

1. The date of birth of the author:
2. The date on which his first literary work was published—the date of his literary birth, so to speak; and
3. The date of death of the author.

Of these, the last is not a practicable one, since the date of death of contemporary authors is an unknowable entity. While the date of literary birth would be the most suitable, this characteristic is not definite. It cannot be easily ascertained and there is likely to be difference of opinion about it. They do not satisfy the Canon of Ascertainability. Hence, the rule uses the date of birth of the author as the focus in the Author Facet.

The following books will be of use in finding the dates of authors:

Language		*Name of the book*
English	..	(1) The Index Volume of the *Cambridge history of English literature.* (2) The Index Volume of the *Dictionary of national biography.* (3) *Who's who.* (4) *Who's who in literature.*
Sanskrit	..	KEITH (A B). *A history of Sanskrit literature.*
Tamil	..	POORNALINGAM PILLAI (M S). *A primer of Tamil literature.*
Telugu	..	VEERESALINGAM PANTHULU (K). *Complete works,* V. 10, Pt I, *Lives of Telugu poets.*
Kanarese	..	NARASIMHACHARYA (R). *Karnataka kavicarite.*
Persian	..	BROWNE (E G). *Literary history of Persia.*
Urdu	..	RAM BABU SAKSENA. *History of Urdu literature.*

Similar sources can be found for authors in other languages.

O33 In Medieval Sanskrit Literature and similar cases, the exact year of birth of the author may not be found. In such cases it would be sufficient if care is taken that the relative sequence of the authors is properly secured. The Author Number may be worked out to some arbitrary year so as to be in consonance with the relative sequence. Similarly, if the year of birth cannot be definitely ascertained in other cases, a probable year may be used.

O34 In the case of certain Ancient Sanskrit and Tamil works, there appears to be no means whatever of conclusively fixing even their centuries (or millennia). Hence, a special illustrative schedule of some of these classics is given in Chapter O of Part 3 where the numbers are worked out by a modified form of (CID).

O35 In the case of modern authors, and particularly in the case of living authors, the year of birth can be found by writing to the persons concerned, if the names are not listed in works of reference.

O36 If the year of birth of a modern author (say born after 1800) cannot be found by any means, the century of birth may be guessed; and the Century Digit should be used as the first Digit of the Author (IN). The later digits of it may be got by (AD).

This Rule has to be resorted to in the case of many modern authors of Indian literature. Even a letter does not bring any response from some of them.

The result of Rule O36 is that authors, whose years of birth are known, will have precedence over those who have to be fixed by (AD).

There are some difficulties in applying (AD). Certain combinations of letters occur often at the beginning of several names. To reach individualisation many letters in the name will have to be used. But this would make the Author Numbers too long. In such cases, the first three letters alone of the name may be retained. In the case of the second, third, etc., of the authors concerned, the digits 1, 2, etc., may be added.

O37 An author is likely to appear in more than one Form Class. In such cases, it will be an advantage if care is taken to see that he gets the same Author Number in each Form Class.

O4 Work Facet

O4 The work contained or treated about in the book should be taken as the focus in the Work Fact.

Here also we should remember what may be termed **Work Inequality**, *viz.*

Work *is not equal to* **Book.**

O41 The Work (IN) should be constructed as follows:—

1 If the number of works of the author does not exceed eight, the works should be arranged in chronological sequence or, if it is impossible, in any arbitrary sequence, and the numbers 1, 2, 3,...8, respectively should be assigned to the works.

2 If the number of works of an author is greater than eight but does not exceed sixty-four, the works should be arranged in

chronological sequence or, if it is impossible, in some convenient sequence and they should be divided successively into groups of eight each, and the numbers 1, 2, 3...8, respectively should be assigned to the groups. Such a number may be termed Group Number. Then to get the actual Work (IN) of the works in any group, 1, 2, 3...8, respectively should be put after the Group Number; thus, each Work (IN) will consist of two digits, the first digit indicating the group into which the book falls and the second indicating the work in the group.

3 If the number of works is greater than sixty-four but does not exceed 512, the same device may be extended. That is, the Work (IN) will consist of three digits, the first digit showing the major group of 64 works into which the work falls, the second digit showing the sub-group of the major group into which the book falls, and the third digit indicating the work in the sub-group.

Examples:—In the case of an author whose number of works does not exceed eight, the Work Number of the 6th work will be '6', that of the 7th will be '7', and so on.

In the case of an author the number of whose works is greater than eight but does not exceed 64, the 6th work will have the number '16', 7th will have '17' the 15th will have '27', the 16th will have '28', 54th will have the number '76' the 63rd will have the number '87', and so on.

O7 Classic Device

O7 The [ClD] may be applied to any [CN] ending with Criticism Number, when warranted.

1 This rule is particularly applicable in the case of Sanskrit Literary Criticism. An illustrative list of (ClD) is given in Part 3.

O9 Common Isolates

O9 In addition to and in slight modification of the [ACI] given in Chapter 2 of the Schedules, the following also may be used in Literature.

d Index of titles of works.

e Index of first lines.

O9*w* In the case of a biography of an author, who is assignable to more than one form of Literature, the Form Number part of the (CN) should be that one with which the author is most associated.

Though Shakespeare and Kalidasa are both dramatists as well as poets they are more associated with Drama. Hence their biographies should be placed in the Form Division Drama. Although Thomas Hardy and Walter Scott are both novelists as well as poets, their biographies should be placed in the Form Division Fiction. Similarly, although G K Chesterton is a prose writer, a novelist as well as a poet, his biography should be placed in the Form Division Other Forms of Prose.

O9*w*1 If a book contains the biography of a single author, the Digit *w* should be added after the Author Number and it need not be fitted with a Chronological Facet.

O9*w*2 If a book contains biographies of several authors, the digit *w* should be added after

1 the Form (IN) if all the authors belong to one Form;

2 the Language (IN) if all the authors belong to one Language but to different Forms, and

3 the (MC) Digit O if the authors belong to several languages.

O9*w*3 If the authors in a collected biography have not been selected from the angle of a particular subject, the digit *w* should be divided by (CD), using the (LED) in which the youngest of the authors was born.

O9*w*4 If the authors in a collected biography have been selected from the angle of a particular subject, the digit *w* should be first divided by (SD) and thereafter by (CD).

O9*x* The Digit *x* should be treated in the same way as *w*.

O9*x*1 Even in the case of a selection from a single author, *x* may be divided by (SD), if warranted.

O9:*g* The Posteriorising Common Energy Isolate Number " : *g* " should be treated in the same way as *x*, except that when the main purpose of the book is not giving critical studies of individual authors but giving only an exposition of the principles of criticism, the criticism number should not be divided by (CD).

Examples

English is taken as the **Favoured Language.**

O,1:*g*	Poetic criticism
O—,1*x*N3	Anthology of English poems (The youngest author born in 1932)
O—,1*x*(Δ)N3	Anthology of English mystical poems (The youngest author born in 1932)
O—,1:*g*(S:55)	Love in English poetry
O—,2J64,51	*Hamlet*
O—,2J64,51:*g*	Criticism of *Hamlet*
O—,2J64,51:*g*(S)	Psychology of *Hamlet*

O121,1G65:*g*	Criticism of Dante
O15,1D40:*g*	Criticism of Kalidasa's poetry
O15,1D40,8	Kalidasa: *Nalodaya*
O15,2D40,1	Kalidasa: *Sakuntala*
O152,1J34*w*	Life of Tulasidas
O152,1J34,1	Tulasidas: *Ram charitmanas*
O41,1E37*x*	Works of Su Tung-Po

CHAPTER P

LINGUISTICS

P0 Facets

Facet	*Term*	(IN) *by*
[P]	Language	Enumeration
[P2]	Variant. Stage	Enumeration. (CD)
[P3]	Element	Enumeration
[E] [2P]	Problem	Enumeration

P29 Language Facet

P290 If a book treats of a variant of a language such as a dialect or a slang or a jargon, the Language Number should be divided by the addition of the appropriate Number taken from the List of Variants given in Chapter P of the Schedules.

P2901 A comma should separate the variant Facet and [P3].

P29D If the book treats of a specific dialect peculiar to a definite geographical division, the Dialect Number may be further divided by the addition of the Geographical Number appropriate to the area in which it is current.

P29J After the Jargon Number, the Geographical Number and Century Number corresponding to the place and period of origin of the jargon may be put if necessary. A comma should separate the (GN) and Century Number.

P29Z If both Stage Number and Variant Number are warranted, the Variant Number should follow the Stage Number; and a comma should separate them.

P2A Stage Facet

P2A0 The Stage of the language, forming the subject-matter of the book, should be got by (CD). The century of the commencement of the Stage should be used as the epoch.

By way of illustration and for convenience of reference, the Stages of some of the languages are given in Schedule P in Part 2.

P2A0A In the case of books dealing with the grammar of a single Veda, the stage digit 'A' should be preceded by a number, the first digit representing the Veda and the later digits, the recension concerned. If a book deals with more than one recension of a Veda, the second digit or the Recension digit as it may be called, should be zero. The Veda digit and the Recension digit should be taken from Chapter Q of the Schedules.

P4 Problem Facet

P44 If the Problem Number is '4' or '5' or a subdivision of '5' and if the Element Number is '3', the Element Number may be omitted.

This is to economise in notation. Since most of the dictionaries will have the Problem Number '4' and the Element Number '3' and since dictionaries are books that are frequently used, the idea is that the number in such cases should be made as short as possible. Care has also been taken to see that no ambiguity arises as a result of this special provision.

It may be asked whether an Element Number other than '3' is likely to precede the Problem Number '4'. The answer is 'yes'. Take, for example, a Dictionary of Phrases, or a Dictionary of Idioms, or a Dictionary of Proverbs. In these cases, the Element Number will be '4', '5' and '6' respectively.

P48 A dictionary of Special Terms used in a particular subject should be placed in the subject concerned and its number should be got by (SD). That is, a colon should be put after the number representing the particular science or subject, and thereafter P followed by the number of the language concerned should be added within circular brackets.

P487 In the case of surnames, the dictionary should be placed in the Generalia Class *w*.

P48U In the case of place-names, the dictionary should be placed in the (MC) U.

P9 Common Isolates

P9*k* In the case of ordinary dictionaries giving the meaning of words, phrases, idioms and proverbs, the language part of the Book Number should represent the language in which the meaning is given, or the first of the languages if the meaning is given in two or more languages.

P9:(G) If the main purpose of a book is that of giving not a descriptive but a comparative account, its class number should be worked out to the fullest extent, otherwise appropriate, and " :(G)" should be added thereafter.

P9:(G)1 If particularly necessary, the number " :(G) " may be fitted with a Chronological Facet, the focus being the latest century to which the study is brought in the book.

P91 To distinguish different standards in practising materials, Standard Facet may be prefixed to Book Number.

See examples 11 to 13 and 15 to 16 below.

Examples of Class Numbers

P111,9D56175	Yorkshire dialect
P111,9D56175,1:1	Pronunciation in Yorkshire dialect
P111,9J44,L	Anglo-Indian jargon
P111,9J44,L,4	Dictionary of Anglo-Indian jargon (Hobson-Jobson)
P111,J,9D56175	Modern Yorkshire dialect
P111,J3:1*k*	Modern English pronouncing dictionary
P15,25A	Taittirīya Prātisākhyā
P15,C3:291	Composition of words in classical Sanskrit
P152:4*k*	Hindi dictionary
P31,9D4498:4	Semasiology of Jaffna Tamil
P31,J9 (3) N60	Tamil reader, standard 3, 1960
P31,J9 (3) *w*3 N60	Tamil story reader, standard 3, 1960
P31,J9 (5) N60	Tamil reader, standard 5, 1960
P4:(G)	Comparative study of Asian languages
P (1) 31, J9 (2) N60	Tamil copybook, standard 2, 1960
P (3) 31, J9 (6) N60	Tamil shorthand practice book, grade 6, 1960

CHAPTER Q

RELIGION

Q0 Facets

Facet	*Term*	(IN) *by*
[P]	Religion	Enumeration, (GD) and (CD)
[E] [2P]	Problem	Enumeration

Q1 Religion Facet

Q1 In any major Religion, the sects which have their own special religious practices and institutions should be shown as subdivisions of the major Religion.

For example, the different Vedas and their respective *sakhas* or recensions are shown in Chapter Q of the Schedules as successive subdivisions of '1 Hinduism (Vedic)'. So also the different Vaishnavite, Saivite, etc., sects, with specialised sacred books, rituals and organisations, have been shown as subdivisions of '2 Hinduism (Post Vedic)'. So also in the case of Jainism, Buddhism, Christianity, Muhammadanism, etc., some illustrative sects are as far as possible enumerated.

Q2 Problem Facet

Q201 " FARQUHAR (J. K.): *Outline of the religious literature of India* " may be usefully consulted in finding out the Sacred Books, the Theological Works, etc., relating to the Religion Divisions '1' to '4' and their subdivisions. But this book gives also the purely philosophical treatises of the Indian Schools of Philosophy. Hence, care must be taken not to bring such philosophical books into the (MC) Q Religion.

Q21 It may be explicitly stated that the *Sthalapuranas* of India should be accommodated in the Problem Division '38', this number being divided by (GD). The Geographical Number of the locality treated in the book but omitting the initial digit or digits representing the whole of India should be used in the (GD).

Q211 It should also be remembered that during the last three centuries many poems, particularly Tamil ones, have used *Sthalapuranas* as themes. These should be classed in poetry and not in Religion.

Q22 The Sacred Books of different Religions are likely to fall into different groups. In Chapter Q of Part 3 the Sacred Books of some religions are given by way of illustration. The digit '2' should be subdivided similarly for other religions. If the Sacred Books do not fall into any such groups, the subdivisions of '2' may be constructed in the same manner as the Work Number in the (MC) O Literature.

Q224 There are said to be innumerable *Tantras* belonging to Saktaism and Buddhism. Several of them are now being printed. But there is no authentic or agreed list of them. Hence it may be well to individualise them in the way in which Work Numbers are constructed in the (MC) O Literature assuming that the number of *Tantras* exceeds 64, i.e., working on a three-digit basis.

Q23 It may be remarked that books on the Theology of a Religion are likely to contain philosophical matter. One should not be misled by this fact to place such theological books in the (MC) R Philosophy. Only a book which treats exclusively of the philosophical aspect of the Theology of a Religion should be put in ' R3 Metaphysics ' and further fitted with a subject Facet as provided for in the rules for the subdivision of ' R3 Metaphysics.'

Examples of Class Numbers

Q125:21	Taittirīya samhita
Q222:451	Pancharatra ecclesiology
Q3:336	Rebirth according to Jainism
Q4:33	Buddha
Q45:7	Japanese Mahayana sects
Q6:445	Christian worship
Q7:26	Muslim traditions

CHAPTER R

PHILOSOPHY

R0 It is not possible to enunciate any relevant characteristics which may be made the basis of classification of Philosophy as a whole. In fact, we have to divide, in the first instance, along canonical lines. Some of the (CC) admit of classification on the basis of definite and appropriate characteristics. The ninth subdivision of each division is usually reserved for special topics about which some considerable literature exists. The terms used in Philosophy are very elusive. Many shades of difference are discernible in the use of the same term by different philosophers. Baldwin's *Dictionary of philosophy* and James Hastings' *Encyclopaedia of religion and ethics* may be of use in deciding the appropriate (CN) of books in Philosophy.

R3 Metaphysics

R30 Facets

Facet	*Term*	(IN) *by*
[P]	View	Enumeration
[P2]	Subject	(SD)

R4 Ethics

R40 Facets

Facet	*Term*	(IN) *by*
[P]	Topic	Enumeration
[P2]	Controlling principle	Enumeration

R42 Family Ethics of Hindus will be R42, (Q2). 'Treatment of animals according to Jains' will be R47, (Q3). If a book deals with Ethics as determined by sociological considerations, its number will be R4,(Y). On the other hand, a book which deals with Ethics as determined by statutory laws will be R4, (Z).

R6 Indian Philosophy

R60 Facets

Facet	*Term*	(IN) *by*
[P]	System	Enumeration
[P2]	(1) For R61 to R64 Canonical (with their own facets)	As for R
	(2) For R65 to R6893 Basic Text (in the first octave)	Enumeration
	Canonical with their own facets (in the second octave)	As for R

R601 The division 'R6' has been set apart for Indian Philosophy. So also the division 'R7' may be set apart for any other system or school of philosophy in which the library specialises.

R602 Special places have been given for Indian Philosophy as there is a considerable amount of literature on it. But it is open to libraries, whose collections are different, to use 'R6' and 'R7' for such Philosophical Systems as are represented most in their collections.

R65 The books in the Divisions 'R65' to 'R68' fall into two classes, viz., those that are direct expositions and those that take the form of a commentary on certain basic texts.

R650 In the case of books, taking the form of commentaries on basic texts, the Basic Text Focus should be used. Examples are given in Part 3.

R697 Classic Device

R697 The literature in Indian Philosophy abounds in classical treatises with a long hierarchy of commentaries and sub-commentaries. Hence a fairly long illustrative list of classes by (CID) is included in Part 3.

Examples of Class Numbers

R14	Symbolic logic
R3,(Q)	Philosophy of religion
R4,(Q6)	Christian ethics
R641,14	Symbolic logic in Nyaya Philosophy
R65,5	Brahma-sutra
R66,914	Symbolic logic in Advaita Philosophy

CHAPTER S

PSYCHOLOGY

S0 Facets

Facet	*Term*	(IN) *by*
[P]	Entity	Enumeration
[E] [2P]	Problem	Enumeration

S1 Entity Facet

S1 The terms used in [P] require some explanation. The following give a rough indication of the denotation of these terms.

S11 The term 'child' should be given the second meaning given in the *New English dictionary* namely "a young person of either sex below the age of puberty," i.e., below fourteen years in the case of a male and twelve years in the case of a female. The class '11 New Born' should include children below eight months, the class '12 Toddler' children between eight months and one year, the class '13 Infant' children under seven, and the class '15 Pre-adolescent' children above seven years but below the age of puberty.

S12 The class '2 Adolescent' should include males between the years fourteen and twenty-five and females between the years twelve and twenty-one.

S14 The Division '4 Vocational' should include classes of persons belonging to different vocations and this may be subdivided by (SD).

S16 The connotation of the class '6 Abnormal' is indicated by its subdivisions.

S17 The Division '7 Race' may, wherever necessary, be subdivided as Y7 in Sociology.

SA It may be repeated that when a System Facet occurs in the (CN), a comma should precede [P].

SA1 It may also be repeated that the (IN) 'A' should be used in the System Facet, if several systems are treated.

Examples of Class Numbers

S15:524	Anger of children
S55:524	Anger of women
SM9,55:524	Psycho-analysis of anger of women

CHAPTER T

EDUCATION

T0 Facets

Facet	*Term*	(IN) *by*
[P]	Educand	Enumeration
[E]	Problem	Enumeration
[2P]	Subject (for 3 Teaching Technique, 4 curriculum, and 5 Educational Measurement in [E])	(SD)
[2P2]	Method	Enumeration

T1 Educand Facet

T1 It may be observed that the foci in the Educand Facet of the (MC) T Education are mnemonic with those of the Entity Facet of the (MC) S Psychology.

T3 Subject Facet

T3 In the application of (SD) to [2P], the modification in " P Linguistics " given in Chapter T of the Schedules should be borne in mind.

TA and TA1 Similar to Rules SA and SA1.

Examples

T:3,1	Audio-visual method
T:3(B2)	Method of teaching algebra
T:3(B2),1	Audio-visual method of teaching algebra
T15:3(B2),1	Audio-visual method of teaching algebra in elementary schools
T2:3(P5),3	Medium of instruction for teaching foreign language in secondary schools
TN3.44.N5	Basic schools in India in 1950's
TN3,15:3(B2)	Method of teaching algebra in Basic elementary schools

CHAPTER U

GEOGRAPHY

U0 Facets

Facet	*Term*	(IN) *by*
P	Geography	Enumeration

U1 Geography Facet

The term ' Geography ' is a very elusive one. According to the *Encyclopaedia Britannica*, it is a synthetic science. " The characteristic task of geography is to investigate the control exercised by the forms and vertical relief of the surface of the lithosphere directly or indirectly on the various mobile distributions." The *New English Dictionary* defines it as " The Science which has for its objects the description of the earth's surface, treating of its form and physical features, its natural and political divisions, the climate, productions, populations, etc., of the various countries."

Accordingly, [P] includes Mathematical Geography, Physical Geography, Bio-Geography, Anthropo-Geography and Economic Geography. We have also included the Science of Meteorology. Another feature is that ' Travels ' also is included in it. It is only General Travel Books that are to be accommodated in this division.

U2 Theoretical material may call for an Energy Facet. The Schedule for this will be given in the fascicule U of Depth Classification.

U3 Space Facet will be necessary in all cases except theoretical books.

U4 [T] may not be applicable in all cases. But, it will certainly be applicable when the (IN) in [P] is ' 6 ' or ' 8 '. Normally, the [LED] covered should be used as the epoch in constructing the Chronological Number, unless the context is against it.

Examples

U2855.42.N5	Rainfall in Japan brought upto 1950's
U30r287	Bio-climatics
U5.44.N5	Historical geography of India brought upto 1950's
U8.65:N3	West African travels brought upto 1930's
U8:(Z44Q7,155)	Pakistan law of passports for aliens

CHAPTER V

HISTORY

V0 Facets

Facet	*Term*	(IN) *by*
[P]	Community	(GD)
[P2]	Part	Enumeration
[E]	Problem	Enumeration

V1 Community Facet

V10 If a book deals with the science of History or of the science of any Problem Isolate of History but does not give the history either of the world as a whole, or of any Community, no Community Number should be put.

There are books which give an account of the methodology or the content or the history, etc., of History as an art or science. Again there may be biographies of historians. Evidently such books may not admit of any Community Isolate.

V1-1 It may be repeated that the focus in the Community Facet of a book on different countries of the world is the disjunctive one represented by 1-1.

V26 If a book deals with a specific Local Body, its Community Number should be worked out to the necessary number of digits to represent the geographical area of the Local Body.

V3 Problem Facet

V319 In the case of a book dealing with the Foreign Policy of a State in regard to some other Specific State, [S] should be added after the Problem Number 19. The Focus in it should be the other State.

V3191 In the case of a book dealing with the Foreign policy of a State in relation to some other State and in regard to a Specific Subject, a Bias Phase should be added after [S]. The focus in it should be the specific subject of the Foreign Policy.

V32 The line of demarcation between the Problem Isolate '2 Constitutional' and the (MC) W Political Science is not an easy one. A book, whose primary interest is tracing the history or giving a descriptive account of the constitution of a country or of any of its specific constitutional parts forming the foci of the 'Part Facet' and which, if at all, leads to the enunciation of certain general constitutional principles only in a subsidiary way or as a by-product of the narration of history, should be put in the (MC) V History and given the appropriate Part and Problem Numbers. On the other hand, a book, whose primary interest is that of studying or giving an exposition of contitutional principles as such and in which the constitutions or the constitutional aspects of particular countries come in only incidentally for illustrative purposes, should be put in the (MC) W Political Science. In particular, all books dealing with the theory of election and election methods should be invariably put in the (MC) W Political Science.

V4 Time Facet

It may be stated explicitly that except in the case of a book dealing with the science of History or some aspect of it, [T] should occur in the (CN) of a book in "V History". Ordinarily, the focus in [T] will be the (LED) covered.

V9 Common Isolate

V9*s* In the case of a book giving only tables of Kings, Ministers, etc., the (CI) *s* should be added to the (CN) of the book got otherwise and the digits should be fitted with a Facet whose focus is the (LED).

V9*y*7 The biography of a King, a President, a Minister, a Legislator, a Leader of a Political Party, a Person who has been known as one who has fought for Political Rights and a Person whose name is best associated with functioning of Local Bodies, a member of diplomatic service, etc. should be placed in the appropriate subdivision of the Part Number and fitted with the (ACI) Number *y*7.

Examples

(India is taken as Mother Country and Great Britain as Favoured Country)

V1-3,1:3.N3	The functions of the head of British Empire brought upto 1930's
V1N4,2.N5	The executive of the United Nations brought upto 1950's
V2,16:2.N5	Constitution of Local Bodies in India brought upto 1950's
V211:16.N5	Relation of State government to Local Bodies in the Madras State brought upto 1950's
V3:19.5.N5	Britain's European policy brought upto 1950's
V3:19.50*b*X.N5	British European economic policy brought up to 1950's
V3:2:(Z).N5	British constitutional law brought upto 1950's
V41:710*b*Q4	Buddhist archaeology of China
V53,1*y*7L69	Life of Napoleon
V53,2*y*7L49	Life of Mirabeau
V5(W4),3:3.N5	Functions of legislature in European monarchies brought upto 1950's
V6-52.N3	History of the Italian possessions in Africa brought upto 1930's

CHAPTER W

POLITICAL SCIENCE

W0 Facets

Facet	*Term*	(IN) *by*
[P]	Type of state	Enumeration
[P2]	Part	Enumeration
[E]	Problem	Enumeration

W2 It will be observed that the Part and Problem Classes of 'W Political Science' are quite parallel to those of 'V History'. A reference may be made to the commentary V32 of chapter V of this part, with regard to the line of demarcation between 'V History' and 'W Political Science'

Examples of Class Numbers

W*a*N3	Bibliography of political science brought upto 1930's
W*k*	Dictionary of political science
W*x*C61*c*	Concordance to the *Arthasastra* of Kautilya
W:5	Civic rights and duties
W:58(Q)	Freedom of conscience
W:91N:3	Counting in proportional representation
W4,1*v*1.N5	History of kingship in the world brought upto 1950's
W4,1:(R)	Philosophy of kingship
W41:591	Allegiance in an absolute monarchy
W691:58(Q)	Freedom of conscience in communistic state
W691,45	Party in opposition in communistic state
W95:3	Functions of a World State

CHAPTER X

ECONOMICS

X0 Facets

Facet	*Term*	(IN) *by*
[P]	Business	Enumeration
[E] [2P]	Problem	Enumeration

X1 Business Facet

X14 'Transport' occurs both in the Business and the Problem Facets. In the former, books on the business of 'Transport,' as such, should be accommodated while the latter should hold only books that deal with the process of the actual transport of specific commodities, involving, as it does, the details indicated in the focus '4' of the Problem Facet in Chapter X of the Schedules.

X17 The Business Isolate '7' and its subdivisions may not admit of all the General Problem Isolates given in Chapter X of the Schedules. Hence a special schedule of Problem Isolates applicable to the Business Isolate '7' and its subdivisions is given at the end of the General Problem Isolate '7' in Chapter X of the Schedules.

X2 Problem Facet

X29 'Personnel management' is made an independent focus in the Problem Facet and not included in the focus '8 Management' as the subject is a vast one and Literary Warrant would justify saving a digit thereby. The old name for this isolate was "Labour Problem".

X290 The isolates under '9 Personnel Management' are arranged in the three sectors: *Least concrete sector* 1 to 922; *More concrete sector* 9A to 9W; and *Still more concrete sector* A to R. If the book covers more than one sector, the (IN) of each sector should be made a Level of [2P] after 9 in [E]. The more concrete sector should be made the earlier level.

Examples

X:9	Personnel management
X:936	Profit sharing
X:99P	Clerical staff
X:99P,36	Profit-sharing by clerical staff
X:9K5	Alien staff
X:9K5,36	Profit-sharing by alien staff
X:9K5,9P	Alien clerical staff
X:9K5,9P,36	Profit-sharing by alien clerical staff

X297 Similarly three sectors are shown under '7 Industrial relation' in the first sector of '9 Personnel management'. Their use is similar.

Examples

X:976	Arbitration in personnel relation
X:979D	Strike
X:979D,6	Arbitration in strike
X:97D	Trade union
X:99P,76	Arbitration in the relation of clerical staff
X:99P,79D	Strike of clerical staff
X:99P,79D,6	Arbitration in strike of clerical staff
X:9K5,9P,79D,6	Arbitration in strike of alien clerical staff

X3 Space and Time Facets

X3 A book, dealing with the Science of Economics but does not deal with an account of any specific economic problem in any particular geographical area, will not admit of [S] and [T]. On the other hand, all descriptive and historical books will need [S] and [T].

X31 A book on the Economic History of a country will have no Business and Problem Facets. [S] and [T] will come after the (MC) digit X.

Example

X.44.N5 Economic condition of India in the 1950's

X8 Phase

X8 For a book dealing with any Economic Relation between two countries, [S] should have an (IN) with Intra-Facet Relation.

Example

X:53.440r56.N5 The influence of British tariff on Indian tariff brought upto 1950's

X9*e* Books on weights and measures should be given the class number X:5*e*.

CHAPTER Y

SOCIOLOGY

Y0 Facets

Facet	*Term*	(IN) *by*
[P]	Group	Enumeration
[E] [2P]	Problem	Enumeration
[2E] [3P]	Secondary problem	Enumeration. Differentiated

Y1 Group Facet

Y17 The Group Isolate 7 and its subdivisions are to hold the classes Anthropology and Ethnology.

Y19: The Class 'Y Sociology' may frequently require the application of the Auto-Bias Device in the construction of Group Numbers.

Examples of Class Numbers

Y:411:5(Z)	Prohibition by legislation
Y:433:6.73.N5	Treatment of unemployment in U.S.A. brought upto 1950's
Y:47:2.73.N5	The etiology of social tension in U.S.A. brought upto 1950's
Y31:7:7	Rural development
Y72-78:424.N5	The moral degeneration of the Australian primitives brought upto 1950's
Y73(P1):434:68	Charity for the poor among the Aryans

CHAPTER Z

LAW

Z0 Facets

Facet	*Term*	(IN) *by*
[P]	Community	(GD) for a nation and any other localised community and (SD) for other cultural groups
[P2]	Law I	Enumeration
[P3]	Law II	Enumeration. Differentiated

Z1 Community Facet

Z1 French Law and Australian Law will be represented by Z53 and Z8, while Hindu Law, Canon Law of Christians, and Muslim Law will be represented by Z (Q2), Z (Q6), and Z (Q7) respectively.

Again the federal law of the United States will be Z73 whereas the law of California will be Z7351. So also in the case of the special law of a particular sect of a religion, the religion focus should be sharpened to the necessary extent.

Z11 For international law, the (IN) in the Community Facet should be 1 if it covers the whole world, or the (IN) of any other appropriate area if it covers only a part of the world.

Examples.—American international law will be Z7, while International law will be Z1.

It may be stated here that this rule relates to Public International Law, i.e., to law which governs situations in which all the parties concerned are States or Governments, politically independent of one another.

Z12 It may be stated explicitly that if a book gives the Municipal Laws of several countries of the world, its number should be Z1-1 or Z4-1 or Z5-1 etc., as the case may be.

Z2 Law Facet I

Z2 The terms used to denote the foci in the Law Facet I are applicable to International as well as Municipal Law. Wherever it is not so, the analogous terms should be understood.

Z25 Some of the subdivisions of '5 Crime' are by a modified form of (SD). Further subdivisions may be obtained in an analogous manner.

Z26 The focus '6 Conflict of laws. Private international law' in the Law Facet I has been taken away from 'Public international law,' as it is said to have greater affinity to 'Municipal Law' than to 'International Law'.

Z2A The (IN) A to D of the Law Facet I relate to war conditions They should be sharpened by adding to them such of the other foci in the Law Facet I as are applicable to them.

The appropriate terms for the derived composite classes will be obvious e.g., Z1,C265 is the number for 'Prize law.'

Z3 Law Facet II

Z3 The terms used to denote the foci in Law Facet II are applicable to International as well as Municipal Law. Whenever it is not so, the analogous terms should be understood.

Z9 Common Isolates

Z9*y*7 A law report should be fitted with the (ACI) Number *y*7. The report of a particular case may require the Chronological Facet, its focus being worked out to three digits and the date of commencement of the trial being used as the epoch. A periodical law report may require the further (ACI) Number *m*.

INDEX

Note.—The reference is to Sections and Chapters

COLON CLASSIFICATION

BY

S R RANGANATHAN

PART 2

SCHEDULES OF CLASSIFICATION

SARADA RANGANATHAN ENDOWMENT
FOR LIBRARY SCIENCE
Bangalore 560 078

Shiyali Ramamrita **RANGANATHAN** (1892)

First Edition 1933
Second Edition 1939
Third Edition 1950
Fourth Edition 1952
Fifth Edition 1957
Sixth Edition 1960
Reprinted 1963
(with amendments)
Reprinted 1964
Reprinted 1969

2:51N3
*q*N60·2

CHAPTER 02

BOOK NUMBER

Facet formula for book-number

[L] [F] [Y] [A]. [V]—[S]; [C]: [Cr]

Foci in

Form of F

Facet

*a*1	Systematical
*a*5	Alphabetical
*a*6	Chronological
b	**Index**
*b*1	Systematical
*b*5	Alphabetical
*b*51	Title
*b*55	Subject
*b*57	Author
c	**List**
*c*1	Systematical
*c*2	Numerical
*c*3	Geographical
*c*4	Conventional
*c*5	Alphabetical
*c*51	Title
*c*55	Subject
*c*57	Name
*c*6	Chronological
*c*9	Other types
*c*94	Printer
*c*96	Publisher
d	**Data book**
*d*2	Pattern
*d*3	Recipe
f	**Picture**
*f*2	Sculpture
*f*3	Engraving
*f*4	Graphic art
*f*5	Painting
*f*95	Photograph
*f*953	Cinema film
*f*9533	Sound film
*f*954	Negative
*f*955	Transparent picture
*f*994	Block
g	**Plan**
*g*1	Section
*g*2	Elevation
*g*3	Relief
*g*6	Diagram
h	**Graph**
*h*1	Line
*h*2	Histogram
*h*3	Perspective
*h*6	Schematic
j	**Parody**
k	**Adaptation**
m	**Catechism**
n	**Opinion**
*p*1	Lecture
*p*2	Dialogue
*p*3	Discussion
*p*5	Debate
*p*7	Symposium
q	**Code**
v	**Practical**
*w*1	Verse
*w*2	Drama
*w*3	Fiction
*w*4	Letter
*w*7	Champu
x	**Quotation**
*x*4	Press cutting

CHAPTER 1

MAIN CLASS

z	**Generalia**
1	**Universe of Knowledge**
2	**Library Science**
3	**Book Science**
4	**Journalism**
A	**Natural Sciences**
AZ	**Mathematical Sciences**
B	**Mathemetics**
BZ	**Physical Sciences**
C	**Physics**
D	**Engineering**
E	**Chemistry**
F	**Technology**
G	**Biology**
H	**Geology**
HX	**Mining**
I	**Botany**
J	**Agriculture**
K	**Zoology**
KX	**Animal Husbandry**
L	**Medicine**
LX	**Pharmocognosy**
M	**Useful Arts**
Δ	**Spiritual Experience and Mysticism**
MZ	**Humanities and Social Sciences**
MZA	**Humanities**
N	**Fine Arts**
NX	**Literature and Language**
O	**Literature**
P	**Linguistics**
Q	**Religion**
R	**Philosophy**
S	**Psychology**
Σ	**Social Sciences**
T	**Education**
U	**Geography**
V	**History**
W	**Political Science**
X	**Economics**
Y	**Sociology**
YX	**Social Work**
Z	**Law**
	Illustrative
(: *g*)	**Criticism technique**
(*p*)	**Conference technique**
(*r*)	**Administration report technique**
(P)	**Communication theory**
(X)	**Management**

CHAPTER 2

COMMON ISOLATE

21 **Anteriorising Common Isolate** (*Applicable before Space Facet*)

Number	*Term*	*Facet formula*
a	Bibliography	*a*[T]
c	Concordance	
d	Table	
e	Formula	
f	Atlas	*f*[T]
k	Cyclopaedia	*k*[P], [P2]
m	Periodical	*m*[P], [P2]
n	Serial	*n*[P], [P2]
p	Conference proceedings	*p*[P], [P2]
v	History	*v*[S]. [T]
w	Biography	
	General	*w*[S], [T]
	Individual	*w*[P]
	Autobiography	*w*[P], 1
	Ana	*w*[P], 2
	Letters	*w*[P], 4
x	Works (Collection or Selection)	
	General	*x*[S], [T]
	Individual	*x*[P]
*y*1	Programme of instruction	
*y*2	Syllabus	
*y*3	Synopsis	
*y*4	Scope	
*y*7	Case study	same as for *w*
*y*8	Digest	

22 Anteriorising Common Isolate (*Applicable only after Space Facet*)

Number	*Term*	*Facet formula*
r	Administration report	
s	Statistics (if periodical)	*s*[T]

23 Anteriorising Common Isolate (*Applicable only after Time Facet*)

s	Statistics (if stray)	*v*	Source material
		*v*5	Literature
t	Commission report	*v*6	Tradition
*t*4	Survey	*v*7	Archaeology etc., (as in V History)
*t*5	Plan		
*t*6	Ideal	*v*8	Archive (as in V History)

25 Posteriorising Common Isolate: Energy Common Isolate

*b*1	Calculating	*f*3	Experiment
*b*2	Designing	*f*4	Discussion
*b*6	Measuring		
		g	Criticism
*c*1	Weighing	*p*	Drafting
		r	Reporting
f	Investigation	*u*	Surveying
*f*2	Observation		

27 Posteriorising Common Isolate: Personality Common Isolate

(C1), [P], [P2]: [E]

b	**Profession**	*f*2	Observational
		*f*3	Experimenting
d	**Institution**	*f*4	Discussional
		*f*7	Yogic (Asrama)
e	Educational (in which the subject, represented by the host class, is taught)	*g*	Learned society
		h	Industrial body
*e*2	Lower	*k*	Commercial body
*e*4	Higher	*w*	Administrative department of Government
f	**Investigating**		

CHAPTER 3

TIME ISOLATE

31 Isolate in [T]: Chronological Division

A	Before 9999 B C	K	1600 to 1699 A D
A1	Eozoic	L	1700 to 1799 A D
A2	Palaeozoic	M	1800 to 1899 A D
A3	Mesozoic	N	1900 to 1999 A D
A4	Cainozoic	P	2000 to 2099 A D
A5	Quarternary	Q	2100 to 2199 A D
		R	2200 to 2299 A D
B	9999 to 1000 B C	S	2300 to 2399 A D
C	999 to 1 B C	T	2400 to 2499 A D
D	1 to 999 A D	U	2500 to 2599 A D
		V	2600 to 2699 A D
E	1000 to 1099 A D	W	2700 to 2799 A D
F	1100 to 1199 A D	X	2800 to 2899 A D
G	1200 to 1299 A D	YA	2900 to 2999 A D
H	1300 to 1399 A D		
I	1400 to 1499 A D	YB	3000 to 3099 A D
J	1500 to 1599 A D	YC	3100 to 3199 A D

32 Isolate in [T2]: Featured Time

c	**Day-time**	*n*5	Autumn
d	**Night**	*n*7	Winter
e	**Twilight**		
		p	Meteorological period
n	**Season**	*p*1	Dry
*n*1	**Spring**	*p*5	Wet
*n*3	**Summer**	*p*8	Snow

CHAPTER 4

SPACE ISOLATE

41 Isolate in [s]: Geographical Division

1	**World**
1-0	**Empire**
	To be divided by (GD)
	(*Illustrative*)
1-52	Roman empire
1-56	British empire
16	Atlantic countries
161	Mediterranean countries
167	Baltic countries
17	Pacific countries
19	**By Zone**
191	Equatorial
192	Tropical
1923	South
1927	North
193	Sub-tropical
195	Temperate
197	Sub-arctic
198	Arctic
19A	**By Orientation**
19B	East
19C	Near
19D	Middle
19E	Far
19F	South-east
19G	South
19L	South-west
19M	West
19R	North-west
19S	North
19W	North-east
19X	Inside
19Y	Outside
1A	Near-Sovereign Formation
	To be divided by (CD)
	(*Illustrative*)
1N	League of Nations area
1N4	United Nations area
1N48	The Commonwealth area
	Division by (SD)
	(*Illustrative*)
1(P111)	English speaking countries
1(Q7)	Muslim countries
2	**Mother country**
3	**Favoured country**

4	**Asia**
41	**China**
4111	Kiang-su
4112	An-hwei
4113	Che-kiang
4121	Kiang-si
4122	Fu-kien
4131	Kwang-tung
4132	Kwang-si
4141	Yun-nan
4142	Kwei-chow
4143	Hu-nan
4151	Sze-chwan
4152	Hu-peh
4153	Shen-si
4161	Ho-nan
4162	Shan-si
4163	Kan-su
4171	Chih-li
4181	Shan-tung
42	**Japan**
421	Honshu
422	Shikoku
423	Kyushu
428	Hokkaido
4295	Formosa
43	**Southeast Asia**
431	**Indo-China**
4311	Annam
4312	Laos
4313	Viet Nam
4315	Cambodia
4317	Tongking
433	**Thailand**
435	**Malay States**
43591	Singapore
436	**Indonesia**
4361	Moluccas
4362	Celebes
4363	Java
4365	Sumatra
4367	Borneo
43691	Anamba isles
43692	Natuna isles

438 **Burma**
43811 Northern Shan States
43812 Southern Shan States
43813 Karenni
43814 Salween
43821 Thaton
43822 Amherst
43823 Tavoy
43824 Mergui
43831 Toungoo
43832 Pegu
43833 Tharrawaddy
43834 Hanthawaddy
43835 Insein
43836 Pyapon
43837 Myaungmya
43838 Ma-ubin
43841 Bassein
43842 Henzada
43843 Sandoway
43844 Prome
43851 Kyaukpyu
43852 Minbu
43853 Pakokku Hill Tracts
43854 Pakokku
43855 Akyab
43856 North Arakan
43861 Chin Hills
43862 Lower Chindwin
43864 Katha
43865 Shwebo
43871 Myitkyina
43873 Bhamb
43881 Ruby Mines
43882 Mandalay
43883 Kyankse
43884 Meiktila
43885 Yamethin
43886 Magwe
43887 Thayetmyo
43888 Myingyan
43889 Sagaing

44 **India**
As before 1956
441 **Madras** (**excluding the Indian States**)
4411 **Eastern districts**
44111 Madras
44112 Chingleput
44113 South Arcot
44114 Tanjore

4413 **Southern districts**
44132 Ramnad
44133 Tinnevelly
44134 Madura
44135 Trichinopoly
44136 Coimbatore
44137 Nilgiris

4415 **West Coast**
44153 Malabar
44154 South Kanara

4416 **Ceded Districts**
44161 Cuddapah
44162 Anantapur
44163 Bellary
44165 Kurnool

4418 **Andhra Desa**
44181 Nellore
44182 Guntur
44183 Kistna
44184 Godavari, West
44185 Godavari, East
44186 Vizagapatam
44187 Ganjam (*Before*) 1936

4419 **Central Districts**
44191 Salem
44192 North Arcot
44193 Chittoor

442 **South** (**excluding Madras**)
4421 Pudukkottai
4422 **Travancore**
4423 **Cochin**
4424 **Mysore**
4425 **Hyderabad**
4426 **Coorg**

4431 **Bombay**
443111 Ahmadnagar
443112 Sholapur
443113 Akalkot
443114 Jath
443115 Jamkhandi
443116 Bijapur
443121 Dharwar
443131 North Kanara
443141 Belgaum
443142 Sangli
443143 Savantvadi
443144 Kolhapur
443151 Ratnagiri
443152 Kolaba
443153 Satara
443154 Aundh
443155 Bhor
443156 Poona
443157 Thana
443158 Jawhar
443161 Surat
443162 Broach
443163 Kathiawar
443164 Palanpur

443165 Mahikanta
443171 Khandesh, West
443172 Khandesh, East,
443173 Nasik
443181 Ahmadabad

443182 Baroda
443183 Kaira
443184 Panch Mahals
443185 Rewakantha

4432 Baluchistan
443211 Kachhi
443212 Jhalawan
443231 Lasbela
443232 Makran
443251 Kharan
443252 Chagai
443253 Sarawan
443271 Zhob
443272 Loralai

4433 Sind

4435 North West Frontier
443511 Kohat
443512 Banu
443521 Dera Ismail Khan
443541 Agencies and tributary areas
443571 Hazara
443572 Peshawar

4436 Punjab
443611 Ambala
443612 Karnal
443613 Rohtak
443621 Gurgaon
443631 Hissar
443632 Montgomery
443633 Bahawalpur
443641 Multan
443642 Muzaffargarh
443643 Jhang
443644 Lyallpur
443651 Dera Ghazi Khan
443652 Mianwali
443653 Shahpur
443654 Gujranwala
443656 Shekhpura
443661 Gujarat
443663 Jhelum
443664 Attock
443665 Rawalpindi
443671 Amritsar
443672 Sialkot
443673 Gurudaspur
443674 Kapurthala State
443681 Hoshiarpur
443682 Kangra
443683 Chamba
443684 Simla
443685 Simla States
443686 Mandi and Suket
443687 Sirmur
443691 Punjab States
4436911 Patiala
4436912 Faridkot
4436913 Kalsia State
4436914 Dujana State
443692 Ferozepore
443693 Lahore
443694 Jullundur
443696 Ludhiana

444 Himalayan regions
4441 Kashmir
4442 Himachal Pradesh
4445 Nepal
4446 Sikkim
4447 Bhutan

445 North India

4451 Delhi

4452 United Province=Uttar Pradesh
445211 Azamgarh
445212 Ballia
445213 Benares
445214 Ghazipur
445215 Jaunpur
445221 Mirzapur
445222 Allahabad
445223 Partabgarh
445231 Banda
445232 Hamirpur
445233 Jhansi
445234 Jalaun
445235 Etawah
445236 Cawnpore
445237 Fatehpur
445241 Hardoi
445242 Farrukhabad
445243 Mainpuri
445244 Agra
445245 Muttra
445246 Aligarh
445247 Etah
445251 Budaun
445252 Bulandshahr
445253 Meerut
445254 Muzaffarnagar
445255 Moradabad
445256 Rampur
445257 Bareilly
445261 Saharanpur
445262 Dehra Dun

445264 Garhwal
445265 Almora
445266 Nainital
445267 Bijnor
445271 Sitapur
445272 Shahjahanpur
445273 Pilibhit
445274 Kheri
455275 Bahraich
445276 Gonda
445281 Basti
445282 Gorakhpur
445291 Unao
445292 Lucknow
445293 Bara Banki
445294 Rae Bareli
445295 Sultanpur
445296 Fyzabad

4453 Bihar and Orissa (*Before bifurcation—1936*)

445311 Santal Parganas
445312 Manbhum
445315 Singhbhum
445316 Balasore
445331 Cuttack
445335 Angul
445336 Feudatory States of Orissa
445351 Sambalpur
445352 Ranchi
445353 Palamau
445355 Shahabad
445371 Saran
445372 Champaran
445373 Muzaffarpur
445374 Darbhanga
445375 Monghyr
445376 Bhagalpur
445377 Purnea
445391 Hazaribagh
445392 Gaya
445393 Patna

4454 Orissa (*After bifurcation in 1936*=**Utkal**)

44541 Cuttack
44542 Puri
44543 Ganjam
44544 Korapet
44545 Sambalpur
44547 Balasore

4461 Assam

446112 Naga Hills
446114 Manipur
446131 Lushai Hills
446151 Sylhet
446153 Garo Hills
446171 Goalpara
446172 Kamrup
446173 Darrang
446174 Nowgong
446175 Sibsagar
446191 Khasi and Jaintia Hills
446192 Cachar

4462 Bengal

446211 Mymensingh
446212 Dacca
446213 Tipperah
446214 Tripura
446215 Chittagong Tracts
446217 Noakhali
446231 Backergunge
446232 Khulna
446233 Twenty-four Parganas
446234 Howrah
446236 Midnapore
446251 Hooghly
446252 Bogra
446253 Burdwan
446254 Birbhum
446255 Murshidabad
446256 Malda
446257 Dinajpur
446271 Darjeeling
446272 Jalpaiguri
446273 Cooch Behar
446275 Rangpur
446291 Pabna
446292 Faridpur
446293 Jessore
446295 Nadia
446296 Rajshahi

4471 Central Provinces=Madhya Pradesh

447111 Bilaspur
447112 Raipur
447113 Kanker
447114 Drug
447121 Bastar
447131 Nandgaon
447132 Chanda
447133 Yeotmal
447134 Akola
447135 Wardha
447136 Nagpur
447137 Bhandara
447141 Amraoti
447142 Buldana
447143 Nimar
447151 Betul
447152 Hoshangabad
447153 Narsinghpur
447154 Chhindwara
447155 Seoni
447161 Saugor

447162 Damoh
447163 Jubbulpore
447171 Mandla
447172 Chang Bhakar
447173 Korea
447181 Surguja
447182 Jashpur
447183 Udaipur
447184 Rajgarh
447185 Chhathisgarh feudatory states
447191 Balaghat

448 Central India and Rajputana

4481 Central India = Madhya Bharat
448111 Rewah
448112 Maihar
448113 Panna
448114 Ajaigarh
448118 Other Eastern states
448151 Gwalior
448152 Bhopal
448154 Indore
448158 Other Western states

4482 Rajputana
448211 Kotah
448212 Jhalawar
448231 Shajapur
448232 Mandasor
448241 Banswara
448242 Dungarpur
448243 Mewar
448251 Sirohi
448252 Marwar
448253 Jaisalmer
448261 Bikaner
448271 Jaipur
448281 Alwar
448282 Bharatpur
448291 Bundi
448292 Ajmer-Merwara

449 Islands
4491 Andamans
4492 Laccadive Islands

After 1956

441 Southern States
4411 Madras (Tamil Nadu)
4412 Kerala
4413 Mysore (Karnataka)
4416 Andhra Pradesh

443 Western States
4431 Bombay
4435 Maharashtra
4436 Gujarat
4437 Rajastan

444 North Western States
4443 Punjab (East)
4445 Himachal Pradesh
4447 Jammu and Kashmir

445 Northern States
4452 Uttar Pradesh
4455 Madhya Pradesh

447 Eastern States
4471 Orissa
4473 Bihar
4475 Bengal (West)
4477 Assam

448 Centrally Administered Areas
4481 Delhi

4497 Himalayan States
44971 Bhutan
44973 Sikkim
44974 Nepal

4498 Ceylon

44Q7 Pakistan

44Q71 East Pakistan

44Q72 East Bengal
44Q721 Chittagong Division
44Q7211 Cittagong Hill Tracts
44Q7212 Chittagong
44Q7213 Noakhali
44Q7214 Tipperah
44Q7215 Sylhet
44Q722 Dacca Division
44Q7221 Mymensingh
44Q7222 Dacca
44Q7223 Faridpur
44Q7224 Bakrangaj
44Q723 Rajshahi Division
44Q7231 Rangpur
44Q7232 Dinajpur
44Q7233 Bogra
44Q7234 Rajshahi
44Q7235 Pabna
44Q7236 Nadia
44Q7237 Jessore
44Q7238 Khulna

44Q73 West Pakistan

44Q74 Sind

44Q741 Thar Parkar
44Q742 Hyderabad
44Q743 Karachi
44Q744 Dadu
44Q745 Nawabshah
44Q746 Khairpur
44Q747 Larkana
44Q748 Sukkur
44Q7491 Upper Sind Frontier

44Q75 Baluchistan
44Q751 Kachhi
44Q752 Jhalawan
44Q753 Lasbela
44Q754 Makran
44Q755 Kharan
44Q756 Chagai
44Q757 Nuski
44Q758 Sarawan
44Q7591 Quetta
44Q7592 Zhob
44Q7593 Loralai
44Q76 North West Frontier
44Q761 Dera Ismail Khan
44Q762 South Waziristan
44Q763 North Waziristan
44Q764 Bannu
44Q765 Kohat
44Q766 Peshawar
44Q767 Mardan
44Q768 Swat
44Q7691 Dir
44Q7692 Chitral

44Q77 West Punjab
44Q7711 Sialkot
44Q7712 Gujaranwala
44Q7713 Sheikhpura
44Q7714 Lahore
44Q7715 Lyllpur
44Q7731 Montgomery
44Q7732 Multan
44Q7733 Bahawalpur
44Q7734 Muzaffargarh
44Q7735 Dehra Gazhi Khan
44Q7736 Jhang
44Q7737 Shahpur
44Q7738 Mianwali
44Q7771 Gujrat
44Q7772 Jhelum
44Q7773 Attock
44Q7774 Rawalpindi

45 Persia (Iran)

46 Arabian Peninsula

461 Arabia
4611 El-hasa
4613 Hadhramaut
4614 Nejd
4615 Hejaz
4617 Syrian Desert
462 Oman
464 Aden

465 Palestine
4651 Jordan
4653 Israel
4655 Lebanon

466 Syria

467 Iraq (Mesopotamia)
46791 Babylonia
46792 Assyria

47 Asia Minor

48 Siberia
4893 Armenia

49 Other Asian countries

491 Afghanistan

494 Manchuria

495 Korea

496 Mangolia

497 Sinkiang

498 Tibet

5 Europe

51 Greece

52 Italy
5291 Sicily
5292 Malta

53 France

54 Spain and Portugal

541 Spain

542 Portugal

55 Germany
5541 Saar Basin

56 Great Britain and Ireland

561 England
56111 Norfolk
56112 Suffolk
56113 Essex
56114 Hertford
56115 Bedford
56116 Northampton
56117 Cambridge
56118 Huntingdon
56121 Surrey

56122 Kent
56123 Sussex
56124 London
56131 Berks
56132 Hamp
56133 Wilts
56134 Dorset
56141 Devon
56142 Cornwall
56143 Somerset
56151 Oxford
56152 Gloucestor
56153 Monmouth
56154 Hereford
56155 Shropshire
56156 Derby
56157 Worcester
56158 Warwick
56161 Stafford
56162 Cheshire
56163 Lancashire
56171 Westmorland
56172 Cumberland
56173 Northumberland
56175 Yorkshire
56176 Nottingham
56177 Durham
56181 Lincoln
56182 Leicester
56183 Rutland

562 Wales
5621 Radnor
56212 Brecknock
5622 Glamorgan
5623 Carmarthen
5624 Pembroke
5625 Cardigan
5626 Montgomery
5627 Merioneth
56281 Carnarvon
56282 Denbigh
56283 Flint
56291 Anglesey

563 Scotland
56311 Fife
56312 Kinross
56313 Clackmannan
56314 Stirling
56321 West Lothian (Linlithgow)
56322 Mid Lothian (Edinburgh)
56323 East Lothian (Haddington)
56324 Berwick
56327 Peebles
56331 Lanark
56332 Selkirk
56333 Roxburgh
56334 Dumfries
56341 Kircudbright
56342 Wigtown
56343 Ayr
56351 Renfrew
56352 Dumbarton
56353 Argyll
56354 Perth
56371 Inverness
56372 Ross and Cromarty
56373 Sutherland
56374 Caithness
56381 Nairn
56382 Moray (Elgin)
56383 Banff
56384 Aberdeen
56385 Kincardine
56386 Angus (Forfar)

5639 Islands
56391 Bute
56392 Orkney Islands
56393 Shetland

564 Ireland
5641 Leinster
564111 Dublin
564112 Kildare
564113 Wicklow
564121 Wexford
564122 Carlow
564131 Kilkenny
564151 Queen's Co. (Leix)
564152 King' Co.
564153 West Meath
564161 Lontgford
564181 Louth
564182 Meath
5643 Munster
56431 Waterford
56432 Cork
56433 Kerry
56434 Limerick
56435 Clare
56437 Tipperary
5645 Connaught
56451 Roscommon
56453 Galway
56455 Mayo
56457 Sligo
56458 Leitrim
5647 Ulster
56471 Monoghan
56472 Cavan
56473 Donegal
5648 Northern Ireland
56481 Antrim
56482 Down
56483 Armagh
56486 Fermanagh

56487	Tyrone
56488	Londonderry
57	**Scandinavia**
571	**Sweden**
572	**Denmark**
573	**Norway**
574	Iceland
575	Finland
58	**Russia**
591	**Turkey**
59191	Cyprus
592	**Balkan States**
5921	**Rumania**
5922	**Bulgaria**
5923	**Yugo-slavia**
5925	**Czecho-slovakia**
5927	**Albania**
5931	**Austria**
5932	**Hungary**
594	**Switzerland**
595	**Poland**
596	**Netherlands**
5961	**Belgium**
5962	**Holland**
5966	**Luxemberg**
5971	**Lithuania**
5973	**Latvia**
5975	**Esthonia**
6	**Africa**
611	**Tanganyika**
612	**Mozambique**
613	**Rhodesia**
6133	**Southern Rhodesia**
615	**Nyasaland**
63	**Union of South Africa**
631	Transvaal
632	Natal
633	Orange Free State
634	Cape of Good Hope
641	**Belgian Congo**
642	**South West Africa**
643	**Angola**
65	**West Africa**
653	**French West Africa**
654	**Nigeria**
655	**Ashanti**
656	**Liberia**
657	**Ghana**
658	**Gambia**
6591	**Sierra Leone**
661	**Rio de Oro**
663	**Morocco**
671	**Algeria**
673	**Tunisia**
674	**Libya**
677	**Egypt**
6771	**Sinai**
678	**Sudan**
681	**Eritrea**
682	**Abyssinia**
683	**British Somaliland**
685	**Italian Somaliland**
687	**Kenya**
688	**Uganda**
69	Islands
691	**Madagascar**
692	**Socotra**
693	**Mauritius**
698	**Zanzibar**
7	**America**
71	**North America**
7191	**Greenland**
72	**Canada**
7211	Novā Scotia
7212	New Brunswick
722	Ontario
723	Manitoba
724	Saskatchewan
7251	Alberta
7252	British Columbia
7253	Yukon
726	North West Territory
728	Quebec
7291	Prince Edward Islands
7292	Newfoundland

73	**United States**
7311	New York
7312	Pennsylvania
7313	New Jersey
7314	Delawar
7315	Maryland
7317	Virginia
7318	Kentucky
7321	North Carolina
7322	South Carolina
7323	Georgia
7324	Florida
7325	Alabama
7326	Louisiana
7327	Mississippi
7328	Tennessee
7331	Texas
7332	Oklahoma
7333	Kansas
7334	Nebraska
7335	Missouri
7336	Arkansas
7341	New Mexico
7342	Arizona
7343	Colorado
7344	Wyoming
7351	California
7352	Nevada
7353	Oregon
7354	Idaho
7355	Utah
7361	Washington
7363	Montana
7371	North Dakota
7372	South Dakota
7373	Minnesota
7374	Wisconsin
7375	Iowa
7376	Illinois
7377	Indiana
7381	Michigan
7382	Ohio
7383	Vermont
7384	Connecticut
7385	Massachusetts
7386	New Hampshire
7387	Maine
7391	Rhode Island
74	**Mexico**
7414	**Yucatan**
75	**Central America**
751	Guatemala
752	British Honduras
753	Salvador
755	Nicaragua
758	Costa Rica
76	Alaska

77	Panama
791	**South America**
7911	**Uruguay**
7913	**Argentine Republic**
7914	**Chile**
7915	**Paraguay**
79161	**Bolivia**
79162	**Peru**
79163	**Ecuador**
79164	**Colombia**
79171	**Venezuela**
79172	**British Guiana**
79173	**Dutch Guiana**
79174	**French Guiana**
7918	**Brazil**
79198	**Falkland Isles**
792	**West Indies**
7921	**Trinidad**
7922	**Windward and Seaward Islands**
7924	**Porto Rico**
7925	**Haiti**
7926	**Jamaica**
7927	**Cuba**
7928	**Bahamas**
8	**Australia**
81	**Queensland**
82	**New South Wales**
8291	**Hunter Islands**
83	**Victoria**
84	**South and Central Australia**
85	**Western Australia**
86	**North Australia**
89	Islands
8921	Tasmania
93	**Land within Pacific Ocean**
931	Philippine and other associated islands
933	New Guinea
934	Melanesia

2·16

935	Micronesia		**The Oceans**
9358	Solomon Islands		
936	Polynesia	**95**	**Indian**
9365	Samoa		
9368	Fiji	**96**	**Atlantic**
937	New Zealand		
9391	Aleutian Islands	**97**	**Pacific**
9392	Hawaii	**983**	**Antarctic**
9473	**Spitsbergen**	**987**	**Arctic**

42 Isolate in [S2]

1	Geosphere	2	Mountain
124	Forest	3	City (Town, Village)
137	Delta	5	Hydrosphere
14	Island	54	Lake
16	Valley	6	River

Note: Any specific isolate should be individualised by (AD).

GEOGRAPHICAL INDEX

CHAPTER 5

LANGUAGE ISOLATE

1 **Indo-European**

11 **Teutonic**

11011 Gothic
110153 Low Frisian
110155 Old Frisian
111 English
112 Dutch
113 German
114 Swedish
115 Norwegian
116 Danish
117 Icelandic

12 **Latin**

121 Italian
122 French
123 Spanish
124 Portuguese
128 Celtic
1283 Welsh
1285 Irish
1287 Scotch, Gaelic

13 **Greek**

14 **Slavonic**

141 Lethic
142 Russian
143 Bulgarian
144 Illyrian
1441 Slav
1442 Servian
145 Polish
146 Bohemian

15 **Sanskrit**

151 Prakrt
1511 Pali
1512 Maharastri
1516 Ardhamagadhi
1517 Magadhi
1518 Apabhramsa
15198 Sinhalese
152 Hindi
153 Panjabi
154 Kashmiri
155 Marathi
156 Gujarati
157 Bengali
158 Assamese
1591 Oriya
1595 Nepalis

16 **Iranian**

161 Avestic
162 Pahlavi
164 Persian
165 Afghan (Pushtu)
168 Urdu

17 Armenian
18 Albanian
191 Tockarish
192 Phyrigian
197 Hittite

2 **Semitic**

21 Babylonian including Syriac
22 Assyrian
24 Aramaic
25 Hebrew
26 Phoenician
28 Arabic

3 **Dravidian**

31 Tamil
32 Malayalam
33 Kanarese
34 Tulu
35 Telugu
36 Kui
38 Brahui
39 Toda, etc.

4 **Other Asian languages**

5 **Other European languages**

6 **Other African languages**

7 **Other American languages**

8 **Other Australian languages**

9 **Other oceanic languages**

Divisions 4-9 *to be divided by* (GD)

(*Illustrative*)

467 Sumerian

99 **Artificial languages**

To be divided by (CD)

(*Illustrative*)

99M Solresol

99M7	Lingualumina	99N	Interlingua 'Latino Sina flex'
99M8	Volapuk	99N1	Ido
99M84	Blaia Zimondal	99N2	Hom-idyomo
99M86	Cabe Aban		
99M87	Esperanto		

CHAPTER 6

PHASE, INTRA-FACET, and INTRA-ARRAY RELATION

Intra-Array	*Intra-Facet*	*Phase*	*Nature of Relation*
t	*j*	*a*	General
u	*k*	*b*	Bias
v	*m*	*c*	Comparison
w	*n*	*d*	Difference
y	*r*	*g*	Influencing

CHAPTER 9*a*

GENERALIA BIBLIOGRAPHY

a **[P], [P2] [P3], [P4]**

Foci in [P]

1 **By mode of production**
11 Tablet
12 Manuscript
128 Archive
13 Sound book
14 Printed book
15 Photo-reproduction
151 Micro
1511 Film strip
1512 Film roll
152 Photostat
17 Map
18 Raised type

2 **By script**

(*To be divided by language*)

3 **By language**

(*To be divided by language*)

4 **By nature of publication**
43 Book (conventional)
44 Newspaper
45 Recreative
46 Periodical
47 Reference book
48 Patent
494 Thesis
4994 Not-written book
4995 Book written but not existing

5 **By agency of production**
54 University
55 Government
58 Private

6 **By age of publication**
61 Old
66 Current

7 **By edition**
71 First
74 Proscribed
75 De luxe
77 Autograph

8 **By social group of readers**

(*To be divided as in* Y *Sociology*)

95 **Translation**

(*To be divided first by the language of the original and then by the language of the translation. A hyphen should be inserted between the two language numbers*)

991 **By size**
9911 Oversize
9912 Miniature
9917 Pamphlet

Foci in [P2]

1 List of publications in a geographical area
2 Library catalogue
3 Publisher's catalogue
4 Bookseller's catalogue
5 Catalogue of exhibition
7 Reading list

Foci in [P3] and [P4]

See Chapter 9a of the Rules

CHAPTER 92

LIBRARY SCIENCE

2 [P]; [M]: [E] [2P]

Foci in [P]

1 **Trans-local**

11 World
13 Nation
14 Region
15 State
16 Division

2 **Local**

21 District
22 City

3 **Academical**

31 Elementary school
32 Secondary school
33 College
34 University
36 Research

4 **Business**

42 Industry
44 Newspaper office
45 Commerce
48 Government department

Others by (SD)

(*Illustrative*)

4(Q) Religious
4(X81) Insurance

5 **Subscription**

6 **Special class**

61 Child
63 Prisoner
64 Hospital
65 Woman
68 Blind
695 Seafarer

95 **Contact**

97 **Private**

Foci in [M]

Same as *Foci in* [P] for

Generalia Bibliography

Foci in [E] *cum* [2P]

1 Book selection
2 Organisation
3 Function
4 Co-operation

5 **Technical treatment**

51 Classification
55 Cataloguing

6 **Circulation**

61 Consultation
62 Lending
7 Reference service

8 **Administration**

81 Book Selection
811 Source
815 Indent
82 Order
84 Accession
85 Preparation
88 Maintenance
97 Documentation

CHAPTER B

MATHEMATICS

Canonical divisions

B1 **Arithmatic**

B2 **Algebra**

B3 **Analysis**

B4 **Other methods**

B5 **Trigonometry**

B6 **Geometry**

B7 **Mechanics**

B8 **Physico-mathematics**

B9 **Astronomy**

B1 **Arithmetic**

B11 Lower arithmetic
B111 Numeration
B112 Notation
B113 Arithmetical operation
B114 Approximation

B12 **Concept of number**

B13 **Integer (theory of numbers)**

B13 [P], [P2]: [E] [2P]

Foci in [P]

1 Prime number
2 Number defined by factor properties
21 Highly composite number
5 Number defined by partition properties

Foci in [P2]

1 Primality and divisibility
2 Distribution
3 Diophantine equation

Special equations by (CD) (*illustrative*)

3K Pell's equation
5 Form including partition

Special forms by (CD) (*illustrative*)

5K Fermat's last theorem
5L Goldbach's theorem
5L5 Waring's problem
9 Associated arithmetic function

9A Special arithmetic functions by (CD) (*illustrative*)

9L θ function
9M μ function
9M9 Merten's function
9N Multiplicative function

Foci in [E] *cum* [2P]

1 Elementary arithmetical method
2 Algebraic method
21 Elementary algebraic method
22 Method of rational approximations by continued fraction
23 Congruence
25 Method of algebraic form
28 Method of probability
3 Analytical method
36 Method of infinite series and product
38 Method of complex variable
39 By the use of special function

(*to be divided as* B39)

6 Geometrical method

B15 **Algebraic number and ideal number**

(*to be divided as* B13)

B16 **Complex and hyper-complex number**

(*to be divided as* B13)

B18 **Transcendental number**

B2 **Algebra**

B21 Elementary algebra, *i.e.*, not involving infinite processes
B213 Fundamental operation and law
B215 Ratio and proportion, variation
B216 Progression
B217 Permutation and combination

B22 **Continued fraction**

B221 Finite

B23 **Theory of equation**

B23 [P]: [E]

Foci in [P]

1 Simple (Linear)
2 Quadratic
3 Cubic
4 Biquadratic
5 Simultaneous
7 *nth* degree
8 Transcendental
9 Special

Special equations by (CD) (*illustrative*)

9M Abelian equation
9M7 Sylow equation

Foci in [E]

1 Numerical solution
3 Symmetric function
4 Elimination, (Resultant)
5 Formal solution
6 Graphical solution
7 Existence of solution, (Galois theory)

B24 Determinant

B245 Matrix

Special determinants by (CD) (*illustrative*)

B24M Alternant

B25 Higher algebra (form, transformation, invariant, etc.)

B25 [P], [P2]: [E] [2P]

Foci in [P]

2 Binary
3 Ternary
4 Quaternary
7 *n*-nary

Foci in [P2]

1 Linear
2 Quadratic
3 Cubic
7 *nth* degree

Foci in [E] *cum* [2P]

1 Linear transformation
18 Special invariant
2 Quadratic transformation
28 Special invariant
3 Cubic transformation
38 Special invariant
7 *n*-ic transformation
78 Special invariant
8 Special transformation

Special transformations by (CD) (*illustrative*)

8M Cremona transformation

B27 Group

B271 Finite group

B28 Statistics

B281 Probability
B2813 Normal equation
B2817 Sampling
B2818 Theory of attribute
B282 Frequency curve
B283 Histograms
B284 Average and index number
B285 Correlation
B286 Periodogram analysis
B287 Sequential analysis
B288 Programme (Design of experiment)

B2A Systems of Algebra by (CD)

B3 Analysis

B31 Foundation

B311 Number
B3111 Ordinal
B3113 Cardinal
B3114 Transfinite

B313 Function-space

B313N Hilbert space
B316 Topology

B32 Calculus

B321 Differential
B324 Partial differentiation
B325 Integral calculus
B3255 Definite integral
B328 Multiple integral

B33 Differential and integral equation

B33 [P], [P2], [P3]: [E] [2P]

Foci in [P]

1 Ordinary
2 Simultaneous
3 Total differential
4 Partial
5 Integral

Foci in [P2]

1 Linear
2 Quadratic
3 Cubic
4 Quartic
5 Quintic
6 Sextic
7 *n*th degree

Foci in [P3]

1 First order
2 Second
3 Third
4 Fourth
5 Fifth
6 Sixth
7 *n*th

Foci in [E] *cum* [2P]

1 Numerical solution
5 Formal solution
52 Algebraic theory
53255 Solution by definite integral
56 Solution by infinite series
58 Singular solution
6 Graphical solution
7 Existence of solution

B34 Continuous group

B35 Differential form

B36 Infinite series

B361 Sequence
B362 Series of positive terms
B363 Alternative series
B365 Infinite product
B369 Divergent series

Special series by (CD) (*illustrative*)

B36M Fourier's
B36M3 Dirichlet's

B37 Real variable

B37 [P]: [E] [2P]

Foci in [P]

1 Single variable
2 Two
7 *n*

Foci in [E] *cum* [2P]

1 Integral

Special theories by (CD) (*illustrative*)

1M Cauchy
1M5 Riemann
1N Lebesgue

2 Analytic representation
22 As a continued fraction
23 As a definite integral
26 As an infinite series
265 As an infinite product
4 Singularity
5 Distribution of value
7 Maximum-minimum principle
8 Inequality and mean value
92 Family of functions

B38 Complex variable

B38 [P]: [E] [2P]

Foci in [P]

1 Single variable
2 Two
7 *n*

Foci in [E] *cum* [2P]

1 Cauchy's theorem (complex integration)
2 Analytic representation
22 Approximation by polynomial
23 As a contour integral
26 As an infinite series
265 As an infinite product
3 Analytic continuation
4 Singularity
41 Pole
45 Essential singularity
5 Distribution of value
59 Exceptional value
6 Conformal representation (uniformisation)
7 Maximum-minimum principle
8 Inequality and mean value
92 Family of functions

B39 Special function

B391 Elementary function defined by a finite number of algebraic operations
B392 Integral of algebraic function

Subdivisions by (CD) (*illustrative*)

B392L Hyperbolic function
B392L8 Elliptic function
B392M Hyperelliptic function
B392N Prym function
B393 Function defined by contour integral

Subdivisions by (CD)

(*illustrative*)

B393L Eulerian function (gamma function)
B393M Lie function
B393M2 Bessel function (cylindrical harmonic)
B394 Function defined by differential and integral equation

Subdivisions by (CD)

(*illustrative*)

B394L Laplace function, Legendere function (spherical harmonic)
B394M Green's function (harmonic function)
B394M3 Lame's function (ellipsoidal harmonic)
B394M7 Mathieu's function
B396 Function defined by infinite series and product

Subdivisions by (CD)

(*illustrative*)

B396M Hypergeometric series (Hermite's function)
B396M3 Integral function
B396M5 Zeta function
B397 Function defined by group, (Automorphic function)
B398 Function of position defined in the manner of Riemann
B399 Function qualitatively defined
B399M Meromorphic function
B399N Quasi-analytic function
B399N2 Almost periodic function

B4 Other Calculus

B41 Finite difference
B42 Variation
B43 Functional analysis
B44 Graphical (nomography)
B45 Quaternion
B46 Vector etc.
B463 Tensor (Absolute)
B466 Vector
B48 Operational
B491 Mathematical calculation

B5 Trigonometry

B52 Plane
B53 Spherical

B6 Geometry

B6 [P]: [E] [2P]

Foci in [P]

1 Line

2 Plane

21 Configuration essentially made up of points and straight lines only
22 Curve of the second degree
23 Third
24 Fourth
25 Fifth
27 Algebraic curve in general
28 Transcendental curve

3 Three dimensions

31 Configuration essentially made up of points, straight lines and planes only
32 Surface of the second degree
33 Cubic
34 Quartic
36 Curve in space
39M Knot

4 Four dimensions

5 Five dimensions

7 *n* dimensions

Foci in [E] *cum* [2P]

1 Enumerative geometry
2 Algebraic
23 Elementary co-ordinate
25 With the use of higher algebra
3 Differential
32 Infinitesimal
34 With the aid of vectors
35 Higher differential
4 Practical
5 Descriptive
6 Pure
7 Projective including differential projective
91 Foundation

B6A Systems of Geometry by (CD)

B6M Non-Euclidean

B6M3 Elliptic
B6M5 Hyperbolic
B6N Line-complex

B7 Mechanics

B7 [P]: [E] [2P]

Foci in [P]

1 **Solid**

11 **Particle**

117 System of particles (chain)
12 Surface
127 System of surfaces (flexible surface)

13 **Rigid body**

137 System of rigid bodies (jointed frame)
15 Elastic body
19 Special system
192 Top, (gyroscope)
193 Ballistic
196 Pendulum

5 **Liquid**

51 Perfect
55 Compressible
56 Viscous

8 **Gas**

Foci in [E] *cum* [2P]

1 **Fundamental principle**

11 Inertia
111 Centre
112 Moment
12 D'Alembert's
13 Hamilton's. Least action

15 **Archimedes'**

151 **Centre of pressure**

162 Virtual velocity
163 Virtual work

2 **Statics**

291 Floating body

3 **Motion, Dynamics**

31 Kinematics
32 Kinetics
321 Single force. Central force
322 Multiple force
324 Impulse
34 Constrained motion
35 Irrotational
351 Streamline
353 Turbulent
354 Discontinuous
39 Rotational
391 Motion of solid (in liquid and gas)

5 **Vibration**

55 Wave
61 Tautochrone
63 Brahystochrone
66 Isochronism

B8 Physico-Mathematics

B83 Potential function and attraction
B85 Wave function

B9 Astronomy

B9 [P]: [E] [2P]

Foci in [P]

1 **Earth**

2 **Moon**

3 **Sun**

4 **Planet**

41 Mercury and infra-Mercurial
42 Venus
43 Mars
44 Asteroid
45 Jupiter
46 Saturn
47 Uranus
48 Neptune
49 Trans-Neptunian

5 **Meteor and comet**

51 Meteor
52 Comet
55 Zodiacal light

6 **Star**

61 Constellation
62 Double
63 Multiple
64 Cluster. (nebulae)
641 Milky way

7 **Planetary system**

78 Satellite
7894 Artificial

Foci in [E] *cum* [2P]

1 **Chronology**

11 Year
112 Lunar
113 Solar
12 Month
122 Lunar
123 Solar
13 Week
14 Day
142 Lunar
143 Solar
1431 True solar
1432 Mean solar

1435 **Equation of time**
146 Sidereal day
15 Subdivision of day
16 Time reckoning
161 Sidereal time
162 Local
165 Standard
1652 Summer

17 **Calendar**
18 Era
194 Duration of daylight

2 **Geodetic astronomy**
21 Geographical position
22 Meridian
23 Longitude
24 Latitude

5 **Spherical astronomy**
51 Celestial sphere (co-ordinate)
513 Right ascension
514 Declination
52 Reduction to centre of earth
521 Refraction
5212 Dip of horizon
5215 Twilight
522 Parallax
53 Correction for movement of earth
531 Aberration
532 Annual parallax
535 Star reduction
55 Position of the pole
56 Ecliptic
563 Longitude
564 Latitude

57 **Eclipse**
575 Occultation
578 Transit
58 Calculation of ephimerides

6 **Physical astronomy (astrophysics)**
61 Position
611 Movement
62 Constant
621 Dimension (figure)
622 Mass
623 Density
624 Distance
63 Rotation (surface)
631 Rotation
635 Surface
6358 Atmosphere
642 Temperature
643 Radiation
652 Brightness
653 Spectroscopy
67 Age
68 Constitution

7 **Theoretical astronomy (celestial-mechanics)**
72 Orbit
73 Problem of three bodies
74 Perturbation (planetary theory)
75 Perturbation, (lunar theory)
76 Rotation (figure of equilibrium)
77 Perturbed rotation
78 Tide

8 **Cosmogony**
95 Radio-astronomy
995 Cosmic ecology

CHAPTER C

PHYSICS

Canonical divisions

C1 **Fundamentals**
C2 **Properties of matter**
C3 **Sound**
C4 **Heat**
C5 **Light. Radiation**
C6 **Electricity**
C7 **Magnetism**
C8 **Cosmic hypothes**

C1 Fundamentals

C13 Matter
C11 Weight
C18 Gravitation
C14 Energy
C15 Space
C166 Time

C2 Properties of Matter

C2 [P], [P2]

Foci in [P]

1 Solid
15 Glass
16 Crystal
5 Liquid
8 Gas

Foci in [P2]

13 Density

2 Elasticity

21 Linear
22 Areal
23 Volume
25 Shape
251 Bending

4 Surface tension

47 Capillarity
6 Plasticity
91 Friction
92 Viscosity
93 Diffusion

7 Pressure

76 Vacuum

8 Structure

C3 Sound

C3 [P]: [E] [2P]

Foci in [P]

1 Audible sound
2 Infra sound
5 Ultra sound

Foci in [E] *cum* [2P]

1 Generation

2 Propagation

21 Velocity
22 Reflection
23 Refraction
28 Intensity

3 Frequency

31 Pitch
33 Musical scale
35 Resonance
358 Resonator
38 Analysis

5 Interference (beat. diffraction)

7 Acoustics

71 Absorption

8 Nature

C4 Heat

C4: [E] [2P]

Foci in [E] *cum* [2P]

1 Generation

2 Transference

23 Convection
24 Conduction
25 Radiation

27 Absorption

28 Calorimetry etc.

281 Calorimetry
282 Quantity of heat
283 Specific heat

3 Thermometry

4 Expansion of body

5 **Change of state**
51 Fusion
511 Solidification
512 Melting point
513 Change of volume during fusion
514 Latent heat of fusion
52 Sublimation
55 Vaporization (evaporation, ebullition)
551 Liquefaction
552 Boiling point
554 Latent heat of vaporization
58 Critical state
582 Critical point

7 **Thermodynamics**

8 **Nature of heat**

C5 Radiation

C5 [P]: [E] [2P]

Foci in [P]

1 **Light**
12 Red
13 Orange
14 Yellow
15 Green
16 Blue
17 Indigo
18 Violet
2 Ultra violet
3 X
4 Gamma
6 Infra red
7 Hertzian
91· Source
911 Monochromatic

Foci in [E] *cum* [2P]

1 Generation

2 **Propagation**
21 Velocity
22 Reflection
23 Refraction
28 Photometry

3 **Dispersion (spectroscopy)**
3:1 Technique of the spectrum
32 Continuous spectrum
33 Band spectrum
34 Line spectrum
35 Hyperfine structure
38 Effects

Special effects by (CD) (*illustrative*)
38M Kerr effect
38M9 Zeeman
38N Stark
38N2 Compton
38N28 Raman

5 **Interference etc**
51 Interference
55 Diffraction
58 Scattering

6 **Double refraction (polarization)**
65 Elliptic
68 Rotatory

7 **Absorption etc.**
71 Absorption
72 Emission
73 Luminescence
74 Fluorescence
75 Phosphorescence

8 **Nature of light**

Special theories by (CD) (*illustrative*)
8K Corpuscular
8K9 Wave
8M Elastic solid
8M6 Electromagnetic
8N Quantum

C6 Electricity

C6 [P]: [E] [2P]

Foci in [*P*]

2 **Current**
23 Direct
24 Alternating
242 Two-phase
243 Three-phase
248 Multiphase
25 Weak

3 **Statical electricity**
42 Piezo-electricity

Foci in [E] *cum* [2P]

1 **Generation**
11 Primary cell
12 Induction

2 **Propagation**
21 Conduction
211 Dielectric

25 Radiation
28 Secondary cell

3 Potential

4 Transformation into other form of energy

44 Thermo-electricity
45 Photo-electricity
47 Magneto-electricity

8 Nature of electricity

C7 Magnetism

C7 [P]: [E]

Foci in [P]

2 Dia
3 Para
4 Ferro
5 Terrestrial

Foci in [E]

2 Intensity

8 Nature of magnetism

C8 Cosmic Hypotheses

C81 Time, space
C82 Energy, matter
C83 Matter
C84 Energy
C85 Space
C86 Time

C9A Specials

C9B1 Molecular ray
C9B2 Atom

C9B3 Nucleus

Foci in [P]

1 Neutron
2 Nutrino
5 Proton (β ray)
7 Meson
8 Cosmic ray

Foci in [E] *cum* [2P]

Similar to those for C5 Radiation with the following additions

11 Fission
12 Fusion
77 By-product
774 Waste-product

C9B4 β ray
C9B41 Positron
C9B5 Electron

C9B6 Surface Physics
C9B71 High vacuum
C9B78 High pressure

C9D1 Low temperature
C9D8 High temperature

C9F1 Low potential
C9F8 High potential

CA Systems by (CD)

(*illustrative*)

CK Gravitation theory
CM Kinetic theory
CM6 Ether theory
CM65 Electromagnetic theory
CM9 Electron theory
CM96 Radio activity
CN Relativity
CN1 Quantum theory
CN2 Wave mechanics. (statistical mechanics)

CHAPTER D

ENGINEERING

D [P], [2P] [P2]: [E]

Foci in [*P*]

1 **Civil engineering**

2 **Irrigation and drainage work**

24 Underground water
26 River
27 Tank
28 Drainage
284 Subsoil

3 **Building**

31 Wood
32 Earth
324 Refractory material
33 Brick
34 Stone
341 Granite
343 Sand stone
35 Cement
36 Reinforced concrete
38 Steel and other metal
39 Other
391 Plywood
394 Cave

4 **Transport—track**

41 Land

411 **Road**

4111 Wood paved
4112 Earth
4113 Macadam
41131 Water bound
41132 Tar bound
4114 Stone paved
4115 Cement
4116 Reinforced concrete
4117 Asphalt
4119 Other kind

415 **Rail Road**

4151 Street
4152 Light
4153 Ordinary
41531 Narrow gauge
41532 Metre gauge
41533 Standard gauge
41534 Broad gauge
4154 Underground
4156 Mountain

416 **Bridge**

4161 Wood
4162 Suspension
4163 Masonry
4164 Stone
4165 Culvert
4166 Reinforced concrete
4168 Steel
4169 Other bridge
41698 Cantilever

4194 **Tunnel**

42 **Water way**

421 Inland canal
423 River
424 Inter-oceanic canal
425 Ocean
4254 Submarine

43 **Air way**

44 **Rope way**

5 **Transport—vehicle**

51 Land
511 Carried by muscular power
5111 Palanquin
5112 Chair
5113 *Doly*
512 Drawn by muscular power
5121 Country cart
5122 Spring cart
5125 Cycle
513 Drawn by mechanical power
5132 Motor truck
5133 Motor car
5135 Motor cycle
515 Railroad vehicle
5151 Tram car

5153 **Railway carriage**

51532 Railway truck
515321 Open truck
515322 Parcel van
515323 Animal van
515325 Oil van
515328 Trucks for heavy goods
51533 Passenger carriage
515331 Saloon
515332 Higher class carriage

515333	Lower class carriage
515334	Military carriage
515335	Dining car
515336	Tourist carriage
52	**Water vehicle**
521	Boat
523	Steam boat
525	Ship
5251	Sailing ship
5253	**Steam and motor ship**
52532	Cargo ship
525325	Oil ship
52533	Passenger ship
52534	Men-of-war
5254	Submarine
53	**Air vehicle**
531	Dirigible
535	Aeroplane
54	Stratosphere vehicle
58	Space vehicle
6	**Mechanical engineering**
62	**Principle of mechanism**
621	Shafting
6211	Shaft
62115	Flexible shaft
6212	Bearing
62121	Journal bearing
62122	Pillow block, Hanger. Bracket
62123	Pivot bearing
62124	Collar bearing
62125	Ball and roller bearing
622	Belt gearing
6221	Pulley
6222	Belting
6223	Belt shifter
6224	Rope transmission
6225	Chain gearing
6226	Link belting
623	Toothed gearing. Cam
624	Screw
625	Spring
626	Valve gear
627	**Lubrication**
6291	Governor (Regulation and control)
6292	Speed and revolution indicator
6296	Dynamo-meter
635	**Hydraulic**
6351	Water wheel
6353	Piston engine
6355	Turbine
638	**Pneumatic**
6381	Windmill
6385	Turbine
6387	Compressed air
64	**Heat**
641	**External combustion engine (steam engine)**
643	Piston engine
645	Turbine
646	**Internal combustion engine**
6465	Oil engine
6466	Diesel engine
6467	Gas engine
6468	Hot air engine
65	**Electronic**
66	**Electrical**
663	Direct current
664	Alternating current
6642	Two-phase
6643	Three-phase
6648	Multi-phase
665	Weak current
67	Magneto
7	**Nuclear engineering**
8	**Municipal (sanitary) engineering**
85	**Water supply**
851	**Source and head work**
8514	Underground
85141	Well
85144	Artesian well
8517	River
8518	Reservoir. Tank. Lake
854	**Pollution**
855	**Purification**
8551	Mechanical treatment
85511	Settling
85512	Filtration
855121	Natural
855122	Sand
855128	Domestic filter
8552	Physical treatment
85525	Ultra violet ray
85526	Electrical
8553	Chemical treatment

(To be divided by substance used as in 'E Chemistry')

856 **Distribution**
8561 Pumping station
8562 Water tower
8564 Pipe
85641 Main pipe
85645 House connection
85698 Prevention of waste

86 **Sewage**
862 House connection
864 Sewer
865 Pumping station
866 Sewage disposal
8662 Irrigation, Sewage farm
8664 Disposal into stream, sea, etc.
8665 Purification
8666 Septic tank

88 **Municipal refuse**
882 House collection
885 Street cleaning
886 Refuse disposal

Foci in [P2]

For **2 Irrigation** *and its subdivisions in* [P]

1 Source (catchment)
2 Head work
3 Surplus work
4 Distributive work
5 Cross-drainage work
8 Flood protecting and river training work

For **3 Building** *and its subdivisions in* [P]

1 **Earth work**

2 **Foundation**
3 Floor

4 Support
41 Wall
45 Pillar

5 Stairway

6 **Roof**
61 Beam and truss
62 Rafter
63 Roof covering

7 **Window**
72 Window frame
75 Window grating
78 Window shutter

8 **Door**
82 Door frame
85 Hinge
88 Door proper
89 Fastening device

9 Ventilation, etc.
91 Domestic water supply
92 House drainage
93 Ventilation
94 Heating. Cooling
95 Lighting
98 Sanitary fitting
996 Lightning protection

For **411 Road** *and its subdivisions in* [P]

1 **Earth work**
2 Foundation

3 **Surface**
4 Gradient
5 Curve
6 Pavement
7 Berm, avenue, etc.
8 Gate, trap
9 Other part
92 Drainage arrangement
94 Signal

For **415 Railway** *and its subdivisions in* [P]

1 **Earth work**
2 Foundation

3 Surface
31 Ballast
33 Sleeper
35 Rail

4 Gradient
5 Curve
6 Bank, cutting
7 Berm

8 **Station yard**
85 Point and crossing
87 Platform
9 Other part
92 Drainage
94 Signal

For **416 Bridge** *and its subdivisions in* [P]

1 **Earth work**

2 Foundation
4 Pier. abutment, and wing wall
5 Wind brasing, parapet, etc.
6 Bridge proper
8 Approach. River training work

For **42 Waterway** *and its subdivisions in* [P]

1 Earth work. Dredging
4 Lock
7 Towpath
8 Harbour
87 Jetty, Pier
88 Dock
94 Signal

For **43 Airway** *and its subdivisions in* [P]

8 Aerodrome
94 Signals

For **5 Vehicle** *and its subdivisions in* [P]

1 Wheel and tyre
2 Axle
5 Spring
6 Body
61 Step
63 Floor
64 Support
65 Stairway
66 Roof
67 Window
68 Door
7 Propelling arrangement
8 Braking arrangement

For **6 Mechanical Engineering** *and its subdivisions in* [P]

1 Generation
2 Transmission
3 Transformation
4 Traction
To be subdivided on the analogy of Division **5** *in* [P]
5 Illumination
6 Machinery
7 General machinery
71 Lift
711 Jack. Derrick
712 Elevator
72 Hoisting
73 Conveying
74 Pressing
78 Servomechanism
8 Machine tool
81 Planing
811 Planer
812 Shaper
813 Slotting
814 Grooving
82 Turning
821 Lathe
824 Screw cutting
825 Milling
831 Saw
835 Shear
84 Perforating
841 Punching
8418 Multiple
845 Drilling
851 Filing
852 Emery wheel
853 Grind stone
854 Abrasive
86 Bending including straightening
87 Hammer
88 Crushing
8(1) Other machinery
Divisions by [SD] *(illustrative)*
8(2:55) Information retrieving
8(B) Computor
3(D2:1) Excavating
8(D85) Pumping
8(M14) Printing
8(M7) Textile
8(MC421) Refrigerating
8(MJ38) Flouring
8(MJ381) Rice husking
8(P:795) Translating

For **64 Heat engine** *and its subdivisions in* [P]

1 Generation
12 Engine room
121 Engine
15 Fuel

For **65 Electronic Engineering** *in* [*P*]

4 Wireless
41 Location

43 Broadcasting
45 Television
47 Telegraphy
48 Telephony

For **66 Electrical Engineering** *and its subdivisions in* [P]

1 Generation
11 Prime mover and its adjuncts
1135 Hydraulic
114 Heat Engine
1194 Chimney
12 Generating room
121 Generator
Special type indicated by (CD)
122 Cable to the bus room
123 Metering transformer
1234 Circuit breaker
125 Switch-gear
126 Condenser well
13 Bus structure
131 Bus
132 Feeder
133 Metering transformer
134 Circuit breaker
14 Transformer
15 Switch-gear
16 Control room
18 Storage
191 Substation

2 Transmission
21 Overhead
24 Underground
254 Submarine
29 Special problem
291 Corona
292 Insulation
294 Short circuit
296 Lightning protection

3 Transformation
31 Voltage
32 Current
33 Frequency
34 Phase
36 A. C. to D. C. and *vice versa*
38 Motor

4 Transport
In addition to the divisions under '**5 transport**' *in* [P] *the following*
47 Telegraphy
48 Telephony

For **7 Nuclear Engineering**

1 **Generation**
11 **Fission**
12 **Fusion**
13 **Reactor**
15 **Fuel**
7 **By-product**
74 Waste-product

Foci in [E] *cum* [2P]

1 Applied mechanics

11 Structural
111 Beam. Cantilever
112 Column
113 Frame
114 Moving load
115 Retaining wall
116 Slab
117 Arch
118 Wind stress
1194 Chimney

13 Graphical statics

15 Hydraulics
151 Catchment
155 Flow
1551 In pipe
1552 In channel

18 Pneumatics
185 Flow
1851 In tube
1858 Air current

2 Surveying
21 Levelling
22 Land surveying
221 Theodolite survey
28 Aerial surveying

32 Strength of material

35 Elastic stability

4 Design. Drawing

5 Specification. Quantity

6 Estimate

7 Construction (execution)

71 Earthwork and excavation

76 Form-work
8 Working, etc.
81 Testing
82 Maintenance
825 Renewal

83 Working
85 Repair
96 Relief. Rescue

Divisions of Common Isolate digit 'e'

(illustrative)

(For Work Division **66***)*

*e*1 **Resistance metre**
*e*11 Ohm meter
*e*12 Resistance-box
*e*16 Wheatstone's bridge
*e*2 Voltage meter
*e*21 Volt meter
*e*211 Voltage detector
*e*3 Current meter
*e*31 Ammeter
*e*32 Coulombmeter
*e*33 Ampere hour meter
*e*34 Voltameter
*e*4 Quantity meter
*e*41 Watt meter
*e*5 Energy meter
*e*51 Watt hour meters
*e*52 Power-factor meter

CHAPTER E

CHEMISTRY

E [P:] [E] [2P]

Foci in [P]

1 Inorganic substance

10 Group 0

100 Helium (He)
101 Neon (Ne)
102 Argon (A)
104 Krypton (Kr)
106 Xenon (Xe)
109 Radon (Rn)
Niton (Nt)

11 Group 1

110 Hydrogen (H)
1109 Lithium (Li)
111 Sodium (Na)
112 Potassium (K)
1129 *Ammonium*
113 Copper (Cu)
114 Rubidium (Rb)
115 Silver (Ag)
116 Cesium (Cs)
117 Dyspriosium (Dy) or (Ds)
1179 Holmium (Ho)
118 Gold (Au)
1191 Francium (Fr)

12 Group 2

120 Beryllium (Be)
121 Magnesium (Mg)
122 Calcium (Ca)
123 Zinc (Zn)
124 Strontium (Sr)
125 Cadmium (Cd)
126 Barium (Ba)
127 Erbium (Er)
1279 Thulium (Tm) or (Tu)
128 Mercury (Hg)
129 Radium (Ra)

13 Group 3

130 Boron (B)
131 Aluminium (Al)
132 Scandium (Sc)
133 Gallium (Ga)
134 Yttrium (Yt) or (Y)
135 Indium (In)
136 Lanthanum (La)
137 Ytterbium (Yb)
1379 Lutecium (Lu)
138 Thallium (Tl)
1391 Actinium (Ac)
1392 Promethium (Pm)

14 Group 4

140 Carbon (C)
141 Silicon (Si)
142 Titanium (Ti)
143 Germanium (Ge)
144 Zirconium (Zr)
145 Tin (Sn)
146 Cerium
1469 Praseodymium (Pr)
147 Celtium (Ct) or (Hf)
148 Lead (Pb)
149 Thorium (Th)

15 Group 5

150 Nitrogen (N)
151 Phosphorus (P)
152 Vanadium (V)
153 Arsenic (As)
154 Columbium (Cb)
Niobium (Nb)
155 Antimony (Sb)
156 Neodymium (Nd)
157 Tantalum (Ta)
158 Bismuth (Bi)
159 Protoactinium (Pa)

16 Group 6

160 Oxygen (O)
161 Sulphur (S)
162 Chromium (Cr)
163 Selenium (Se)
164 Molybdenum (Mo)
165 Tellurium (Te)
166 Samarium (Sm)
1669 Europium (Eu)
167 Tungsten (W)
168 Polonium (Po)
1691 Uranium (U)
1692 Neptunium (NP)
1693 Plutonium (Pu)
1694 Americium (Am)
1695 Curium (Cm)
1696 Berkelium (Bk)
1697 Californium (Cf)

17 Group 7

170 Fluorine (F)

171 **Chlorine (Cl)**
172 **Manganese (Mn)**
173 **Bromine (Br)**
174 **Technetium (Jc)**
175 **Iodine (I) or (J)**
176 **Gadolinium (Gd)**
1769 Terbium (Tb)
177 Rhenium (Re)
178 Astatine (At)

18 **Group 8**
182 Iron (Fe)
1829 Nickel (Ni)
183 Cobalt (Co)
184 Ruthenium (Ru)
1849 Palladium (Pd)
185 Rhodium (Rh)
187 Osmium (Os)
1879 Platinum (Pt)
188 Iridium (Ir)

191 Metal
1911 Noble metal
1917 Radio-active metal
192 Rare element
1921 Lantharides (Rare earths)
1923 Aetinides (Transuranic)
193 Alloy
195 Non-metal
196 Isotope
198 Gas
1981 Air

2 **Hydroxyl. Basic oxide**

(*To be divided by the constituent element and its valency*)

27 **Binary other than water, which is neither hydroxyl nor acid nor salt**

(*To be divided successively by the two constituent elements and their respective valencies*)

2710 **Hydride**

3 **Acid. Acidic oxide**

(*To be divided by the constituent elements and its valency*)

4 **Salt**

(*To be divided by the constituent elements and their respective valencies*)

5 **Organic substance**

6 **Aliphatic compound**
61 **Paraffin**
611 Methane
612 Ethane
613 Propane
614 Butane
615 Pentane
616 Hexane
618 *n*th homologue

63 **Olefine**
632 Ethylene
633 Propylene
634 Butylene
638 *n*th homologue

64 **Di-olefines or allene**
641 Allene

65 **Acetylene series**
651 Acetylene
658 *n*th homologue

68 **Carbohydrate**
681 Monosaccharide
6811 Pentose (eg arabinose)
6813 Hexose (eg glucose)
682 Disaccharide
6821 Maltose
683 Trisaccharide
688 Polysaccharide

6891 Pentosan
6892 **Starch**
6893 Gum
6894 **Cellulose**
6898 Glucoside

7 **Aromatic compound**
71 Benzenoid
711 Benzene
712 Naphthalene
713 Anthracene
718 Polynuclear system

72 Non-benzenoid
73 Cyclo-pentadine
74 Tropane
79 Alycyclic

8 **Heterocyclic compound**
84 Oxygen ring
85 Nitrogen ring
86 Sulphur ring
88 Other ring

9 **Bio-substance**
92 Alkaloid
92J Vegetable alkaloid
92K Animal alkaloid
92Z Amino acid
92Z1 Polypeptide
92Z2 **Protein**
92Z2J Vegetable protein

92Z2K Animal protein
94 Fat
95 Pigment
96 Lipin

97 Vitamin
971 Vitamin A
972 Vitamin B
973 Vitamin C
974 Vitamin D
975 Vitamin E
977 Vitamin G

981 Chlorophyll
9814 Porphyrine
982 Enzyme
9821 Oxidase
9822 Hydrolytic enzyme
986 Hormone
993 Creatine and creatinine
994 Pectin
996 Sterol
998 Tannin

Other substances by (SD)

Foci in [P2]
for substance numbers
5, 6, 7 *and* **8** *in* [P]

1 Halogen derivative
2 Hydroxyl (alcohol, phenol)
28 Derivative of alcohol
281 Ether
2831 Aldehyde
285 Ketone

3 Organic acid
38 Derivative of acid
383 Ester
385 Anhydride

5 Nitrogen compound
51 Amino-compound
537 Azo-compound
55 Diazo-compound
7 Nitro-compound
59 Other nitrogen compound
591 Cyanogen compound

6 Sulphur compound

8 Compound with other element

Foci in [E] cum [2P]

1 General
11 Preparation

14 Atomic weight. Molecular weight
17 Periodic system

2 Physical chemistry
21 Chemical combination and action
211 Law of chemical combination
213 Chemical kinetics
2131 Combustion. Flame
2133 Phase rule
2136 Ionisation
214 Chemical affinity
215 Valency
218 Molecular structure

22 Solution
2201 Solubility
221 Solid
225 Liquid
228 Gas

23 Mixture
231 Alloy
232 Absorption (surface phenomena)

235 Colloid
236 Emulsion
237 Osmosis
238 Aerosol
2381 Occlusion

24 Chemical thermo-dynamics
25 Photochemistry
26 Electrochemistry
27 Magnetochemistry

28 Stereochemistry, etc.
281 Allotropy
282 Isomerism
296 Radiochemistry

3 Analytical chemistry
33 Qualitative
34 Quantitative
35 Volumetric

Foci in [2P2] *for* 3 of [E]

1 Macro
2 Semi-micro
3 Micro
5 Spot (ultra-micro)
6 Commercial
7 Non-destructive

A Method
B Physical
C Mechanical
C1 Gravimetric
C3 Volumetric

D	**Thermal**
E	**Radiation**
E1	Colorimetry
E3	Diffraction
E4	Polarimetry
E5	Absorption
E52	Ultra-violet
E53	X-ray
E56	Infra-red
E7	Raman-spectra
E81	Nephelometry
E82	Turbidimetry
F	Electrical
G	Magnetic
H	Nuclear
J	Chemical
M	Kinetic
N	Titrimetry
T	Electrochemical
T1	Polarography
T5	Mass spectroscopy
T6	PH measurement
X	Biological
4	**Synthesis**
5	**Extraction**
8	**Manipulation**
81	Oxidation. Reduction
82	Hydration. Dehydration
831	Crystallisation
832	Sublimation
833	Sedimentation
835	Distillation
84	Temperature
845	Humidity
85	Indicator and test paper
856	Polarisation
86	Electrical method
87	Fermentation
871	Direct
872	Indirect
877	Symbiotic
88	Catalysis
89	Other methods
891	Reagent
892	Filtration
893	Assaying
894	Fatigue study
895	Protection. Painting. Colouring
896	Glass blowing
897	Absorption
898	Recovery of waste
91	Nomenclature. Classification
98	Polymerisation
E9A	**Specials**
E9G	Biochemistry

CHAPTER F

TECHNOLOGY

F [P]: [E] [2P]

***Foci in* [P]**

Same as in **E chemistry** *and in addition the following*

4414	Refractory material
4416	Enamel
52	Plastic
527	Celluloid
53	Food
54	**Alcohol**
547	Wine
548	Beer
55	**Fuel**
551	Coal
555	Petroleum
5552	Petrol
558	Fuel gas
5591	Matches
5594	Explosive
56	**Drug**
57	**Textile**
573	Artificial silk
58	**Dye**
5895	Paint
5897	Tanning material
594	Poison
596	Spice (condiment)
5964	Vinegar
94	**Fat and oil**
943	Edible oil
944	Miscible oil
9491	Wax
9495	Candle
9495	Drying oil
9496	**Soap**
94966	Washing
949695	Liquid
949696	Medicated
949697	Disinfectant
94972	**Perfume**
95	**Cosmetic**
951	Face
952	Hair
9533	Ankle
9567	Hand
9568	Finger

Foci in [E] *cum* [2P]

See Chapter **F** of the Rules

CHAPTER G

BIOLOGY

G [P]: [E] [2P]

Foci in [P]

1	**Basic and regional (Life)**
11	Cell
111	Cell membrane
1115	Cilia
112	Cytoplasm
1121	Cytoplasm proper
1122	Centrosome
1123	Chondriosome
1124	Metaplastic body
113	**Nucleus**
1131	Nuclear membrane
1132	Chromation, Linin
1133	Nuclear acids
1134	Nuclear sap, karyolymph
1135	Nucleoli
11351	Karyosome
11352	Plasmosome
1137	Golgi apparatus
116	**Gene**
12	Tissue

Other divisions same as in **L Medicine** *and* **I Botany** *as the case may be*

91	**Protista**
9193	Benefic
9194	Pathogenic
95	Ecological group (*Illustrative*)
951	Land organism
9511	Subterranean
95121	Desert
95122	Prairy
95124	Forest
93131	Coastland
95137	Delta
9514	Island
9515	Marsh
9518	Mountain
955	Hydro-biology
9551	Underground
9553	Salt Water
95531	Coastal
95534	Land sea
9555	Marine biology
9557	Fresh water
95574	Lake (limnology)
95576	River
958	Atmospheric organism

Foci in [E] *cum* [2P]

1	**Preliminaries**
11	Nomenclature, classification
12	Natural history
13	Popular description
14	Picture
17	Collecting
18	List
19	**Microscopy**
192	Sectioning
195	Fixing
196	Mounting
198	Staining
1995	Microphotography
2	**Morphology**
3	**Physiology**
32	**Absorption**
33	**Metabolism**
331	Anabolism
332	Katabolism
33C	Physical effect
33C2	Material vibration and movement
33C4	Heat production
33C5	Radiation production, Mitogenetic radiation
33C6	Electrical effect
33C7	Magnetic effect
33E	Chemical effect
341	Inanition
345	Water fasting
346	**Fasting**

Each of the above three to be divided as **33**

35	Excretion
36	Transpiration
394	Fatigue

4	**Pathology**
	(*To be sub-divided as in* **L Medicine**)
5	**Ecology**
51	Preliminaries
511	Nomenclature
515	Classification
52	State control
527	Conservation
54	Prevention of diseases and injuries
55	Environment
551	Ground
555	Water
556	Season
5561	Spring
5563	Summer
5565	Autumn
5567	Winter
558	Air
5593	Vibration
5594	Heat
5595	Light
55955	Radioactive radiation
5599	Heavenly body
56	Interrelation (Social life)
563	Protective colouration
5637	Mimicry
564	Parasitism
565	Intolerance (struggle)
566	Succession
567	Symbiosis
571	Abode
573	Nutrition
575	Cleanliness (toilet)
576	Regulation of habit
58	Migration
59	Other habits
6	**Genetic** (**phylogeny**)
61	Heredity
62	Variation
63	Mutation
64	Hybridisation
65	Survival of the fittest
66	**Evolution**
67	**Reproductive method**
671	Abiogenesis
672	Hermaphrodite
674	Parthenogenesis
675	Sexual
676	Asexual
677	Alternation of generation
7	**Development** (**Ontogeny**)
8	**Manipulation**
G9A	**Specials**
G9B	Embryo
G9C	Child
G9D	Adolescent
G9E	Old age

CHAPTER H

GEOLOGY

Canonical divisions

H1 **Mineralogy**
H2 **Petrology**
H3 **Structural geology**
H4 **Dynamic geology**
H5 **Stratigraphy**
H6 **Palaeontology**
H7 **Economic geology**
H8 **Cosmic hypothesis**

H1 MINERALOGY

H1 [P]: [E] [2P]

Foci in [P]
as in **E Chemistry**
and the following additional isolates

9 **Precious stone**
91 Diamond
92 Ruby and sapphire
921 Ruby
922 Sapphire
931 Opal
95 Topaz
96 Spinel
98 Pearl
9944 Agate

Foci in [E] *cum* [2P]

1 **Preliminaries**
Subdivisions as in
G BIOLOGY
and the followithng additional isolates

15 Prospecting
155 Occurrence
16 Genesis
164 Artificial production

8 **Crystallography**
811 Nomenclature
8115 Classification
82 Structure
821 Isometric
822 Tetragonal
823 Hexagonal
8235 Trigonal and rhombohedral
824 Orthorhombic
825 Monoclinic
826 Triclinic
84 Irregularities
841 Twinning (gliding plane)
844 Pseudosymmetry
85 Inclusions
864 Artificial production

H2 Petrology

H2 [P]: [E]]2P]

Foci in [P]

1 **Igneous rock**

11 **Volcanic rock**

113 **Rock containing quartz and feldspars**
1131 Obsidian
1132 Rhyolite
1133 Dacite

114 **Rock containing feldspars**
1141 Pitchstone
1142 Trachyte
1143 Andesite
1144 Basalt
1145 Tachylyte

115 **Rock containing feldspars and feldspathiods**
1151 Phonolite
1152 Leucitophyre
1153 Limburgite

119 **Other volcanic rocks**

15 **Hypabyssal rock**
1511 Aplites
1512 Porphyries
1513 Lamprophyres
1531 Granophyre
1532 Felsite

154 **Rock containing feldspars alone**
1541 Dolerite
1543 Tinguaite

17 **Plutonic rock**
171 Arizonite, Silexite

173 **Rock containing quartz and feldspars**
1731 Granite
1733 Tonalite. Granodiorite

174 **Rock containing feldspars**
1741 Syenite
1744 Diorite
1747 Anorthite
1748 Gabbros

175 **Rock containing feldspars feldspathiods, etc.**
1751 Nepheline syenite
1752 Threalite
1753 Teschenite
1756 Ijolite
1758 Periodotite picrite
179 Other plutonic rocks

2 **Metamorphic rock**

21 **Rock due to regional metamorphism**
211 Rock derived from igneous rock
213 Rock derived from sedimentary rock
2131 Crystalline schist
2132 Slate
2133 Marble
2134 Steatite

23 **Contact metamorphism**
231 Limestone
233 Shale and slate
235 Conglomerate and sand

3 **Sedimentary rock**
31 **Rudaceous**
311 Conglomerate
312 Breccia

32 **Arenaceous**
321 Sandstone
322 Grit
323 Arkose
324 Quartzite
325 Gannister
326 Greywacke
327 Silt stone

33 **Argillaceous**
331 Clay
3311 Fire clay
3312 Fuller's clay
3313 Aeolian clay
3314 Abyssal clay
3315 Volcanic clay
3316 Residual clay
332 Mudstone
333 Shale
335 Marl
336 Calcareous shale

34 Chemical origin
3422 Calcareous
34221 Calcite
3423 Dolomite
3451 Phosphatic rock

3482 **Ferruginous**
34821 **Bedded iron ore**
34823 **Bog iron ore**

35 **Rock due to organic origin**

3522 **Calcareous**
35221 Limestone
35222 Dolomitic limestone
35223 Oolite and pisolitic limestone
35224 Abyssal ooze
35225 Chalk

3540 **Carbonaceous**
35401 Peat
35402 Lignite

35403 **Coal and anthracite**
35404 Cannel and torbanite

35406 **Oil shale**

35407 **Asphalt and asphaltic impregnation**

3541 **Silicious**
35411 Chert and flint
35413 Silicious earth

5 **Meteorite**

Foci in [E] *cum* [2P]
(*Same as those for mineralogy except* ' 8 ')

H3 Structural Geology

H31 **Stratification**
H32 Joint and cleavage
H33 Fault and folding
H34 Metamorphism
H35 Vein, dike, neck, bosse
H36 Mountain building, orogeny

H4 Dynamic Geology

H41	**Hypogene. Internal dynamics**
H411	Volcano
H412	Geyser, hot spring
H413	Movement and earth's crust
H4131	Slow depression, upheaval
H4132	**Earthquake**
H418	Other internal actions
H42	**Epigene or superficial action. External dynamics**
H421	Glaciology
H422	Action of water
H4221	Rain
H4223	Flood
H4224	Underground water
H4225	Ocean
H4227	River
H4228	Lake
H423	Action of air
H424	Land slide
H426	Action of plant
H427	Action of animal
H428	Action of man

H5 Stratigraphy

H51	**Archean eozoic. Pre-cambrian**
H52	**Primary. Palaeozoic**
H521	Cambrian
H522	Ordovician
H523	Silurian
H524	Evonian
H525	Carboniferous
H526	Permian
H53	**Secondary. Mesozoic**
H531	Triassic
H533	Jurassic
H534	Cretaceous
H54	**Tertiary. Cainozoic**
H541	Eocene
H542	Oligocene
H543	Miocene
H544	Pliocene
H55	**Quaternary**
H551	Pleistocene
H555	Holocene. Recent

H7 Economic Geology

H 7 [P]: [E] [2P]

CHAPTER HZ

MINING

HZ [P], [P2]: [E] [2P]

Foci in [P]

See Chapter HZ of the Rules

Foci in [P2]

1 Pit
2 Shaft
3 Tunnel
4 Underground road
5 Underground vehicle
7 Hoist
8 Surface transport

Foci in [E] *cum* [2P]

1 Preliminary
11 Excavation
12 Quarrying
13 Drilling (blasting)
14 Deep boring
15 Shaft sinking
16 Tunnelling (drifting)
17 Stopping
18 Timbering (masonry lining)

2 Ore dressing
21 Preliminary operation
22 Hand dressing
23 Crushing (stamping engine)
24 Screening
25 Jigging (ore concentrator)
26 Slime treatment
27 Magnetic separation
28 Washing
29 Dressing work

4 Danger and accident
41 Fire damp
42 Mine fire
43 Crushing (fall of ground)
44 Accident to miner
45 Flooding

5 Health Measure
52 Drainage
53 Ventilation
54 Heating. Cooling
55 Lighting

CHAPTER I

BOTANY

I [P], [P2]: [E] [2P]

Foci in [P]

1 **Cryptogamia**

2 **Thallophyta**

21 Protophyta (bacteria, yeast, microbes)

22 **Algae (sea-weeds)**

221 Cyanophyceae (blue-green algae)

223 Chlorophyceae (green algae)

225 Phaeophyceae (brown algae)

227 Rhodophyceae (red algae)

23 **Fungi**

231 Myxomycetes (slime fungi-mycetozoa)

233 Phycomycete (mould)

235 Ascomycete (green mould)

237 Basidiomycete

2371 Smut

2372 Rust

2375 Mushroom

2376 Phalloides

27 **Lichen**

3 **Bryophyta**

31 Hepaticae (liverwort)

311 Marchantiale

313 Jungermanniale

315 Anthocerotale

32 Musci. Moss

321 Sphagnale

323 Andreaeale

325 Bryale

4 **Pteridophyta**

41 Ophioglossaceae

42 Filicineae (fern)

43 Equisetineae (horsetail)

44 Lycopodineae (clubmoss)

45 Psilotaceae

5 **Phanerogamia (flowering plant)**

6 **Gymnosperm**

61 Cycadaceae (cycad family)

63 Ginkgoaceae

65 Coniferae (pine family)

67 Gnetaceae

7 **Monocotyledon**

71 **Microspermae**

711 Hydrocharitaceae

712 Burmanniaceae

715 Orchidaceae

72 **Epigynae**

721 Scitamineae

722 Bromeliaceae

723 Haemodoraceae

724 Iridaceae

725 Amaryllidaceae

726 Taccaceae

728 Dioscoreaceae

73 **Coronarieae**

731 Roxburghiaceae

732 Liliaceae

733 Pontederiaceae

734 Philydraceae

735 Xyridaeceae

736 Commelinaceae

737 Mayaceae

738 Rapataceae

74 **Calycinae**

741 Flagellariaceae

743 Juncaceae

75 **Palmae**

76 **Nudiflorae**

761 Pandanaceae

762 Cyclanthaceae

763 Typhaceae

764 Aroideae

768 Lemnaceae

77 **Apocarpeae**

771 Triuridaceae

772 Alismaceae

774 Naiadaceae

78 **Glumaceae**

781 Eriocaulonaceae

782 Centrolepideae

783 Restionaceae

785 Cyperaceae
786 Gramineae

8 Dicotyledon

811 Ranales
8111 Ranunculaceae
8112 Dilleniaceae
8113 Calycanthaceae
8114 Magnoliaceae
8115 Anonaceae
8116 Menispermaceae
8117 Berberidaceae
8118 Nymphaeaceae

812 Parietales
8121 Sarraceniaceae
8122 Papaveraceae
8123 Fumariaceae
8124 Crucifeae
8125 Capparidaceae
8126 Cistaceae
8127 Resedaceae
8128 Violaceae
81291 Canellaceae
81292 Bixineae

813 Polygallales
8131 Pittosporeae
8132 Tremandreae
8134 Polygalaceae
8136 Vochysiaceae

814 Caryophyllales
8141 Caryophyllaceae
8143 Frankeniaceae
8145 Tamariscineae
8147 Portulaceae

815 Guttiferales
8151 Elatineae
8153 Hypericineae
8154 Guttiferae (clusiaceae)
8156 Ternstroemiaceae
8157 Dipterocarpaeceae
8158 Chlaenaceae

816 Malvales
8161 Malvaceae
8162 Sterculiaceae
8163 Tiliaceae

821 Geraniales
8211 Lineae
8212 Humiriaceae
8213 Malpighiaceae
8214 Zygophyllaceae
8215 Geraniaceae
8216 Rutaceae
8217 Simarubeae
8218 Ochnaceae
82191 Burseraceae
82192 Meliaceae
82193 Chailletiaceae

822 Olacales
8221 Olacineae
8222 Ilicineae
8223 Cyrilleae
8225 Phytocreneae
8227 Aquifoliaceae

823 Celastrales
8231 Celastrineae
8233 Hippocastanaceae
8234 Stackhousiaceae
8236 Rhamnaceae
8238 Ampelideae (vitaceae)

824 Sapindales
8241 Sapindaceae
8243 Aceraceae
8244 Staphyleae
8245 Sabiaceae
8246 Anacardiaceae

831 Rosales
8311 Rosaceae
8312 Connaraceae
8313 Leguminosae
8314 Saxifragaceae
8315 Crassulaceae
8316 Droseraceae
8317 Hamamelidaceae
8318 Bruniaceae
83191 Halorageae

832 Myrtales
8321 Myrtaceae
8323 Rhizophoraceae
8324 Combretaceae
8325 Melastomaceae
8326 Lythraceae
8328 Onagraceae

833 Passiflorales
8331 Passifloreae
8332 Samydaceae
8333 Loaseae
8334 Turneraceae
8335 Datisceae
8336 Cucurbitaceae
8337 Begoniaceae

834 Ficoidales
8341 Cactaceae
8344 Mesembryanthaceae (ficoideae)

835	**Umbellales**
8351	Umbelliferae
8355	Araliaceae
8357	Cornaceae
841	**Rubiales**
8411	Caprifoliaceae
8412	Rubiaceae
842	**Asterales**
8421	Valerianaceae
8422	Dipsaceae
8423	Calycereae
8424	Compositae
843	**Campanales**
8431	Stylideae
8432	Goodeniaceae
8433	Campanulaceae
844	**Ericales**
8441	Vacciniaceae
8442	Ericaceae
8443	Monotropeae
8445	Epacrideae
8446	Diapensiaceae
8448	Lennoaceae
845	**Primulales**
8451	Plumbagineae
8452	Primulaceae
8453	Myrsineae
846	**Ebenales**
8461	Sapotaceae
8462	Ebenaceae
8463	Styraceae
851	**Gentianales**
8511	Oleaceae
8512	Salvadoraceae
8513	Apocynaceae
8514	Asclepiadaceae
8515	Loganiaceae
8516	Gentianaceae
852	**Polemoniales**
8521	Polemoniaceae
8522	Hydrophyllaceae
8523	Boragineae
8524	Convolvulaceae
8526	Solanaceae
853	**Personales**
8531	Scrophularineae
8532	Orobanchaceae
8533	Lentibularieae
8534	Columelliaceae
8535	Gesneraceae
8536	Bignoniaceae
8537	Pedalineae
8538	Acanthaceae
861	**Lamiales**
8611	Myoporineae
8612	Selagineae
8613	Verbenaceae
8614	Labiateae
871	**Plantagineae**
88	**Monochlamydeae**
881	**Curvembryeae**
8811	Nyctagineae
8812	Illecebraceae
8813	Amarantaceae
8814	Chenopodiaceae
8815	Phytolaccaceae
8816	Batideae
8817	Polygonaceae
8821	Podostemaceae
883	**Multiovulatae terrestres**
8831	Nepenthaceae
8832	Cytinaceae
8833	Aristolochiaceae
884	**Micrembryeae**
8841	Piperaceae
8842	Chloranthaceae
8843	Myristiceae
8844	Monimiaceae
885	**Daphnales**
8851	Laurineae
8852	Proteaceae
8853	Thymeleaceae
8854	Penaeaceae
8855	Elaeagnaceae
886	**Achlamydosporeae**
8861	Loranthaceae
8862	Santalaceae
8863	Balanophoreae
887	**Unisexuales**
8871	Euphorbiaceae
8872	Balanopseae
8873	Urticaceae
8874	Platanaceae
8875	Leitnerieae
8876	Juglandeae
8877	Myricaceae
8878	Casuarineae
8891	Cupuliferae

89 **Ordine anomali**
891 Salicineae
892 Lacistemaceae
893 Empetraceae
894 Ceratophylleae

95 **Ecological groups**

Same as in **G Biology** *with the following additions*

952 Creeper
953 Climber
9597 Insectivorous plant

Foci in [P2]

1 **Basic and regional**
11 Cell
12 Tissue
13 Root
131 Root hair
132 Secondary root
133 Primary root
14 Stem
142 Cotyledonous bud
147 Apical bud
148 Growth ring
15 Leaf
16 Flower
17 Fruit
178 Seed
197 Formative regions, Meristem

(*For the functional system of organ, the foci* ' 2 ' *to* ' 8 ' *in* [P] *of L Medicine are to be used as far as applicable*)

Foci in [E] *cum* [2P] *as in* **G Biology** *with the following addition*

8 **Paleobotany**

BOTANY: INDEX TO NATURAL GROUPS

CHAPTER J

AGRICULTURE

J [P]: [E] [2P]: [2E]

Foci in

Utility Array of [P]

1 Decoration
2 Feed
3 Food
4 Stimulant
5 Oil
6 Drug
7 Fabric
8 Dye, Tan
91 Adhesive
92 Manure
93 Vegetable
94 Sugar producing

Foci in

Part Array of [P]

1 Sap
2 Bulb
3 Root
4 Stem
5 Leaf
6 Flower
7 Fruit
8 Seed
97 Whole plant

Foci in [P]

1 Horticulture

15 Foliage

16 Floriculture
169 Bulb (Botanical)
16911 Lily
16912 Tulip
16913 Daffodil
197 Whole plant

2 Feed
25 Leaf
251 Grass

3 Food

31 Sap
311 Sugarcane

32 Bulb
321 Onion

33 Root
331 Beetroot
332 Turnip
333 Carrot
334 Radish
3391 Yam

34 Stem
341 Potato
342 Elephant-yam
346 Arrowroot

35 Leaf
3511 Rhubarb
3512 Spinach
3513 Cabbage
3521 Lettuce

36 Flower
361 Cauliflower

37 Fruit
371 Apple
372 Orange
373 Musa
3731 Plantain
374 Grape
3751 Mango
3752 Pineapple
3755 Date palm
3759 Fig
37943 Tomato
3795 Gourd

38 Seed
381 Rice
382 Wheat
383 Oat
384 Rye
385 Corn
386 Barley
387 Millet

388 Pulse

389 Nut
38911 Walnut
3896 Cashewnut

4 Stimulant

41 Sap
412 Palmyra

45	**Leaf**
451	Tea
452	Tobacco
47	**Fruit**
471	Opium
48	**Seed**
481	Coffee
482	Cocoa
484	Cola
5	**Oil**
53	**Root**
531	Khas khas
54	**Stem**
541	Sandalwood
55	**Leaf**
551	Lemon grass
56	**Flower**
561	Rose
562	Jasmine
563	Violet
564	Lavender
57	**Fruit**
571	Olive
58	**Seed**
581	Groundnut
582	Cocoanut
584	Sesame
585	Castor
586	Indian rape
6	**Drug**
61	**Sap**
613	Frankincense
62	**Bulb**
621	Garlic
64	**Stem**
641	Cinchona
642	Cinnamon
643	Camphor
645	Ginger
646	Turmeric
65	**Leaf**
651	Curry leaf
652	Peppermint
66	**Flower**
661	Clove
662	Saffron
67	**Fruit**
671	Black pepper
674	Chillies
675	Coriander
68	**Seed**
681	Mustard
683	Nutmeg
684	Cardamom
688	Nux-vomica
7	**Fabric**
71	**Sap**
711	Rubber
74	**Stem**
741	Jute.
742	Flax
743	Hemp
748	Bamboo
7491	Rattan
75	**Leaf**
751	Sisal hemp
78	**Seed**
781	Cotton
8	**Dye, Tan**
85	**Leaf**
851	Indigo
87	**Fruit**
871	Marking nut
872	Divi divi
91	**Adhesive**
911	**Sap**
9111	Gum arabic

Foci in [E]

1	Soil
2	Manure
3	Propagation
4	Disease
5	Development
6	Breeding
7	Harvesting
91	Nomenclature
915	Classification
92	Morphology
93	Physiology
95	Ecology

For **1 Soil** of [E]

Foci in [2E]

2	Tillage
4	Damage
6	Improvement
7	Conservation

For **2 Manure** of [E]

Foci in [2P]

1	Green
2	Farm

3 Municipal refuse
4 Fertilizer
41 Nitrogenous
42 Phosphatic
43 Potassic
47 Trace element
5 Organic
9 Products
95 Oil cake

Foci in [2E]

2 Collecting
3 Application
6 Compositing
8 Storing

For **3 Propagation** of [E]

Foci in [2P]

As in Part Array of [P]

Foci in [2E]

3 Sowing
5 Transplanting
8 Storing

For **4 Disease** of [E]

Foci in [2P]

As in " L Medicine "

For **7 Harvesting** of [E]

Foci in [2P]

As in Part Array of [P]

Foci in [2E] *cum* [2P]

2 Recovery
3 Stacking
4 Threshing
5 Cleaning
6 Curing
7 Yield
8 Storing
84 Cold storage
97 Use

J9A **Specials**
J9D Dry farming
J9S Soilless farming

JA **Systems**
JB Forestry

CHAPTER K

ZOOLOGY

K [P]: [E] [2P]

Foci in [P]

1 **Invertebrata**

2 **Protozoa**

21 **Sarcodina**
211 Rhizopoda
212 Foraminifera
213 Heliozoa
214 Radiolaria
215 Proteomyxa
216 Mycetozoa

23 **Sporozoa**
231 Telosporidia
235 Neosporidia

25 **Flagellata**

27 **Infusoria**
271 Ciliata (ciliophora)
275 Suctoria (tentaculifera)

3 **Porifera**
31 Calcarea
32 Myxospongia
33 Hexactinellida
34 *Octactinellida*
35 *Heteractinellida*
36 Demospongia

4 **Coelenterata**

41 **Hydrozoa**
411 Eleutheroblastea
412 Milleporina
413 Gymnoblastea (anthomedusæ)
414 Calyptoblastea (lepto medusæ)
415 Stylasterina
416 Trachomedusæ
417 Narcomedusæ
418 Siphonophora
419 Graptolitoidea

43 **Scyphozoa, Scyphomedusæ**
431 Cubomedusæ
433 Stauromedusæ
435 Coronata
437 Discophora

45 **Anthozoa. Actinozoa**
451 Alcyonaria
452 Stolonifera
453 Coenothecalia
454 Alcyonacea
455 Gorgonacea
4551 Pseudaxonia
4553 Axifera
456 Pennatulacea
4561 Pennatuleæ
4562 Spicatæ
4563 Verticilladeæ
4564 Renilleæ
4565 Veretilleæ
457 Zoantharia
4571 Edwardsiidea
4572 Actiniaria
45721 Actinlina
45722 Stichodactylina
4573 Madreporaria
45731 Entocnemaria
45732 Cyclocnemaria
4574 Zoanthidea
4575 Antipathidea. Antipatharia
4576 Cerianthidea

48 **Ctenophora**
481 Tentaculata
482 Cydippidea
483 Lobata
484 Cestoidea
485 Platyctenea
487 Nuda

5 **Echinodermata**

51 **Eleutherozoa**

52 **Asteroidea**
521 Spinulosa
522 Velata
523 Paxillosa
524 Valvata
525 Forcipulata

53 **Ophiuroidea**
531 Streptophiuræ
532 Zygophiurae
533 Cladophiuræ

54 **Echinoidea**
541 Endocyclica
542 Clypeastoridea
5421 Protoclypeastroidea
5422 Euclypeastroidea
543 Spatangoidea

55 **Holothuroidea**
551 Aspidochirotæ

552	Elasipoda
553	Pelagothuriidæ
554	Dendrochirotæ
555	Molpadiida
556	Synaptidæ
56	**Pelmatozoa**
57	**Crinoidea**
572	Inadunata
573	Articulata
576	Camerata
58	**Extinct classes**
581	*Thecoidea (edrioasteroidea)*
582	*Carpoidea*
583	*Cystoidea*
584	*Blastoidea*
6	**Vermes**
61	**Platyhelminthes**
611	Turbellaria
6111	Polycladida
6112	Tricladida
6113	Rhabdocoelida
613	Trematoda
6131	Monogenea
6132	Digenea. (Malacocotylea)
615	Cestoda
617	Mesozoa
62	**Nemertinea**
621	Protonemertini
623	Mesonemertini
625	Metanemertini
627	Heteronemertini
63	**Nemathelminthes**
631	Nematoda
633	Nematomorpha
635	Acanthocephala
637	Chætognatha
64	**Rotifera**
641	Flosculariaceæ
642	Melicertaceæ
643	Bdelloida
644	Asplanchnaceæ
645	Scirtopoda
646	Ploima
6461	Illoricata
6462	Loricata
647	Seisonaceæ
648	Gastrotricha
6481	Euichthydina
6482	Apodina
649	Kinorhyncha
65	**Annelida**
651	Chaetopoda
652	Polychæta. Myzostomaria
6521	Phanerocephala
65211	Nerediformia
65212	Spinoniformia
6523	Terebelliformia
6524	Capitelliformia
6525	Scoleciformia
6526	Cryptocephala
65261	Sabelliformia
65262	Hermelliformia
6527	Myzostomaria
653	**Oligochaeta**
6531	Microdrili
6532	Megadrili
654	**Hirudinea**
6541	Rhynchobdellæ
6544	Gnathobdellæ
655	**Gephyrea**
6551	Sipunculoidea
6553	Priapuloidea
6555	Echiuroidea
6557	Epithetosomatoidæ
656	Archiannelida
66	**Phoronis**
67	**Polyzoa**
671	Entoprocta
672	Ectoprocta
6721	Gymnolaemata
6725	Phylactolaemata
7	**Mollusca**
71	**Pelecypoda**
711	Protobranchiata
712	Filibranchiata
713	Pseudolamellibranchiata
7131	Anomiacea
7135	Arcacea
7137	Mytilacea
714	Eulamellibranchiata
7141	Submytilacea
7142	Tellinacea
7143	Veneracea
7144	Cardiacea
7145	Pholadacea
7147	Anatinacea
715	Septibranchiata
73	**Amphineura**
731	Polyplacophora
733	Apolocophora
75	**Gasteropoda**
753	Prosobranchiata
7531	Diotocardia
7532	Monotocardia
755	Opisthobranchiata
7551	Tectibranchiata
7555	Ascoglossa
756	Nudibranchiata
7561	Pteropoda
757	Pulmonata

7571 Basommatophora
7575 Stylommatophora

76 Scaphopoda

77 Cephalopoda
771 Dibranchiata
7711 Octopoda
7712 Decapoda
775 Tetrabranchiata
7751 Nautiloidea
7753 Ammonoidea

78 Brachiopoda
781 Ecardines
785 Testicardines

8 Arthropoda

81 Crustacea
811 Entomostraca

812 Branchiopoda
8121 Phyllopoda
8122 Cladocera

813 Copepoda
8131 Gymnoplea
8132 Podoplea

814 Cirripedia
8141 Pedunculata
8142 Operculata
8143 Acrothoracica
8144 Ascothoracica
8145 Apoda
8146 Rhizocephala
8147 Ostracoda

815 Malacostraca
8151 Anaspidacea
8152 Mysidacea
8153 Cumacca
8154 Isopoda
81541 Chelifera
81542 Flabellifera
81543 Valvifera
81544 Asellota
81545 Oniscoida
81546 Epicarida
81547 Phreatoicida

8155 Amphipoda
81551 Crevettina
81552 Læmodipoda
81553 Hyperina
8156 Stomatopoda
8157 Euphausiaca
8158 Decapoda
81581 Macrura
81582 Anomura
81583 Brachyura

816 *Trilobites*

83 Onychophora. Peripatus. Prototracheata

84 Myriapoda

841 Chilognatha. Diplopoda

843 Chilopoda

845 Schizotarsia

846 Symphyla

847 Pauropoda

86 Insecta

861 Aptera
8611 Thysanura
8612 Collembola

862 Orthoptera
8621 Orthoptera cursoria
8625 Orthoptera saltatoria

863 Neuroptera
8631 Mallophaga
8632 Pseudo-neuroptera
8633 Neuroptera amphibiotica
8634 Newroptera planipennia
8635 Trichoptera

864 Hymepoptera
8641 Hymenoptera sessili ventres
8643 Hemenoptera petiolata
8645 Tubulifera
8647 Aculeata

865 Coleoptera
8651 Lamellicornia
8652 Adephaga. Caraboidea
8653 Polymorpha
8654 Heteromera
8655 Phytophaga
8656 Rhynchophora
8657 Strepsiptera

867 Lepidoptera
8671 Rhopalocera
8675 Heterocera

871 Diptera
8711 Orthorrhapha nemocera
8712 Orthorrhapha brachycera
8713 Cyclorrhapha aschiza
8714 Cyclorrhapha schisophora
8715 Pupipara

874 Aphaniptera
8741 *Pulicidae*

876 Thysanoptera
8761 Terebrantia

877 Hemiptera
8771 Heteroptera
8772 Homoptera
8774 Anoplura

88 Arachinida

881 Delobronchiata. Merostomata

8811	Xiphosura
8813	*Eurypterida gigantostraca*
882	**Embolobranchiata**
8821	Scorpionidea
8822	Pedipalpi
8823	Araneae
8824	Palpigradi
8825	Solifugæ, solpugæ
8826	Chernetidea. Chernetes Pseudoscorpiones
8827	Podogona. Ricimulie
883	**Phalangidea. Opiliones**
8831	Cyphophthalmi
8832	Mecostethi. Laniatores
8833	Plagiostethi. Palpatores
884	**Acarina. Acari. Acaridea**
8841	Vermiformia
8842	Astigmata
8843	Metastigmata
8844	Heterostigmata
8845	Prostigmata
8846	Notostigmata
885	**Tardigrada**
886	**Pentastomida**
888	**Pycnogonida. Podosomata. Pantopoda**
9	**Prochordata and vertebrata**
91	Prochordata
911	Hemichordata
9111	Enteropneusta
91111	Pterobranchia
91113	Phoronidea
913	Urochordata. Tunicata
9131	Larvacea
9133	Ascidiacea
91331	Ascidiæ simplices
91332	Ascidiæ compositæ
91333	Merosomata
913336	Holo mata
91335	Ascidiae luciae
9135	Thaliacea
91351	Cyclomyaria
91353	Hemimyaria
915	Cephalochordata
917	**Craniata**
9171	Cyclostomata
91711	Myxinoides
91715	Petromyzontes
92	**Pisces**
922	**Elasmobranchii**
9221	*Pleuropterygii*
9222	*Ichthyotomi*
9223	*Acanthodei*
9224	Plagiostomi
92241	Selachii
92245	Batoidei
923	**Holocephali**
925	**Teleostomi**
9251	Crossopterygii
92511	*Osteolepida*
91515	Cladistia
9252	Chondrostei
9253	Holostei
9254	Teleostei
92541	Malacopterygii
92542	Ostariophysi
92543	Symbranchii
92544	Apodes
92545	Haplomi
92546	Heteromi
92547	Catosteomi
92548	Percesoces
925491	Anacanthini
925493	Acanthopterygii
925494	Opisthomi
925495	Pediculati
925496	Plectognathi
926	**Dipneusti. Dipnoi**
927	*Palaeospondylidae*
928	*Ostracodermi*
9281	*Heterostraci*
9282	*Osteostraci*
9283	*Anaspida*
93	**Amphibia**
931	**Stegocephali**
9311	Stegocephali lepospondyli
93111	Branchiosauri
93113	Aistopodes
9312	Stegocephali temnospondyli
9313	Stegocephali stereospondyli
932	**Lissamphibia**
9321	Apoda
9323	Urodela
9325	Anura
93251	Aglossa
93255	Phaneroglossa
94	**Reptilia**
941	**Proreptilia**
942	**Prosauria**
9421	Microsauri
9425	Prosauri
94251	Protorosauri
94255	Rhynchocephali
943	**Theromorpha**
9431	Pareiasauri
9433	Theriodontia
9435	Anomodontia
9437	Placodontia

944	**Chelonia**
9441	Atheca
9445	Theocophora
94451	Cryptodira
94453	Pleurodira
94455	Trionychoidea
945	**Dinosauria**
9451	Sauropoda
9453	Theropoda
9455	Orthopoda
94551	Stegosauri
94555	Ornithopoda
9457	Ceratopsia
946	**Crocodilia**
9461	Pseudosuchia
9463	Parasuchia
9465	Eusuchia
947	**Plesiosauria**
9471	Nothosauri
9475	Plesiosauri
948	**Ichthyosauria**
9481	Ichthyosauri
9491	Pterosauria
94911	Pterosauri
949111	Pterodactyli
949115	Pteranodontes
9492	Pythonomorpha
94921	Dolichosauri
94925	Mosasauri
9493	Sauria
94931	Lacertilia
949313	Geckones
949315	Lacertæ
949316	Chamæleontes
94932	Ophidia
96	**Aves**
961	Archæornithes
962	**Neornithes**
9621	Neornithes ratitae
96211	**Ratitae**
962111	Struthiones
962112	Rheæ
962113	Megistanes
962114	Apterges
962115	Dinornithes
962116	Aepyornithes
96212	**Stereornithes**
962121	*Mesembriornis*
962122	*Diatryma*
962123	*Dasornis*
929124	*Remiornis*
962125	*Gastornis*
9622	Neornithes odonotolcæ
96221	Hesperornithes
96225	Enaliornithes
9623	Neornithes carinatæ
96231	Ichthyornithes
96232	Colymbiformes
962321	Colymbi
962325	Podicipedes
96322	Sphenisciformes
963221	Sphenisci
96323	Procellariiformes
963231	Tubinares
9633	**Ciconiiformes**
96331	Steganopodes
96332	Ardeæ
96333	Ciconiæ
96334	Phoenicopteri
9634	Anseriformes
96341	Palamedeæ
96345	Anseres
9635	**Falconiformes**
96351	Cathartæ
96353	Accipitres
9636	**Tinamiformes**
96361	Tinami
9637	**Galliformes**
96371	Mesitæ
96373	Turnices
96375	Galli
96377	Opisthocomi
9638	**Charadriiformes**
96381	Limicolæ
96382	Lari
96384	Alcæ
96385	Pterocles
96387	Columbae
964	**Cuculiformes**
9641	Cuculi
9645	Psittaci
965	**Coraciiformes**
9651	Coraciæ
9652	Striges
9653	Caprimulgi
9654	Cypseli
9655	Colii
9656	Trogones
9657	Pici
966	**Passeriformes**
9661	Passeres anisomyodæ
96611	Subclamatores
96615	Clamatores
9662	Passeres diacromyodæ
96621	Suboscines
96625	Oscines
97	**Mammalia**
971	**Monotremata**

972	**Marsupialia**
9721	Diprotodontia
9725	Polyprotodontia
973	**Edentata**
9731	Xenarthra
9735	Nomarthra
974	**Sirenia**
975	**Cetacea**
9751	Mystacoceti
9752	Odontoceti
9753	Archæoceti
976	**Ganodonta**
978	**Ungulata**
9781	Condylarthra
9782	Amblypoda
9783	Ancylopoda
9784	Typotheria
9785	Toxodontia
9786	Proboscidæ
9787	Hydracoidea
9788	Perissodactyla
97891	Litopterna
97892	Artiodactyla
9791	**Carnivora**
97911	Fissipedia
97912	Pinnipedia
9792	**Credonta**
9793	**Rodentia**
97931	Simplicidentata
97935	Duplicidentata
9795	**Insectivora**
97951	Insectivora vera
97955	Dermptera
9796	**Chiroptera**
97961	Megachiroptera
97965	Microchiroptera
9797	**Primates**
97971	Lemuroidea
97975	Anthropoidea
995	**Ecological groups**
9954	Wild animal
9958	Flying animal

Foci in [E] *cum* [2P]
as in " G Biology "
with the following additions

591	Relation to young ones
595	Courting

ZOOLOGY: INDEX TO NATURAL GROUPS

Neornithes odontolcae 9622
Neornithes ratitae 9621
Neosporidia 235
Nerediformia 62511
Neuroptera 863
— amphibiotica 8633
— planipennia 8634
Nomarthra 9735
Nothosauri 9471
Notostigmata 8846
Nudibranchiata 756

Octactinellida 34
Octopoda 7711
Odontoceti 9752
Oligochaeta 635
Oniscoida 81545
Onychophora 83
Operculata 8142
Ophidia 94932
Ophiuroidea 53
Opiliones 883
Opisthobranchiata 755
Opisthocomi 96377
Opisthomi 925494
Ornithopoda 94555
Orthopoda 9455
Orthopetera 862
Orthoptrea cursoria 8621
— saltatoria 8625
Orthorrhapha brachycera 8712
— nemocera 8711
Oscines 96625
Ostariophysi 92532
Osteolepida 92511
Osteostraci 9282
Ostracoda 8147
Ostracodermi 928

Palaeospondylidae 927
Palamedeae 96341
Palpatores 8833
Palpigradi 8824
Pantopoda 888
Parasuchia 9463
Pareiasauri 9431
Passeres anisomyodae 9661
— diacromyodae 9662
Passeriformes 966
Pathogenic K[P], 8694
Pauropoda 847
Paxillosa 523
Pediculati 925495
Pedipalpi 8822
Pedunculata 8141
Pelagothuriida 553
Pelecypoda 71
Pelmatozoa 56
Pennatulacea 456
Pennatuleae 4561
Pentastomida 886
Percesoces 92548
Periapatus 83
Perissodactyla 9788
Petromyzontes 9171
Phalangidea 883
Phanerocephala 6521
Phaneroglossa 93255
Phoenicopteri 96334
Pholadacea 7146
Phoronidea 91113
Phoronis 66
Phreatoicida 81547
Phylactolaemata 6725
Phyllopoda 8121
Phytophaga 8655
Pici 9657
Pinnipedia 97912
Pisces 92
Placodontia 9437
Plagiostethi 88333
Plagiostomi 9224
Platyctenea 485
Platyhelminthes 61
Plecotognathi 925496
Plesiosauri 9475
Plesiosauria 947
Pleurodira 94453
Pleuropterygii 9221
Ploima 646
Podicipedes 962325
Podogona 8827
Podoplea 8132
Podosomata 888
Polychaeta 652
Polycladida 6111
Polymorpha 8653
Polyplacophora 731
Polyprotodontia 9725
Polyzoa 67
Porifera 3
Priapuloidea 6553
Primates 9797
Proboscidae 9786
Procellariformes 96323
Prochordata 91
Proreptilia 941
Prosauri 9425
Prosauria 942
Prosobranchiata 753
Prostigmata 8845
Proteomyza 215
Protobranchiata 711
Protoclypeastroidea 5421
Protonemertini 621
Protorosauri 94251
Prototracheata 83

CHAPTER KZ

ANIMAL HUSBANDRY

KZ [P]: [E] [2P]: [2E] [3P]

Foci in
Utility Array of [P]
Same as in
J Agriculture
with the following alteration

2 Cattle
4 Traction
5 Pet (game)

Foci in
Part Array of [P]

1 Secretion. Extracts like oil
2 Bone
3 Flesh
4 Whole animal
5 Egg
6 Connective tissue
7 Skin
8 Hair. Nail

Foci in [P]

112 Coral
122 Pearl oyster
142 Aquarium fish
3 **Food**
31 **Secretion**
311 **Cow**
312 She buffalo
313 She goat
33 **Flesh**
331 Beef cattle
332 **Fish**
333 Goat and sheep
334 Pig
337 Turkey
3392 Oyster
35 **Egg**
351 **Fowl**
352 Duck
4 **Traction**
441 Bull
442 **Horse**
445 Mule
446 Camel
447 Elephant
449 Reindeer
5 **Pet**
541 Dog
542 Cat
546 Parrot
6 **Drug**
611 **Bee**
612 Fish yielding medicinal oil
7 **Fabric**
711 **Silkworm**
783 Sheep
788 Fox
8 **Dye**
811 Lac insect

Foci in [E]

1 Feeding
2 Morphology
3 Physiology
4 Disease
5 Hygiene
6 Breeding
7 Produce
8 Training
91 Nomenclature
915 Classification
96 Pharmacognacy

For **1 Feeding in** [E]
Foci in [2*P*]
To be got by (SD)
Foci in [2E]

11 Nomenclature
15 Classification
3 Preparation
7 Administering
8 Storing

For **4 Disease in** [E]
Foci in [2P] *and* [2E] *cum* [3P]
As in " L Medicine "

For **7 Harvest**
Foci in [2P]
(*Illustrative*)
For 31 of [P]

1 Milk
3 Butter
4 Ghee
5 Buttermilk
8 Cheese

For 35 of [P]

5 Egg
6 Yolk

Foci in [2E] *cum* [3P]
As in " J Agriculture "

CHAPTER L

MEDICINE

L [P]: [E] [2P]

	Foci in [P]
1	**Basic and regional**
11	Cell
12	Tissue
13	**Lower extremity**
131	Toe
132	Foot
133	Ankle
134	Leg
135	Knee
136	Thigh
137	Pelvic region
14	**Abdomen**
141	Iliac
1411	Right
1415	Left
143	Hypogastric
144	Umbilical
145	Lumbar
1451	Right
1455	Left
147	Epigastric
148	Hypochondriac
1481	Right
1485	Left
1493	Diaphragm
15	**Thorax**
151	Right
153	Front
155	Left
157	Back
16	**Upper extremity**
161	Shoulder
162	Axilla
163	Arm
164	Elbow
165	Forearm
166	Wrist
167	Hand
168	Finger
17	**Neck**
177	Throat
18	**Head**
181	Face
183	**Ear**
1831	Pinna
1832	External auditory meatus

1833	Tympanic cavity
1834	Tympanic membrane
1835	Eustachian tube
1836	Tympanic ossicle
1837	Osseous labyrinth
1838	Membraneous labyrinth
185	**Eye**
1851	Coat
18511	Eyelid
18512	Cornea
18513	Sclerotic
18514	Iris
18515	Ciliary process
18516	Choroid
18517	Retina
1852	Parts
18521	Aqueous humour
18522	Crystalline lens
18523	Vitreous humour
1856	Lachrymal gland
18562	Lachrymal sac
18565	Tears
18571	Lachrymal duct
18572	Nasal duct
187	**Scalp**
192	**Joint**
198	Storage region
2	**Digestive system**
21	**Mouth**
211	Lips
212	Cavity of the mouth
2121	Floor of the mouth
2123	Cheek
2125	Palate
21251	Uvula
21252	Soft palate
21253	Hard palate
2127	Jaw
213	Tongue
214	**Tooth**
21411	Gum
21412	Enamel
2142	Part
21421	Root
21422	Neck
21423	Crown
2143	Kinds of teeth
21431	Milk teeth

21432 **Canine**
21433 Lateral incisor
21434 Central incisor
21435 First molar
21436 Second molar
2145 Dentine
2146 Pulp cavity
245 Fauces

216 **Salivary gland**
2161 Parotid gland
21617 Parotid duct
2162 Submaxillary gland
21627 Submaxillary duct
2163 Sublingual gland
2164 Mucous gland
219 Tonsil

22 **Pharynx**

23 **Esophagus**

24 **Stomach**
245 Gastric secretion
246 Gastric gland
2461 Cardiac gland
2463 Pyloric gland
248 Orifice and valve
2481 Cardiac orifice
2482 Pyloric orifice
24828 Pyloric valve

25 **Intestine**

26 **Small intestine**
266 Intestinal gland
2661 Brunner's gland
2662 Solitary gland
2663 Peyer's gland
268 Ileo cæcal valve

27 **Large intestine**
272 Part
2721 Cæcum
27219 Vermiform appendix
2722 Colon
2723 Rectum
2724 Anal canal
276 Solitary gland
278 Houston's valve

291 **Liver**
2915 Bile
2917 Bile duct
292 Gall bladder
2927 Cystic duct

293 **Pancreas**
2935 Pancreatic secretion
2937 Pancreatic duct

3 **Circulatory system**
31 Percardium

32 **Heart**

33 **Vena cava**
331 Superior vena cava
332 Inferior vena cava

34 **Aorta**

35 **Blood**
358 Haemoglobin
36 Vein
(*To be divided locally*)
37 Artery
(*To be divided locally*)
38 Capillary
(*To be divided locally*)

39 **Lymphatic vessel**
391 Thoracic duct
392 Right lymphatic duct
394 Others
(*To be divided locally*)
395 Lymph
396 Lymphatic gland
(*To be divided locally*)
398 Lymphatic valve

4 **Respiratory system**

41 **Nose**
411 Outer nose
412 Nasal fossæ

42 **Larynx**

43 **Trachea**

44 **Bronchi**
441 Right bronchus
4415 Right intra-pulmonary bronchus
445 Left bronchus
4455 Left intra-pulmonary bronchus

45 **Lung**
4511 Pleura
46 Pleural sac
48 Mediastinum

5 **Genito-urinary system**

51 **Kidney**
513 Sinus
515 Urine
517 Ureter
52 Bladder
53 Urethra

54 **Sexual organ**

55 **Female genital organ**
551 Ovary
5515 Egg
552 Fallopian tube

553 Uterus
554 Vagina
555 External organ
5551 Vulva
55511 Labium
5552 Perineum
556 Breast

56 Male genital organ
561 Testes
5611 Scrotum
5621 Epididymis
5622 Vas deferens
5623 Ejaculatory duct
565 Seminal vesicle
5655 Spermatozoa
5661 Prostate gland
5662 Cowper's gland
567 Penis

6 Ductless gland
61 Suprarenal
62 Spleen
63 Thymus
64 Para thyroid
65 Thyroid
66 Hypophysis
661 Anterior
662 Posterior
67 Pineal
68 Others
(*To be divided locally*)

7 Nervous System
71 Central
72 Brain
721 Meninges
7211 Dura mater
7212 Arachnoid mater
7213 Pia mater
722 Parts
7221 Cerebrum
7222 Cerebellum
7223 Pons
7224 Medulla oblongata
73 Spinal cord
731 Spinal meninges

74 Nerves
75 Peripheral nerve
(*To be divided locally*)
76 Sensory nerve
(*To be divided locally*)
77 Motor nerve
(*To be divided locally*)
78 Autonomic nerve
781 Sympathetic nerve
(*To be divided locally*)
795 Cerebro-spinal fluid

8 Other systems

82 Bone
821 Periosteum
822 Bone proper
8221 Substantial
8222 Cancellous
8223 Cavity
825 Marrow

83 Muscle

86 Connective tissue
861 Connective tissue proper
8611 Lining membrane
86111 Serous
86112 Synovial
86113 Mucous
8613 Protecting brane
8614 Basement
8615 Reticular tissue
8616 Ligament
8617 Tendon
866 Cartilage

87 Skin
871 Epidermis
872 Corium
875 Pigment
876 Glands of the skin
8761 Sebaceous gland
8762 Sweat gland
88 Hair, etc.
881 Hair
882 Scale
883 Nail

Foci in [E] *cum* [2P]

1 Preliminaries
11 Nomenclature
13 Nursing home
14 Hospital
15 Sanatorium
17 Anæsthetization
19 Microscopy
192 Sectioning
195 Fixation
196 Mounting
198 Staining

2 Morphology

3 Physiology
To be subdivided as in "G Biology" with the following modifications:

Subdivisions when applied to

L9F Female Medicine

3 Obstetrics

31	**Pregnancy**
313	Diagnosis
3135	Multiple pregnancy
314	**Pathology of pregnancy**
3142	Vomiting
3143	Varices
31451	Albuminuria
31455	Complications due to abnormalities in the generative tract
3147	Convulsion
31471	Insanity of pregnancy
31495	Extra-uterine pregnancy
32	**Foetus**
324	Diseases of the fœtus
3291	Death of fœtus
331	Chorian
332	Amnion
333	Placenta
334	Umbilical cord
34	**Abortion**
341	Natural
345	Artificial
35	**Labour**
351	Presentation
3511	Vertex
3512	Face and brow
3513	Lower extremity
3515	In multiple pregnancy
352	Second stage
353	Third stage
354	**Abnormal labour**
3542	Due to foetus
3543	Due to anomalies of expelling forces
3544	Due to passage and obstacles
357	**Obstetric operation**
3571	Dilatation
3574	For inversion of uterus
3577	Use of forceps
3578	Embryotomy
36	**Puerperal state**
3641	Puerperal infection
3646	Mastitis
37	Post-puerperal
393	**Ordinary (non-pregnant) physiology**
394	**Birth control**
4	**Disease**
5	**Public health and hygiene**
51	**Vital statistics**
515	Birth
5191	Death
52	**State control**
521	Habitation *To be subdivided as in* " NA Architecture "
522	Animals *To be subdivided as in* " KZ Animal Husbandry "
523	Food. Beverage *To be subdivided as* [P] of " E Chemistry " *and* " F Technology "
524	Intoxicant. Poison *To be subdivided as* 523
525	Conveyance
526	Medicine *To be subdivided as* 523
54	**Prevention of diseases in general** *To be subdivided as* " 4 Disease "
5497	Prevention of accident
55	**Public hygiene**
551	Ground
555	Water
556	Season (*Divide by season*)
558	Air
57	**Personal hygiene**
571	Residence
5711	Floor. Wall, etc.
5712	Water supply
5713	Ventilation
5714	Heating. Cooling
5715	Light
5718	Drainage
57197	Furniture
572	Exercise and recreation
573	**Food**
5731	Underfeeding
5732	Overfeeding
5736	Fasting
574	Intoxicant. Stimulant
575	Bath. Toilet. Cleanliness
576	Regulation of habit
577	Clothing *To be subdivided as in* [P] *of* " M7 Textiles "
578	Sleep

7 **Development Ontogeny**
8 Physical fitness

For **4 DISEASE in [E]**
Foci in [2P]

1 **General**
11 Atrophy
12 Hypertrophy
13 Hemorrhage
14 Fever
15 Inflammation
17 Pain
18 Spasm
19 Other

2 **Infection**
21 Tuberculosis
22 Syphilis
23 Virus
24 Bacteria
25 Metaphyta
26 Protozoa
27 Metazoa

3 **Parasite**
32 Algae
33 Fungus
36 Vermes
38 Insect

4 **Poison**
41 Snake poison
To be further divided as [P] *of* 'E Chemistry'

5 **Functional disorder**
51 Under functioning
52 Over functioning
53 Complicated functioning
537 Allergy
56 Non-functioning
565 Non-functioning due to external causes

6 **Nutrition**
61 Deficiency
62 Excess

7 **Structural**
71 Abnormality
711 Size
712 Shape
713 Position
714 Fixation
715 Number
716 Total absence
718 Opening
72 Tumour
721 Hypertrophy
722 Inflammatory
723 Cyst
724 Non-malignant
7241 Osteoma
7242 Chondroma
7243 Myoma
7245 Myxoma
72462 Lipoma
72463 Fibroma
7247 Papilloma
7248 Adenoma
725 Malignant tumours
7251 Osteosarcoma
7252 Chondrosarcoma
7253 Myosarcoma
7255 Myxosarcoma
72562 Liposarcoma
72563 Fibrosarcoma
7257 Carcinoma
7258 Adenosarcoma
73 Hernia
74 Ulcer
75 Abscess
76 Gangrene
77 Wound

8 **Foreign matter**
81 Solid
85 Fluid
88 Gas

9 **Other**
91 Fire
92 Asphyxia
921 Smoke
941 Low temperature
942 High temperature
951 Draught
952 Excess of rain
954 Hail
983 Wind
986 Lightning

Specific disease
(*Illustrative*)

L:423 Pox
L:4231 Small pox
L:4232 Chicken pox
L:4233 Measles
L:4631 Scurvy
L:4632 Beriberi
L12:26 Obesity
L14:485 Ascites
L191:46 Gout
L2161:423 Mumps
L24:451 Anorexia
L25:4241 Typhoid
L25:4242 Bacillary dysentery
L25:4251 Cholera
L25:4262 Amœbic dysentery
L25:4371 Tapeworm

L25:4372	Hookworm
L25:4373	Round worm
L25:4374	Thread worm
L25:451	Constipation
L25:452	Diarrhoea
L25:474	Dysentery (general)
L291:453	Jaundice
L292:481	Gallstone
L2927:481	Biliary colic
L293:46	Diabetes
L34:411	Angina pectoris
L35:411	Anæmia
L35:4111	Secondary
L35:4112	Chlorosis
L35:4113	Pernicious
L35:4114	Splenic
L35:4115	Leucemia
L35:4231	Typhus
L35:4261	Malaria
L35:4262	Sleeping sickness
L35:4263	Yellow fever
L37:411	Arteriosclerosis
L37:4711	Aneurysm
L39:4371	Filarial elephantiasis
L39:481	Elephantiasis
L396:412	Hodgin's disease
L396:4241	Bubonic plague
L4:4241	Influenza
L4:4242	Whooping cough
L41:4241	Diptheria
L44:453	Asthma
L45:424	Pneumonia
L4511:485	Empyema
L51:453	Albuminuria
L51:481	Renal colic
L61:411	Addisons' disease
L62:4261	Kala-azar
L65:4711	Goitre
L65:4716	Cretinism. Myxœdema
L66:472	Acromegaly
L7:51	Neurasthenia
L7:52	Insomnia
L71:453	Epilepsy
L711:424	Cerebro-spinal meningitis
L72:4241	Tetanus
L73:417	Neuralgia
L76:411	Paralysis
L76:453	Chorea
L81:463	Rickets
L87:485	Edema
L875:4716	Albinism

Foci in [2*E*] *cum* [3P]

1	**Nursing**
2	**Etiology**
3	**Symptom and diagnosis**
31	Clinical
32	Physical method
325	Microscope
3253	X-ray
33	Chemical method
4	**Pathology**
402	Physical method
403	Chemical method
411	Examination of cell
412	Examination of tissue
424	Examination of gastric content
427	Examination of faeces
44	Examination of sputum
45	Examination of urine
4798	Post-mortem examination
5	**Preventive step**
51	Epidemiology
55	Control measure
56	Immunology
6	**Therapeutics**
61	Method of administration
6121	By mouth
6123	By rectum
616	Injection
6161	Epidermal
6163	Intramuscular
6166	Intravenal
62	Physicotherapy
624	Thermotherapy
625	Radiotherapy
6252	Ultra-violet therapy
6253	X-ray therapy
626	Electrotherapy
627	Magnetotherapy
63	Pharmacotherapy
63129	Radiumtherapy
64	Physiological therapy
642	Regulation of diet
6426	Fast cure
6434	Blood letting
6435	Cupping
644	Respiratory remedy (*Pranayamam*)

65	Hydrotherapy
662	Serumtherapy
663	Vaccine therapy
67	Organotherapy
68	Aerotherapy
69	Other cure
691	Psychotherapy
7	**Surgery**
75	Prosthesis
76	Amputation
77	Excision
8	**Diet regulation**
9	Other
91	After care
97	First aid
L9A	**Specials**
L9B	Embryo
L9C	Child
L9D	Adolescent
L9E	Old age
L9F	Female
L9H	Tropical
L9T	Aviation
L9V	War
L9X	Industrial
LA	**Systems** *by* **[CD]** (*Illustrative*)
LB	Ayurveda
LC	Siddha
LD	Unani
LL	Homoeopathy
LM	Naturopathy

CHAPTER LZ

PHARMACOGNOSY

Canonical Divisions

LZ3	**Pharmacology**
LZ5	**Pharmacopoeia**
LZ8	**Pharmacy**

LZ3 Pharmacology

LZ3 [P]: [E] [2P]

Foci in [E]

2	Stimulation
3	Depression
5	Irritation
6	Desnulescence
7	Osmosis
8	Replacement
91	Antibioticaction

LZ5 Pharmacopoeia

LZ5 [P], [P2]

Foci in [P2]

1	Official
2	Secondary
3	Tertiary

CHAPTER M

USEFUL ARTS

M1 **Book production and description**

M13 Paper-making
M14 Printing, etc.
M141 Type founding
M142 Composition
M143 Printing
M1435 Off-set
M144 Book illustration
M145 Ink manufacture
M148 Typewriting
M15 Book-binding
M16 Publishing
M17 Book selling
M18 Book description

M3 **Domestic science**
M31 Cooking
M32 Serving
M37 Beauty culture

M4 Smithy
M5 Carpentry
M6 Glass industry

M7 **Textiles**

M7 [P]: [E] [2P]

Foci in [*P*]

1 Cotton
2 Wool
3 Silk
4 Flax
5 Other vegetable fibre
6 Metal yarn

Foci in [E] *cum* [2P]

1 Preliminaries
11 Sorting. Ginning
12 Beating. Scouring
13 Carding
15 Oiling. Washing
2 Spinning
3 Twisting
4 Bleaching. Dyeing
5 Sizing
7 Weaving
8 Textile printing

M8 Dress making
M92 Masonry
M95 Photography
M97 Leather industry
M98 Packaging

Further foci by (SD)
(*Illustrative*)

MB1 Calculating machine, etc.
MB9 Horology
MC3 Gramophone
MC5 Opticians' trade
MD12 Clay industry
MD13 Bricklaying
MD132 Lime-sand brick
MD5124 Horse-riding
MD5133 Motor-driving
MD521 Boat-rowing
MD525 Navigation
MD53 Aviation

MJ7 **Rope making**

MJ7 [P]: [E] [2P]

Foci in [P]

1 Cotton
2 Coir
3 Hemp
4 Flax
5 Jute
6 Sissal
97 Other vegetable fibre
98 Metal

Foci in [E] *cum* [2P]

Same as in " M7 Textiles "

MNR Musical instrument making
MV4 Science of war
MV41 Military science
MV45 Naval science
MV48 Airfight
MX411 Traffic regulation in road

MY **Physical training, sports, games, Use of leisure. Hobby**

MY1 **Physical training**
MY11 Callisthenics
MY12 Heavy exercise

MY2 **Athletics**
MY21 Ball game
MY211 Thrown by hand
MY2115 Basket ball
MY2116 Volley ball
MY212 Driven by foot
MY2121 Football
MY2122 Rugby

MY213	Thrown with racket
MY2131	Tennis
MY2132	Badminton
MY214	Driven by bats
MY2141	Cricket
MY2142	Base ball
MY2143	Hockey
MY2144	Croquet
MY2145	Golf
MY2146	Polo
MY22	Competitive sport
MY221	Tug of war
MY222	Throwing games
MY223	Stilt walking
MY224	Jumping
MY225	Running
MY226	Cycling
MY227	Motoring
MY23	Children's game
MY24	Fighting sport
MY241	Boxing
MY242	Fencing
MY243	Archery
MY244	Shooting
MY245	Wrestling
MY25	Aquatic sport
MY251	Swimming
MY252	Boating
MY254	Skating
MY256	Water polo
MY26	Mountain climbing
MY28	Airsport
MY284	Aviation
MY3	**Indoor amusement, games**
MY31	Card
MY32	Chance game
MY321	Dice
MY322	Chess
MY33	Billiards
MY34	Occupational amusement
MY35	Play with doll and toy
MY36	Jugglery
MY37	Mimicry
MY4	**Mental pastime**
MY43	Cross-word puzzle
MY5	**Animal racing**
MY6	**Hunting**
MY65	Fishing
MY68	Bird-hunting
MY7	Scouting
MY8	Club life
MY92	Propaganda
MY93	Betting, lottery
MY95	Circus
MYX46	Philately

CHAPTER △

SPIRITUAL EXPERIENCE AND MYSTICISM

△ **[P], [P2] : [E] [2P]**

Foci in [P]

1	**Integral,** (*Purna*)
2	**Hindu**
22	Hatha
23	Jnāna
24	Karma
25	Bhakti
26	Rāja
28	Siddhar (of South India)
3	**Jain**
4	**Buddhistic**
42	Mahāyāna (Indian)
421	Vajrayāna
426	Sahajayāna
428	Mantrayāna
44	Shingon
45	Amita
46	Zen
47	Mahavairocana
5	**Judaic**
6	**Christian**
63	Gnostic
7	**Islamic**
73	Sufi
8452	Mithraism
8513	Neoplatonic

Foci in [P2]

11	God
12	Angel. Devil
14	Man
15	Fairy
16	Disembodied soul
2	Nature

To be Subdivided as in [P3] of " ND Sculpture "

5	Space
6	Time

Foci in [E] *cum* [2P]

1	**Nomenclature**
18	Symbolism
3	**Technique**
34	Breath control
36	Meditation
5	Vision
6	Tradition
7	Interpretation and relation
8	**Occultism**
83	Manifestation
831	Materialisation
833	Clairaudience
834	Telepathy
835	Clairvoyance
838	Writing
84	Transformation
86	**Prophecy**
862	Physiognomy
8625	*Macca Sāstra*
8627	Palmistry
8628	Phrenology
864	Astrology
866	Precognition
9692	Omen
87	Magic and witchcraft
872	Sympathetic
874	Ceremonial
893	Voice

CHAPTER N

FINE ARTS

Canonical divisions

NA **Architecture**
NB Town planning
NC Plastic art
ND **Sculpture**
NE Lapidiary art
NF Numismatic art
NG Mould art
NH Ceramic art
NJ Inlay art
NL Embroidery
NK Toy making
NM **Graphic Art**
NN Engraving
NP Drawing
NQ **Painting**
NR **Music**
NS Dance
NT **Theatre**
NU Puppet play
NV Shadow play
NW Cinema
NX Talkie

NA ARCHITECTURE

NA [P], [P2] [P3], [P4]: [E]
Foci in [P], [P2] *taken together*
(*Illustrative*)

NA41 **Chinese**
NA42 **Japanese**
NA44 **Indian**
NA44,C Buddhist
NA44,D Calukyan
NA44,E Jain
NA44,J Moghul
NA441 Dravidian
NA441,G Pallava
NA45,C Persian
NA45,D Selucid and Sassanian
NA46 **Saracenic**
NA461 Arabian
NA463,C Jewish
NA47,A Babylonian
NA47,B Assyrian
NA47,D Byzantine
NA492 Syrian
NA5 **European**
NA5,D Romanesque
NA5,F Gothic
NA5,J Renaissance
NA51 **Greek**
NA51,A Minoan and Mycenean Pelasgic
NA51,C Hellenic
NA513,C Corinthian
NA517,C Doric
NA519,C Ionian
NA52 **Italian**
NA52,C Etruscan
NA52,D Roman
NA52,E Tuscanian
NA56 **British**
NA561D Anglo-Saxon
NA561,E Norman
NA561,H Early English
NA561,J Tudor
NA563 **Scottish**
NA563,G First period
NA563,H Second period
NA563,I Third period
NA563,J Fourth period
NA564 **Irish**
NA564,D Celtic
NA564,G Mediaeval
NA677 **Egyptian**
NA74,F **Aztec**

Foci in [P3]

2 **Building**
22 Library building
To be divided as the [P] *of* "2 Library Science"
3 **Dwelling**
31 Rural
33 Urban
35 City
37 Castle
39 Other groupings
391 Detached
393 Attached
399 Workmen
4 **Hotel, etc.**
43 Restaurant
44 Hotel
45 Inn
5 **City hall**
6 **Museum**

7 **General office building**

8 **Sepulchral Monument**

8(A) **Other buildings**

(*To be divided by* (SD)

Foci in [P4]

3 Floor
4 Support
41 Wall

45 **Pillar**
453 Base
455 Shaft
458 Capital
46 Arch
5 Stairway
6 Roof
Gable
Roof covering
631 Tile

633 **Ceiling**
64 Flat roof

65 **Dome**

66 **Spire**

67 **Tower**

7 **Window**
71 Compass
72 Offertory
73 Rose
74 Venetian
79 Other types
8 Door

9 Other features

91 **Cornice**

92 **Frieze**
94 Fire place
98 Chimney

99 **Decoration**
992 Decoration in relief
993 Veneering
994 Mosaic
995 Painted decoration
996 Stained glass
999 Other modes

Foci in [E]

1 Location
2 Composition
3 Plan
4 Elevation
5 Section
6 Perspective
8 Model

NB TOWN PLANNING

NB [P], [P2] [P3], [P4]: [E]

Foci in [P3]

1 Village
3 Town
5 City
7 Metropolis

Foci in [P4]

1 Zone
3 Landscape
4 Avenue
5 Market
6 Public resort
61 Public worship
62 Public bath
64 Promenade
65 Playground
66 Park
691 Theatre
7 Monument
8 Cemetry
9 Other parts

Foci in [E]

As for " NA Architecture "

ND SCULPTURE

ND [P], [P2] [P3]; [M]: [E] [2P]

Foci in [P3]

1 **Human figure**
11 Equestrian statue
18 Bust

2 **Nature**
21 Earth
216 Mountain
25 water
254 Lake
256 River
28 Sky

Subdivide as in

[P] of " B 9 Astronomy " and in addition

288 Cloud

3 **Landscape**
4 Plant
5 Animal

6 **Scene**

7 **Numismatics**
71 Coin
72 Medal
74 Seal

8 Sepulchre
81 Effigy
8(A) Other subjects

To be divided by (SD)

9(Q)	**Iconography**
	Foci in [M]
1	Wood
3	Marble
4	Stone
5	Bronze
6	Other metals
7	Terracotta
8	Ivory
9	Other materials
	Foci in [E] *cum* [2P]
4	Design
5	Making of cast
8	Modelling
9	Others
98	Preservation

NN ENGRAVING

Canonical Divisions

NNB	Line
NND	Stipple
NNF	Mezzotint
NNH	Aquatint
NNK	Etching
NNM	Lithography

NQ PAINTING

NQ [P], [P2] [P3]; [M]: [E] [2P]

Foci in [P3]

As for " ND Sculpture "

	Foci in [M]
1	Wood
2	Paper
3	Fresco
4	Stone
5	Metals
6	Glass
7	Canvas
8	Ivory
9	Other surfaces
	Foci in [E] *cum* [2P]
1	Composition
2	Colour
3	Water-colour
4	Oil-colour
5	Gouache
6	Distemper
7	Encaustic
9	Other topics
98	Preservation

NR MUSIC

NR [P], [P2] [P3]; [M]: [E] [2P]

	Foci in [P3]
1	Word. Libertto
18	Notation
2	Form
6	Keeping time, *tālam*
91	Dramatic music
92	Orchestral music
	Foci in [M]
2	**Wind instrument**
21	Pipe
22	Flute
23	Organ
24	Claironet
25	Oboe
26	Bassoon
27	Bagpipe
28	Trumpet
29	Others
291	Harmonium
3	**Stringed instrument**
31	*Vina*
32	Violin
34	Piano
35	Harp
36	Lute
39	Others
4	**Percussion instrument**
41	Drum
42	Kettle-drum
43	Cymbals
9	Others
91	Vocal

CHAPTER O

LITERATURE

O [P], [P2] [P3], [P4]

Foci in [P]

As the Language Divisions
in Chapter 5

Foci in [P2]

1 Poetry
2 Drama
3 Fiction, including short stories
4 Letters (literature written in the form of letters)
5 Oration
6 Other forms of prose
7 Campu

Foci in [P3]

1 To be got by (CD)
2 For authors born later than 1800, if year of birth cannot be found out at all, (CD) to be worked only to one digit. Thereafter, (AD) may be used.

Foci in [P4]

See Rule in Chapter O of Part 1

CHAPTER P

LINGUISTICS

P [P], [P2] [P3]: [E] [2P]

Foci in [P2]

9A **Variant**
9B Slang
9D Dialect
9J Jargon

A **Stage**

Foci in [P], [P2] *taken together* (*Illustrative*)

111,D Old English
111,E Middle English
111,J Modern English
113,D Old German
113,E Middle German
113,J Modern German
114,D Old Swedish
114,J Modern Swedish
115,D Old Norse
115,J Modern Norwegian
117,D Old Icelandic
117,J Modern Icelandic
122,A Old French
122,F Middle French
122,H Modern French
1295,D Old Irish
1295,E Middle Irish
1295,N Modern Irish
15,A Ancient or Vedic Sanskrit
15,B Epic Sanskrit
15,C Classical Sanskrit
31,A Ancient Tamil
31,D Sangam Tamil
31,J Modern Tamil
33,A Ancient Kanarese
33,E Old Kanarese
33,J Modern Kanarese

Foci in [P3]

1 **Isolated sound. Phoneme**
11 Vowel
111 Back
115 Mixed
118 Front

Common isolates for
11 and its subdivisions

01 Close
03 Half Close
05 Half open
07 Open
08 Nasal
13 Dipththong
15 Consonant
151 Glotted
152 Circular
153 Velar
154 Palatal
155 Post-dental alveolar
156 Predental
157 Labiodental
158 Bilabial

Common isolates for
15 and its subdivisions

01 Plosive
02 Lateral
03 Rolled
04 Fricative
05 Semi-vowel
08 Nasal
16 Voiced consonant
To be subdivided as '**15**'
17 Unvoiced consonant
To be subdivided as '**15**'

2 **Syllable**
203 Formative, element. Prefix. Suffix. Infix
27 Specific syllable

3 **Word**
301 Root
302 Stem
303 Compound word
305 Loan word

31 **Noun**
311 Concrete
312 Proper
313 Common
314 Class
315 Collective
316 Material
317 Abstract

32 **Adjective**
321 Proper
322 Descriptive
323 Quantitative
324 Demonstrative
325 Distributive

33 Numeral
331 Cardinal
335 Ordinal
34 Pronoun
341 Personal
344 Demonstrative
345 Relative
346 Interrogative
35 Verb
351 Finite form
353 Infinitival form
354 Infinitive
356 Gerund
357 Participle
359 Special form
3591 Auxilliary
3594 Defective
3597 Anomalous
36 Adverb
361 Simple
365 Relative
366 Interogative
37 Preposition
371 Simple
372 Compound
373 Participial
377 Disguised
38 Conjunction
381 Subordination
385 Co-ordination
391 Interjection
397 Specific words
4 Phrases
To be divided as '3'
5 Clauses
To be divided as '3'
6 Sentences
601 Simple
605 Compound
607 Complex
7 Pieces of composition
To be divided as [P2] *of* "O Literature"
794 Anagram
795 Translation
8 Punctuation
9 Meterials for practice, readers
To be divided if necessary **by grades**
Foci in [E] *cum* [2P]
1 Phonology, (sound, phonetics)
12 Accent
122 Stress (quantity)
123 Pitch (quality)
13 Conditional change. Combinative change, *e.g.*, Umlaut, Verner's Law
14 Sudden change. Loss, Appearance
15 Changes due to analogy
16 Unconditional change. Isolative change *e.g.*, Grimm's Law
18 Representation
2 Morphology (structure)
21 Number
22 Gender
23 Case
24 Degree of comparison
25 Person
26 Mood
27 Tense
28 Derivation (if applied to *words*). Transformation (if applied to *sentences*).
291 Composition (if applied to *words*). Synthesis (if applied to *sentences*).
3 Syntax (function)
301 Number
302 Gender
303 Case
304 Degrees of comparison
305 Person
306 Mood
307 Tense
31 Function by accent
33 Analysis
331 Subject
332 Adjuncts to subject
335 Predicate
336 Adjuncts to predicate
38 Function by position
4 Meaning (for a given element) (semasiology)
5 Element for a given idea
52 Adaptation of existing element
53 Coining
58 Borrowing
7 Composition
75 Figure of speech (imagery)
795 Translating
P(1) Calligraphy
P(3) Shorthand
P(6) Typewriting

CHAPTER Q

RELIGION

Q [P]: [E] [2P]

Foci in [P]

1 **Hinduism, Vedic**

11 **Rigvedic**
111 Aitareyin
112 Kausitakin

12 **Yajur Vedic**
121 Black Yajur Vedic
122 Kathaka
123 Kapisthala Katha
124 Maitrayaniya
125 Taittiriya
126 White Yajur Vedic or (Vajasaneyin)
127 Madhyandina
128 Kanva

13 **Sama Vedic**
131 Tandin
132 Talavakara (Jaiminiya)
133 Ranayaniya

14 **Atharva Vedic**
141 Saunakiya
142 Paippalada

2 **Hinduism, Post Vedic**

21 **Smartaism**
213 Dattatreyism

22 **Vaisnavism**
221 Bhagavata
2212 Madhva
2213 Vallabhaism
2215 Radhait
22151 Visnuswamin
22152 Nimbarka
2216 Caitanya
222 Pancaratra
2221 Sri Vaisnava
22211 Vadagalai
22212 Tengalai
2222 Manbahu
223 Narasimha
224 Rama

23 **Saivism**
231 Pasupata
2311 Lakulisa-pasupata
2312 Kapalika
2313 Goraksanathi
2315 Natha
2316 Rasesvara
232 Agamic Saivism
233 Kasmir Saivism
234 Virasaivism

24 **Ganapatysim**

25 **Saktaism**
251 Right handed
255 Left handed
256 Kaulacarin

26 **Sanmukaism**

28 **Sauraism**
29 Other
298 Hanumatseva
2998 Village god-worship

Other Post Vedic Religions by (CD) (*Illustrative*)

29J Sad
29M2 Bramo Samaj
29M6 Prarthana Samaj
29M8 Arya Samaj

3 **Jainism**

31 **Svetambara**
311 Pujera
312 Dhundai
313 Terapanthi

32 **Digambara**
321 Bispanthi
323 Terapanthi
324 Samaiyapanthi
325 Gumanpanthi
326 Totapanthi

4 **Buddhism**

41 **Hinayana**
411 Mahasanghika
412 Mahisasaka
413 Lokottaravadin
414 Sarvastivadin
415 Mulasarvastivadin
416 Dharmagupta
417 Sammitiya

4182 **Hinkyknk (Japan)**
41821 Kusha
41822 Pitsu
41823 Jojitsu

42 **Mahayana (Indian and general)**

43 **Lamaism. (Mahayana, Tibet)**

44 **Mahayana, China**
441 Ch'an
442 Chiao-men
443 Lu
444 T'ien t'ai
445 Hsien shou or Huayen
446 Tz'en or Fa Hsiang
448 Ching t'u

45 **Mahayana, Japan**
451 Hosso
452 Sanron
453 Kegon
454 Tendai
455 Jodo
456 Shin
457 Nichiren
458 Shingon
4596 Zen

5 **Judaism**
51 Palestine
52 Babylonian
58 Zionist

6 **Christianity**
61 Early church
611 Greek
613 Armenian
618 Russian
62 Roman Catholic
63 Protestant
64 Presbyterian
65 Puritan
66 Quaker
68 *Others by* (CD) (*Illustrative*)
68J3 Baptist
68L4 New Church
68L6 Methodists
68M6 Christian Science

7 **Muhammadanism**
71 Sunni
711 Heneifi
712 Shafi'l
713 Maliki
714 Henbeli
72 Shi'ah
73 Mu'sazilite
77 Wahabi
78 *Others by* (CD) (*Illustrative*)
78M5 Bahaism
78M9 Ahamadiya

8 **Other Religions**

Divided by (GD) *and by* [FD] (*Illustrative*)

8411 Pre-confucianism
8412 Confucianism
8413 Lao-Tseism. Taoism
8421 Shintoism
8441 Sikhism
8451 Zoroastrianism
8452 Manichaeism

QA **Universal religion**

To be individualised by (CD) (*Illustrative*)

QM Theosophy

Foci in [E] *cum* [2P]

1 **Mythology, etc.**

2 **Scripture**
25 Sayings
26 Tradition

Subdivisions for

'1 Hinduism (Vedic)'

21 Samhita
22 Brahmana
23 Aranyaka
24 Upanishad

Subdivisions for

'2 Hinduism (Post-vedic)'

21 Relevant selection from Veda
22 Relevant selection from Purana
23 Samhita. Agama. Tantra
24 Upanisad

3 **Theology**
31 God
311 *Avasara*
315 *Avatara*
32 Angel. Devil
324 *Navagraha* (Planet)
33 Founder of religion
332 Consecrated saint
34 Man. Soul
35 Salvation
351 Predestination
352 Freedom. Free-will
353 Faith
354 Repentance
355 Regeneration
356 Grace
36 Eschatology
361 Death
362 Intermediate state
363 Judgment
364 Heaven
365 Hell
366 Rebirth

367	Eternity
368	Immortality
369	Other topics
37	Universe
38	*Sthala* (local) ***purana***
39	Other topics
396	Revelation
4	**Religious practice** (*Kalpasutra* in Vedic religion)
41	**Personal**
411	Initiatory
412	Meditative
413	Evangelistic
414	Worship
4146	Prayer
415	Symbolism
416	Sacred furniture (*Sulvasutra* in Vedic religion)
417	Hymns
4173	*Namavali*
418	Sacred formula. Incantation
419	Other topics
4192	Ritual
4193	Gift
4194	Appeasement
4195	Expiation
4196	Devotion
4198	Pilgrimage
42	**Sacrament** (*Grhyasutra in* Vedic religion)
423	Baptism
426	Confirmation
427	Marriage
428	Obsequies
4284	Pollution
4288	Anniversary rite
42891	*Sati*
429	Other topics
43	Holy day
433	Fast
437	Vigil
44	Didactic (*Dharmasutra* in Vedic religion)
447	Monkhood
448	Penance
45	Public worship
451	Ecclesiology
452	Consecration
454	Worship
456	Sacred furniture
457	Festival
458	Temple priest
46	*Gotrapravara* in Vedic religion
49	Other topics
494	Sacrifice
495	Holy water
5	**Preaching, etc.**
51	Preaching
52	Sermon
53	Pastoral visitation
57	Society for parish work
6	**Religious institution**
61	Religion and its relation to other institutions
62	Ecclesiastical polity
621	Clergy
6211	Apostolic succession
6212	Papacy
6213	Episcopate
6214	Lay ministry
65	Mission
67	Monastic order
68	Religious association
681	Religious society for men and women
6811	Men
6815	Women
69	Other topics
7	**Religious sect**
8	**Heresy and persecution**

CHAPTER R

PHILOSOPHY

Canonical divisions

R1 **Logic**
R2 **Epistemology**
R3 **Metaphysics**
R4 **Ethics**
R5 **Aesthetics**
R6 **Favoured System (1)**
(*In what follows*
Indian philosophy)
R7 **Favoured System (2)**
R8 **Other Systems** ***by*** **(GD)**

R1 **Logic**
R11 Inductive
R12 Deductive
R13 Dialectic
R14 Symbolic
R16 Genetic
R17 Scientific method
R19 Special topic
R191 Definition
R192 Inference
R193 Judgment. Proposition
R194 Fallacy. Sophism
R195 Ambiguity
R198 Probability
R199 Categories

R2 **Epistemology**
R21 Sources of knowledge
R211 Sense-perception
R212 Inference
R2125 Analogy
R213 Verbal testimony
R2133 Tradition
R215 Presumption
R22 Nature of knowledge
R24 Validity of knowledge
R29 Special topic
R292 Truth and error
R299 Categories

R3 **Metaphysics**
R3 [P], [P2]
Foci in [P]

1 Absolute
2 Idealism and realism
21 Idealism
25 Realism
3 Materialism
4 Rationalism. Free thought
5 Monism and pluralism
51 Monism
55 Pluralism
6 Teleology
7 Value
9 Other special views
To be got by (SD)
(*Illustrative*)
9(G) Genetic
9(Y) Humanism

Foci in [P2]
To be got by (SD)

R4 **Ethics**
R4 [P], [P2]
Foci in [P]

1 **Personal ethics**
11 Truth and falsehood
12 Humility. Egoism. Modesty. Pride
13 Temperance
14 Gentleness. Cruelty. Tolerance. Envy. Sweetness. Anger
15 Chastity. Celibacy, Adultery. Immoral habits.
16 Gratefulness and ungratefulness
17 Diligence and sloth
18 Courge. Cowardliness. Firmness. Weakness
19 Other qualities
2 **Family ethics**
21 Husband and wife. Marriage. Divorce
211 Husband
215 Wife
217 Marriage
2175 Polygamy. Adultery
2178 Break-up of marriage
22 Parent and child
221 Parent
2211 Father
2213 Foster father
2214 Step-father
2217 Foster mother
2218 Step-mother
225 Child
2251 Son
2253 Foster son

2254 Step-son
2255 Daughter
2257 Foster daughter
2258 Step-daughter
23 Guardian and ward
231 Guardian
235 Ward
24 Dependent relative
241 Conduct towards dependent relative
245 Conduct of dependent relative
25 Other relatives
251 Conduct towards other relatives
255 Conduct of other relatives
26 Guest. Host
261 Host
265 Guest
28 Domestic servant
281 Conduct towards domestic servant
285 Conduct of domestic servant

3 Social ethics
32 Truth and slander
33 Philanthropy and humanity
34 Etiquette
341 Entertainment
342 Wedding
343 Card
344 Conversational
345 Letter-writing
346 Travelling
347 Club
348 Funeral
37 Friendship. Courtship
3W State ethics (Sub-divisions as in 'W' Political Science)

4 Professional and business ethics

To be divided by Professions

6 Ethics of leisure and amusement

To be divided as 'MY'

7 Conduct towards animal

9 Special topics

91 Good and evil
911 Good
915 Evil
918 Compromise

92 Truth and falsehood
921 Truth
925 Falsehood
928 Compromise

93 Right and wrong
931 Right
935 Wrong
938 Compromise

94 Happiness and sorrow
941 Happiness
945 Sorrow
948 Compromise

96 Progress, Perfection
961 Progress
965 Perfection
968 Compromise
98 Compromise in genera

Foci in [P2]

1 Egotism. Altruism
11 Egotism
15 Altruism
3 Conscience
6 Teleology
7 Value

Other divisions to be got by (SD)

R5 Aesthetics

R6 Indian philosophy

R6 [P], [P2] [P3], [P4]

Foci in [P]

1 Hindu philosophy

2 Vaisesika. Nyaya
21 Vaisesika
25 Nyaya

3 Sankhya. Yoga
31 Sankhya
35 Yoga

4 Purva mimamsa
41 Bhatta mimamsa
45 Prabhakara mimamsa

5 Vedanta

6 Advaita
63 Pratyabhijna
634 Virasaiva

7 Visistadvaita
72 Vaisnava
73 Saivasiddhanta

8 Dvaita
89 Others
891 Bhedabheda
892 Dvaitadvaita
893 Suddhadvaita

9 Other Indian schools
91 Carvaka
93 Jaina
94 Buddhistic
941 Hinayana
942 Vaibhasika
943 Sautrantika
945 Mahayana
946 Yogacara
947 Madhyamika

Foci in [P2]

For R65 to R6893

0 Upanishad
1 Rigvedic
2 Yajurvedic
3 Samavedic
4 Atharvavedic

(*with their respective sub-divisions*)

5 Brahmasutra
6 Bhagavad Gita
7 Bhagavata
8 Mahabharata and its parts
9 Other texts

CHAPTER S

PSYCHOLOGY

S [P]: [E] [2P]

Foci in [P]

1 Child
11 New born
12 Toddler
13 Infant
15 Pre-adolescent

2 Adolescent
21 Boy
25 Girl

3 Post-adolescent
35 Middle age
38 Old age

4 Vocational

5 Sex
51 Male
55 Female
58 Eunuch

6 Abnormal
61 Genius
62 Idiot
63 Insane
64 Sick and infirm
65 Criminal
67 Deaf and dumb
68 Blind
6916 Left-handed

7 Race
To be divided by (GD)
76 Negro

8 Social
To be subdivided as [P] *of* "Y Sociology"

9 Animal (genetic)

Foci in [E] *cum* [2P]

1 Nervous reaction
To be divided as [P] 7 of "L Medicine"
21 Static sense
22 Taste
23 Hearing
24 Smell
25 Sight
255 Colour sense
27 Touch
28 Cutaneous sense
29 Other senses
291 Other organic senses
294 Location sense
296 Direction sense

3 Characters of consciousness
31 Attention
311 Apperception
315 Selection
318 Abstraction
32 Association
34 Work, fatigue
35 Habit. Accommodation, Aptation. Complacency
38 Time relation of consciousness. Mental chronometry

4 Cognition. Conception
41 Conception of idea
42 Conception of time, space and motion
43 Memory. Imagination. Remembering. Forgetting
44 Resoning. Thinking. Judgment. Belief
45 Reflection. Self-consciousness
46 Normal illusion. Normal suggestion
47 Opinion

5 Feeling. Emotion. Affection
51 Pleasantness. Unpleasantness
52 Emotion
521 Laughter
523 Joy
524 Anger
526 Fear
53 Affection. Hatred
55 Love
56 Anxiety
57 Sentiment. Interest

6 Conation. Movement
61 Dynamo-genesis. Inhibition
62 Instinct. Impulse (imitation and play)
63 Reflex action
64 Conscience
65 Volition. Effort
68 Special motor functions
682 Speech. Song
6821 Soliloquy

6822 Dialogue
6823 Debate
6825 Public speech
6828 Song
683 Walking
685 Seeing
686 Handwriting. Drawing.

7 Personality
71 Vitality
72 Intelligence
73 Ability
7395 Transfer of ability
74 Character
743 Fairmindedness
75 Temperament
76 Intuition
77 Opinion
78 Psychic powers
791 Longevity
793 Endurance
794 Immunity
795 Acclimatization
796 Drug habit

8 Metapsychology
81 Sleep
811 Dream
813 Hallucination
815 Unconscious. Subconscious
851 Hypnotism. Mesmerism
852 Suggestion
86 Psycho-therapy (alternative)

Foci in [2E] *cum* [3P]

Applicable to [E] '2' and '3'

2 Anatomy
3 Physiology
31 Reflex function
35 Automatic function
4 Pathology
5 Psycho-physics
6 Psychometry

SA Systems by (CD) (*Illustrative*)

SM Experimental
SM9 Psycho-analytic
SN Gestalt
SN1 Behaviouristic
SN14 Individualistic
SN17 Refexology
SN2 Eidetict. Typological
SN8 Field
SN36 'We'

CHAPTER T

EDUCATION

T [P]: [E], [2P], [2P2]

Foci in [P]

1	**Pre-secondary**
13	Pre-school child
15	Elementary
2	**Secondary**
25	Intermediate
3	**Adult**
31	Literate
35	Foreigner
38	Illiterate
4	**University**
42	Pass
43	Honours
45	Post-graduate
48	Research
5	**Sex**
51	Male
55	Female
6	**Abnormal**
61	Genius
62	Idiot
63	Insane
65	Criminal
67	Deaf and dumb
673	Stammerer
68	Blind
7	**Backward classes**
9	Other classes

To be divided by (SD) (*Illustrative*)

9(Y31)	Rural community
9(Y4)	Vocation
9(Y52)	Aristocracy
9(Y54)	Military class

Foci in [E] *cum* [2P]

1	**Nomenclature**
2	**Curriculum**
3	**Teaching technique**

Foci in [2P2]

1	Audio-visual
13	Audio
133	Gramophone
136	Radio
15	Visual
3	Medium of instruction
31	Mother tongue
32	Bilingualism
35	Foreign medium
38	Classical medium
4	Heuristic method
5	Catechism
7	Case study. (Observation)
8	Experiment
91	Direct method
92	Dramatisation
93	Story method
95	Pictorial method
96	Play method
97	Lecture method
98	Discussion method
4	**Student's work**

Foci in [2P2]

1	Home work
2	Library work
3	Study method
4	Field work
5	Examination work
6	Competition
7	Group work
8	Correspondence course
5	**Educational measurement**

Foci in [2P2]

1	Intelligence test

Subdivisions by the (CD) (*Illustrative*)

1N	Binet Simon
1N1	Terman
1N2	Block-design test
1N24	Form board and performance test
1N26	Drawing test
1N3	Brain test
1N31	Merrill-Palmer test
2	Achievement test
5	Examination
55	Marking
7	Interview. *Viva voce*
8	Diploma

6 **Physical education**
64 Medical inspection
65 Games
7 **Student's life**
71 Students organisation
711 International
72 Hostel
76 Leisure
8 **Management**

As in [E] of "X Economics" and in addition

892 Admission
893 Fees, scholarship
894 Research fellowship
895 Term. Holiday. Attendance
896 Time-table

Foci in [2P]

To be got by (SD) *with the following modification*

In the case of Linguistics omit the stage number and instead of the language number put the following:

1 Mother tongue
5 Foreign language
8 Classical language

TA **Systems** by (GD)
TJ Commenius. Object teaching
TL Rousseau's school
TL2 Kant's school
TL5 Pestalozzi's school
TL6 Fichte's school
TL7 Herbart's school
TL8 Froebel's kindergarten
TL9 Mann's school
TM Manual training
TN Plantoon school
TN1 Montessori school
TN3 Basic. Wardha

CHAPTER U

GEOGRAPHY

U [P]. [S]. [T]

Foci in [P]

1	**Mathematical geography**
11	Cartograpuy
111	Scale
112	Delineation of the ground
114	Measurement of distance
115	Map printing
117	Maps with a special purpose
12	Map projection
13	Relief map
14	Globe
16	Movement of earth. Season
161	Spring
162	Summer
163	Autumn
164	Winter
18	Topographical survey
181	Land survey
182	Latitude and longitude
1823	Longitude
1824	Latitude
185	Hydrographical survey
2	**Physical geography**
21	**Geomorphology**
25	**Oceanography**
251	Extension
252	Surface
253	Ocean floor
254	Oceanic deposit
255	Properties of the sea water
2552	Physical
2553	Chemical
256	Oceanic circulation
2562	Currents
27	Straubosphere (dust)
28	**Meteorology**
281	Weather
282	Atmospheric pressure
283	Wind
2831	Velocity
22835	Storm
284	Temperature
85	Humidity
2853	Cloud
2855	Rainfall
2856	Dry condition
286	Other physical and chemical phenomena
2862	Physical
28627	Magnetic
2863	Chemical
287	Climate
288	Cosmic meteorology
2891	Weather forecasting
29	Other regions
294	Stratosphere
296	Ionosphere
98	Space
23	**Biogeography**
33	Paleogeography
35	Floral
36	Faunal
37	Reaction of organism and environment
4	**Anthropogeography**
41	Race-distribution
42	Migration
421	Inland
425	Emigration
426	Immigration
45	Population
47	Reaction of man and environment (Human geogrphy)
5	**Political geography**
54	Military geography
6	**Economic geography**
641	Trade route
6415	Railway
6425	Oceanic route
6435	Air route
67	Resource (alternative)
671	Natural
672	Industrial
8	**Travel. Expedition. Voyage**

CHAPTER V

HISTORY

V [P], [P2]: [E] [2P]. [T]

Foci in [P]

To be got by (GD)

Foci in [P2]

1 Head
11 Viceroy
12 Governor

2 Executive
21 First Minister

3 Legislature
31 First house
32 Second house

4 Party
41 Party in office
45 Party in opposition
4A Specific parties by (CD)

6 Local body
61 Urban
63 Larger rural
64 Primary rural
68 *Ad Hoc* body for special function

To be divided by (SD)

7 Judiciary

8 Civil Service

91 Consembly

93 Functional body

To be divided by (SD)

Foci in [E] *cum* [2P]

1 Policy
11 Home
12 Federal
13 Constituent State
16 Local Body
17 Colonial
18 Mandatory
19 Foreign
191 Diplomacy
1914 Espionage
194 War
1941 Defence
1944 Armament
195 Peace
1954 Disarmament

2 Constitution

3 Function
33 *Laissez-faire*
35 State Control

Other subdivisions by (SD) (*Illustrative*)

3(Q) State and religion
3(T) State and education
3(X4) State and transport facility
3(X4'5) State and railway

4 Relation of the state with special classes of people
44 Refugee
45 Foreigner
47 Backward class
48 Minority

5 Relation of the state with citizen (civil right and duty)
51 Struggle for independence
511 Liberty of person
512 Liberty of family

To be subdivided as [P2] 12 *of* "Z Law"

52 Right of property
53 Freedom of contract
54 Freedom of public meeting
55 Franchise
56 Sanctity of private correspondence
57 Freedom of expression of opinion
58 Other rights

To be divided by (SD) (*Illustrative*)

58(Q) Freedom of belief and conscience
58(T) Education
58(U42) Liberty of migration and movement
58(W28) Equal eligibility for office
58(X) Freedom of trade and industry
58(Y5) Work
58(Y8) Freedom of association
58(Z) Equality before law
59 Duty

591	Loyalty. Allegiance
594	Military service
59	Other duties
6	**Source**
66	Tradition
67	Literature
68	Language
7	**Archaeology. Epigraphy, etc.**
71	Archaeology
72	Epigraphy. (Inscription)
73	Numismatics. (Seal)
74	Genealogy
75	Heraldry
76	Chronology
8	**Archives**
91	Election method
911	Nomination
912	Polling
913	Counting
914	Declaration of the result
915	Objection petition
918	Returning officer
91A	**Systems** by (CD) (*Illustrative*)
91M	Proportional representation

CHAPTER W

POLITICAL SCIENCE

W [P], [P2] : [E] [2P]

Foci in [P]

1	Anarchy
2	Primitive
3	Feudal
4	**Monarchy**
41	Absolute
46	Limited
5	Oligarchy
6	**Democracy**
61	Representative
62	Direct
64	Dictatorship
691	**Communism**
7	Utopia
8	Change of form of st
81	Revolution
87	Passive resistance (non-violence)
94	Nationality
95	World State

Foci in [P2] and [E] *cum* [2P]
Same as for " V History "

CHAPTER X

ECONOMICS

X [P]: [E] [2P]

Foci in [P]

3 Communication
31 Post
35 Telegraph
36 Telephone

4 **Transport**
41 Land
411 Road, highway
412 Vehicle drawn by muscular power
4122 Rickshaw
413 Motor vehicle
415 Railway
4151 Street
4153 Provincial
4155 International

42 Water
421 Canal
423 River
424 Lake
425 Oceanic
4251 Coastal
428 Port
4288 Dock

43 Air

5 **Commerce**

51 **By state**
511 Primitive
512 Retail
5121 Hawker
5128 Bigger retailer
518 Wholesale
5181 Seller
5182 Buyer

52 **By structure**
521 Chain-store
528 Department store

54 **By transport**
(*to be divided as* 4)

55 **By geography**
551 Inland
555 Foreign

56 **By finance**
561 Cash
562 Credit
5691 Barter

57 **By personality**
571 Private to private
573 Person to his own State
575 Person to foreign State
577 State to State

6 **Credit**

61 **Money**
611 By denomination
615 International

62 **Bank**
621 Central. Reserve
6212 Federal reserve
622 Industrial
625 Commercial
6251 Consumer
626 Mortgage
6261 Land
6266 Pawn
627 Savings bank
628 Lottery. Chit fund
6291 International settlement
6295 Foreign

64 **Money market**

65 **Investment**
651 Stock
652 Security
6521 State
6526 Municipal
6529 Industrial

7 **Public finance**
71 Budget

72 **Tax**
721 Poll
722 Property
723 Land
7232 Irrigation
724 Income
7241 Investment
7242 Government Bond
7243 Business

To be divided by business

7244 Salary
7245 Foreign income
725 Profession
726 Inheritance
7281 Capital levy
7282 Gift tax

7285 Expenditure tax

729 **Indirect tax**

Tax on article of consumption; raw material and manufacture

7291 Sale
7292 Stamp duty
7293 Licence fee
7295 Custom duty

73 State-owned property

74 Commercial and industrial undertaking

75 **Public loan**
751 State policy
752 Form
753 Sinking fund
755 Foreign loan and debt

76 **Expenditure**
79A Specials
79C Local finance
79E State finance
79F Federal finance

81 **Insurance**
811 Child
813 Life
815 Marriage
816 Maternity
818 Industrial
819 Accident
8191 Fire
8192 Unemployment
8194 Sickness
8195 Marine
8196 Bad debt. Credit
8198 Fidelity
81994 War risk

82 Promotion
83 Advertisement
88 Warehousing

8(A) **Industry**

Divisions by (SD) (*Illustrative*)

8(F182) Iron
8(F551) Coal
8(J) Agricultural economics
8(JA) Lumber
8(M13) Paper
8(M6) Glass
8(M7) Textile
8(MJ452) Cigar

Foci in [M]

For **61 Money in [P]**

1 Gold
2 Silver
4 Paper
5 Bimetallism

Foci in [E] *cum* [2P]

1 **Consumption**
16 Standard of living
17 Economic conservation
176 Saving

2 **Production**
26 Cost of production
27 Resource
271 Natural
272 Industrial
28 Management of production
294 Location

3 **Distribution**
31 Personal. National income
32 Functional
321 Consumer
322 Land. Rent
325 Trader. Commission
326 Capitalist. Interest
328 Organiser. Profit
329 Labour. Wage

3A **Systems** by (GD)
3M Socialism
3N Social credit

4 **Transport**
41 Packing
42 Collection. Distribution
44 Haulage
446 Rate, freight
45 Warehousing
46 Cost of entire transport
48 Management

5 **Trade**
51 Marketing
511 Survey
512 Canvassing
513 Advertising
515 Futures marketing
516 Competition
517 Monopoly
518 Dumping

53 **Tariff**
531 Protection
5311 Imperial preference
533 Free trade
535 Export duty
536 Import duty

54 **Export. Import**
545 Export
546 Import
55 Controlled trade
555 Import control
556 Export control

56 **Financing**

57	**Foreign exchange**
575	Balance of trade
576	Balance of payment
58	Management of commerce
6	**Financing**
7	**Value**
73	Supply and demand. *Laissez-faire*
731	Demand
732	Supply
74	Business cycle
741	Boom
742	Depression
746	Recovery measure
75	Artificial control. Planned economy
76	Price
8	**Management**
81	Top management
82	Board of management
87	Executive
89A	Production management
89C	Standards management
89K	Location
89L	Lay-out
89M	**Work study**
89M1	Motion study
89M4	Fatigue study
89M5	Rest period
89MA	Working conditions
89P	Production engineering
89Q	Production control
89Q8	Quality control
89R	Execution
89S	Inspection
89T	Material control
89TX	Salvaged material
89U	Purchase
89V	Stores
89X	Plant
	(*More concrete sector of* 89)
89ZB	Development
89ZC	Laboratory stage
89ZD	Pilot stage
89ZE	Prototype stage
8C	**Finance and accounts**
8D	**Finance**
8DB	Net-worth
8DD	General reserve
8DR	Profit
8E	Budget
8F	**Accounts**
8G	Book-keeping
8H	Accountancy
8HW	Balance sheet
8HX	Profit and loss statement
8H(Z6)	Bankruptcy account
8J	Audit
8K	**Cost accounts**
8K9J	Prime cost
8K9M	Overhead
8L	Estimating
8M	**Office management**
8M4	Correspondence
8M6	Committee work
8M8	Filing
8N	Public relation
8NV	Relation with Government
9	Personnel management (Labour problems)
	(*Least Concrete sector of* 9)
91	Job evaluation
915	Job classification
916	Job rating
92	Merit rating
93	**Wage**
931	Base rate
932	Wage differential
934	Piece rate
935	Incentive plan
936	Profit-sharing
937	Stock ownership
94	**Safety measure**
95	**Employment and service**
951	Labour source
952	Recruitment
953	Status
954	Discipline
955	Hours
956	Leave
957	Termination
958	**Social security**
9581	Pension
9582	Provident fund
9583	Workman's compensation
9585	**Social benefit**
95851	Unemployment
95854	Medical
95855	Maternity
9588	**Social insurance**
96	**Employee services**
962	Housing
967	Recreation
97	**Industrial relation**
	(*Least Concrete sector of* 97)
971	Morale maintenance
972	Collective agreement
973	Negotiation
975	Mediation
976	Arbitration
977	Adjudication

978 Settlement

(*More concrete sector of* 97)

979A Strained relation
979B Grievance
979C Dispute
979D Strike
979W Lock-out

(*Still more concrete sector of* 97)

97B Employee

97D Trade union
97K National trade union
97M International trade union
97W Employer union

991 Labour market
9911 Under-employment
9912 Over-employment
9915 Full employment

(*More Concrete sector of* 9)

99A Grades

99B Manual (wage-earning)
99C Unskilled
99D Semi-skilled
99G Supervisory (Foreman)

99N Intellectual (salaried)
99P Clerical
99R Creative (research)
99T Technical
99V Administrative
99W Policy-making

(*Still more concrete sector of* 9)

9A Type of labour
9B Child

9F Female
9F5 Married
9F6 Pregnant
9F7 With children

9G By time
9G4 Part-timed
9G5 Seasonal

9H By area
9H1 Rural
9H5 City

9J By origin
9J2 Migrant
9J4 Refugee
9J5 Emigrant
9J6 Immigrant
9K5 Alien

9N Non-paid
9N2 Slave
9N3 Apprentice
9N4 Forced
9N5 Compulsory
9P Abnormal
9P4 Disabled
9P8 Blind
9Q Prisoner

For **" 62 Bank " in [P]**

1 Lending
11 Rate of interest
2 Reserve
3 Discount
5 Cheque

The rest as in General

For **" 72 Taxation " in [P]**

1 Incidence
11 Equal taxation
12 Proportional taxation
124 Specific
127 *Ad valorem*
13 Progressive taxation

2 Exemption

3 Distribution
32 Double taxation

5 Effect

X9A Specials
X9B Small scale
X9D Large scale
X9S Private enterprise
X9V Public utility
X9W Public enterprise

XA Systems by (CD)

(*Illustrative*)

XB War economics
XM Co-operative
XM2 Socialism
XN1 Syndicalism
XN Communism
XN19 Technocracy

CHAPTER Y

SOCIOLOGY

Y [P]: [E] [2P]: [2E] [3P]

Foci in [P]

1 **By age and sex**
11 Child
To be subdivided as in "S Psychology"
12 Youth
13 Old person
15 Woman
16 Man

2 **Family**
To be subdivided as in "R4 Ethics"

3 **By residence**
31 Rural
33 Urban
35 City
38 Nation
394 Refugee
396 Mountain

4 **By occupation**
41 Profession
45 Commerce
46 Leisured
48 Leader
49 Working class
491 Serf
492 Slave

5 **By birth or status**
51 Royalty
52 Aristocracy
53 Middle class
54 Military class
55 Alien
57 Slum
58 Minority
591 By title of distinction
592 By caste
5922 Twice-born, *Dvija*
5923 Brahman
5324 Kshatriya
5925 Vaisya
5926 Sudra
5927 Harijan
594 Hybrid

6 **Abnormal and defective**
To be subdivided as in "S Psychology"

7 **Race as a social group**
71 **Prehistoric**
7114 Tertiary
7115 Quaternary
714 Stone age
7142 Eolithic
7143 Paleolithic
7144 Mesolithic
7145 Neolithic
718 Metal age
7183 Copper and bronze
7188 Iron
7196 Lost race
71961 Gandvan
71963 Lemurian
71965 Atlantic race

72 **Primitive**

73 **Ethnological division**
738 Gypsy
Other divisions by (SD) (*Illustrative*)

73(MY6) Nomadic

73(P1) Aryan
73(P11) Teutonic
73(P114) Nordic
73(P128) Celtic
73(P14) Slav
73(P15) Indian
73(2) Semitic
73(P25) Hebraic
73(P28) Arabic
73(P3) Dravidian
73(P41) Mongolian
73(Q2) Hindu
73(Q5) Jewish
73(Q7) Muslim

74 to 79 **Territorial division**
To be got by (GD)

8 **By association**
81 Secret society
82 Freemason
83 Friendly society
84 Monastery
85 Nunnery

9 **Others**
To be subdivided by (SD)

Foci in [E] *cum* [2P]

1 **Civilisation. Culture**

2 **Physical character and feature**

21 Weight

22 **Measurement**

221 Linear

222 Area

223 Volume

23 **Proportion**

24 **Abnormality**

241 Size

2411 Dwarf

2412 Giant

242 Shape

243 Position

244 Fixation

245 Number

246 Total absence

247 Lateral interchange

25 **Colour**

27 **Functioning**

2922 Taste

2924 Smell

2927 Touch

293 Strength

294 Temperature

3 **Activity**

To be divided as [P] *of* " R4 Ethics " *with the following modification*

34 **Ceremonial**

341 Childhood

3411 Naming

342 Adolescence

343 Adulthood

344 Old age

345 Funeral

346 Anniversary

348 Inauguration

To be subdivided by (SD) (*Illustrative*)

348(D) Building

348(U8) Travel

348(W,21) Coronation

Other ceremonials by (SD)

35 ' As if ' activity

351 Folklore

354 Superstition

356 Custom

Each division of 35 *to be subdivided as* [P2] *of* △ *and by* (SD)

36 Festival

37 Opinion

38 **Symbolism**

381 Material. Totem. Flag

382 Idea

383 Sound

384 Graphic

386 Gesture

388 Script

Each division of 38 *to be subdivided as* [P2] *of* △ *and by* (SD)

Other Activities or Attitudes
To be got by (SD)

4 **Social pathology**

41 **Intemperance**

411 Alcoholism

412 Tobacco habit

413 Opium habit

414 Other drug habits

42 **Degeneration**

421 Physical

423 Mental

425 Moral

426 Spiritual

43 **Destitution**

431 Widowhood

432 Orphanhood

433 Unemployment

434 Poverty

435 Disaster

4351 Fire

4353 Famine

4354 Pestilence

4355 Flood

436 Earthquake

437 Accident

438 War

44 **Social evil**

45 **Crime**

To be subdivided as in " Z Law "

46 Short life

48 Disunion

484 Espionage

49 Other ills

492 Slavery

495 Refugee

Further divisions by (SD)

5 **Demography**

51 Under-population

52 Over-population

55 Sex-proportion

56 Age-proportion

58 Distribution

581 Sparseness

585 Concentration

7	**Personality**
	To be divided as in "S Psychology"
8	**Equipment**
81	**Habitat**
	To be divided as [P3] "NA Architecture"
82	**Utensil**
823	Cooking
825	Drinking
828	Storing
83	**Implement**
831	Fire
	Other divisions by (SD) (*Illustrative*)
83(C4)	Hearing device
83(C5)	Light. Lamp
83(J)	Agricultural implement
83(M7)	Textile implement
83(P18)	Writing implement
84	**Transport—track**
	To be divided as 4 *of* [P] *of* "D Engineering"
85	**Transport—vehicle**
	To be divided as 5 *of* [P] *of* "D Engineering"
86	**Ornament**
	To be divided as 1 *of* [P] *of* "L Medicine" (*Illustrative*)
8631	Toe ring
8633	Anklet
8637	Waist cord
8666	Bangle
8668	Ring
867	Necklace
8683	Ear ring
8684	Nose ring
	Crown. Head ornament
8688	Ornament for hair
8697	Tattooing
87	Furniture
872	Fittings
88	**Apparel**
91	**Nomenclature etc.**
	To be divided as in "G Natural Science"

Foci in [2E] *cum* [3P]

For **1, 3, 7, 8** *of* [E]

1	**Nomenclature, etc.**
	To be divided as in "G Natural Science"
5	Influence. Contact
6	Genetic or comparative study
62	Variation. Natural selection
65	Hybridisation (cultural)
7	**Conservation. Improvement.**
75	Ecological method
76	Phylogenetic method
77	Ontogenetic method

For **4** *of* [E]

1	Nomenclature, etc.
2	Etiology
3	Diagnosis
4	Experimentation
5	Prevention

Subdivisions by (SD) (*Illustrative*)

5(G)	Eugenical
5(Q)	Religious
5(T)	Educational
5(U)	Congregational
5(X)	Occupational
5(Y)	Family system
5(Z)	Legislative
6	Treatment
61	Detection. Police
62	Prison
63	Banishment
64	Extermination
65	Asylum. Correction
66	Work house
67	Relief work
68	Charity
69	Other methods
691	Corporeal punishment

For **5** *of* [E] *same as for* **4** *of* [E] *with suitable modifications in Terminology*

CHAPTER Z

LAW

Z [P], [P2], [P3], [P4]

Foci in [P]
To be got by (GD) *and by* (SD).

Foci in [P2]

1	**Legal person**
11	**By age and sex**
111	Minor
113	Adult
115	Female
1151	Unmarried
1152	Married
1153	Pardanahin
1154	Widow
12	**By fiduciary relation**
122	Marriage
1221	Husband and wife
1227	Divorce
1228	Concubinage
123	Parent and child
1234	Child by mixed marriage
1235	Adopted child
1238	Illegitimate child
128	Guardian and ward
13	**By residence**
131	National
134	Without nationality
135	Alien
1351	Domiciled
1354	Refugee
14	**By occupation**
141	Serf
142	Slave
145	Diplomatic staff
1451	International staff
148	Public servant
15	**By status**
151	Royalty
152	Minister
153	Legislator
155	Pope
16	**Abnormal**
162	Illiterate
163	Lunatic
164	Drunkard
165	Criminal
166	Bankrupt
167	Deaf and dumb
168	Blind
17	**State**
171	Sovereign
1712	Federal
1713	Constituent
1717	Colony
1718	Mandatory. Trustee
172	Tribal
173	Neutral
1734	Armed neutral
175	Alien
1751	Allied
1755	Enemy
18	**Association**
181	Corporate
1815	Foreign
182	Unincorporate
1823	Friendly Society
18231	Club
1826	Charitable institution
1827	Learned Body
1828	Business Body
186	Local Body
187	Other Statutory Body
191	Idol
192	Mutt. Temple. Mosque. Church
193	Police
194	Armed force
1941	Army
1945	Navy
1948	Air
197	Benami
2	**Property**
21	**Immovable. Territory**
211	Land
2113	Mine. Mineral
215	Sea
2153	Territorial waters
2157	River. Lake
21573	Of common interest
2158	Harbour
218	Air
24	Treasure trove
25	**Servitude**
251	Support
252	Boundary. Fence
253	Produce. Profits *a prendre*
254	Right of way

255 Water
256 Fishery
258 Air and light
2591 Prospective

26 Movable
264 Arms
265 Ship
2654 Salvage

267 Immaterial
2671 Goodwill
26712 Business location
26717 Name
26718 Business name
2673 Design. Patent
2674 Copyright
2675 Trade mark
2676 Trade name
2677 Chose in action

27 Licence

28 Exterritoriality
281 Diplomatic office
2811 Residence of diplomatic agent
282 Pope's residence
284 Army quarter

292 Joint family property
293 Impartible property
293 Neutral property
294 Cantonment
2991 Lost property

3 Contract. Treaty

31 Contract creating relation
311 Master and servant
312 Business contract
313 Agency
314 Power of attorney
315 Partnership
318 Auction agent

32 Contract relating to property
321 Indemnity
3213 Surety
322 Gift
323 Exchange
324 Trust

33 Contract relating to immovable property
331 Mortgage
333 Lease
335 Sale

34 Contract relating to movable property
341 Pledge
342 Bailment
343 Hire purchase
345 Sale
346 Debtor and creditor
35 Third party contract
36 Quasi contract
37 Extradition

4 Tort
41 to 47 on the analogy of 51 to 57
472 Libel
494 Custody of dangerous animal and thing
496 Quasi-tort

5 Crime

51 Against person
511 Homicide
5111 Suicide
5112 Murder
51121 Infanticide
5113 Man-slaughter

512 Hurt, etc.
5121 Hurt
5122 Assault
5123 Battery
5124 False imprisonment
5125 Abduction (Kidnapping)
51262 Slavery
51263 Forced labour

5141 Intimidation
5142 Annoyance

515 Against woman
5151 Rape
5152 Offending modesty
5153 Procuring abortion

517 Against marital status

52 Against property
5211 Arson
5212 Mischief
5215 Extortion
5221 Dacoity
5222 Robbery
5223 Theft
5224 Receiving stolen property

5231 Cheating
5232 Misappropriation
5238 Breach of trust

524 Trespass
5242 House-breaking

527 Against immaterial property
5275 Against trade mark
5277 Forgery
52774 Using forged document

53 Breach of contract
54 Negligence and rashness

545	**Contributory negligence**
548	**Breach of duty**
55	Public nuisance
555	Fraud
557	Malicious prosecution
57	Against reputation
571	Slander
572	Libel
58	Against public peace
582	Unlawful assembly
582	Rioting
583	Affray
595	Piracy
5Q	Against religion
5W	Against state
5W1	Against king
5W2	Against minister
5W3	Against member of legislature
5W4	Waging war against state
5W5	Adhering to enemy of the state
5W6	Betrayal of state secret
5W7	Promoting class hatred
5W8	Against public servant
5W84	Against army, etc.
5X	Relating to weights and measures
5X61	Relating to coin and government stamp
5Z	Against public justice
5Z7	Against regulative law
5ZA	War crime

The following may be added to any Isolate under **5**

04	Abetment
6	**Conflict of laws**
	All the divisions of **Z** *based on* **[P2]** *and in addition the following*
66	Choice of law
7	**Cause of action**
71	Civil action
75	Criminal proceedings
751	Summary trial
753	Summons case
754	Warrant case
755	Sessions case
8	**Court**
81	Supreme Court
83	High Court
831	Appellate Side (Chancery)
832	Original Side (King's Bench)
834	Admiralty
835	Divorce
836	Probate
84	Subordinate Court
85	Sessions Court
86	Quasi Court
87	Arbitration Tribunal
898	Itinerant Court
91	**Jurisprudence**
916	Legal maxim
92	**Source**
921	Sacred
922	Custom
923	Convention
924	Equity
925	Case-law
926	Fiction in law
927	Common law
928	Enactment
9281	Amendment
9287	Codification
9298	Administrative law
93	**Interpretation**
94	**Evidence**
941	By source
9411	Direct
9412	Circumstantial
9414	Hearsay
9415	Confession
9944	By channel
9441	Oral
9448	Documentary
947	By validity
9471	Primary
9472	Secondary
9491	Nisi Prius
95	**Remedy and sanction**
9511	Death
9512	Penal servitude, transportation
9513	Imprisonment
9514	Whipping
9521	Confiscation
9522	Fine
9531	Preventive detention
9532	Recognizance
9533	Police inspection
9534	Probation
9541	Borstal treatment
9542	Detention in inebriate retreat
9591	Restitution
9592	Damages
9593	Administration of estate
9594	Injunction
9595	Specific performance
9596	Control of document

9597 Declaratory order
9598 Writs
95981 Mandamus
95982 Certiorari
95983 Habeas corpus
95984 Prohibition
95993 Maintenance

97 Regulative law
To be subdivided by (SD)
(*To be used for cross reference only*)

98 Document
981 Deed
985 Negotiable instrument

A War

B Land

C Naval

D Air

All the earlier divisions of [P2] *are applicable after* **A, B, C** *and* **D**

Foci in **[P3]**

For **1 Legal Person** *in* [P2]

1 Capacity. Jurisdiction
15 *Ultra vires*
16 Right of legation
Other divisions by (SD)
5 Alienation
6 Succession

For **2 Property** *in* [P2]

1 Ownership
14 Limited
145 Woman's Estate
1456 Stridhana
16 Perpetuities
195 Pre-emption
2 Possession

3 Landlord and tenant

4 Disposition other than by contract
41 Will. Cession
414 Trusts
4145 Public
42 Gift
43 Exchange
44 Conquest
45 Acquisition by State
46 Compulsory sale. Annexation. Seizure
47 Occupation
48 Discovery
493 Covenant running with the property
494 Fraudulent transfer

6 Succession
61 Intestate
63 Testamentary
64 Perpetuity
68 Executor
691 Primogeniture

93 Boundary
931 Natural
933 Coast
936 Mountain
937 River
938 Lake
9391 Artificial

For **3 Contract** in [P2]

1 Capacity
11 to 197 *as in* [P2]
198 Executor

2 Form

21 Oral
211 Executory

213 Implied
214 By conduct
216 By custom
217 By law

28 **Deed**

3 **Formation**
31 Offer
37 Acceptance. Ratification
38 Consideration

4 **Illegal**
41 Statutory
414 Stock exchange
415 Insurer
416 Money lender
417 Waging
418 Lottery
42 Restraint of marriage
43 Champerty and maintenance
44 Immoral
45 Criminal
46 Restraint of trade
48 Against public policy

5 **Voidable**
51 Fraud
52 Misrepresentation
53 Condition and warranty

54 **Uberimae fideli**
541 Insurance
542 Sale of land
543 Surety
545 Partnership
548 Company
55 Duress

6 **Frustration**
61 Vis major

7 **Discharge**
71 Performance
72 Payment
73 Accord and satisfaction
74 Release
75 Alteration
76 Death
77 Belligerency
[illegible] Limitation
794 Set-off
795 Breach
797 Judgment

8 **Remedy**
83 Specific performance
84 Rectification
85 Injunction
87 Recision
91 Assignment

For **7 Cause of Action** in [P2]

1 **Procedure**
11 Civil
15 Criminal
16 Arbitration

2 **Jurisdiction**
21 Forum
22 Res judicata. Autrefois acquit. Autrefois convict
26 Limitation
27 Jurisdiction award

3 **Institution**

4 **Preliminary**
41 Pleadings
4113 Process
4115 Communication to accused
412 Written statement. Plea
413 Discovery
414 Preliminary disposal
414 Production of document
417 Issue. Charge. Discharge
419 Inter-locutory proceeding
4191 Affidavit
4194 Commission for evidence
4196 Interim relief
4198 Receiver

5 **Trial**
51 Burden of proof
52 Deposition
521 Oath
524 Cross examination
525 Re-examination
54 Compromise

55 **For sessions case**
551 Committal proceedings
5514 List of defence witnesses
5515 Committal
552 Sessions trial
553 Appointment juror
554 Reading of committal evidence
555 Inspection of place of offence
557 Verdict of jury

7 **Judgment and decree**
71 Contested
72 Consent
73 Ex parte
75 Award
78 Declaratory
795 Foreign

Foci in [P3]

For **8 Court** of [P2]

1 **Bench**
11 Judge

15 Jury
17 Assessor
2 Master
4 Clerk of the Crown
5 Bar
51 Attorney-General
53 Advocate
54 Solicitor
8 Executive
81 Registrar
82 Sheriff
84 Bailiff
85 Coroner
87 Commission
88 Receiver

For **94 Evidence** in [P2]

3 Admissibility
4 Estoppel
5 Relevancy
7 Weight

For **A, B, C, D, War** *in* [P2]

1 Declaration of war
193 Notification to neutral state
2 Martial law
3 Belligerent measures. Warfare
31 Invasion
32 Stratagem
33 Siege. Blockade
34 Espionage
35 Prohibited weapons, methods and actions
4 Wounded and sick
5 Intercourse of belligerents
51 Truce
52 Capitulation
53 Cartel
54 Safe conduct
6 Prisoners of war
8 Cessation of hostility

Foci in [P4]

For **7 Judgment and decree in** [P3]

2 Partition
3 Specific performance
34 Restitution
5 Injunction
51 By nature
56 By duration
564 Temporary
566 Perpetual

Foci in [E] *cum* [2P]

For **98 Document** in [P2]

1 Drafting
12 Precedents
2 Execution
3 Registration
4 Rectification
5 Cancellation

INDEX TO SCHEDULES

HOW TO USE THE INDEX

This is an alphabetical index to the fundamental constituent terms in the Schedules of Classification contained in this Part but not to the derived composite terms (vide *Prolegomena to library classification*)

The number given against an entry requires some explanation. The first letter or digit represents a Common Isolate if it is a lower case and a Main Class if it is a numeral or a capital letter. If the number begins with a capital letter followed by a numeral, it is the number of a Canonical Class.

The following key to the contractions will be of use:—

(ACI)	=	Anteriorising Common Isolate
(BN)	=	Book Number
(LD)	=	Language Division
(PCEI)	=	Posteriorising Common Energy Isolate
(PCPI. Asf)	=	Posteriorising Common Personality Isolate after Space Facet
(PCI. Atf)	=	Posteriorising Common Isolate after Time Facet
[E]	=	Energy Facet
[2E]	=	Second Round Energy Facet
[M]	=	Matter Facet
[M2]	=	Second Level Matter Facet
[2M]	=	Second Round Matter Facet
[P]	=	Personality Facet
[P2]	=	Second Level Personality Facet
[P3]	=	Third Level Personality Facet
[2P]	=	Second Round Personality Facet
[S]	=	Space Facet
[T]	=	Time Facet

The following interpretation of the index number is illustrative:—

1.	Abdomen G [P], K [P2], L [P], 14	=	"Abdomen" has the Isolate Number 14 in the Personality Facet of G Biology, Second Level Personality Facet of K Zoology, and Personality Facet of L Medicine.
2.	Abduction Y [E], 45125. Z [P2], 5125	=	"Abduction" has the Isolate Number 45125 in the Energy Facet of Y Sociology. It has also the Isolate Number 5125 in the Second Level Personality Facet of Z Law.
3.	Abelian equation B23 [P], 9M	=	"Abelian equation" has the Isolate Number 9M in the Personality Facet of B23 Algebraic equation.
4.	Abelian function B392M	=	"B392M" is the number for Abelian function.

INDEX TO SCHEDULES

5. Abnormal S, T [P], 6. X [E], 9P. Z [P2], 16 = " Abnormal " has the Isolate Number 6 in the Personality Facet of S Psychology and T Education. It has also the Isolate Number 9P in the Energy Facet of X Economics, and 16 in the Second Level Personality Facet of Z Law.

6. Abnormal structure L [E], 4 [2P], 71. Y [E], 24 = " Abnormal structure " has the Isolate Number 71 in the Second Round Personality Facet for Isolate Number 4 of the Energy Facet of L Medicine. It also has the Isolate Number 24 in the Energy Facet of Y Sociology.

7. Acromegaly L66: 472 = " Acromegaly " has the Class Number L66: 472.

8. Administrative institution (PCPI. Asf), *w* = *w* is the Isolate Number for " Administrative institution." It should be applied after the Space Facet as a Posteriorising Common Personality Isolate.

9. Administrative report (ACI. Asf), *r* = *r* is the Isolate Number for " Administrative report." It should be applied after Space Facet as an Anteriorising Common Isolate.

10. Advertisement X [P], 83; [E], 513 = " Advertisement " has the Isolate Number 83 in the Personality Facet of X Economics. It has also the Isolate Number 513 in its Energy Facet.

11. Afghan (LD), 165 = " Afghan language " has the Isolate Number 165.

12. Agriculture J = " Agriculture " has the Main Class Number J.

In general, [2P] should be taken as understood after [E] wherever it occurs.

COLON CLASSIFICATION

BY

S R RANGANATHAN

PART 3

SCHEDULES OF CLASSICS AND SACRED BOOKS WITH SPECIAL NAMES

SARADA RANGANATHAN ENDOWMENT
FOR LIBRARY SCIENCE
Bangalore 560 078

Shiyali Ramamrita **RANGANATHAN** (1892)

First Edition 1933
Second Edition 1939
Third Edition 1950
Fourth Edition 1952
Fifth Edition 1957
Sixth Edition 1960
Reprinted 1963
(with amendments)
Reprinted 1964
Reprinted 1969

2:51N3
*q*N57·3

The Author is indebted to Mahāmahopadhyāya Professor **S. Kuppuswami Sastriar** (1880-1943) for help in constructing this Schedule

L MEDICINE

LA Systems of Medicine

LB Ayurveda System

Divisions by the Classic Device (*Illustrative*)

LBx1,1	*Caraka-saṁhitā*
LBx1,1,1	Patañjali's commentary
LBx1,1,2	Cakra-pāṇi-datta: *Caraka-tāṭparya-dīpikā* or *Āyur-veda-dīpikā*
LBx1,1,3	Hari-candra's commentary
LBx1,1,4	Siva-dāsa: *Caraka-tattva-pradīpikā*
LBx1,1,5	Gaṅgā-dhara: *Jalpa-kalpa-taru*
LBx2,1	Vāg-bhaṭa I: *Aṣṭāṅga-saṅgraha*
LBx2,1,1	Aruṇa-datta's commentary
LBx3,1	Vāg-bhaṭa II: *Aṣṭāṅga-hṛdaya*
LBx3,1,1	Aruṇa-datta: *Sarvāṅga-sundara*
LBx3,1,2	Hemādri or Kāma-deva: *Āyur-veda-darśana*
LBx3,1,3	Āśādhara-sallakṣaṇa: *Aṣṭāṅga-hṛda-yoddyota*
LBx3,1,4	Candra-candana: *Padārtha-candrikā*
LBx3,1,5	Dāmodara: *Saṅketa-mañjarī*
LBx3,1,6	Rāma-nātha Vaidya: *Aṣṭāṅga-hṛdaya-ṭīkā*
LBx3,1,7	*Bāla-prabodhikā*
LBx3,1,8	*Hṛdaya-bodhikā*
LBx3,1,M80	Hari-kṛṣṇa Mullick: *Vāg-bhaṭārtha-kaumudi*
LBx3,1,M90	Yaśodānandan Sarkār: *Pradīpa*
LBx4,1	Bhela: *Bhela-samhitā*
LBx5,1	Sārṅga-dhara: *Śārṅgadhara-samhitā*
LBx5,1,1	Ādha-malla: *Śārṅgadhara-dīpikā*
LBx6,1	Bhāva Mirśa: *Bhāva-prakāśā*
LBx7,1	*Nava-nāvanitakam*
LBx8,1	Yogānanda-nātha: *Āyur-ve..a-sūtra*
LBxD40,1	Nāgārjuna: *Rasa-vaiśeṣik ..tra*
LBxM13,1	Parameśvara: *Hṛdaya-priya*

LB:4 Disease

LB:4x1,1	Mādhava-kara: *Mādhava-nidāna*

LB:4:6 Therapeutics

LB:4:6x1,1	Cakra-pāṇi-datta: *Cikitsā-sāra-saṁhitā*

LB:4:7 Surgery

LB:4:7x2,1	*Suśruta-saṁhitā*
LB:4:7x2,1,1	Cakra-pāṇi-datta: *Bhānu-matī*
LB:4:7x2,1,2	Gayādāsa: *Nyāya-candrikā* or *pañjikā*
LB:4:7x2,1,3	Jejjaṭācārya's commentary
LB:4:7x2,1,4	Bhāskara's commentary
LB:4:7x2,1,5	Mādhava's commentary
LB:4:7x2,1,6	Brahma deva's commentary
LB:4:7x2,1,7	Dallaṇācārya: *Nibandha-saṅgraha*
LB:4:7x2,1,8	Ubhalta's commentary
LB:4:7x3,1	*Bhoja-tantra* or *Bhoja-samhitā*

LB:4:91 After-Care

LB:4:91x1,1	*Jīvaka-tantra*
LB:4:91x2,1	*Parvataka-tantra*
LB:4:91x3,1	*Bandhaka-tantra*
LB:4:91x4,1	*Hiraṇyākaṣva-tantra*
LB:4:91xM90,1	Rama-varier: *Arogya-kalpa-druma*

LB:4:441 Snake-Poison

LB:441:6x1,1	*Kāśyapa-samhitā*

LB:6 Pharmacognosy

LB:6x2,1	*Kāka-caṇdīsvara-tantra*
LB:65x1,1	*Muktāvali*
LB:67x1,1	Cakra-pāṇi-datta: *Cakra-datta* or *Dravya-guṇa-saṅgraha*
LB:68x1,1	Vāg-bhaṭa (son of Siṃha Gupta); *Rasa-ratna-samuccaya*
LB:68x2,1	*Rasādhyāya*

△SPIRITUAL EXPERIENCE AND MYSTICISM

△2 Hindu

△2x4 Yōga Upaniṣads

△2x5,11 *Avadhūta-gītā*

△22 Hatha-Yoga

△22x3,1 *Gheraṇḍa-saṁhitā*

△22x4,1 Svātmārāmā-svāmin: *Haṭha-yōga-pradīpikā*

△25 Bhakti-Yoga

△25x1,1 Nārada: *Bhakti-sūtra*

△25x2,1 Sāṇḍilya

△25xD60,1 Paṭṭinattu Pillai

△25xD65,1 Pattiragiriyār

△25xK00,1 Tāyumānavar

△25xM23,1 Rāmalingaswāmi-gal

△26 Raja-Yoga

△26x4 Rāja-yoga Upani-ṣads

△26x4,11 *Maṇḍala-Brāhma-ṇopaniṣad*

△28 Siddhars of South India

△28x12 Rāma-devar

△28x13 Kumba-muni

△28x14 Iḍaikkāḍar

△28x15 Dhanvantiri

△28x16 Vālmīki

△28x17 Kamala-muni

△28x18 Bhoga-nāthar

△28x21 Macca-muni

△28x22 Koṇkaṇār

△28x23 Patañjali

△28x24 Nandi-deva

△28x25 Bodha-guru

△28x26 Pāmbātti

△28x27 Cattai-muni

△28x28 Sundarānanda-devar

△28x31 Kuḍumbai Sittar

△28x32 Gorakkar

△28x33 Ahappey Sittar

△28x41 Sattiya-nāthar

△28x42 Saṭoka-nāthar

△28x43 Ādi-nāthar

△28x44 Anādi-nāthar

△28x45 Vahuli-nāthar

△28x46 Mataṅga-nāthar

△28x47 Maccendra-nāthar

△28x48 Kaṭendra-nāthar

△3 Jain

△3xD50,1 Yōgīndu-dēva: *Paramātma-prakāśa*

△4 Buddhistic

△41 Hina-Yana

△41:3x1,1 Yōgāvacāra: *Manual*

△42 Maha-Yana

△42:3x2,1 Dharmēndra: *Yōgāvatārōpadeśa*

△42:87x1,1 *Tathāgata-guhyaka* or *Guhya-samāja*

△42:87x2,1 *Pañca-krama*

△42:87x4,1 *Mañjusrīmūla-kalpa*

△42:87x5,1 *Caṇḍa-mahāroṣana-tantra*

△42:87x6,1 *Śri-cakra-sambhāra-tantra*

△42:87x7,1 Indra-bhūti: *Jñāna-siddhi*

△42:87x8,1 *Sādhana-mālā*

△42:87x91,1 *Tisavastik*

△42:87x92,1 *Dākārṇava*

△47 Maha-Vairocana

△47x1,1 *Mahā-vairōcana-sūtra*

△5 Judaic

△5:8x1,1 *Zohar*

△73 Sufi

△73xD40,1 Abu Bakr-al-Kala-badhi

△73xE58,1 Al-Ghazzali

△73xG07,1 Jalal-ud-din Muhammad Rumi

△73xI14,1 Nūruddin-Abdur-Rahman Jami

△841 Chinese

△841xD77,1 *Secret of golden Jower*

△8513 Neo-Platonic

△8513x1,1 Hermes: *Hermetica*

△8513xD20,1 Plotinus

△8513xI60,1 Ebreo (Leone)

N FINE ARTS

NA Architecture

NA44x1,1	*Mānasāra*

NR Music

NR44x1,1	Sārṅgadeva: *Saṅgīta-ratnākara*
NR44x2,1	Dattila-muni: *Dattila*
NR44x3,1	Mātaṅga-muni: *Bṛhad-deśi*
NR44x4,1	Pārśava-deva: *Saṅgīta-samaya-sāra*
NR44x5,1	Nārada: *Saṅgīta-makaranda*
NR44xJ20,1	Rāmā-mātya: *Svara-mela-kalā-nidhi*
NR44xK12,1	Ahobala: *Saṅgīta-pārijāta*
NR44,Kx6,1	Venkaṭā-makhin: *Catur-daṇḍi-prakāśikā*
NR441,Kx09,1	Soma-nātha: *Rāgā-vibodha*

NS Dance

NS44x1,1	Nandikeśvara: *Abhinayā-darpaṇa*

O LITERATURE

O111,2J64:*g*(*w*) Shakespeare Controversy

O111,2J64:*g*(*w*1)	Bacon—Shakespeare
O111,2J64:*g*(*w*2)	Rutland—Shakespeare
O111,2J64:*g*(*w*3)	Derby—Shakespeare
O111,2J64:*g*(*w*4)	Oxford—Shakespeare

O13,1:*g* Greek Literary Criticism

O13,1:*gx*1,1	Aristotle: *Poetics*

O15:*g* Sanskrit Literary Criticism (Alamkara)

O15:*gx*1,1	**Bharata:** *Nāṭya-śāstra*
O15:*gx*1,1,3	Abhinava-gupta: *Abhinava-bhāratī* or *Nāṭya-veda-vivṛti*
O15:*gx*2,1	**Bhamaha:** *Bhāmahālaṅkāra* or *Kāvyālaṅkāra*
O15:*gx*3,1	**Dandin:** *Kāvyā-darśa*
O15:*gx*3,1,1	Taruṇā-vācaspati: *Kāvyā-darśa-ṭīkā*
O15:*gx*3,1,2	*Hṛdayaṅ-gama*
O15:*gx*3,1,3	Vādi-jaṅghāla: *Śrutānupālinī*
O15:*gx*3,1,4	Hari-nātha Mahopādhyāya: *Mārjana*
O15:*gx*3,1,8	Jīvānanda-vidyā-sāgara Bhaṭṭācārya: *Kāvyā-darśa-ṭīkā*
O15:*gx*4,1	**Udbhata:** *Kāvyālaṅkāra-sāra-saṃgraha*
O15:*gx*4,1,1	Pratīhārendu-rāja: *Laghu-vṛtti*
O15:*gx*4,1,3	Rājānaka Tilaka: *Vivṛti*
O15:*gx*5,1	**Vamana:** *Kāvyālaṅkāra sūtra-vṛtti*
O15:*gx*5,2	Gopendra Tippa Bhūpāla: *Kāmadhenu*
O15:*gx*6,1	**Rudrata:** *Rudraṭālaṅkāra*
O15:*gx*6,1,2	Nami Sādhu: *Rudraṭālaṅkāra-ṭippaṇa*
O15:*gx*6,1,5	Āśādhara's commentary
O15:*gx*7,1	**Ananda-vardhana:** *Dhvanyāloka*
O15:*gx*7,1,3	Abhinava-gupta: *Kāvyāloka-locana*
O15:*gx*7,1,3,1	Parameśvarācārya: *Locana-vyākhyā-kaumudī*
O15:*gx*7,1,3,2	S. Kuppu-svāmi Śāstri: *Upa-locana*
O15:*gx*8,1	**Mammata:** *Kāvya-prakāśa*

O15:*gx*8,1,1	Ruyyaka: *Saṅketa*
O15:*gx*8,1,2	Māṇikya-candra: *Saṅketa*
O15:*gx*8,1,3	Bhaṭṭa-gopāla: *Sāhitya-cūḍāmaṇi*
O15:*gx*8,1,4	Ratneśvara's commentary
O15:*gx*8,1,5	Viśva-nātha: *Darpaṇa*
O15:*gx*8,1,6	Vidyā-cakravartin: *Bṛhat-ṭīkā* or *Sampradāya-prakāśinī*
O15:*gx*8,1,7	Govinda Thakkūra: *Pradīpa*
O15:*gx*8,1,7,1	Vaidya-nātha: *Pradīpa-prabhā*
O15:*gx*8,1,7,2	Nāgoji Bhaṭṭa: *Pradīpoddyota*
O15:*gx*8,1,8	Vāmanācārya's commentary
O15:*gx*D85,1	Rudra Bhaṭṭa: *Śṛṅgāra-tilaka*
O15:*gx*D90,1	Ajita-senācārya: *Alaṅkāra-cintāmaṇi*
O15:*gx*D91,1	**Raja-sekhara:** *Kāvya-mīmāṁsā*
O15:*gx*D92,1	Mukula Bhaṭṭa: *Abhidhāvṛtti-mātṛkā*
O15:*gx*E25,1	**Ksemendra:** *Aucitya-vicāra-carcā*
O15:*gx*E50,1	Kuntala: *Vakrokti-jīvita*
O15:*gx*E51,1	**Mahima-bhatta:** *Vyakti-viveka*
O15:*gx*E51,1,1	*Vyakti-viveka-vyākhyā*
O15:*gx*E55,1	**Bhoja:** *Sarasvatī-kaṇṭhābharaṇa*
O15:*gx*E55,1,1	Ratneśvara: *Ratna-darpaṇa*
O15:*gx*E55,1,2	Jagadhara: *Ṭīkā*
O15:*gx*E55,2	Bhoja: *Śṛṅgāra-prākāśa*
O15:*gx*E60,1	Mammaṭa: *Śabda-vyāpāra vicāra*
O15:*gx*E89,1	**Hema-candra:** *Kāvyānuśāsana*
O15:*gx*F20,1	**Ruyyaka:** *Alaṅkāra-sarvasva*
O15:*gx*F20,1,1	Jaya-ratha: *Alaṅkāra-sarvasva-vimarśinī*
O15:*gx*F20,1,2	Samudra-bandha: *Alaṅkāra-sarvasva-vyākhyā*
O15:*gx*F20,1,3	Vidyā-cakravartin: *Sañjīvinī*
O15:*gx*F20,1,4	Maṅkhuka: *Alaṅkāra-sūtra-vṛtti*
O15:*gx*F20,2	Ruyyaka: *Sāhitya-mīmāṁsā*
O15:*gx*F25,1	**Vag-bhata I:** *Vāghbaṭālaṅkāra*
O15:*gx*F25,1,2	Simha-deva-gaṇi's commentary
O15:*gx*F90,1	Sāradā-tanaya: *Bhāva-prakāśa*
O15:*gx*G42,1	Arisiṁha: *Kavitā-rahasya* or *Kāvya-kalpa-latā*
O15:*gx*G42,1,1	Amara-candra: *Kavi-sikṣā-vṛtti*

O15:*gx*G90,1	**Vag-bhata II:** *Kāvyānuśāsana*
O15:*gx*G90,1,1	Vāg-bhaṭa: *Alaṅkāra-tilaka*
O15:*gx*H00,1	Deveśvara: *Kavi-kalpa-latā*
O15:*gx*H00,1,1	Vecārāma Sārvabhauma's commentary
O15:*gx*H00,1,2	Rāma-gopāla Kavi-ratna's commentary
O15:*gx*H10,1	**Jaya-deva:** *Candrāloka* or *Pīyūṣa-varṣa*
O15:*gx*H10,1,1	Pradyotana Bhaṭṭa: *Candrāloka-prakāśa-śaradāgama*
O15:*gx*H10,1,2	Viśveśara or Gāgā-bhaṭṭa: *Rākāgama* or *Sudhā*
O15:*gx*H10,1,3	Vaidya-nātha Pāyaguṇde: *Ramā*
O15:*gx*H10,1,4	Virūpākṣa: *Śāradā-śarvarī*
O15:*gx*H15,1	**Vidya-dhara:** *Ekāvalī*
O15:*gx*H15,1,1	Malli-nātha: *Taralā*
O15:*gx*H16,1	**Vidya-natha** *Pratāpa-rudra-yaśo-bhūṣaṇa*
O15:*gx*H16,1,1	Kumāra-svāmin: *Ratnā-paṇa*
O15:*gx*H30,1	Singa-bhūpāla: *Rasārṇava-sudhākara*
O15:*gx*H35,1	**Visva-natha:** *Sāhitya-darpaṇa*
O15:*gx*H35,1,2	Rāma-caraṇa Tarka-vāgīśa: *Vivṛti*
O15:*gx*H35,1,4	Gopī-nātha: *Prabhā*
O15:*gx*H50,1	**Bhanu-datta:** *Rasa-taraṅginī*
O15:*gx*H50,1,1	Gaṅgā-rāma Jadi: *Naukā*
O15:*gx*H50,2	**Bhanu-datta:** *Rasa-mañjarī*
O15:*gx*H50,2,1	Ānanda Paṇḍita: *Vyaṅgyārtha-kaumudī*
O15:*gx*H50,2,2	Nāgeśa Bhaṭṭa: *Prakāśā*
O15:*gx*H50,2,3	Śeṣa-cintāmaṇi: *Parimala*
O15:*gx*H50,2,4	Gopālācārya: *Vikāsa*
O15:*gx*H50,2,5	Dravida Gopāla Bhaṭṭa: *Rasikarañjanī*
O15:*gx*H50,2,7	*Āmoda*
O15:*gx*H50,2,M80	Badari-nātha Sarma: *Surabhi*
O15:*gx*J24,1	**Kavi-karna-pura:** *Alaṅkāra-kaustubha*
O15:*gx*J24,1,1	Viśva-nātha-cakravartin: *Alaṅkāra-kaustubhasāra-bodhini*
O15:*gx*J24,1,2	*Alaṅkāra-kaustubha-kiraṇa*
O15:*gx*J32,1	Rūpa Gosvāmin: *Ujjvala-nīlamaṇi*
O15:*gx*J32,1,1	Jīva Gosvāmin: *Locana-rocanī*

O15:*gx*J32,1,2 Viśva-nātha-cakravartin: *Ānanda-candrikā* or *Ujjvala-nīlamaṇi-kiraṇa*
O15:*gx*J35,1 Gaṅgānanda Maithila: *Karṇa-bhūṣaṇa*
O15:*gx*J50,1 **Appaya Diksita:** *Kuvalayānanda*
O15:*gx*J50,1,1 Vaidya-nātha Tatsat: *Alaṅkāra-candrikā*
O15:*gx*J50,1,2 Āśādhara: *Alaṅkāra-dīpika*
O15:*gx*J50,1,3 Gaṅgā-dharādhvarin or Gaṅgā-dhara-vāja-peyin: *Rasika-ramani*
O15:*gx*J50,1,4 Nāgoji Bhaṭṭa: *Alaṅkāra-sudhā*
O15:*gx*J50,2 **Appaya Diksita:** *Citra-mīmāṁsā*
O15:*gx*J50,3 **Appaya Diksita:** *Vṛtti-vārtika*
O15:*gx*J60,1 Keśava Miśra: *Alaṅkāra-śekara*
O15:*gx*J64,1 Prabhā-kara Bhaṭṭa: *Rasa-pradīpa*
O15:*gx*J90,1 Kavi-candra: *Kāvya-candrikā*
O15:*gx*K36,1 Rāja-cūḍāmaṇi Dikṣita: *Kāvya-darpaṇa*
O15:*gx*K40,1 Nṛsimha-kavi: *Nañja-rāja-yaśo-bhuṣaṇa*
O15:*gx*K75,1 **Jagan-natha:** *Rasa-gaṅgādhara*
O15:*gx*K75,1,1 Nāgeśā-Bhaṭṭa: *Guru-marma-prakāśikā*
O15:*gx*K75,2 Jagan-nātha: *Citra-mīmāṁsā-khaṇḍana*
O15:*gx*L00,1 Viśveśvara Bhaṭṭa: *Alaṅkāra-kaustubha*
O15:*gx*L10,1 Cirañjīvi Bhaṭṭācārya: *Kāvya-vilāsa*
O15:*gx*L20,1 Cirañjīvi Bhaṭṭācārya: *Śṛṅgāraḍākini*
O15:*gx*L30,1 Kṛṣṇa Sarman: *Maṇḍāra-maranda-campu*
O15:*gx*M31,1 Acutarāya: *Śāhitya-sāra*
O15:*gx*M50,1 Kṛṣṇa Brahma-tantra Para-kāla-svāmin: *Alaṅkāra-maṇi-hāra*

O15,1A Ancient Sanskrit Poetry

O15,1A1 Rāmāyaṇa
O15,1A2 Mahābhārata

O15,2:*g* Criticism of Sanskrit Drama

O15,2:*gx*D98,1 Dhanañjaya: *Daśa-rūpaka*
O15,2:*gx*D98,1,1 Dhanika: *Ava-loka*
O15,2:*gx*G43,1 Sāgara-nandin: *Nāṭaka-lakṣaṇa-ratnakōśa*
O31,1A **Sanganul**
O31,1B *Eṭṭut-tokai*
O31,1B1 *Naṛṛinai*

O31,1B2	*Kurun-tokai*
O31,1B3	*Ainguru-nūrū*
O31,1B4	*Patirrup-pattu*
O31,1B5	*Pari-pādal*
O31,1B6	*Kalit-tokai*
O31,1B7	*Aga-nānūru*
O31,1B8	*Pura-nānūru*
O31,1B9	*Pattup-pāṭṭu*
O31,1B911	*Tirumurukār-rup-pāḍai*
O31,1B912	*Porunārārrup-paḍai*
O31,1B921	*Ciru-pāṇarrup-paḍai*
O31,1B922	*Perum-pāṇarrup-paḍai*
O31,1B931	*Mullaip-pāṭṭu*
O31,1B932	*Maturaik-kāñchi*
O31,1B941	*Neḍunal-vāḍai*
O31,1B942	*Kuruñchip-pāṭṭu*
O31,1B951	*Paṭṭinap-pālai*
O31,1B952	*Malaipaṭu-kaṭām*
O31,1C	*Padineṇ-kīzhk-kaṇakku*
O31,1C21	*Nāladiyār*
O31,1C22	*Nān-maṇik-kaṭikai*
O31,1C3	*Nā-nāṛpatu*
O31,1C31	*Innā-nāṛpatu*
O31,1C32	*Iniyavai-nāṛpatu*
O31,1C33	*Kār-nāṛpatu*
O31,1C34	*Kala-vazhi-nāṛpatu*
O31,1C4	*Ain-tiṇai*
O31,1C41	*Ain-tiṇai-aimpatu*
O31,1C42	*Ain-tiṇai-ezhupatu*
O31,1C43	*Tiṇai-mozhi-aimpatu*
O31,1C44	*Tiṇai-mālai-nūṛṛaimpatu*
O31,1C5	*Tiruk-kural*
O31,1C51	*Arattup-pāl*
O31,1C52	*Porut-pāl*
O31,1C53	*Kāmattup-pāl*
O31,1C61	*Tiru-katukam*

O31,1C62 *Acārak-kovai*
O31,1C63 *Pazha-mozhi*
O31,1C64 *Ciru-panca-mūlam*
O31,1C65 *Mutu-mozhik-kānchi*
O31,1C66 *Elādi*
O31,1C67 *Kainilai*
O31,1C9 Pancha-kavyam
O31,1C91 *Cīvaka-cintāmaṇi*
O31,1C92 *Cilap-padikāram*
O31,1C93 *Maṇi-mekalai*
O31,1C94 *Valaiyāpaṭi*
O31,1C95 *Kuṇḍala-keci*

O33,1:*g* **Kanarese Poetics and Prosody**

O33,1:*gx*1,1 *Kavirāja-mārgam*
O33,1:*g*(P)*x*1,1 Nāga-varma: *Chandombudhi*
O33,1:*g*(P)*x*2,1 *Nandi-chandas*

O35,1:*g*(**P**) **Telugu Prosody**

O35,1:*g*(P)*x*1,1 Bhīma-kavi (Vemula-vāda): *Kavi-janāśrayamu*
O35,1:*g*(P)*x*2,1 Ananta: *Anantuni-chandamu* or *Chando-darpaṇamu*
O35,1:*g*(P)*x*3,1 Tātam-bhaṭṭa (Mannulakṣaṇakavi): *Sulakṣaṇa-sāramu*
O35,1:*g*(P)*x*4,1 Kastūri-raṅgayya: *Anandaraṅga-rātchandamu*
O35,1:*g*(P)*x*94,1 Subrahmaṇya Śāstri (A): *Kavyā-darśamu*
O35,1:*g*(P)*x*J45,1 Rāma-badra Kavi: *Kavi-jana-sanjīvinī*

Vedic Sanskrit

P15,10A Rg-Vedic

P15,10Ax1,1	Saunaka: *Ṛgveda-prātiśakhyā*
P15,10A3:28x1,1	Yāska: *Nirukta*
P15,10A3:28x1,1,2	Durgāçārya: *Ṛjvartha*
P15,10A3:28x1,1,4	Skanda-svāmin's commentary
P15,10A3:28x1,1,5	Maheśvara's commentary
P15,10A3:28x1,1,6	Deva-rāja-yajvan's commentary
P15,10A4:28x1,1	*Nighantu*

P15,20A Yajur Vedic

P15,25A Taittiriya

P15,25Ax1,1	*Taittirīya-prātiśākhyā*
P15,25A:1x1,1	Vyāsa: *Vyasa-śikṣā*
P15,25A:1x8,1	Srīvatsāṅkara: *Sapta-lakṣaṇa*

P15,26A Vajasaneya

P15,26Ax1,1	Kātyāyana: *Vājasa-nēya-prātiśākhyā*

P15,30A Sama-Vedic

P15,30Ax1,1	*Sāma-veda-prātiśākhyā*
P15,30Ax2,1	*Puṣpa-sūtra*
P15,30Ax3,1	*Pañca-vidha-sūtra*

P15,40A Atharva-Vedic

P15,40Ax1,1	*Atharva-veda-prātiśākhyā*

Classical Sanskrit

P15,Cx1,1	**Panini:** *Aṣṭādhyāyi*
P15,Cx1,1,1	Kātyāyana or Vararuci: *Vṛtti*
P15,Cx1,1,2	**Patanjali:** *Mahā-bhāṣya*
P15,Cx1,1,2,1	Kaiyyaṭa: *Mahā-bhāṣya-pradīpa*
P15,Cx1,1,2,1,1	Nāgoji Bhaṭṭa or Nāgeśa Bhaṭṭa: *Mahā-bhāṣya-pradīpoddyota*
P15,Cx1,1,2,1,2	Iśvarānanda: *Mahā-bhāṣya-pradīpa-vivaraṇa*
P15,Cx1,1,3	**Jayaditya** or **Vamana-jayaditya:** *Kāśika-vṛtti*
P15,Cx1,1,3,1	Hara-datta Miśra: *Pada-mañjarī*
P15,Cx1,1,3,2	Jinendra: *Kāśikā-vṛtti-pañcikā* or *Nyāsa*

P15,Cx1,1,4	**Bhartrhari:** *Dīpikā*
P15,Cx1,1,5	**Bhattoji Diksita:** *Sabda-Kaustubha*
P15,Cx1,1,5,1	Bālaṁ-bhaṭṭa or Vaidya-nātha Pāyaguṇḍe: *Prabhā*
P15,Cx1,1,6	**Bhattoji Diksita:** *Siddhānta-kaumudī, Laghu-kaumudī, Madhya-kaumudī*
P15,Cx1,1,6,1	Bhaṭṭoji Dīkṣita: *Mano-ramā, Prauḍha-mano-ramā*
P15,Cx1,1,6,1,1	Hari Dīkṣita: *Śabdha-ratna, Laghu-śabdha-ratna*
P15,Cx1,1,6,1,1,1	Bālaṁ-bhaṭṭa or Vaidya-nātha Pāyaguṇḍe: *Bhāva-prakāśikā*
P15,Cx1,1,6,1,2	Kauṇḍa Bhaṭṭa: *Prauḍha-mano-ramā-khaṇ-dana*
P15,Cx1,1,6,2	Jñānendra Sarasvati: *Tattvabodhinī*
P15,Cx1,1,6,3	Nāgoji Bhaṭṭa or Nāgeśa Bhaṭṭa: *Śabdendu-śekhara, Laghu-śabdendu-śekhara*
P15,Cx1,1,6,3,1	Bālaṁ-bhaṭṭa or Vaidya-nātha Pāyaguṇḍe: *Ciaasthi-mālā*
P15,Cx1,1,6,4	Jayakṛṣṇa: *Subodhinī*
P15,Cx1,1,6,5	Vāsudeva Dīkṣita: *Bāla-manoramā*
P15,Cx1,1,7	**Rama-candracarya:** *Prakriyā-kaumudī*
P15,Cx1,1,7,1	Viṭṭhalācārya: *Prakriyā-kaumudī-prasāda*
P15,Cx1,1,7,2	Jayanta: *Tattva-canara*
P15,Cx1,1,E00	Dharma-kīrti: *Rupāvatāra*
P15,Cx1,1,F90	Purusottama-deva: *Bhāṣā-vṛtti*
P15,Cx1,1,K10	Annam-bhaṭṭa: *Vyākaraṇa-mitā-kṣara*
P15,Cx1,1,M40	Oram-bhaṭṭa: *Vyākaraṇa-dīpikā*
	P15,Cx19, Paribhasas
P15,Cx191,1	Śiradeva: *Paribhāṣā-vṛtti*
P15,Cx192,1	Bhāskara Bhaṭṭa: *Laghu-paribhāṣā-vṛtti*
P15,Cx193,1	*Paribhāṣārthā-saṁgraha*
P15,Cx193,1,1	Svayam-prakāsānanda: *Candrikā*
P15,Cx194,1	Nāgoji Bhaṭṭa or Nāgeśa Bhaṭṭa: *Paribhā-ṣendu-śekhara*
P15,Cx194,1,1	Bālam-bhaṭṭa or Vaidya-nātha Pāyaguṇḍe *Paribhāṣendu-śekhara-kauśika*

P15,Cx195,1	Nīla-kaṇṭha Dīṣita: *Paribhāṣā-vṛtti*
P15,Cx2,1	**Candra-gomin**: *Candra-vyākaraṇa*
P15,Cx2,1,1	Candra-gomin: *Candra-vṛtti*
P15,Cx2,1,5	Kāśyapa: *Bālāvabodha*
P15,Cx3,1	**Jainendra** or **Indra** or **Deva-nandi** or **Pujya-pada-svami**: *Jainendra-vyākaraṇa*
P15,Cx3,1,1	Deva-nandi: *Mahāvṛtti*
P15,Cx3,1,2	Soma-deva: *Śabdārṇava-candrikā*
P15,Cx3,1,3	Abhaya-nandi: *Mahāvṛtti*
P15,Cx3,1,4	Sruta-kīrti: *Pañca-vastu*
P15,Cx4,1	**Saka-tayana**: *Sabdānuśāsana*
P15,Cx4,1,1	Sāka-ṭāyana: *Amogha-vṛtti*
P15,Cx4,1,2	Prabha-candrācārya: *Nyāsa*
P15,Cx4,1,3	Yakṣa-varmā: *Cintāmaṇi*
P15,Cx4,1,3,1	Ajita-senācārya: *Maṇi-prakāśikā*
P15,Cx4,1,3,2	Maṅga-rāsa: *Cintāmaṇi-pratipada*
P15,Cx4,1,3,3	Sāmanta-bhadra: *Tippanī*
P15,Cx4,1,3,5	Abhaya-candrācārya: *Prakriyā-saṅgraha*
P15,Cx4,1,3,6	Daya-pāla: *Rupa-siddhi*
P15,Cx5,1	**Hema-candra**: *Śabdānuśāsana*
P15,Cx5,1,1	Hema-candra: *Śabdānuśāsana-bṛhad-vṛtti*
P15,Cx5,1,1,1	*Nyāsa*
P15,Cx5,1,1,2	*Dhuṇḍhikā* or *Bṛhad-vṛtti*
P15,Cx5,1,1,3	Devendra-sūri: *Haima-laghu-nyāsa*
P15,Cx5,1,1,4	*Śabda-mahārṇava-nyāsa*
P15,Cx5,1,5	Vinaya-vijaya-gaṇi: *Haima-laghu-prakriyā*
P15,Cx5,1,5,1	Vimala-vijaya-gaṇi: *Haima-prakāśa*
P15,Cx5,1,6	Megha-vijaya: *Haima-kaumudī*, *Candra-prabhā*
P15,Cx5,1,7	Puṇya-sundara-gaṇi's commentary
	P15,Cx59, Paribhasas
P15,Cx591,1	Hema-haṁsa-vijaya-gaṇi's commentary
P15,Cx591,1,1	Hema-haṁsa-vijaya-gaṇi: *Nyāyārtha-mañjūṣa*
P15,Cx6,1	**Sarva-varman**: *Kātantra-sūtra-pāṭha*
P15,Cx6,1,1	Durga-siṁha: *Kātantra-vṛtti*
P15,Cx6,1,1,1	Vardha-māna: *Kātantra-vistāra*

P15,Cx6,1,1,1,1	Pṛthvī-dhara's commentary
P15,Cx6,1,1,2	Trilocana-dāsa: *Kātantra-vṛtti-pañcikā*
P15,Cx6,1,1,2,1	Jina-prabha-sūri: *Jina-prabodha*
P15,Cx6,1,1,2,2	Kuśala's commentary
P15,Cx6,1,1,2,3	Rāma-candra's commentary
P15,Cx6,1,1,3	Mahā-deva: *Śabda-siddhi*
P15,Cx6,1,6	Bhaṭṭa Jagaddhara: *Bāla-bodhinī*
P15,Cx6,1,6,1	Ugra-bhūti: *Bāla-bodhinī-nyāsa*
P15,Cx6,1,7	Chichu-bhaṭṭa: *Laghu-vṛtti*
P15,Cx7,1	**Narendracarya**: *Sārasvata-sūtra*
P15,Cx7,1,1	Anubhūti-svarūpācārya: *Sārasvata-prakriyā*
P15,Cx7,1,1,1	Kuñjarā's commentary
P15,Cx7,1,1,2	Amṛta-bhārati: *Subodhikā*
P15,Cx7,1,1,3	Kṣemendra's commentary
P15,Cx7,1,1,4	Candra-kīrti: *Dīpikā*
P15,Cx7,1,1,5	Mādhava's commentary
P15,Cx7,1,1,6	Vāsu-deva Bhaṭṭa: *Sārasvata-prakāśa*
P15,Cx7,1,1,7	Maṇḍana's commentary
P15,Cx7,1,1,8	Megha-ratna's commentary
P15,Cx7,1,1,J50	Dhaneśvara's commentary
P15,Cx7,1,1,J70	Jagan-nātha: *Śāra-pradīpika*
P15,Cx7,1,J90	Kāśīnātha: *Sārasvata-bhāṣya*
P15,Cx7,1,1,J95	Bhaṭṭa Gopāla's commentary
P15,Cx7,1,1,K20	Sahaja-kīrti: *Sārasvata-prakriyā-vārtikā*
P15,Cx7,1,1,K50	Haṁsa-vijaya-gaṇi: *Śabdārtha-candrikā*
P15,Cx7,1,1,K80	Rāma-bhaṭṭa: *Rāmabhaṭṭi* or *Vidvat-prabodhinī*
P15,Cx7,1,2	Rāma-candrāśrama: *Siddhānta-candrikā*
P15,Cx7,1,2,1	Lokeśa-kara: *Tattva-dīpikā*
P15,Cx7,1,2,2	Sadānanda-gaṇi: *Subodhinī*
P15,Cx7,1,3	Tarka-tilaka Bhaṭṭācārya's commentary
P15,Cx7,1,4	Jinendu or Jina-ratna: *Siddhānta-ratna*
P15,Cx7,1,5	Raghu-nātha: *Laghu-bhāṣya*
P15,CxF60,1	**Vopa-deva or Bopa-deva** *Mugdhabodha*
P15,CxF60,1,5	Rāma-tarka-vāgīśa's commentary
	P15,CxF609 Paribhasas
P15,CxF6091,1	Rāma-candra Vidyā-bhūṣaṇa: *Paribhāṣāvṛtti*

P15,C*x*K20,1	Nārāyaṇa Bhaṭṭa: *Prakriyā-sarvasvam*
P15,C*x*K20,1,3	*Prakāśikā*
	P15,C:22 Gender
P15,C:22*x*1,1	**Panini**: *Liṅgānuśāsana*
P15,C:22*x*1,1,1	Vara-ruci: *Liṅgā-viśeṣa-vṛtti*
P15,C:22*x*1,1,3	Vāmana: *Liṅgānuśāsana*
P15,C:22*x*2,1	**Candra-gomin**: *Liṅgānuśāsana*
P15,C:22*x*4,1	**Saka-tayana**: *Liṅgānuśāsana*
P15,C:22*x*5,1	**Hema-candra**: *Liṅgānuśāsana*
P15,C:22*x*5,1,1	Śrīvallabha Vācanācārya: *Durgapada-prabodha*
P15,C:22*x*D50,1	Harsa-vardhana: *Liṅgānuśāsana*
	P15,C:3 Syntax
P15,C:3*x*4,1	**Bhartr-hari**: *Vākya-pradipa*
P15,C:3*x*5,1	**Konda-Bhatta**: *Vaiyākaraṇa-bhūṣaṇa*
P15,C:3*x*5,1,1	Harivallabha: *Bhūṣaṇa-sāradarpaṇa*
P15,C:3*x*5,1,1,1	Vaidya-nātha Pāyaguṇḍe or Bālaṁbhaṭṭa: *Laghu-bhūṣaṇa-kānti*
P15,C:3*x*6,1	**Nagesa Bhatta** or **Nagoji Bhatta**: *Vaiyākaraṇa-siddhānta-māñjūṣā*
P15,C:3*x*6,1,1,1	Vaidya-nātha Pāyaguṇḍe or Bālaṁbhaṭṭa: *Kalā*
	P15,C:4 Meaning
P15,C:4*x*1,1	**Amara-simha**: *Amra-kośa* or *Nāmalingānuśāsana*
P15,C:4*x*1,1,1,1	Kṣīra-swȧmin: *Amara-kośodghāṭana*
P15,C:4*x*1,1,2	Sarvānanda Vandya-gatīya: *Tikāsarvasva*
P15,C:4*x*1,1,3	Subhūti or Subhūti-candra: *Kāmādhenu*
P15,C:4*x*1,1,4	Bṛhaspati or Rāya-mukaṭa: *Pada-candrikā*
P15,C:4*x*1,1,5	Bhānuji Dīkṣita: *Vyākhyā-sudhā* or *Rāmāśrami*
P15,C:4*x*1,1,6	Nārāyaṇa Śarman: *Amara-kośa-pañjikā* or *Padārtha-kaumudī*
P15,C:4*x*1,1,F90	Maheśvara: *Amara-viveka*
P15,C:4*x*1,1,L90	*Guru-bāla-prabodhikā*
P15,C:4*x*2,1	**Yadava-prakasa**: *Vaijayantī*

P15,C:4x3,1	**Mahesvara**: *Viśva-prakāśa*
P15,C:4x4,1	**Sasvata**: *Anekārtha-samuccaya*
P15,C:4x5,1	**Hala-yudha**: *Abhidhāna-ratna-mālā*
P15,C:4x6,1	**Trikanda-sesa**: *Kośa-samuccaya*
P15,C:4xF60,1	Keśava: *Kalpadru-kośa*
P15,C:4xF90,1	Keśava-svāmin: *Nānārthārṇava-śaṃkṣepa*
	P15,C:3 Word
P15,C301x1,1	**Panini**: *Dhātu-pāṭha*
P15,C301x1,1,1	Maitreya-rakṣita: *Dhātu-pradīpa* or *Tantra-pradīpa*
P15,C301x1,1,2	Bhīma-sena's commentary
P15,C301x1,1,3	Kṣīra-svāmin: *Dhātu-vṛtti*
P15,C301x1,1,4	Mādhavācārya or Sāyanācārya: *Mādhavīya-dhātu-vṛtti*
P15,C301xF60,1	Bopa-deva or Vopa-deva: *Kavikalpa-druma*
P15,C301xF60,1,1	Bopa-deva or Vopa-deva: *Kāmadhenu*
P15,C302x1,1	**Panini**: *Gaṇa-pāṭha*
P15,C302x1,1,2	Kṣīra-svāmin: *Gaṇa-vṛtti*
P15,C302x1,1,3	Vardha-māna: *Gaṇa-ratna-mahodadhi*
P15,C303x1,1	**Panini**: *Uṇādi-sūtra*
P15,C303x5,1	**Hema-candra**: *Uṇādi-sūtra*
P15,C303xL70,1	Bharata Mallika: *Kārakōllāsa*
P15,C31:2x5,1,1	Amara-candra: *Syādi-samuccaya*
P15,C35:2x5,1,1	Guṇa-ratna-sūri: *Kriyā-ratna-samuccaya*
	Prakrta
P151x2,1	**Vara-ruci**: *Prākṛta-sūtras*
P151x2,1,1	Bhāmaha: *Prākṛta-prakāśā*
	Tamil
	P31,A Ancient Tamil
P31,Ax1	Agastyar or Agattiyar
	P31,D Middle Tamil
P31,Dx1,1	Tolkāppianar: *Tolkāppiam*
P31,Dx1,1,1	Ilampūraṇar: *Commentary*
P131,Dx1,1,2	Kallāḍanār: *Commentary*
P31,Dx1,1.3	Perāśiriyar: *Commentary*
P31,Dx1,1,4	Senā-varaiyar: *Commentary*

3,19

P31,Dx1,1,5	Naccinārkkiniyar: *Commentary*
P31,Dx1,11	*Ezhut-adhikāram*
P31,Dx1,13	*Śol-adhikāram*
P31,Dx1,14	*Porul-adhikāram*
P31,Dx2	Iraiyanār
P31,Dx2,1	*Ahapporul*
P31,Dx2,1,1	Nakkirar: *Commentary*
	P31,D:4 Meaning
P31,D:4x1,1	*Adi-divākaram*
P31,D:4x1,1,1	Divā-karar: *Śendan-divākaram*
P31,D:4x2,1	Gaya-karar: *Gayakaram*
P31,D:4x3,1	Piṅgaḷar: *Piṅgaḷa-nighaṇṭu*
P31,D:4x4,1	Aṇḍip-pulavar: *Āśiria-nighaṇṭu*
P31,D:4x5,1	Maṇḍala-puruḍar or Vīra Maṇḍalavar: *Cūdāmani-nighaṇṭu*
	P31,J Modern Tamil
P31,Jx1,1	**Pava-nandi Munivar**: *Nannūl*
P31,Jx1,1,1	Mayilai-nāthar: *Urai*
P31,Jx1,1,2	*Nannūl-āśiriya-virutti*
P31,Jx1,1,3	Subrahmaṇya Dīkṣitar: *Prayoga-vivekam*
P31,Jx1,1,4	Swāmi-nātha Deśikar: *Illakkaṇak-kòttu*
P31,Jx1,1,5	Sankara-nama-sivāyar: *Urai*
P31,Jx1,1,8	Narkavi Rājanambī: *Ahap-porul-vilakkam*
P31,JxK40,1	Vaidya-nātha Deśikar: *Ilakkaṇa-vilakkam*
	P31,J:4 Meaning
P31,J:4xJ96,1	Cidambara-revaṇa Siddhar: *Akarādi-nighaṇṭu*
P31,J:4xL95,1	Subrahmaṇya Bhārati: *Poruṭṭogai-nighaṇṭu*
P31,J:4xM00,1	Muttu-swami Pillai: *Nānārtha-dīpikai*
	Kanarese
	P33:E Ancient Kanarese
P33,E:4x1,1	Nāga-varma: *Abhidhāna-vastu-kōśa*
P33,E:4xH50,1	*Karṇāṭaka-śabda-sāra*
	Telugu
	P35,E Ancient Telugu
P35,Ex1,1	Nannaya-bhaṭṭācārya: *Andhra-śabdha-cintamaṇi*

P35,Ex1,1,1	Ahobala-paṇḍita: *Ahobala-paṇḍitīyamu* or *Kavi-śiro-bhūṣaṇamu*
P35,Ex1,1,2	Narasiṃha-rāja Siṃhudu Balārisiṃha: *Kavi-janāñjanamu*
P35,Ex1,1,3	Appa-kavi: *Appa-kāvīyamu*
P35,Ex1,1,7	Bāla-saraswati: *Bāla-sarasvatīyamu*
P35,Ex1,1,8	Rāma-śāstry: *Udyotinī*
P35,Ex2,1	Atharvaṇācārya: *Atharvana-kārikāvāli*
P35,Ex3,1	Ketana-kavi: *Andhra-bhāśā-bhūṣanamu*
P35,Ex4,1	Peddanna: *Kāvyālankāra-cūḍamaṇi*
P35,Ex5,1	Timmaya: *Sarva-lakṣṇa-sāra-saṇgrahamu*
P35,Ex6,1	Sūra-kavi or Sūraya (Aḍidamu): *Kavi-śamsaya-vicchedamu*
P35,ExM60,1	Cinnaya Sūri (Paravastu): *Bālavyākaraṇamu*
P35,ExM60,1,1	Saṅkara Raṅgayya and Venkaṭarāma Sāstri (Kalluri): *Bālavyākaraṇa-guptārtha-prakāśikā*

P35,E:4 Meaning

P35,E:4x1,1	Lakṣmaṇuḍu (Paiḍipāṭi): *Andhra-nāma-saṅgrahamu*
P35,E:4x2,1	Kastūri Raṅgayya: *Sāmba-nighaṇṭu*
P35,E:4x3,1	Venkanna (Koti): *Andhra-bhāṣār-ṇavamu*
P35,E:4x6,1	Sūrya (Aḍidamu): *Andhra-nāma-śeṣamu*

Q RELIGION

Q 1 Vedic

Q 11 Rg-Veda

	Kalpasūtra
Q11:4x1,1	Āśvalāyana
	Kauṣītakin
	Brahmana
Q112:22	Śāṅkhyāyana
	Kalpasūtra
Q112:4x2,1	Śaṅkhyāyana

Q12 Yajur-Veda

Q124	Maitrāyanīya
	Kalpasūtra
Q124:4x1,1	Mānava
Q124:4x2,1	Kāṭḥaka
Q124:4x3,1	Varāha

Q125 Taittiriya

	Samhita
Q125:214	Ekāgnikānda
	Mantrapraśna
	Mantrapātha
	Upanishad
Q125:25	Narāyana, Yajnik
Q125:26	Svetāśvatarā
	Kalpasūtra
Q125:4x1,1	Baudhāyana
Q125:4x2,1	Āpastamba
Q125:4x3,1	Bhāradvāja
Q125:4x4,1	Hiraṇyakeśin
Q125:4x5,1	Vādhūla

Q126 Vajasaneya

	Kalpasūtra
Q126:4x6,1	Vaikhānasa

Q 127 Madhyandina

	Brahmana
Q127:22	Satapātha
	Upanishad
Q127:24	Bṛhadāranyaka
Q127:25	Īsāvaśya
	Kalpasūtra
Q127:4x1,1	Kātyāyana
Q127:4x2,1	Pāraskara

Q 131 Sama Veda

Q131	Tāndin
	Samhitā
Q131:211	Arcika
Q131:212	Aranyaka
Q131:213	Uttarācika
Q131:214	Stobha
Q131:215	Veyagāna
Q131:216	Aranyagāna
Q131:217	Uhagāna
Q131:218	Rahasyagāna
	Brahmana
Q131:22	Samvidhana
Q131:221	Pancaviṁsa
Q131:222	Sadviṁsa
Q131:224	Arseya
Q131:225	Chāndogya
Q131:226	Devatādhyāya
	Upanishad
Q131:24	Chāndogya
	Kalpasūtra
Q131:4x1,1	Māṣaka
Q131:4x2,1	Lāṭyāyana
Q131:4x3,1	Gobhila

Q131:4x5,1 Chāndogya

Q132 Talavakara

Upaniṣad

Q132:24 Kena

Kalpasūtra

Q132:4x1,1 Jaiminīya

Q133 Ranayaniya

Kalpasūtra

Q133:4x2,1 Drāhyāyaṇa

Q133:4x3,1 Khādira

Q133:4x5,1 Gautama

Q14 Atharva-Veda

Q141 Saunakiya

Upaniṣad

Q141:24 Prasna

Q141:25 Mundaka

Q141:26 Māndūkya

Kalpasūtra

Q141:4x1,1 Kauśika

Q141:4x2,1 Vaitāna

Q 2 Hinduism (Post-Vedic)

Dharma-sastras

Q2:4x1,1 **Manu**

Q2:4x1,1,1 Medhātithi

Q2:4x1,1,2 Kullūkabhaṭṭa

Q2:4x1,1,3 Govindarāja

Q2:4x1,1,4 Nandana

Q2:4x1,1,5 Sarvajña Nārāyaṇa

Q2:4x1,1,6 Nārāyaṇa

Q2:4x1,1,7 Rāghavendra

Q2:4x1,1,8 Rāmacandra

Q2:4x2,1 **Yajnavalkya**

Q2:4x2,1,1 Viśvarūpa

Q2:4x2,1,2 Mitākṣara

Q2:4x2,1,2,1 Subodhinī

Q2:4x2,1,2,2 Pramitākṣara

Q2:4x2,1,2,3 Bālambhaṭṭī

Q2:4x2,1,3 Aparārka or Aparāditya

Q2:4x2,1,4 Sūlapāṇi

Q2:4x2,1,5 Mitramiśra

Q2:4x3,1 Vāsistha

Q2:4x4,1 Parāśara

Q2:4x5,1 Nārada

Q2:4x6,1 Hārīta

Q2:4x7,1 Viṣṇu

Q2:4xD75,1 Asahāya

Q2:4xH80,1 Vidyā-kara Vāja-peyi: *Nityācāra-paddhati*

Q2:4xK26,1 Kamalākara Bhaṭṭa: *Nirṇaya-sindhu*

Q2:4xL50,1 Kāśi-nātha: *Dharma-sindhu*

Q2:4y8 Digest

Q2:4y8x6,1 Gopi-nātha: *Saṁskāra-ratna-mālā*

Q2:4y8xF50,1 Devana Bhaṭṭa: *Smṛti-candrikā*

Q2:4y8xI50,1 Nara-siṁha Vāja-peyi: *Nityācāra-pradipa*

Q2:4y8xJ20,1 Raghu-nātha: *Smṛti-tattva*

Q2:4y8xJ30,1 Viśvambhara Tripāṭhi: *Smṛti-sārod-dhāra*

Q2:4y8xK20,1	Mitra Miśra: *Vīra-mitrodaya*
Q2:4y8xK70,1	Ratnākara: *Jayasimha-kalpa-druma*
Q2:4y8xL25,1	Ananta Bhaṭṭa: *Vidhāna-pārijāta*
	Q2:41 Personal Religious Practice
Q2:41y8xG60,1	Hemādri: *Catur-varga-cintāmaṇi*
Q2:41y8xI60,1	Gadā-dhara: *Gadādhara-paddhati*
Q2:41y8xK30,1	Vaidya-nātha Dikṣita: *Smṛti-muktā-phala*
	Q2:4193 Religious Gift
Q2:4193y8xJ40,1	Govindānanda: *Dāna-kriya-kaumudi*
Q2:4193y8xJ61,1	Bhaṭṭa Nīla-kaṇṭha: *Dāna-mayūkha*
	Q2:4195 Expiation
Q2:4195y8xJ50,1	Nāgeśa Bhaṭṭa: *Vrātya-prāyaścitta-nirṇaya*
Q2:4195y8xK60,1	Nāgojī Bhaṭṭa: *Prayaś-cittendu-śekhara*
	Q2:4198 Pilgrimage
Q2:4198y8xH30,1	Vācas-pati Miśra: *Tīrtha-cintāmaṇi*
Q2:4198y8xI82,1	Dala-pati Rāja: *Nṛsimha-prasāda-tīrtha-sāra*
Q2:4198y8xJ80,1	Bhaṭṭojī Dīkṣita: *Tri-sthalī-setu*
	Q2:42 Sacrament
Q2:42y8xE55,1	Sridharācārya: *Smṛtyārtha-sāra*
Q2:42y8xH25,1	Caṇḍeśvara Thakūra: *Gṛhastha-ratnākara*
Q2:42y8xH75,1	Madana-pāla: *Madana-pārijāta*
Q2:42y8xJ61,1	Saṅkara Bhaṭṭa: *Samskāra-mayūkha*
	Q2:428 Obsequies
Q2:428y8xF70,1	Aniruddha Bhaṭṭa: *Hāra-latā*
Q2:428y8xK80,1	Divā-kara Bhaṭṭa: *Srāddha-candrikā*
	Q2:4284 Pollution
Q2:4284y8xI96,1	Adityācārya: *Saḍaśīti*
Q2:4284y8xL20,1	Bhaṭṭa Raghu-nātha: *Tṛmśac-chloki*
	Q2:4288 Anniversary Rite
Q2:4288y8xL25,1	Seṣa-kṛṣṇa Paṇḍita: *Dharmānu-bandhi-śloka-caturdaśi*
	Q2:43 Holy Day
Q2:43y8xF10,1	Jīmūta-vāhana: *Kāla-viveka*
Q2:43y8xL50,1	Vāsudeva-ratha: *Smṛti-prakāśa*
	Q2:45 Public Worship
Q2:45y8xI26,1	Nārāyaṇa: *Tantra-samuccaya*

Q21 Smartaism.

Relevant Selections from Vedas

Q21:21x1,1 Puruṣa-sūktam

Q21:22 *Purāna*

Q21:221 Brahma
Q21:222 Mārkaṇḍeya
Q21:223 Bhaviṣya
Q21:2231 Bhaviṣyottara
Q21:224 Vāmana
Q21:225 Brahmāṇḍa
Q21:2251 Adhyātma Rāmāyaṇa
Q21:2252 Rāma-gītā
Q21:226 Yoga-vāśiṣṭha Rāmāyaṇa, Jñāna-vāśiṣṭha
Q21:227 Ānanda Rāmāyaṇa
Q21:228 Adbhuta Rāmāyaṇa

Q22 Vaisnavism

Q22*w Devotee*

Q22*wx*1,1 Mahī-pati: *Bhakta-vijaya*
Q22*wx*1,2 Mahī-pati: *Bhakta-līlāmṛta*
Q22*wx*2,1 Candra-datta: *Bhakta-mālā*

Q22:22 *Purāṇa*

Q22:221 Padma
Q22:2211 Siva-gītā
Q22:222 Viṣṇu
Q22:223 Bhāgavata
Q22:224 Nārada
Q22:2241 Nārada-upa-purāṇa
Q22:225 Brahma-vaivarta
Q22:226 Varāha
Q22:227 Garuḍa
Q22:2271 Viṣṇu-dharmottara
Q22:228 Hari-vaṁśa
Q22:2291 Kalki
Q22:2292 Narasiṁha
Q22:2293 Bhārgava

Q22:417 *Hymn*

Q22:417*x*1 Nalayira-divya-prabandham
Q22:417*x*1 First thousand
Q22:417*x*1,11 Tirup-pallāṇḍu (Periyāzhvār)
Q22:417*x*1,12 Tiru-mozhi (Periyāzhvār)
Q22:417*x*1,13 Tirup-pāvai (Āṇḍāl)
Q22:417*x*1,14 Nācchiyār-tiru-mozhi (Āṇḍāl)
Q22:417*x*1,15 Perumāl-tiru-mozhi (Kula-śekhara Āzhvār)
Q22:417*x*1,16 Tiru-chanda-viruttam (Tirumazhiśai Āzhvār)
Q22:417*x*1,17 Turi-mālai (Toṇḍaraḍip-poḍi-Āzhvār)
Q22:417*x*1,18 Tirup-palli-ezhucci (Toṇḍaraḍip-poḍi-Āzhvār)

Q22:417x1,191	Amalanādippirān (Tiruppāṇ Āzhvār)
Q22:417x1,192	Kaṇṇinuṇ-śirut-tāmbu (Madurakavi Āzhvār)
Q22:417x1,2	Second thousand
Q22:417x1,21	Periya-tiru-mozhi (Tirumaṅgai Āzhvār)
Q22:417x1,22	Tiruk-kurun-tāṇḍagam (Tirumaṅgai Āzhvār)
Q22:417x1,23	Tiru-neḍun-tāṇḍagam (Tirumaṅgai Āzhvār)
Q22:417x1,3	Third thousand
Q22:417x1,31	Mudal-tiru-vandādi (Poigai Āzhvār)
Q22:417x1,32	Iraṇḍān-tiru-vandādi (Pūdattāzhvār)
Q22:417x1,33	Mūnrān-tiru-vandādi (Pēyāzhvār)
Q22:417x1,34	Nān-mungan-tiru-vandādi (Tirumazhiśai Āzhvār)
Q22:417x1,35	Tiru-viruttam (Nammāzhvār)
Q22:417x1,36	Tiru-vāsiriyam (Nammāzhvār)
Q22:417x1,37	Periya-tiru-vandādi (Nammāzhvār)
Q22:417x1,38	Tiru-vezhuzkūṟ-ṟirukkai (Tirumaṅgai Āzhvār)
Q22:417x1,391	Siriya-tiru-maḍal (Tirumaṅgai Āzhvār)
Q22:417x1,392	Periya-tiru-maḍal (Tirumaṅgai Āzhvār)
Q22:417x1,4	Fourth thousand
Q22:417x1,41	Tiru-vāy-mozhi (Nammāzhvār)
Q22:417x1,42	Irā-mānuśa *Nūṟ-ṟandādi*
	Q22:417 *Nāmāvali*
Q22:4173x1	*Viṣṇu-sahasra-nāma*
Q22:4173x1,1	Saṅkara: *Commentary*
Q222	**Pancarata**
	Q222:23 *Samhitā*
Q222:231	Pauṣkara
Q222:232	Sāttvata
Q222:233	Ahirbudhnya
Q222:234	Jaya
Q222:235	Padma
Q222:236	Parameśwara
Q222:237	Iśwara
Q222:2391	Brahma
Q222:2392	Nārada
Q222:23921	Bṛhad-dharma
Q222:2393	Ānanda
Q23	**Saivism**
	Q23w *Devotee*
Q23wx1	Śekkizār: *Periya-purāṇam*
Q23:21	*Relevant Selections from the Vedas*
Q23:21x1	Rudra

Q23:21x2 Camaka

Q23:22 *Purāṇa*

Q23:221 Vāyu
Q23:222 Agni
Q23:223 Linga
Q23:224 Gaṇeśa
Q23:2244 Gaṇeśa-gītā
Q23:225 Matsya
Q23:226 Skanda
Q23:2261 Sūta-saṁhitā
Q23:2262 Brahma-gītā
Q23:227 Kūrma
Q23:2271 Īśwara-gītā
Q23:28 Saura
Q23:2291 Siva

Q23:417 *Hymn*

Q23:417x1 Tevāram
Q23:417x2 Sambandar
Q23:417x3 Appar
Q23:417x4 Sundarar
Q23:417x5 Māṇikka-vācagar
Q23:417x6 Tiru-visaip-pa
Q23:417x7 Tirup-pal-lāṇḍu
Q23:417x8 Tirumūlar: *Tiru-mandiram*
Q23:417x93 Eleventh Tiru-murai (padino-ran-tiru-murai)

Q232 Agamic Saivism

Q232:23 *Agama*

Q232:2311 Kāmika
Q232:2312 Yogaja
Q232:2313 Cintya
Q232:2314 Kāraṇa
Q232:2315 Ajita
Q232:2316 Dipta
Q232:2317 Sūkṣma
Q232:2318 Sahasraka
Q232:2321 Aṁśumān
Q232:2322 Suprabhā
Q232:2331 Vijaya
Q232:2332 Niśvāsa
Q232:2333 Svāyambhuva
Q232:2334 Āgneyaka (Āgney, Anala-Anila)
Q232:2335 Bhadra (Vīra)
Q232:2336 Raurava
Q232:2337 Mākuṭa
Q232:2338 Vimala
Q232:2341 Candra-hāsa (Candra-jñāna)
Q232:2342 Mukha-yug-bimba (Bimba)
Q232:2343 Udgīta (Prodi-Gītā)
Q232:2344 Lalita
Q232:2345 Siddha
Q232:2346 Santāna
Q232:2347 Narasimha (Sarvokta, Sar-vottra)
Q232:2348 Parameśvara
Q232:2351 Kiraṇa
Q232:2352 Para (Pārahita, Vātuḷa)

Q233 Kasmir Saivism

Q233:231 Mālini-vijaya
Q233:231,1 Abhinava-gupta: *Vārttika*
Q233:232 Svac-chanda
Q233:232,1 *Uddyota*
Q233:233 Vijñā-Bhairava

Q233:234	Ucchūṣmara-Bhairava
Q233:235	Ānanda-Bhairava
Q233:236	Mṛgendra
Q233:237	Mātanga
Q233:237,1	*Vṛtti*
Q233:238	Śiva-sūtra
Q233:238,1	*Vṛtti*
Q233:238,2	Bhāskara: *Vārtika*
Q233:238,5	Kṣema-rāja: *Vimarsini*
Q233:2391	Netra
Q233:2392	Naiśvāsa
Q233:2393	Svāyam-bhuva
Q233:2394	Rudra-yāmala
Q233:2395	Spanda-sūtra (Spanda-kārikā)
Q233:2395,1	Kallata: *Vṛtti* (*Spanda-sarvasva*)
Q233:2895,2	Rāmakanṭha: *Vivṛti*
Q233:2395,3	Utpala II: *Pradīpika*
Q233:2395,4	Kṣemarāja: *Spanda-sadoha*
Q233:2395,5	Kṣemarāja: *Spanda-nirṇaya*
Q234	**Virasaivism**
Q234xK50,1	Prabhu-liṅga-līla
Q234:22	Padma-rāja purāṇam
Q25	**Saktaism**
Q25x1,1	Śaṅkara: *Saundarya-laharī*

Q25x1,1,1	Lakṣmī-dhara's commentary
Q25:21	*Relevant selections from the Vedas*
Q25:21x5	Śri-sūktam
Q25:21x6	Durgā-sūktam
Q25:22	*Purāṇa*
Q25:221	Devī-bhāgavata
Q25:222	Bṛhad-dharma
Q25:223	Kālikā
Q25:225	Lalitopākhyāna
Q25:2291	Devī-māhātmya
Q25:4	**Religious Practices**
Q25:4x1,1	Mahīdhara: *Mantra-mahodadhi*
Q25:4173	*Nāmāvali*
Q25:4133x1	*Lalitā-sahasra-nāma*
Q25:4173x1,1	Bhāskara: *Commentary*
Q26	**Sanmukaism**
Q26:417x150,1	Aruṇagiri-nāthar: *Tirup-pugazh*
Q28	**Sauraism**
Q28:22	*Purāṇa*
Q28:221	Āditya
Q28:223	Sāmba
Q3	**Jainism**
Q31	**Svetambara**
Q31y5x1,1	Śubhavijaya-gaṇi: *Praśna-ratnākara*
Q31:21	Canonical works

Q31:211	**Anga**
Q31:21111	Acāra (Āyāra)
Q31:21112	Sūtra-kṛta (Sūryagaḍa)
Q31:21113	Sthāna (Thāna)
Q31:21114	Samavāya
Q31:21115	Bhagavatī
Q31:21116	Jñāta-dharma-katha (Nāya-dhamaṁ-kahā)
Q31:21117	Upāśaka-dāśā (Uvā-sagadasāo)
Q31:21118	Antakṛta-daśā (Antagada-dasāo)
Q31:21121	Anutta-raupa-pātikadaśā (Anutta-rova vāiya-dasāo)
Q31:21122	Praśna-vyākaraṇa (Paṁhā-vā-garaṇa)
Q31:21123	Vipāka (Vivāga)
Q31:21124	Dṛṣṭi-vāda
Q31:212	**Upangas**
Q31:21211	Aupa-pātika (Ovāiya)
Q31:21212	Rāja-praśnīya (Rāya-pase-ṇaiyya)
Q31:21213	Jivābhigama
Q31:21214	Prajñāpanā (Paṇṇavaṇā)
Q31:21215	Sūrya-prajñāpati (Sūriya-paṇ-ṇatti)
Q31:21216	Jambū-dvipa-prajñāpti (Jambūd-dīva-paṇṇatti)
Q31:21217	Candra-prajñāpti (Candapaṇ-ṇatti)
Q31:21218	Nirayāvali (Nirayāvali-yāo) or Kal-pika (Kappi-yāo)
Q31:21221	Kalpāvataṁśikā (Kappavadiṁ-siāo)
Q31:21222	Puṣpikā (Pupphiyāo)
Q31:21223	Puṣpa-cūḍā (Puppha-cūlao)
Q31:21224	Vṛṣni-daśā (Vaṅhidasāo)
Q31:213	**Prakirna** (Painna or Payanna)
Q31:21311	Vīrabhadra Catuḥśaraṇa (Causaraṇa)
Q31:21312	Ātura-pratyā-khyāna
Q31:21313	Bhakta-parijña
Q31:21314	Saṁstāra (San-thāra)

Q31:21315	Tandula-vaitalika; Tandula-vaicarika (Tandula-veyāliya)
Q31:21316	Candā-viyyaya
Q31:21317	Devendra-stava (Devindatthā)
Q31:21318	Gaṇita-vidyā (Gaṇiviyya)
Q31:21321	Mahā-pratyākhyāna
Q31:21322	Vīra-stava (Vīratthaa)
Q31:21323	Gacchācāra prakīrṇaka
Q31:214	**Cheda-sutra**
Q31:2141	Niśitha
Q31:2142	Mahā-Niśitha
Q31:2143	Vyavahāra
Q31:2144	Acara-daśāh or Daśāśrutas kanda or Dasāh-kappavahar
Q31:2145	Bṛhat-kalpa
Q31:2146	Pañca-kalpa
Q31:215	**Nandi and Anuyogadvara**
Q31:2151	Nandi-sūtra
Q31:2152	Anuyogadvāra
Q31:216	**Mula-sutra**
Q31:2161	Uttarādhyayana
Q31:2162	Avaśyaka
Q31:2163	Daśa-vaikālika, Dasa-veyāliya
Q31:2164	Piṇḍa-niryukti
Q31:2167	Ogha-niryukti
Q31:4*x*6,1	*Śrāddha-pratikramaṇa-sūtram*
Q31:41*x*3,11	Haribhadra Sūri: *Dharma-bindu-prakaraṇa*
Q4	**Buddhism**
Q41	**Hinayana**
Q41*x*	General treatises
Q41*x*1,1	Milinda-panha
Q41*x*2,1	Netti-pakaraṇa
Q41*x*3	Dhammapāla: *Mahāṭikā or Paramattha-manjūṣā*
Q41*x*5,1	Buddha-ghoṣa: *Visuddhi-magga*
Q41*x*6,1	Buddha-datta: *Abhidhammā-vatāra*
Q41*x*6,2	Buddha-datta: *Rūparūpa-vibhāga*
Q41*x*6,3	Buddha-datta: *Vinaya-vinic-caya*
Q41:2	**Sacred book (Tripitaka)**

Q41:21	**Vinaya-pitaka**
Q41:21:*gx*5	Buddha-ghoṣa: *Sāmanta-pāsādika*
Q41:211	Sutta-vibhanga
Q41:2111	Pārājika
Q41:2112	Pācittiyā
Q41:212	Khaṇḍakās
Q41:2121	Māhā-vagga
Q41:2122	Culḷa-vagga
Q41:2123	Parivāra
Q41:22	**Sutta-pitaka**
Q41:221	Dīgha-nikāya
Q41:221:*gx*5	Buddha-ghoṣa: *Sumangala-vilāsinī*
Q41:222	Majjhima-nikāya
Q41:222:*gx*5	Buddha-ghoṣa: *Papanca-sūdani*
Q41:223	Saṁyutta-nikāya
Q41:223:*gx*5	Buddha-ghoṣa: *Sāratthapakāsinī*
Q41:224	Anguttara-nikāya
Q41:224:*gx*5	Buddha-ghoṣa: *Manoratha-pūraṇī*
Q41:225	Khuddaka-nikāya
Q41:225:*gx*5	Buddha-ghoṣa: *Khuddaka-nikāyatthakathā*
Q41:22511	Khuddaka-pāṭha
Q41:22511:*gx*5	Buddha-ghoṣa: *Paramattha-jotikā*
Q41:22512	Dhammapada
Q41:22512:*gx*5	Buddha-ghoṣa: *Dhamma-padaṭṭha-kathā*
Q41:22513	Udāna
Q41:22513:*gx*3	Dhammapāla: *Paramattha-dīpanī*
Q41:22514	Itivuttaka
Q41:22514:*gx*3	Dhammapāla: *Itivuttakattha-katha*
Q41:22515	Sutta-nipāta
Q41:22515:*gx*5	Buddha-ghoṣa: *Paramatthajotikā*
Q41:22516	Vimāna-vatthu
Q41:22516:*gx*3	Dhammapāla *Paramattha-dīpanī*
Q41:22517	Peta-vatthu
Q41:22517:*gx*3	Dhamma-pāla: *Paramattha-dīpanī*
Q41:22518	Thera-gāthā
Q41:22521	Therī-gāthā
Q41:22522	Jātaka
Q41:22523	Niddeśa
Q41:22523:*gx*7	*Sad-dhamma-pajjotikā*
Q41:22524	Paṭi-sambhida-magga

Q41:22525	Apadāna
Q41:22526	Buddha-vaṁśa
Q41:22527	Cariyā-piṭakā
Q41:23	**Abhidhamma-piṭaka**
Q41:231	Dhamma-saṅgaṇī
Q41:231:*gx*5	Buddha-ghoṣa: *Aṭṭha-sālinī*
Q41:232	Vibhaṅga
Q41:232:*gx*5	Buddha-ghoṣa: *Sammoha-vinodinī*
Q41:233	Kathā-vatthu
Q41:234	Puggala-paññattī
Q41:235	Dhātu-kathā
Q41:236	Yamaka
Q41:237	Patthāna
Q41:6	**Tradition**
Q41:6*x*6,1	Dhamma-kitti: *Dāṭhā-vaṁśa*
Q41:6*x*7,1	*Thūpa-vaṁśa*
Q41:6*x*E50,1	Upatissa: *Mahā-bodhi-vaṁśa*
Q41:6*x*M20,1	Śāsana-vaṁśa
Q42	**Mahayana**
Q42*x*5,1	*Sad-dharma-puṇḍarīka*
Q42*x*D65,1	Śānti-deva: *Śikṣā-samuccaya*
Q42*x*D65,2	Śānti-deva: *Bodhi-caryāvatāra*
Q5	**Judaism**
Q5:221	Seder Zeraim
Q5:222	Seder Moed
Q5:223	Seder Nashim
Q5:224	Seder Nezikin

Q5:22411	Baba Kamma
Q5:22412	Baba Mezia
Q5:22413	Baba Battra
Q5:225	Kodashim
Q5:226	Tabaroth
Q6	**Christianity**
Q6:21	Bible
Q6:22	Old Testament
Q6:221	Historical books
Q6:222	Poetic books
Q6:2225	Canticles
Q6:223	Prophetic books
Q6:23	New Testament
Q6:231	St. Matthew
Q6:232	St. Mark
Q6:233	St. Luke
Q6:234	St. John
Q6:235	Acts
Q6:236	Epistles
Q6:2361	St. Paul
Q6:2362	James
Q6:2363	Peter
Q6:2364	John
Q6:2365	Jude
Q6:237	Sermon on the Mount
Q6:238	Revelation
Q6:294	Apocrypha
Q8412	**Confucianism**
Q8412:211	Yi Ching
Q8412:212	Śhi Ching
Q8412:213	Shu Ching
Q8412:214	Li He
Q8412:215	Chun Chin
Q8412:216	Analects
Q8451	**Zoroastrianism**

Q8451*x*1,1	Bundahis
Q8451*x*2,1	Selections of Zad Sparam
Q8451*x*3,1	Bahman Yast
Q8451*x*4,1	Shayast-La-Shayast
Q8451*x*5,1	Andaz-i-Atar-pat-i-Maras-pand
Q8451*x*6,1	Arda Viraf
Q8451*x*7,1	Dinkard
Q8451*x*8,1	Gangi-i-Syay-igan
Q8451*x*91,1	Menuk-i-Khrat
Q8451*x*92,1	Sad Dar
Q8451:2	Avesta
Q8451:21	Gāthas
Q8451:22	Vendidad
Q8451:23	Fragments of the Nasks
Q8451:231	Westergard's Fragments
Q8451:232	Zend Fragments
Q8451:233	Tahmura's Fragments
Q8451:234	Fragments of the Erpatistan Nask
Q8451:235	Fragments of the Nirangistan Nask
Q8451:236	Sundry Fragments
Q8451:237	Aogemaide Nask
Q845:24	The Sirozahs, I and II
Q8451:25	The Yasts
Q8451:2511	Ormazd
Q8451:2512	Haptan
Q8451:2513	Ardebehist
Q8451:2514	Khordad
Q8451:2515	Aban
Q8451:2516	Khorshed
Q8451:2517	Mah
Q8451:2518	Tir
Q8451:2521	Gos
Q8451:2522	Mihir
Q8451:2523	Srosh Yast Hadhokht
Q8451:2524	Rashn
Q8451:2525	Farvardin
Q8451:2526	Bahram
Q8451:2527	Ram
Q8451:2528	Din
Q8451:2531	Ashi
Q8451:2532	Ashtad
Q8451:2533	Zamyad
Q8451:2534	Vanant
Q8451:2535	XXI, a Fragment
Q8451:2536	XXII, a Fragment
Q8451:2537	Afrin Paighambar Zartust
Q8451:2538	Vistasp
Q8451:261	Khorshed Nyasis
Q8451:262	Mihir Nyasis
Q8451:263	Mah Nyasis
Q8451:264	Aban Nyasis
Q8451:265	Atas Nyasis

R6 INDIAN PHILOSOPHY

R6*x*1,1	Hari-bhadra: *Ṣaḍ-darśana-samuccaya*
R6*x*2,1	Mādhavācārya: *Sarva-darśana-saṅgraha*
R6*x*3,1	Śaṅkarācārya: *Sarva-siddhānta-saṅgraha*
R6*x*4,1	*Sarva-mata-saṅgraha*
R6*x*5,1	*Prapañca-hṛdaya*

R621 Vaisesika

R621*x*1,1	**Kanada: Vaisesika-sutra**
R621*x*1,1,1	Praśasta-pāda Ācārya: *Padārtha-saṅgraha*
R621*x*1,1,1,1	*Padārtha-tattva-nirṇaya*
R621*x*1,1,1,2	*Dravya-bhāṣya-ṭīkā*
R621*x*1,1,1,4	Śrīdhara: *Nyāyā-kandaḷī*
R621*x*1,1,1,5	Udayaṇācārya: *Kiraṇāvali*
R621*x*1,1,1,5,1	Vardha-mānopādhyāya: *Kiraṇāvali-prakāśa*
R621*x*1,1,1,5,1,2	Raghu-nātha Śiromaṇi: *Kiraṇāvali-prakāśa-dīdhiti*
R621*x*1,1,1,5,2	Padma-nābha-miśra: *Kiraṇāvali-bhāskara*
R621*x*1,1,1,5,3	Bhaṭṭa Vādīndra: *Rasa-sāra*
R621*x*1,1,1,I90	Śaṅkara-miśra: *Praśastapāda-bhāṣyaṭīkā*
R621*x*1,1,1,K30	Jagadiśa Tarkālaṅkāra: *Praśasta-pāda-bhāṣya-sukti*
R621*x*1,1,1,M50	Jaya-nārāyaṇa Tarka-pañcānana: *Vivṛti*
R621*x*1,1,2	Śaṅkara-miśra: *Upaskāra*
R621*x*2,1	**Vallabhacarya: Nyaya-lilavati**
R621*x*2,1,1	Vardha-māna: *Nyāya-līlāvatī-prakāśa*
R621*x*2,1,1,1	*Nyāya-līlāvatī-prakāśa-viveka*
R621*x*2,1,2	Raghu-nātha Siromaṇī: *Nyāya-līlāvatidīdhiti*
R621*x*2,1,4	Śankara Miśra; *Nyāya-līlāvati-kaṇṭhābharaṇa*
R621*x*2,1,8	Bhagī-ratha Ṭhakūra: *Nyāya-līlāvati-vivṛti*
R621*x*D95,1	Sivāditya: *Sapta-padārthī*
R621*x*D95,1,1	Jina-vardhana Śuri: *Commentary*
R621*x*D95,1,2	Mādhava Saraswatī: *Mita-bhāṣiṇī*
R621*x*D95,1,3	Śeṣānanda: *Padārtha-candrikā*

R621*x*D95,1,4	Bhairavendra: *Śiśu-bodhinī*
R621*x*D95,1,5	Bala-bhadra: *Sandarbha*
R621*x*J70,1	Sārva-deva Śūri: *Pramāṇa-mañjarī*
R621*x*K30,1	Gaṅgā-dhara-Śūri: *Kānāda-siddhānta-candrikā*
R621*x*L50,1	Veṇī-datta: *Padārtha-maṇḍana*

R625 Nyaya

R625*x*1,1	**Gautama: Nyaya-sutra**
R625*x*1,1,1	Vātsyāyana: *Nyāya-bhāṣya*
R625*x*1,1,1,1	Uddyota-kara: *Nyāya-vārttika*
R625*x*1,1,1,1,1	Vācaspati-miśra: *Nyāya-vārttika-tātparya-ṭīkā*
R625*x*1,1 1,1,1,1	Udayaṇācārya: *Nyāya-vārttika-tātparya-pari-śuddhi*
R625*x*1,1,2	Jayanta Bhaṭṭa: *Nyāya-mañjarī*
R625*x*1,1,3	Viśva-nātha Pañcānana: *Nyāya-sūtra-vṛtti*
R625*x*1,1,M10	Rādhā-mohan Bhāṭṭācārya: *Nyāya-sūtra-vivaraṇa*
R625*x*2,1	**Bhasarvajna: Nyaya-sara**
R625*x*2,1,1	Vāsudeva: *Nyāya-sāra-pada-pañcikā*
R625*x*2,1,2	Jaya-siṁha-Śūri: *Nyāya-tātparya-dīpikā*
R625*x*3,1	**Udayana: Nyaya-kusumanjali or Kusumanjali**
R625*x*3,1,1	Varada-rāja: *Bodhinī*
R625*x*3,1,2	Vardha-māna: *Nyāya-kusumañjali-prakāśa*
R625*x*3,1,2,2	Ruci-datta-miśra: *Nyāya-kusumāñjali-prakā-śa-makaranda*
R625*x*3,1,3	Hari-dāsa: *Nyāya-kusumāñjali-kārikā-vyākhya*
R625*x*4,1	**Varada-raja Tarkika-raksa**
R625*x*4,1,1	Varada-rāja: *Sāra-saṅgraha*
R625*x*4,1,2	Jñāna-pūrṇa: *Laghu-dīpikā*
R625*x*4,1,3	Malli-nātha-Śūri: *Niṣkanṭaka*
R625*x*5,1	**Kesava-misra: Tarka-bhaṣa**
R625*x*5,1,1	Cennu Bhaṭṭa: *Tarkabhāṣā-prakāśika*
R625*x*5,1,2	Govardhana-miśra: *Tarkabhāṣā-prakāśā*
R625*x*5,1,3	Gaurī-kānta Sārva-bhauma Bhaṭṭā-cārya: *Bhāvārtha-dīpikā*

R625*x*5,1,4	Bāla-candra: *Tarkabhāṣā-prakāśikā*
R625*x*5,1,5	Mādhava-deva: *Tarkabhāṣā-sāramañjarī*
R625*x*5,1,6	Gopi-nātha: *Tarkabhāṣā-bhāva-prakāśikā*
R625*x*5,1,7	Kauṇḍinya Dīkṣita: *Tarkabhāṣā-prakāśikā*
R625*x*5,1,8	Viśva-karman: *Nyāya-pradīpa*
R625*x*6,1	**Gangesa Upadhyaya: Tattva-cintamani**
R625*x*6,1,1	Vardha-mānopādhyāya: *Prakāśa*
R625*x*6,1,2	Jaya-deva: *Aloka*
R625*x*6,1,3	Ruci-datta-miśra: *Tattva-cintāmaṇi-prakāśa*
R625*x*6,1,4	Vāsu-deva-miśra: *Tattva-cintāmaṇi-ṭīkā*
R625*x*6,1,5	Raghu-nātha Śiromani Bhaṭṭācārya: *Dīdhiti*
R625*x*6,1,5,1	Mathurā-nātha: *Commentary on Dīdhiti*
R625*x*6,1,5,2	Bhavānanda Śiddhānta Vāgīśa: *Tattva-cintāmaṇi-dīdhiti-prakāśa*
R625*x*6,1,5,3	Jagadīśa: *Jāgadīśī*
R625*x*6,1,5,4	Gadā-dhara Bhaṭṭācārya: *Tattva-cintāmaṇi-dīdhiti-vivṛti*
R625*x*6,1,5,4,1	Bhīmācārya Ottangadkar: *Gādā-dharī-Pañca-lakṣaṇī*
R625*x*6,1,5,J70	Kṛṣṇa-dāsa Sārvabhauma: *Anumāna-dīdhiti-prasāriṇī*
R625*x*6,1,6	Mathurā-nātha Tarka-vāgīśa: *Tattva-cintāmaṇi-rahasya*
R625*x*6,1,K36	Rāja-cūḍāmaṇi Makhin: *Maṇi-darpaṇa*
R625*x*6,1,K40	Gopi-nātha: *Maṇi-sāra*
R625*x*6,1,M80	Sangameśvara Śāstri: *Sangameśvara-kroḍam*
R625*x*7,1	**Visva-natha Pancanana Bhattacarya: Karikavali or Bhasa paricheda**
R625*x*7,1,1	Viśva-nātha Pañcānana Bhaṭṭācārya: *Muktāvaḷi*
R625*x*7,1,1,1	Mahā-deva and Dina-kara: *Prakāśa*
R625*x*7,1,1,1,1	Rāma-rudra: *Rāmarudrīya*
R625*x*7,1,1,2	Rāma-rudra: *Prabhā*
R625*x*7,1,1,3	Rāma-rudra: *Mañjūṣā*
R625*x*7,1,1,4	Gaṅgā-rāma: *Gaṅgārāma-jhaṭīya*
R625*x*8,1	**Annam-bhatta: Tarka-sangraha**

R625*x*8,1,1	Annam-bhaṭṭa: *Tarka-saṅgraha-dīpikā*
R625*x*8,1,1,1	Nīla-kaṇṭha: *Prakāśikā*
R625*x*8,1,1,1,1	Lakṣmī-narasimha Śāstri: *Bhāskārodaya*
R625*x*D87,1	Jayanta: *Nyāya-kalikā*
R625*x*H50,1	Nigamānta Mahā-deśika: *Nyāya-pariśuddhi*
R625*x*I50,1	Vācas-pati-miśra: *Khandanoddhāra*
R625*x*J40,1	Raghu-nātha: *Padārtha-tattva-nirupaṇa*
R625*x*J40,1,1	Raghu-deva: *Nyāyālaṅkāra*
R625*x*J40,2	Raghu-nātha: *Padārtha-mālā*
R625*x*J50,1	Jānakī-nātha Bhaṭṭācārya: *Nyāya-siddhānta-mañjarī*
R625*x*J50,1,2	Yādavācārya: *Nyāya-mañjarī-sāra*
R625*x*K50,1	Jaya-rāma Bhaṭṭācārya: *Nyāya-siddhānta-māla*
R625*x*M10,1	Rādha-mohan Bhaṭṭācārya: *Nyāyasūtra-vivaraṇa*
R625*x*M30,1	Rākhāl-dās: *Tattva-sāra*
R625,13*x*1,1	Gokula-nātha: *Pada-vākya-ratnākara*
R625,13*x*2,1	Giri-dhara: *Vibhaktyartha-nirṇaya*
R625,13*x*3,1	Jagadīśa: *Śabda-śakti-prakāśa*
R625,13*x*4,1	Gadā-dhara Bhaṭṭācārya: *Vyutpatti-vāda*
R625,13*x*4,1,1	Kṛṣṇa Bhaṭṭa: *Vyutpatti-vāda-vyākhyā*
R625,13*x*4,1,2	Bacca Śarmā: *Vyutpatti-vāda-vyākhyā*
R625,13*x*4,1,3	Sudarśanācārya: *Vyutpatti-vāda-vyākhyā*
R625,13*x*4,2	Gadā-dhara Bhaṭṭācārya: *Sakti-vāda*

R631 Sankhya

R631*x*1,1	**Tattva-samasa**
R631*x*2,1	**Isvara-krsna: Sankhya-karika**
R631*x*2,1,1	Māṭhara: *Māṭhara-vṛtti*
R631*x*2,1,2	Gauḍa-pāda: *Sāṅkhya-kārikā-bhāṣya*
R631*x*2,1,3	Vācas-pati-miśra: *Sāṅkhya-tattva-kaumudī*
R631*x*2,1,3,8	Vaṁśī-dhara-miśra: *Sāṅkhya-tattva-kaumudī-vibhākara*
R631*x*2,1,4	Śāṅkarārya: *Jaya-maṅgaḷa*
R631*x*2,1,5	Nārāyaṇa-tīrtha: *Candrikā*

R631x2,1,8	*Yukti-dīpikā*
R631x3,1	**Kapila: Sankhya-sutra**
R631x3,1,1	Aniruddha: *Sāṅkhya-sūtra-vṛtti*
R631x3,1,2	Vijñāna-bhikṣu: *Sāṅkhya-pravacana-bhāṣya*
R631x3,1,3	Mahā-deva: *Sāṅkhya-sūtra-vṛtti*

R635 Yoga

R635x1,1	**Patanjali: Yoga-sutra**
R635x1,1,1	Vyāsa: *Bhāṣya*
R635x1,1,1,1	Vācas-pati-miśra: *Pātañjala-sūtra-bhāṣya-vyākhyā* or *Tattva-vaiśāradi*
R635x1,1,2	Vijñāna-bhikṣu: *Yoga-vārttika*
R635x1,1,3	Rāghavānanda, Sarasvatī: *Pātañjala-bhāṣya*
R635x1,1,4	Hari-harānanda Āraṇya: *Bhāsvatī*
R635x1,1,L00	Nāgeśa Bhaṭṭa: *Pātañjala-sūtra-vṛtti*
R635x1,1,L50	Sadāśivendra Sarasvatī: *Yoga-sutra-vṛtti* or *Yoga-sudhākara*
R635x1,1,M10	Rāmānanda-yati: *Maṇi-prabha*
R635x1,1,M20	Nārāyaṇa-tīrtha: *Yoga-siddhānta-candrikā*
R635x1,1,M21	*Sūtrārtha-bodhinī*
R635x1,1,M30	Ananta Paṇḍita: *Pātanjala-darśana*
R635x1,1,M40	*Bhāva-gaṇeśīya*
R635x2,1	Bhoja-deva: *Rāja-mārtāṇḍa*
R635x3,1	Vijñāna-bhikṣu: *Yoga-sāra-saṅgraha* or *Jñāna-pradīpa*

R64 Purva Mimamsa

R64x1,1	Jaiminī: *Mīmāṁsā-sūtra*
R64x1,1,1	Śabara: *Śābara-bhāṣya*
R64x1,1,1,1	Maṇḍana: *Mīmāṁsānukramaṇika*
R64xL40,1	Satya-jñānānanda: *Veda-prakāśa*

R641 Bhatta Mimamsa

R641x1,1	**Kumarila Bhatta: Sloka-varttika**
R641x1,1,1	Umbeka or Umveka and Jaya-miśra: *Śloka-vārttika-vyākhyā*

R641x1,1,2	Sucarita-miśra: *Kāśikā*
R641x1,1,3	Pārtha-sārathi-miśra: *Nyāya-ratnākara*
R641x1,2	**Kumarila Bhatta: Tantra-varttika**
R641x1,2,1	Bhaṭṭa Someśvara: *Nyāya-sudhā* or *Raṇakam*
R641x1,3	**Kumarila Bhatta: Tup-tika**
R641x1,3,1	Pārtha-sārathi-miśra: *Tantra-ratna*
R641x4,1	Maṇḍana-miśra: *Vidhi-viveka*
R641x4,1,1	Vācas-pati: *Nyāya-kaṇikā*
R641x5,1	Maṇḍana-miśra: *Bhāvanā-viveka*
R641x5,1,1	Umbeka or Umveka: *Bhāvanā-viveka-vyākhyā*
R641x6,1	Pārtha-sārathi-miśra: *Nyāya-ratnamāla*
R641x6,1,1	Rāmānujācārya: *Nāyaka-ratna*
R641x7,1	Pārtha-sārathi-miśra: *Śāstra-dīpikā*
R641x7,1,1	Rāma-kṛṣṇa-miśra: *Yukti-sneha-prapūraṇi*
R641x7,1,1,1	Rāma-kṛṣṇa-miśra: *Gūḍhārtha-vivaraṇa*
R641x7,1,2	Somanātha: *Mayukha-mālikā*
R641x8,1	Mādhavācārya: *Jaiminīya-nyāya-mālā* or *Mīmāmsādhikaraṇa-nyāya-mālā*
R641x8,1,1	Mādhavācārya: *Nyāya-mālā-vistāra*
R641x91,1	Khaṇḍa-deva: *Bhāṭṭa-dīpikā*
R641x91,1,1	Sambhu Bhaṭṭa: *Prabhā-valī*
R641x91,1,L80	Vāncheśvara Yajvan: *Bhāṭṭa-cintāmaṇi*
R641x91,2	Khaṇḍa-deva: *Mīmāmsā-kaustubha*
R641x91,3	Khaṇḍa-deva: *Bhāṭṭa-rahasya*
R641xJ50,1	Appaya Dīkṣita: *Vidhi-rasāyana*
R641xJ50,1	Appaya Dīkṣita: *Citra-pāṭha*
R641xJ90,1	Nārāyaṇa Bhaṭṭa and Nārāyaṇa Paṇḍita: *Mānameyodaya*
R641xK20,1	Bhaṭṭa Śaṅkara: *Mīmāmsā-bāla-prakāśa*
R641xK30,1	Āpa-deva *Mīmāmsā-nyāya-prakāśa* or *Apadevī*
R641xK30,1,1	Ananta-deva: *Bhaṭṭālaṅkārā*
R641xK30,1,8	Cinna-svāmi Śāstrī: *Mīmāmsā-nyāya-prakāśa-vyākhyā*
R641xK40,1	Gāgā Bhaṭṭa: *Bhāṭṭa-cintāmaṇi*
R641xK60,1	Laughākṣi Bhāskara: *Artha-saṅgraha*

R641*x*K70,1	Rāma-kṛṣṇa Bhaṭṭācārya: *Adhikaraṇa-kaumudī*
R641*x*K90,1	Vaidya-nātha Bhaṭṭa: *Nyāya-bindu*
R641*x*K95,1	Bhāskara Bhaṭṭa: *Bhāṭṭa-candrikā* (a Comm. on Saṁkarṣa-kāṇḍa of *Mīmāṁsā-sūtra*)
R641*x*L00,1	Kṛṣṇa Yajvan: *Mīmāṁsā-paribhāṣā*
R641*x*L10,1	Nārāyaṇa-tīrtha: *Bhāṭṭa-bhāṣā-prakāśa*
R641*x*L30,1	Vāsu-deva Dīkṣita: *Advara-mīmāṁsā-kutūhala-vṛtti*
R641*x*M50,1	Rāmeśvara-sūri: *Subodhinī*
R641,24*x*1,1	Vācas-pati-miśra: *Tattva-bindu*

R645 Prabhakara Mimamsa or Gurumata

R645*x*1,1	Prabhākara: *Bṛhatī*
R645*x*1,1,1	Sālika-nātha: *Ṛju-vimala*
R645*x*5,1	Śālika-nātha: *Prakaraṇa-pañcikā*
R645*x*6,1	Bhava-nātha: *Naya-viveka*
R645*x*K50,1	Nandīśvara: *Prabhākara-vijaya*
R645*x*L00,1	Rāmanujācārya: *Tantra-rahasya*

R65 Vedanta

R65*x*K08,1	Rāma-dāsa: *Dāsa-bodha*

R66 Advaita

R66*x*1,11	**Sankara: Upadesa-sahasri**
R66*x*1,12	Śaṅkara: *Viveka-cūḍāmaṇi*
R66*x*1,13	Śaṅkara: *Aparokṣānubhūti*
R66*x*1,14	Śaṅkara: *Daśa-ślokī*
R66*x*1,14,1	Madhu-sūdana Sarasvatī: *Siddhānta-bindu*
R66*x*1,15	Śaṅkara: *Pañci-karaṇa*
R66*x*1,16	Śaṅkara: *Dakṣiṇāmūrti-stotra*
R66*x*1,17	Śaṅkara: *Vākya-sudhā*
R66*x*2,1	**Maṇdana-misra: Brahma-siddhi**
R66*x*2,1,1	Vācas-pati-miśra: *Brahma-tattva-samīkṣā*
R66*x*2,1,2	Śaṅkha-pāṇi: *Samīkṣā-phakkikā*
R66*x*2,1,3	Cit-sukha: *Brahma-siddhi-vyākhyā*

R66*x*2,1,4	Ānanda-pūrṇa: *Brahma-siddhi-vyākhyā*
R66*x*3,1	**Suresvaracarya: Naiskarmya-siddhi**
R66*x*3,1,1	Ānandānubhava: *Naiṣkarmya-siddhi-vyākhyā*
R66*x*3,1,2	Jñānottama-miśra: *Candrikā*
R66*x*3,1,3	Cit-sukhācārya: *Comm. on Naiṣkarmya-siddhi*
R66*x*3,1,4	Jaya-kṛṣṇa-brahma-tīrtha: *Comm. on Naiṣkarmya-siddhi*
R66*x*4,1	**Vimuktatman: Ista-siddhi**
R66*x*4,1,1	Jñānottama: *Vivaraṇa*
R66*x*4,1,2	Ānandānubhava: *Commentary*
R66*x*5,1	**Sarvajnatman: Sanksepa-sariraka**
R66*x*5,1,1	Rāma-tīrtha: *Anvayārtha-prakāśikā*
R66*x*5,1,2	Puruṣottama-miśra or Puruṣottama Dīkṣita: *Śubodhinī*
R66*x*5,1,3	Nṛsimhāśrama: *Tattva-bodhinī*
R66*x*5,1,4	Rāghavānanda Sarasvatī: *Vidyānanda-varṣiṇī*
R66*x*5,1,5	Madhu-sūdana Sarasvatī: *Commentary*
R66*x*6,1	**Ananda-bodha: Advaita-makaranda or Nyaya-makaranda**
R66*x*6,1,1	Cit-sukhācārya: *Comm. on Advaita-makaranda*
R66*x*6,2	Ānanda-bodha: *Pramaṇa-mālā*
R66*x*6,2,1	*Pramāṇa-mālā-vyākhyā*
R66*x*6,3	Ānanda-bodha: *Nyāya-dīpāvali*
R66*x*6,3,1	Cit-sukhācārya: *Comm. on Nyāya-dīpāvali*
R66*x*7,1	**Sriharsa: Khandana-khanda-khadya or Anirvacaniyata-sarvasva**
R66*x*7,1,1	Cit-sukhācārya: *Commentary*
R66*x*7,1,2	Varada-rāja: *Commentary*
R66*x*7,1,3	Śaṅkara-miśra: *Commentary*
R66*x*7,1,4	Ānanda-pūrṇa: *Khaṇḍana-phakkikā-vibhajana* or *Vidyā-sāgarī*
R66*x*7,1,5	Raghu-nātha: *Commentary*
R66*x*8,1	**Cit-sukharcarya: Advaita-pradipa or Citsukhi**

R66*x*8,1,1	Pratyag-rūpa Bhagavān: *Nayana-prasādinī*
R66*x*91,1	**Madhu-sudana Sarasvati: Advaita-siddhi**
R66*x*91,1,1	Brahmānanda Sarasvati: *Laghu-candrikā*
R66*x*91,1,1,1	Viṭṭhaḷeśopādhyāya: *Comm.* on *Laghu-candrikā*
R66*x*91,1,2	Brahmānanda Sarasvati: *Guru-candrikā*
R66*x*91,1,3	Bala-bhadra: *Advaita-siddhi-vyākhyā*
R66*x*91,1,4	Sadānanda Vyāsa: *Advaita-siddhi-saṅgraha*
R66*x*D70,1	Totakācārya: *Śruti-sāra-samuddha-raṇa*
R66*x*D95,1	Prakāśātman: *Śābda-nirṇaya*
R66*x*D95,1,1	Ānanda-bodha: *Comm.* on *Śābda-nirṇaya*
R66*x*G70,1	Sukha-prakāśa: *Commentary*
R66*x*G80,1	Ānanda-giri: *Tarka-saṅgraha*
R66*x*H10,1	Bhāratī-tīrtha: *Vaiyāsika-nyāya-mālā*
R66*x*H10,1,1	Vidyāraṇya: *Vaiyāsika-nyāya-mālā-vistāra*
R66*x*H50,1	Vidyāraṇya: *Pañca-daśī*
R66*x*H50,2	Vidyāraṇya: *Jīvan-mukti-viveka*
R66*x*H50,3	Vidyāraṇya: *Vivaraṇa-prameya-saṅgraha*
R66*x*I50,1	Lakṣmī-dhara: *Advaita-makaranda*
R66*x*I50,1,1	Svayaṁ-prakāśānanda: *Commentary*
R66*x*I90,1	Śaṅkara-Miśra: *Bheda-ratnam*
R66*x*J10,1	Raṅga-rājādhvarin: *Advaita-mukura*
R66*x*J25,1	Sadānanda: *Vedānta-sāra*
R66*x*J25,1,1	Āpa-deva: *Bāla-bodhinī*
R66*x*J25,1,3	Rāma-tirtha: *Vidvan-mano-rañjanī*
R66*x*J40,1	Narasiṁhāśrama: *Advaita-dīpikā*
R66*x*J40,2	Narasiṁhāśrama: *Bheda-dhikkāra*
R66*x*J40,3	Narasiṁhāśrama: *Nṛsimha-vijñā-pana*
R66*x*J40,4	Narasiṁhāśrama: *Vedānta-tattva-viveka*
R66*x*J50,1	Appaya Dīkṣita: *Śārīraka-nyāya-rakṣāmaṇi*
R66*x*J50,2	Appaya Dīkṣita: *Śiddhānta-leśa-saṅgraha*
R66*x*J50,2,1,1	Acyuta-kṛṣṇānanda: *Siddhānta-leśa-saṅgraha-vyākhyā*
R66*x*J50,3	Appaya Dīkṣita: *Vāda-nakṣatra-mālā* or *Nakṣatra-vādā-vali*

R66xJ80,1	Kāśmiraka Sadānanda Yogi: *Advaita-brahma-siddhi*
R66xJ85,1	Dharma-rāja Dīkṣita: *Vedānta-paribhāṣā*
R66xK00,1	Madhu-sūdana Sarasvatī: *Advaita-ratna-rakṣaṇa*
R66xK00,2	Madhu-sūdana Sarasvatī: *Prasthāna-bheda*
R66xK00,3	Madhu-sūdana Sarasvatī: *Vedānta-kalpa-latikā*
R66xK00,4	Madhu-sūdana Sarasvatī: *Īśvara-pratipatti prakāśa*
R66xK50,1	Raṅgoji-bhaṭṭa: *Advaita-cintāmaṇi*
R66xK60,1	Ananta-deva: *Siddhānta-tattva* or *Vedānta-prakaraṇa*
R66xK70,1	Kṛṣṇānanda Sarasvatī: *Siddhānta-siddhāñjana*
R66xK70,1,1	Bhāskara Dīkṣita: *Ratna-tūlikā*
R66xK85,1	Gaṅgā-dharendra Sarasvatī: *Vedānta-siddhānta-sūkti-mañjarī*
R66xK90,1	*Svā-rājya-siddhi*
R66xL20,1	Brahmānanda Sarasvatī: *Advaita-siddhānta-vidyotana*
R66xL40,1	Tāṇḍavar: *Kaivalyā-nava-nītam*
R66xL40,1,4	Govindar: *Tātparya-dīpikā*
R66xL50,1	Śadāśivendra Sarasvatī: *Siddhānta-kalpa-vallī*
R66xM00,1	Ayyaṇṇā Dīkṣita: *Vyāsa-tātparya-nirṇaya*
R66xM10,1	Narahari: *Bodha-sāra*
R66xM40,1	Cidambara-svāmi: *Advaita-sāstirat-tiraṭṭu*

R66,5 BRAHMA-SŪTRA

R66,5x1,1	**Sankara: Brahmasutra-bhasya**
R66,5x1,1,1	Padma-pāda: *Pañca-pādikā*
R66,5x1,1,1,1	Prakạ̄sātman: *Pañca-pādikā-vivaraṇa*
R66,5x1,1,1,1,1	Akhaṇḍānanda-muni: *Tattva-dīpana*
R66,5x1,1,1,1,2	Cit-sukha: *Vivaraṇa-tātparya-dīpikā*
R66,5x1,1,1,1,3	Nṛsiṁhāśrama-muni: *Bhāva-prakāśikā*
R66,5x1,1,1,1,4	Rāmānanda Sarasvatī: *Vivaraṇopanyasā*
R66,5x1,1,1,2	Amalānanda: *Pañca-pādikā-darpaṇa*

R66,5*x*1,1,1,3 Ānanda-pūrṇa-yati: *Pañca-pādika-ṭikā*
R66,5*x*1,1,2 Vācas-pati-miśra: *Bhāmatī*
R66,5*x*1,1,2,1 Amalānanda: *Kalpa-taru*
R66,5*x*1,1,2,1,1 Appaya Dīkṣita: *Pari-mala*
R66,5*x*1,1,2,1,2 Lakṣmī-nṛsiṁha: *Abhoga*
R66,5*x*1,1,3 *Prakaṭārtha-vivaraṇa*
R66,5*x*1,1,4 Cit-sukha: *Bhāṣya-bhāvā-prakāśa*
R66,5*x*1,1,5 Ānanda-giri: *Sāriraka-bhāṣya-vyākhyā* or *Nyāya-nirṇaya*
R66,5*x*1,1,6 Rāmānanda Sarasvatī or Govindānanda Sarasvatī: *Bhāṣya-ratna-prabhā*
R66,5*x*1,1,6,1 Acyuta-kṛṣṇānanda: *Ratna-prabhā-vyākhyā*
R66,5*x*1,1,7 Kṛṣṇānanda-yati or Advaitānanda: *Brahma-vidyābharaṇa*
R66,5*x*2,1 Vijñāna-bhīkṣu: *Vijñānāmṛta*
R66,5*x*3,1 Rāmānanda Sarasvatī: *Brahmāmṛta-varṣiṇī*
R66,5*x*4,1 Hari Dīkṣita: *Brahma-sūtra-vṛtti*
R66,5*x*5,1 Brahmānanda Sarasvatī: *Vedānta-sūtra-muktāvali*
R66,5*x*6,1 Sadāśivendra Sarasvatī: *Brahma-sūtra-vṛtti*
R66,5*x*J50,1 Appaya Dīkṣita: *Nyāya-rakṣāmaṇi*
R66,5*x*M50,1 Raghu-nātha Sūri: *Saṅkara-pāda-bhūṣana*

R66,6 BHAGAVAD-GĪTA

R66,6*x*1,1 Sankara: Gitabhasya
R66,6*x*1,1,1 Āṇanda-giri: *Vivecana*
R66,6*x*1,1,2 Dhana-pati: *Bhāṣyotkarṣa-dīpikā*
R66,6*x*2,1 Madhu-sūdana Sarasvatī: *Gūḍhārtha-dīpikā*
R66,6*x*6,1 Vedānta-deśika: *Brahmānanda-giri*
R66,6*x*7,1 Hanumān: *Paiśāca-bhāṣya*
R66,6*x*G90,1 Jñāneśvara: *Jñāneśvarī*
R66,6*x*I20,1 Bhaṭṭar: *Bhagavad-gītai*
R66.6*x*I20,2 Bhaṭṭar: *Gūḍārtha-dīpikai*

R66,8 PORTIONS OF MAHABHARATA

R66,8*x*1 Śaṅkara: *Sanatsūjātīya bhāṣya*

R663 Praty-abhijna (Kasmirian)

R663x1,1	**Somananda: Siva-drsti**
R663x1,1,1	Somānanda: *Vṛtti*
R663x1,1,3	Abhinava-gupta: *Sulocana*
R663x2,1	**Utpala: Praty-abhijna-sutra**
R663x2,1,1	Utpala: *Vṛtti*
R663x2,1,1,1	Utpala: *Tīkā* (*Vivṛti*)
R663x2,1,2	Abhinava-gupta: *Praty-abhijñā-vimarśinī* (*Laghu-vṛtti*)
R663x2,1,3	Abhinava-gupta: *Praty-abhijñā-vivṛti-vimarśinī* (*Bṛhadvṛtti*)
R663x2,1,4	Bhāskara: *Śiva-sūtra-vārttika*
R663x2,1,5	Kṣema-rāja: *Praty-abhijñā-hṛdaya*
R663x3,1	**Abhinava-gupta: Tantra-loka**
R663x3,1,1	Jaya-ratha: *Commentary*
R663x3,2	Abhinava-gupta: *Tantra-sāra*
R663x3,3	Abhinava-gupta: *Paramārtha-sāra*
R663x3,3,1	Yoga-rāja: *Commentary*

R6634 Virasaiva advaita

R6634,5x1,1	Śrīpati-paṇḍitācārya: *Śrīkara-bhāṣya*

R672 Visistadvaita (Vaisnava)

R672x1,1	Yāmuna: *Siddhi-traya*
R672x2,1	**Ramanuja: Vedanta-sara**
R672x2,2	Rāmānuja: *Vedānta-dīpa*
R672x2,3	Rāmānuja: *Vedārthā-saṅgraha*
R672x2,3,1	Sudarśana: *Tātparya-dīpikā*
R672x2,3,1,1	Rāma Miśra: *Sneha-pūrti*
R672x3,1	Nāthamuni: *Nyāya-tattva*
R672x4,1	Parāśara Bhaṭṭa: *Tattva-ratnākara*
R672x5,1	Rāma Miśra: *Vivaraṇa*
R672xG68,1	**Vedanta-desika or Venkata-natha: Adhi-karana-saravali**
R672xG68,1,1	Varada-nātha or Kumāra-varadācārya: *Adhi-karaṇa-cintāmaṇi*

R672*x*G68,2	Vedānta-deśika: *Tattva-muktā-kalāpa*
R672*x*G68,2,1	*Tattva-muktā-kalāpa-vyākhyā*
R672*x*G68,3	Vedānta-deśika: *Nyāya-pariśuddhi*
R672*x*G68,3,1	Śaṭhakopa-yati: *Commentary*
R672*x*G68,3,2	Śrīnivāsa-dāsa: *Nyāya-sāra*
R672*x*G68,4	Vedānta-deśika: *Nyāya-siddhāñjana*
R672*x*G68,4,1	Raṅga-rāmānuja: *Nyāya-siddhāñjana-vyākhyā*
R672*x*G68,5	Vedānta-deśika: *Vādi-traya-khaṇḍana*
R672*x*G68,6	Vedānta-deśika: *Śata-dūṣaṇi*
R672*x*G68,6,1	Rāmānuja-dāsa or Mahācārya: *Caṇḍa-māruta*
R672*x*G68,6,2	Nṛsimha-rāja: *Śata-dūṣaṇi-vyākhyā*
R672*x*G68,6,3	Śrīnivāsa: *Sahasra-kiraṇī*
R672*x*G80,1	Pillai Lokācārya: *Tattva-trayam*
R672*x*G80,2	Pillai Lokācārya: *Tattva-śekhara*
R672*x*G90,1	Jñāneśvara: *Amṛtānubhava*
R672*x*K20,1	Venkaṭācārya: *Śiddhānta-ratnāvali*
R672*x*K50,1	Śaṭhamarṣa Srīnivāsa-tātācārya: *Ānanda-tāratamya-khaṇḍanam*
R672*x*K80,1	Śrīnivāsa: *Aruṇā-dhikaraṇa-saraṇa-vivaraṇi*
R672*x*K80,2	Śrīnivāsa: *Oṅkāra-vadārtha*
R672*x*K80,3	Śrīnivāsa: *Jijñāsādarpaṇa*
R672*x*K80,4	Śrīnivāsa: *Jñāna-ratna-prakāśikā*
R672*x*K80,5	Śrīnivāsa: *Natva-darpaṇa*
R672*x*K80,6	Śrīnivāsa: *Tattva-mārtāṇḍa*
R672*x*K80,7	Śrīnivāsa: *Praṇava-darpaṇa*
R672*x*K80,8	Śrīnivāsa: *Virodha-nirodha*
R672*x*K80,9	Śrīnivāsa: *Yatīndra-mata-dīpika*
R672*x*K90,1	Mahācārya or Rāmānujadāsa: *Pārā-śarya-vijaya*
R672*x*K90,2	Mahācārya: *Vedānta-vijaya*
R672*x*K90,3	Mahācārya: *Advaita-vidyā-vijaya*
R672*x*K90,4	Mahācārya: *Sad-vidyā-vijaya*
R672*x*K95,1	Bucci Venkaṭācārya: *Vedānta-kārikā-vali*
R672*x*L20,1	Para-vastu Vedāntācārya: *Vedānta-kaustubha*
R672*x*L25,1	Nṛsimha-deva: *Ānanda-vallarī*

R672*x*L40,1	Raṅga-rāmānuja: *Parapakṣa-nirākṛta*
R672*x*L50,1	Śaṭhakopa-muni: *Brahma-lakṣaṇa-vākyārtha*
R672*x*M20,1	Anantācārya: *Śārīra-vāda*
R672*x*M20,2	Anantācārya: *Samvidekat-vānumāna-nirāsa-vādārtha*
R672*x*M20,3	Anantācārya: *Samāsa-vāda*
R672*x*M20,4	Anantācārya: *Brahmapada-śakti-vāda*
R672*x*M56,1	Ānandāzhvār: *Vedānta-vādā-vali*

R672,5 Brahma-Sūtra

R672,5*x*2,1	**Ramanuja: Sri-bhasya**
R672*x*5*x*2,1,1	Sudarśana: *Śrī-bhāṣya-vyākhyā, Śruta-prakāśa*
R672,5*x*2,1,1,1	Varada-viṣṇu: *Śruta-prakāśa-vyākhyā. Bhāva-prakāśikā*
R672,5*x*2,1,1,2	Lakṣmaṇa: *Guru-bhāva-prakāśā*
R672,5*x*2,1,2	Sudarśana: *Śruta-pradīpika*
R672,5*x*2,1,3	Vedānta-deśika: *Tattva-ṭīkā*
R672,5*x*2,1,4	Sundara-rāja: *Commentary*
R672,5*x*2,1,5	*Nyāya-prakāśikā*
R672,5*x*2,1,6	Raṅga-rāmānuja: *Mūla-bhāvā-prakāśikā*
R672,5*x*3,1	Raṅga-rāmānuja: *Śārīraka-śāstrārtha-dīpikā*
R672,5*x*J50,1	Appaya Dīkṣita: *Naya-mayūkha-mālikā*

R672,6 Bhagavad-Gīta

R672,6*x*1,1	Yāmuna: *Gītārtha-saṅgraha*
R672,6*x*1,1,1	Vedānta-deśika: *Gītārtha-saṅgraha-rakṣā*
R672,6*x*2,1	Rāmānuja: *Bhagavad-gī.ā-bhāṣya*
R672,6*x*2,1,1	Vedānta-deśika: *Tātparya-candrikā*

R673 Saiva Siddhantam

R673*x*1,1	Uyya-vanda-devar I: *Tiru-vundiyār*
R673*x*1,1,1	Uyya-vanda-devar II: *Tiruk-kalirrupādiyār*
R673*x*2,1	**Mey-kanda-devar: Sivajnana-bodham**
R673*x*2,1,1	Aruṇandi Śivācārya: *Śivajñā-siddhi*
R673*x*2,1,6	Umā-pati Śivācārya: *Śiva-prakāśa*
R673*x*2,1,7,1	Śiva-jñāna Yogin: *Drāviḍa-mahā-bhāṣya*

R673x2,1,7,2	Śiva-jñāna Yogin: *Laghu-ṭīkā*
R673x3,1	Aruṇandi Śivācārya: *Irupādirupadu*
R673x4,1	Mana-vācakam-kaḍandān: *Uṇmai-vilakkam*
R673x5,1	Marai Jñāna-sambandar: *Śiva-samaya-neri*
R673x6,1	Umā-pati Śivācārya: *Tiru-varuṭ-payan*
R673x6,2	Umā-pati Śivācārya: *Vinā-veṇbā*
R673x6,3	Umā-pati Śivācārya: *Poṟṟipahroḍai*
R673x6,4	Umā-pati Śivācārya: *Kodik-kavi*
R673x6,5	Umā-pati Śivācārya: *Nenju-viḍu-tūdū*
R673x6,6	Umā-pati Śivācārya: *Uṇmai-neri-viḷakkam*
R673x6,7	Umā-pati Śivācārya: *Sankalpa-nirā-karaṇam*
R673x7,1	Kaṇṇuḍaya Vaḷḷal: *Ozhivil-oḍukkam*
R673x8,1	Śambu-deva: *Śaiva-siddānta-dīpikā*
R673x91,1	Śiva-jñāna Yogi: *Tattuva-prakāśa*
R673x91,1,1	Śiva-jñāna Yogi: *Tattuva-kaṭṭaḷai*

R673,5 Brahma-Sūtra

R673,5x1,1	**Srikantha Sivacarya: Brahma-sutra-bhasya**
R673,5x1,1,1	Appaya Dīkṣita: *Śivārkamaṇi-dīpikā*
R673,5x1,1,2	Nīla-kaṇṭha: *Kriyā-sāra*

R68 Dvaita

R68x1,1	**Ananda-tirtha or Madhvacarya: Tattva-sankhyana**
R68x1,1,1	Jaya-tīrtha: *Tattva-saṅkhyāna-vivaraṇa*
R68x1,2	Ānanda-tīrtha: *Aṇu-bhāṣya*
R68x1,3	Ānanda-tīrtha: *Sarva-mūla*
R68x3,1	Jaya-tīrtha: *Vādā-valī*
R68x120,1	Calāri Seṣācārya: *Pramāṇa-candrikā*
R68x167,1	Vyāsa-tīrtha: *Nyāyāmṛta*
R68x167,1,1	Srīnivāsa: *Nyāyāmṛta-prakāśa*
R68x167,1,2	Rāmācārya: *Nyāyāmṛta-taranginị*
R68x167,2	Vyāsa-tīrtha: *Bhedoj-jīvana*
R68x167,2,1	Śrīnivāsa: *Śarkara*
R68x167,3	Vyāsa-tīrtha: *Tarka-tāṇḍava*

R68xJ20,1	Vana-māli Miśra: *Mādhva-mukhālaṅkara*
R68xK30,1	Viśva-nātha Pancānana Bhaṭṭacārya: *Bheda-siddhi*
R68xL50,1	Venī-dattācārya: *Bheda-jayaśrī*

R68,5 BRAHMA-SŪTRA

R68,5x1,1	**Aṇanda-tirtha: Brahma-sutra-bhasya**
R68,5x1,1,1	Jaya-tīrtha: *Tattva-prakāśika*
R68,5x1,1,1,1	Vyāsa-tīrtha: *Tātparya-candrikā*
R68,5x1,1,1,1,1	Rāghavendra-tīrtha: *Tātparya-candrikā-prakāśā*
R68,5x1,1,1,2	Rāghavendra-tīrtha: *Tattva-prakāśikā-bhāva*
R68,5x1,2	**Ananda-tirtha: Brahma-sutranu-vyakhyana**
R68,5x1,2,1	Jaya-tīrtha: *Nyāya-sudhā*
R68,5x1,2,1,1	Rāghavendra-tīrtha: *Nyāya-sudhā-parimala*
R68,5x1,2,1,2	Keṣava: *Śeṣa-vākyārtha-candrikā*
R68,5x1,2,1,4	Yadupadācārya: *Yādupadīya*
R68,5x1,2,1,8	Śrīnivāsa: *Nyāya-sudhā-ṭippaṇi*

R68,6 BHAGAVAD-GĪTA

R68,6x1,1	Ānanda-tīrtha: *Bhagavad-gitā-bhāṣya*
R68,6x3,1	Rāghavendra: *Vivṛti*

R68,7 BHAGAVATA

R68,7x1,1	Ānanda-tīrtha: *Bhāgavata-tātparya-nirṇaya*
R68,7xK20,1	Vāmana: *Śruti-kalpa-latā*

R68,8 MAHABHARATA

R68,8x1,1	Ānanda-tīrtha: *Mahābhārata-tātparya-nirṇaya*

R6891 Bheda-Bheda

R6891,5x1,1	Bhāskarācārya: *Brahma-sūtra-bhāṣya*
R6891,5x2,1	Bala-deva: *Vedānta-sūtra-bhāṣya* or *Govinda-bhāṣya*

R6892 Dvaitadvaita

R6892x1,1	Nīmbārka: *Daśa-slokī* or *Vedānta-siddhānta-sāra*
R6892x1,1,1	Bhagavat-purusottamācārya: *Vedānta-ratna-mañjūṣā*
R6892x2,1	Ananta-rāma: *Vedānta-tattva-bodha*

R6892,5 BRAHMA-SŪTRA

R6892,5x1,1	**Nimbarka: Vedanta-parijata-saurabha**
R6892,5x1,1,1	Srīnivāsācārya: *Vedānta-kaustubha*
R6892,5x2,1	Devācārya: *Siddhānta-jāhnāvī*
R6892,5x2,1,1	Sundara Bhaṭṭa: *Dvaitādvaita-siddhānta-setukā*

R6892,6 BHAGAVAD-GĪTA

R6892,6x3,1	Keśava-kāśmīrin: *Tattva-prakāśika*

R6893 Suddhadvaita

R6893x1,1	Vallabhācārya: *Tattvārtha-dīpikā*
R6893x1,1,1	*Vidyā-vaijayanti*

R6893,5 BRAHMA-SŪTRA

R6893,5x1,1	**Vallabhacarya: Anubhasya**
R6893,5x1,1,1	Gosvāmi Srī Puruṣottamjee: *Bhāṣya-prakāśā*
R6893,5x1,1,2	*Bāla-bodhini*
R6893,5x1,1,4	Gosvāmi Srī-Puruṣottamjee: *Vedāntā-dhikāraṇa-mālā*
R6893,5x1,1,8	Vraja-nātha Bhaṭṭa: *Marīcikā*

R6893,7 BHAGAVATA

R6893,7x1,1	Vallabhācārya: *Bhāgavata-ṭīkā, Subhodhinī*

R693 Jain Philosophy

R693x1,1	**Umasvati: Tattvarthadhigama-sutra**
R693x1,1,1	Siddha-sena Gani: *Tattvārtha-ṭikā*
R693x1,1,2	Sāmanta-bhadra: *Gandhahasti-maha-bhāṣyā*

R693*x*1,1,3	Pūjya-pāda: *Sarvārtha-siddhi*
R693*x*1,1,4	Akalaṅka: *Tattvārtha-tikā-vyākhyā-laṅkāra*
R693*x*1,1,5	*Rāja-vārttika*
R693*x*1,1,6	Vidyā-nanda: *Śloka-vārttika*
R693*x*1,1,7	Śrivarddha-deva: *Cūḍāmaṇi*
R693*x*2,1	Kunda-kunda: *Saḍ-prābhṛta*
R693*x*2,1,1	Sruta-sāgara: *Commentary*
R693*x*2,2	Kunda-kunda: *Samaya-sāra-prābhṛta*
R693*x*2,2,1	Amṛta-candra: *Commentary*
R693*x*2,3	Kunda-kunda: *Aṣṭa-prābhṛta*
R693*x*2,4	Kunda-kunda: *Pancāsti-kāya* (*Pancat-thiyasāra*)
R693*x*2,4,1	Amṛta-candra: *Commentary*
R693*x*2,5	Kunda-kunda: *Prābhṛta-sāra*
R693*x*2,6	Kunda-kunda: *Pravacana-sāra*
R693*x*2,6,1	Amṛta-candra: *Commentary*
R693*x*2,7	Kunda-kunda: *Niyama-sāra*
R693*x*2,8	Kunda-kunda: *Pavolinī*
R693*x*2,91	Kunda-kunda: *Rayaṇa-sāra*
R693*x*7,1	Malli-ṣeṇa: *Syād-vāda-manjarī*
R693*x*D90,1	Amṛta-candra: *Tattvārtha-sāra*
R693*x*D90,2	Amṛta-candra: *Puruṣārtha-siddhyupāya*
R693*x*D98,1	Nemi-candra: *Dravya-saṅgraha*
R693*x*D98,2	Nemi-candra: *Tri-loka-sāra*
R693*x*D98,3	Nemi-candra: *Gommaṭa-sāra*
R693*x*D98,4	Nemi-candra: *Labdhi-sāra*

R694 Buddhistic Philosophy

R694*kx*1	Kenjiu Kasavara: *Dharma-saṅgraha*
R694*x*8,1	Advayavajra: *Advaya-vajra-saṅgraha*

R6941 Hinayana

R6941*x*3,1	Vasu-bandhu: *Abhidharma-kośa*
R6941*x*3,1,1	Yaśo-mitra: *Sphutarthā-abhidharma-kośa-vyākhyā*

R6941x3,2 Vasu-bandhu: *Gāthā-saṅgraha*
R6941x3,3 Vasu-bandhu: *Paramārtha-saptati*
R6941x4,1 Anuruddha: *Abhidhammattha-saṅgraha*
R6941x4,2 Aṇuruddha: *Nāmarūpa-pariccheda*

R6945 Mahayana

R6945x1,1 *Prajñapti-mata*
R6945x2,1 *Buddhāvatamśaka* including *Gaṇḍavyūha*
R6945x3,1 *Daśa-bhūmika*
R6945x4,1 *Ratna-kūṭa*
R6945x4,6,3 *Kāśyapa-parivarttā*
R6945x5,1 *Samādhirāja* or *Candrapradīpa-sūtra*
R6945x6,1 *Suvarṇaprabhāsa*
R6945x7,1 Aśva-ghoṣa: *Śraddhotpāda-śāstra* (*Awakening of faith*)

R6946 Yogacara

R6946x1,1 Maitreya-nātha: *Abhisamayālaṅkāra*, *Kārikā* or *Prajñā-pāramitopadeśa-śāstra*
R6946x1,2 Maitreya-nātha: *Yogācāra Bhūmi-śāstra* or *Saptadaśa-bhūmi-śāstra* including *Bodhisattva-bhūmi*
R6946x1,3 Maitreya-nātha: *Mahāyāna-sūtrālaṅkāra*
R6946x2,1 Assanga: *Mahāyāna-samparigraha*
R6946x2,2 Assanga: *Prakaraṇa-āryavācā*
R6946x2,3 Assanga: *Mahāyānabhidharma-saṅgīti-śāstra*
R6946x3,1 Vasu-bandhu: *Vimśaṭikā*
R6946x3,2 Vasu-bandhu: *Trimśaṭikā*
R6946x4,1 Śānta-rakṣita: *Tattva saṅgraha*
R6946x4,1,1 Kamala-sīla: *Pañcika*
R6946x5,1 *Lankāvatāra Sūtra*

R6947 Madhyamikas

R6947x1,1 Nāgārjuna: *Mādhyamika sūtras*
R6947x1,1,1 Nāgārjuna: *Akutobhaya*
R6947x1,1,2 Buddha-pālita: *Mūlamādhyamikavītti*
R6947x1,1,3 Bhāva-viveka: *Prajñapradīpa*

R6947*x*1,1,7	Candra-kīrti: *Prasannapadā*
R6947*x*1,2	Nāgārjuna: *Yukti-ṣaṣṭika*
R6947*x*1,3	Nāgārjuna: *Śūnyatā-saptati*
R6947*x*1,4	Nāgārjuna: *Pratītya-samutpāda-hṛdaya*
R6947*x*1,5	Nāgārjuna: *Mahāyāna-viṃśaka*
R6947*x*1,6	*Prajñā-pāramita-sūtra-śāstra*
R6947*x*1,7	*Daśa-bhūmi-vibhāṣā-śāstra*
R6947*x*1,8	*Eka-śloka-śāstra*
R6947*x*2,1	Ārya-deva: *Catuh-śataka*
R6947*x*2,1,7	Candra-kīrti: *Commentary*
R6947*x*2,2	Ārya-deva: *Citta-viśuddhi-prakaraṇa*
R6947*x*2,4	Ārya-deva: *Hasta-vala-prakaraṇa* or *Muṣṭi-prakaraṇa*
R6947*x*2,5	Ārya-deva: *Akṣar-śataka*
R6947*x*3,1	*Sthira-mayī*
R6947*x*4,1	Diṅnāga: *Nyāya-preveśa*
R6947*x*4,2	Diṅnāga: *Pramāṇa-samakhyā*
R6947*x*5	Dharma-pāla
R6947*x*6,1	Dharma-kīrti: *Nyāya-bindu*
R6947*x*6,1,1	Dharmottari: *Nyāya-bindu-ṭīkā*
R6947*x*6,2	Dharma-kīrti: *Santānāntara-siddhi*
R6947*x*6,3	Dharma-kīrti: *Vāda-nyāya*
R6947*x*7,1	Candra-kīrti: *Mādhyamakāvatāra*

INDEX

Ahobala-paṇḍita: *Ahobala-paṇḍitīyamu* or *Kaviśiro-bhūṣaṇamu* P35,E*x*1,1,1
Ahobala-paṇḍitīyamu by Ahobala-paṇḍita P35,E*x*1,1,1
Aiṅguru-nūru O31,IB3
Aiṅ-tiṇai O31,1C4
Aiṅ-tiṇai-aimpatu O31,1C42
Aiṅ-tiṇai-ezhupatu O31,1C42
Ajita-āgama Q232:2315
Ajita-senācārya: *Alaṅkāra-cintāmaṇi* O15:*gx*D90,1
—— *Maṇi-prakāśika* P15:C*x*4,1,3,1
Akalaṅka: *Tattvārtha-ṭīkā-vyākhyālaṅkāra* R693*x*1,1,4
Akarādi-nighaṇṭu by Cidambara-revaṇa Siddhar P31,J:4*x*J96,1
Akhaṇḍānanda-muni: *Tattva-dīpana* R66,5*x*1,1,1,1,1
Akṣara-śataka by Ārya-deva R6947*x*2,5
Akuto-bhaya by Nāgārjuna R6947*x*1,1,1
Alaṅkāra-candrikā by Vaidya-nātha Tatsat O15:*gx*J50,1,1
Alaṅkāra-cintāmaṇi by Ajita-senācārya O15:*gx*D90,1
Alaṅkāra-dīpikā by Āśādhara O15:*gx*J50,1,2
Alaṅkāra-kaustubha by Kavi-karṇa-pūra O15:*gx*J24,1
—— by Viśveśvara Bhaṭṭa O15:*gx*L00,1
Alaṅkāra-kaustubha-kiraṇa O15:*gx*J24,1,2
Alaṅkāra-kaustubha-sāra-bodhinī by Viśva-nātha Cakravartin O15:*gx*J24,1
Alaṅkāra-maṇi-hāra by Kṛṣṇa Brahma-tantra Para-kālasvāmin O15:*gx*M50,1
Alaṅkāra-sarvasva by Ruyyaka O15:*gx*F20,1
Alaṅkāra-sarvasva-vimarśinī by Jaya-ratha O15:*gx*F20,1,1
Alaṅkāra-sarvasva-vyākhyā by Samudra-bandha O15:*gx*F20,1,2
Alaṅkāra-śekhara by Keśava Miśra O15:*gx*J60,1
Alaṅkāra-sudhā by Nāgoji Bhaṭṭa O15:*gx*J50,1,4
Alaṅkāra-sūtra-vṛtti by Maṅkhuka O15:*gx*F20,1,4
Alaṅkāra-tilaka by Vāg-bhaṭa O15:*gx*G90,1,1
Aloka by Jaya-deva R625*x*6,1,2
Al-ghazzali △73*x*E58,1
Amalanādippirān by Tiruppāṇāzhvār Q22:417*x*1,1,91
Amalānanda: *Kalpa-taru* R66:5*x*1,1,2,1

Appaya Dikṣita: *Naya-mayūkha-mālikā* R672,5xJ50,1
—— *Nyāya-rakṣāmaṇi* R66,5xJ50,1
—— *Parimaḷa* R66,5x1,1,2,1,1
—— *Śārīraka-nyāya-rakṣāmaṇi* R66xJ50,1
—— *Siddhānta-leśa-saṅgraha* R66xJ50,2
—— *Śivārkamaṇi-dīpikā* R673,5x1,1,1
—— *Vāda-nakṣatra-mālā* or *Nakṣatra-vādā-vali* R66xJ50,3
—— *Vidhi-rasāyana* R641xJ50,1
—— *Vṛtti-vārttikā* O15:gxJ50,3
Āranyagāna Q131:216
Aranyaka Q131:212
Arattup-pāl O31,1C51
Arcika Q131:211
Arda-viraf Q8451x6,1
Ardebehist Q8451:2513
Arisimha: *Kavitā-rahasya* or *Kāvya-kalpalatā* O15:gxG42,1
Aristotle: *Poetics* O13,1:gx1,1
Ārogya-kalpa-druma by Rāma-vārier LB:4:91xM90,1
Ārseya Q131:224
Artha-saṅgraha by Laugākṣi Bhāskara R641xK60,1
Aruṇa-datta: *Commentary* on *Aṣṭāṅga-saṅgraha* LBx2,1,1
—— *Sarvāṅga-śundara* LBx3,1,1
Aruṇā-dhikaraṇa-saraṇa-vivaraṇi by Śrīnivāsa R672xK80,1
Aruṇagiri-nāthar: *Tirup-pugazh* Q26:417xI50,1
Aruṇandi Sivācārya: *Irupā-Irupadu* R673x3,1
—— *Śivajñāna-siddhi* R673x2,1,1
Ārya-deva R6947x2,1
Āśādhara: *Alaṅkāra-dīpikā* O15:gxJ53,1,2
—— *Commentary* on *Rudraṭālāṅkāra* O15:gx6,1,5
Āśādhara Sallakṣaṇa: *Aṣṭāṅga-hṛda-yoddyota* LBx3,1,3
Asahāya Q2:4xD75,1
Asaṅga R6946x2,1
Ashi-Yast Q8451:2531
Ashtad-Yast Q8451:2532
Āśiria-nighaṇṭu by Aṇdip-pulavar P31,D:4x4,1

Bāla-bodhinī: by Bhaṭṭa Jagad-dhara P15,C*x*6,1,6
Bālabodhinī-nyāsa by Ugra-bhūti P15,C*x*6,1,6,1
Bālacandra: *Tarka-bhāṣā prakāśikā* R625*x*5,1,4
Bala-deva: *Vedānta-sūtra-bhāṣya* or *Govindha-bhāṣya* R6891,5*x*2,1
Bāla-manoramā by Vāsu-deva Dīkṣita P15,C*x*1,1,6,5
Bālam-bhaṭṭa: *Bhāva-prakāśikā* P15,C*x*1,1,6,1,1,1
—— *Cidasthi-mālā* P15,C*x*1,1,6,3,1
—— *Laghu-bhūṣaṇa-kānti* P15,C3*x*5,1,1,1
—— *Paribhāśendu-śekhara-kauśika* P15,C*x*194,1,1
Bālam-bhaṭṭa: *Prabhā* P15,C*x*1,1,5,1
Bālam-bhaṭṭi Q2:4*x*2,1,2,3
Bāla-prabodhikā: LB*x*3,1,7
Balārisimha: *Kavi-janānjanamu* P35,E*x*1,1,2
Bālāvabodha by Kāśyapa P15,C*x*2,1,5
Bāla-vyākaraṇa by Cinnaya-sūri (Para-vastu) P35,E*x*M60,1
Bāla-vyākaraṇa-guptārtha-prakāśikā by Saṅkara Rangayya and Venkata-rāma Śāstri (Kalluri) P35,E*x*M60,1,1
Bandhaka-tantra LB:4:91*x*3,1
Banṣidhara-miśra: *Sāṅkhya-tattva-kaumudī-vibhākara* R631*x*2,1,3,8
Baudhāyana Q125,4*x*1,1
Bhadra-āgāma Q232:2335
Bhagavad-gītā-bhāṣya by Ānanda-tīrtha R68,6*x*1,1
—— by Rāmānuja R672,6*x*2,1
—— by Saṅkara R66,6*x*1,1
Bhāgavata-purāṇa Q22:223
Bhāgavata-tātparya-nirṇaya by Ānanda-tīrtha R68,7*x*1,1
Bhāgavata-ṭikā-subodhinī by Vallabhācārya R6893,7*x*1,1
Bhagavatī-anga Q31:21115
Bhagavat-puruṣottamācārya: *Vedānta-ratna-mañjūṣā* R6892*x*1,1,1
Bhāgī-ratha Thakūra: *Nyāya-līlāvatī-vivṛti* R621*x*2,1,8
Bhairavendra: *Śiśu-bodhinī* R621*x*D95,1,4
Bhakta-līlamṛta by Mahī-patī Q22*wx*1,2
Bhakta-mālā by Candra-datta Q22*wx*2,1
Bhakta-parijña Q31:21313
Bhakta-vijaya by Mahī-pati Q22*wx*1,1
Bhakti-sūtra by Nārada △25*x*1,1

Bhaṭṭācārya (Gadā-dhara) *See* Gadā-dhara Bhaṭṭācārya
Bhaṭṭācārya (Gaurī-kānta Sārva-bhauma) *See* Gaurī-kānta Sārva-bhauma Bhaṭṭācārya
Bhaṭṭācārya (Jānakī-nātha) *See* Jānakī-nātha Bhaṭṭācārya
Bhaṭṭācārya (Jaya-rāma) *See* Jaya-rāma Bhaṭṭācārya
Bhaṭṭācārya (Jīvānanda Vidyā-sāgara) *See* Jīvānanda Vidyā-sāgara Bhaṭṭācārya
Bhaṭṭācārya (Raghu-nātha Śiromaṇi) *See* Raghu-nātha Śiromaṇi Bhaṭṭācārya
Bhaṭṭācārya (Tarka-tilaka) *See* Tarka-tilaka Bhaṭṭācārya
Bhaṭṭācārya (Viśwa-nātha Pancānana) *See* Viśwa-nātha Pancānana Bhaṭṭācārya
Bhāṭṭā-cintāmaṇi by Gāgā-bhaṭṭa R641xK40,1
—— by Vāncheśvara Yajvan R641x91,1,L80
Bhāṭṭā-dīpikā by Khaṇḍa-deva R641x91,1
Bhaṭṭa-gopāla: *Commentary on Sārasvata-prakriyā* P15,Cx7,1,1,J95
—— *Sāhitya-cūdāmaṇi* O15:gx8,1,3
Bhāṭṭālaṅkāra by Ananta-deva R641xK30,1,1
Bhaṭṭar: *Bhagavad-gīta* R66,6xI20,1
—— *Gūḍhārtha-dīpikā* R66,6xI20,1,1
Bhāṭṭa-rahasya by Khaṇḍa-deva R641x91,3
Bhaṭṭa Sankara: *Mīmāmsā-bāla-prakāśa* R641xK20,1
Bhaṭṭa Someśwara: *Nyāya-sudhā* or *Raṇakam* R641x2,1,1
Bhaṭṭa-vādīndra: *Rasa-sāra* R621x1,1,1,5,3
Bhaṭṭoji Dīkṣita: *Manoramā*, *Prauḍha-manoramā* P15,Cx1,1,6,1
—— *Śabda-kaustubha* P15,Cx1,1,5
—— *Śiddhānta-kaumudī*, *Laghu-kaumudī*, *Madhya-kaumudī* P15,Cx1,1,6
—— *Tristhalī-setu* Q2:4198y8xJ80,1
Bhāva Gaṇesīya R635x1,1,M40
Bhāva Miśra: *Bhāva-prakāśa* LBx6,1
Bhavānanda Siddhānta Vāgīśa: *Tattva-cintāmaṇi-dīdhiti-prakāśa* R625x6,1,5,2
Bhāva-nātha: *Naya-viveka* R645x6,1
Bhāvanā-viveka by Maṇḍana Miśra R641x5,1
Bhāvanā-viveka-vyākhyā by Umbeka R641x5,1,1

Brahadāraṇyaka Q127:24
Brahma-deva: *Commentary* on *Suśruta-saṁhitā* LB:4:7x2,1,6
Brahma-lakṣaṇa-vākyārtha by Śaṭhakopa-muni R672xL50,1
Brahmāmṛta-varṣinī by Rāmānanda Sarasvatī R66,5x3,1
Brahmānanda Sarasvatī: *Advaita-siddhānta-vidyotana* R66xL20,1
—— *Brahma-sūtra-vṛtti* R66,5x5,1
—— *Guru-candrikā* R66x91,1,2
—— *Laghu-candrikā* R66x91,1,1
Brahmānanda-giri by Venkaṭa-nātha R66,6x6,1
Brahma-pada-śakti-vāda by Anantācārya R672xM20,4
Brahma--purāṇa Q21:221
Brahma-samhitā Q222:2391
Brahma-siddhi by Maṇḍana Mīsra R66x2,1
Brahma-siddhi-vyākhyā by Ānanda-pūraṇa R66x2,1,4
—— by Cit-sukha R66x2,1,3
Brahma-sūtra-bhāṣya by Ānanda-tīrtha R68,5x1,1
—— by Bhāskarācārya R6891,5x1,1
—— by Rāmānuja R672,5x2,1
—— by Śankara R66,5x1,1
—— by Śrīkaṇṭha Śivācārya R673,5x1,1
Brahma-sūtra-vṛtti by Brahmānanda Sarasvatī R66,5x5,1
—— by Hari Dīkṣita R66,5x4,1
—— by Śadāśivendra Sarasvatī R66,5x6,1
Brahma-sūtrānuvyākhyāna by Ānanda-tīrtha R68,5x1,2
Brahma-tantra Para-kāla-svāmin (Kṛṣṇa) *See* Kṛṣṇa-Brahma-tantra Para-kāla-svāmin
Brahma-tattva-samīkṣā by Vācas-pati Miśra R66x2,1,1
Brahma-tīrtha (Jaya Kṛṣṇa) *See* Jaya-kṛṣṇa Brahma-tīrtha
Brahma-vaivarta-purāṇa Q22:225
Brahma-vidyābharaṇa by Kṛṣṇānanda-yati R66,5x1,1,7
Bṛhaddeśi by Mataṅga-muni NR44x3,1
Bṛhad-dharma-purāṇa Q25:222
Bṛhad-dharma-samhitā Q222:23921
Bṛhat-kalpa-cheda-sūtra Q3:2145
Bṛhad-vṛtti P15,Cx5,1,1,2
Bṛhaspati: *Pada-candrikā* P15,C:4x1,1,4

Dallaṇācarya: *Nibandha-saṅgraha* LB:4:7*x*2,1,7
Dāmodara: *Saṅketa-mañjarī* LB*x*3,1,5
Dāna-kriyā-kaumudī by Govendānanda Q2:4193*y*8*x*J40,1
Dāna-mayūkha by Bhaṭṭa Nīla-kaṇṭha Q2:4193*y*8*x*J61,1
Daṇḍin: *Kāvyādarśa* Q15:*gx*3,1
Darpaṇa by Viśva-nātha O15:*gx*8,1,5
Daśa-bhūmika R6945*x*3,1
Daśa-bhūmi-vibhāṣā-śāstra R6947*x*1,7
Daśa-bodha by Rāma-dāsa R65*x*K08,1
Dasāh-kappa-vahar Q31:2144
Daśa-rūpaka by Dhanañ-jaya O15,2:*gx*D98,1
Daśa-ślokī by Nimbārka R6892*x*1,1
—— by Saṅkara R66*x*1,14
Daśāśruta-skandha Q31:2144
Daśa-vaikālika Q31:2163
Daśa-veyāliya Q31:2163
Dāṭhā-vaṃśa by Dhamma-kitti Q41:6*x*6,1
Dattila NR44*x*2,1
Dattila-muni NR44*x*2,1
Daya-pāla: *Rūpa-siddhī* P15,C*x*:4,1,3,6
Devācārya: *Siddhānta-jāhnavī* R6892,5*x*2,1
Devana Bhaṭṭa: *Smṛti-candrikā* Q2:4*y*8*x*F50,1
Deva-nandi *See* Jainendra
—— *Mahāvṛtti* P15,C*x*3,1,1
Deva-rāja-yajvan: *Commentary* on *Nirukta* P15,10A3:28*x*1,1,6
Devatādhyāya Q131:226
Devendra-sūri: *Haima-laghu-nyāsa* P15,C*x*5,1,1,3
Devendra-stava-prakīrṇa Q31:21317
Deveśvara: *Kavi-kalpa-latā* O15:*gx*H00,1
Devī-bhāgavata Q25:221
Devī-mahātmyam Q25:2291
Devindatthan-prakirna Q31:21317
Dhamma-kitti: *Dāṭhā-vaṃśa* Q41:6*x*6,1
Dhamma-pada Q41:22512
Dhamma-padaṭṭha-kathā by Buddha-ghoṣa Q41:22512:*gx*5
Dhamma-pāla: *Itivutta-kaṭṭha-kathā* Q41:22514:*gx*3

Drāhyayāṇa Q132:4x2,1
Draviḍa Gopāla Bhaṭṭa: *Rasika-rañjanī* O15:gxH50,2,5
Drāviḍa-mahābhāṣya by Sivajñāna-yogi R673x2,1,7,1
Dravya-bhāṣya-ṭīkā R621x1,1,1,2
Dravya-guṇa-saṅgraha by Cakra-pāṇi-datta LB:67x1,1
Dravya-saṅgraha by Nemi-candra R693xD98,1
Dṛṣṭi-vada-anga Q31:21124
Durgācārya: *Ṛjvartha* P15,10A3:28x1,1,2
Durga-pada-prabodha by Srīvallabha Vācanācārya P15,C:22x5,1,1
Durga-simha: *Kātantra-vṛtti* P15,Cx6,1,1
Durgā-sūkta Q25:21x6
Dvaitādvaita-siddānta-setukā R6892,5x2,1

Ebreo (Leone) △8513xI60,1
Ekāgnikānda Q125:214
Eka-śloka-sāstra R6947x1,8
Ekāvalī by Vidyā-dhara O15:gxH15,1
Elādi O31,1C66
Eḷut-tadhikāram P31,Dx101
Epistles Q6:236
Erapatistan-nask Q8451:234
Eṭṭut-tokai O31,1B
Ezhut-adhikāram P31,Dx1,11

Farvardin-Yask Q8451:2525

Gaccācāra-prakīrnaka Q31:21323
Gadā-dhara Bhaṭṭācārya: *Śakti-vāda* R625,13x5,1
—— *Tattva-cintāmaṇī-dīdhiti-vṛiti* R625x6,1,5,4
—— *Vyutpatti-vāda* R625,13x4,1
Gadā-dhara: *Gadā-dhara-paddhati* Q2:41y8xI60,1
Gadā-dhara-paddhati by Gadā-dhara Q2:41y8xI60,1
Gadā-dhara-pañcalakṣaṇī by Bhimācārya Ottangadkar R625x6,1,5,4,1
Gāgā-bhaṭṭa: *Bhaṭṭa-cintāmaṇi* R641xK40,1
—— *Rākāgama* O15:gxH10,1,2
Gaṇa-pāṭha by Pāṇini P15,C302x1,1

Kāśyapa-samhitā LB:441:6x1,1
Kātantra-sūtra-pātha by Śarva-varman P15,Cx6,1
Kātantra-vistāra by Vardha-māna P15,Cx6,1,1,1
Kātantra-vṛtti by Durga-simha P15,Cx6,1,1
Kātantra-vṛtti-pañcikā by Tri-locana-dāsa P15,Cx6,1,1,2
Katā-vattu Q41:233
Kāṭhakā Q124:4x2,1
Kātyāyana Q127:4x1,1
—— *Vṛitti* P15,Cx1,1,1
—— *Vājasaneya-prātiśākhyā* P15,26Ax1,1
Kauṇḍa Bhaṭṭa: *Prauḍha-manoramā-khaṇḍana* P15,Cx1,1,6,1,2
Kauṇḍinya-Dīkṣita: *Tarka-bhāṣā-prakāśikā* R625x5,1,7
Kauśika Q14:4x1,1
Kavi-candra: *Kāvya-candrikā* O15:gxJ90,1
Kavi-janāñjanamu by Narasimharāja Simhudu P35,Ex1,1,2
Kavi-jana-sañjīvinī by Rāma-bhadra Kavi O35,1:g(P)xJ45,1
Kavi-janāśrayamu by Bhīma Kavi (Vemulavāda) O35,1:g(P)x1,1
Kavi-kalpa-druma by Bopa-deva P15,C:301xF60,1
Kavi-kalpa-latā by Deveśvara O15:gxH00,1
Kavi-karṇapūra: *Alaṅkāra-kaustubha* O15:gxJ24,1
Kavi-rāja-mārgam O33,1:gx1,1
Kavi-śamsaya-vicchedamu by Sūra-kavi P35,Ex6,1
Kavi-sikṣā-vṛtti by Amara-candra O15:gxG42,1,1
Kavi-śiro-bhūṣaṇamu by Ahobala Paṇḍita P35,Ex1,1,1
Kavitā-rahasya by Arisimha O15:gxG42,1
Kāvya-candrikā by Kavi-candra O15:gxJ90,1
Kāvya-darpaṇa by Rāja-cūdāmaṇi Dīkṣita O15:gxK36,1
Kāvyā-darśa by Daṇḍin O15:gx3,1
Kāvyā-darśamu by A. Subrahmaṇya Śāstri O35,1:8g(P)x94,1
Kāvyā-darśa-ṭīkā by Jivānanda Vidyā-sāgara Bhaṭṭācārya O15:gx3,1,8
—— by Taruṇa-vācaspati O15:gx3,1,1
Kāvya-kalpa-latā by Arisimha O15:gxG42,1
Kāvyālaṅkāra by Bhāmaha O15:gx2,1
Kāvyālaṅkāra-cūḍāmaṇi by Peddanna P35,Ex4,1
Kāvyālaṅkāra-sāra-saṅgraha by Udbhaṭa O15:gx4,1

Liṅgānuśāsana by Harṣa-vardhana P15,C:22*x*D50,1
—— by Hema-candra P15,C:22*x*5,1
—— by Pāṇini P15,C:22*x*1,1
—— by Śākaṭāyana P15,C:22*x*4,1
—— by Vāmana P15,C:22*x*1,1,3
Liṅga-purāṇa Q23:223
Liṅga-viśeṣa-vṛtti by Vararuci P15,C:22*x*1,1,1
Locana-rocanī by Jīva Go-svāmin O15:*gx*J32,1,1
Locana-vyākhyā-kaumudī by Parameśvarācārya O15:*gx*7,1,3,1
Lokeśakara: *Tattva-dīpikā* P15,C*x*7,1,2,1

Macca-muni △28*x*21
Maccendra-nāthar △28*x*47
Madana-pāla: *Madana-pārijāta* Q2:42*y*8*x*H75,1
Madana-pārijāta by Madana-pāla Q2:42*y*8*x*H75,1
Mādhava: *Commentary* on *Sārasvata-prakriyā* P15,C*x*7,1,1,5
Mādhava: *Commentary* on *Suśruta-saṁhitā* LB:4:7*x*2,1,5
Mādhava Sarasvati: *Mita-bhāṣiṇī* R621*x*D95,1,2
Mādhavācārya: *Jaiminīya-nyāya-mālā* or *Mīmāmsādhi-karaṇa-nyāya-mālā* R641*x*8,1
—— *Nyāya-mālā-vistāra* R641*x*8,1,1
—— *Sarva-darśaṇa-saṅgraha* R6*x*2,1
—— *Mādhavīyā-dhātu-vṛtti* P15,C301*x*1,1,4
Mādhava-deva: *Tarka-bhāṣā-sāra-mañjarī* R625*x*5,1,5
Mādhavākara: *Mādhava-nidāna* LB:4*x*1,1
Mādhava-nidāna LB:4*x*1,1
Mādhavīyā-dhātu-vṛtti by Mādhavācārya P15,C301*x*1,1,4
Madhu-sūdana Sarasvatī: *Advaita-ratna-rakṣaṇa* R66*x*K00,1
—— *Advaita-siddhi* R66*x*91,1
—— *Commentary* on *Samkṣepa-Śārīraka* R66*x*5,1,5
—— *Gūḍhārtha-dīpikā* R66,6*x*2,1
—— *Īśvara-pratī-patti-prakāśa* R66*x*K00,4
—— *Prasthāna-bheda* R66*x*K00,2
—— *Siddhānta-bindu* R66*x*1,14,1
—— *Vedānta-kalpa-latikā* R66*x*K00,3

Mahī-pati: *Bhakta-līlāmṛta* Q22wx1,2
—— *Bhakta-vijaya* Q22wx1,1
Mah-Nyasis Q8451:263
Mah-Yask Q8451:2517
Maithila (Gaṅgānanda) *See* Gaṅgānanda Maithila
Maitreya-nātha R6946x1,1
Maitreya-rakṣita: *Dhātu-pradīpa* or *Tantra-pradīpa* P15,C301x1,1,1
Majjima-nikāya Q41:222
Makuta-āgama Q232:2337
Malaipaṭu-kaṭam O31,1B952
Mālini-vijaya-āgama Q233:231
Mallī-nātha: *Taralā* O15:gxH15,1,1
—— *Niṣkaṇṭaka* R625x4,1,3
Malli-ṣena: *Syād-vāda-mañjarī* R693x7,1
Mammaṭa: *Kāvya-prākāśa* O15:gx8,1
—— *Śabda-vyāpāra-vicāra* O15:gxE60,1
Mānameyodaya by Nārāyaṇa Bhaṭṭa and Nārāyaṇa Paṇḍita R641xJ90,1
Māna-sāra NA44x1,1
Mana-vācakam-kaḍandān: *Uṇmai-viḷakkam* R673x4,1
Maṇḍala-brāhmaṇopaniṣad △26x4,11
Maṇḍala-puruḍar: *Cūḍāmaṇi-nighaṇṭu* P31,D:4x5,1
Maṇḍana: *Commentary* on *Sārasvata-prakriyā* P15,Cx7,1,1,7
—— *Mīmāmsānukramaṇikā* R64x1,1,1,1
Maṇḍanamiśra: *Bhāvanā-viveka* R641x5,1
—— *Brahma-siddhi* R66x2,1
—— *Vidhi-viveka* R641x4,1
Mandāra-makaranda campu by Kṛṣṇa Sarman O15:gxL30,1
Māṇḍukya Q141:26
Maṅga-rāsa: *Cintāmaṇi-pratipada* P15,Cx4,1,3,2
Māṇikka-vācakar Q23:417x5,1
Māṇikya-candra: *Saṅketa* O15:gx8,1,2
Maṇi-mekalai O31,1C93
Maṇi-prabhā by Rāmānanda Yati R635x1,1,M10
Maṇi-prakāśikā by Ajitasenācārya P15,Cx4,1,3,1
Maṇi-sāra by Gopi-nātha R625x6,1,K40

Nannūl-āśiriya-virutti P31,J*x*1,1,2
Nārada: *Dharma-sāstra* Q2:4*x*5,1
— *Bhakti-sūtra* △25*x*1,1
— *Saṅgīta-makaranda* NR44*x*5,1
Nārada-purāṇa Q22:224
Nārada-samhitā Q222:2392
Nārada-upa-purāṇa Q22:2241
Narahari: *Bodha-sāra* R66*x*M10,1
Narasimha-āgama Q232:2347
Nārasimha-purāṇa Q22:2292
Narasimha-rāja Siṃhudu (Balārisiṃha): *Kavi-jañāñ-janamu* P35,E*x*1,1,2
Narasimhāśrama: *Advaita-dīpikā* R66*x*J40,1
— *Bheda-dhikkāra* R66*x*J40,2
— *Nṛsiṃha-vijñāpana* R66*x*J40,3
— *Vedānta-tatva-viveka* R66*x*J40,4
Narasimha-vājapeyi: *Nityācāra-pradīpa* Q2:4*y*8*x*150,1
Nārāyaṇa Q2:1*x*1,1,6
— *Tantra-samuccaya* Q2:45*x*I26,1
Nārāyaṇa Bhaṭṭa and Nārāyaṇa Paṇḍita: *Mānameyodaya* R641*x*J90,1
Nārāyaṇa Śarman: *Amara-koṣa-pañjikā* or *Padārtha-kaumudī* P15,C:4*x*1,1,6
Nārāyaṇa-tirtha: *Bhāṭṭa-bhāṣā-prakāśa* R641*x*L10,1
— *Candrikā* R631*x*2,1,5
— *Yoga-siddānta-candrikā* R635*x*1,1,M20
Nārāyaṇa-upaniṣad Q125:25
Narendrācārya: *Sārasvata-sūtrās* P15,C*x*7,1
Narkavi Rājanambī: *Ahap-porul-viḷakkam* P31,J*x*1,1,8
Naṟṟinai O31,1B1
Nasks Q8451:23
Naṭaka-lakṣaṇa-ratna-kośa by Sāgara-nandin O15,2:*gx*G43,1
Nāthamuni: *Nyāya-tattva* R672*x*3,1
Nāṭva-darpaṇa by Śrīnivāsa R672*x*K80,5
Nātya-śāstra **by Bharata O15:*gx*1,1**
Nātya-veda-vivṛti by Abhinava-gupta O15:*gx*1,1,3
Naukā **by Gaṅgā-rāma O15:*gx*H50,1,1**

Prabhā-kara: *Bṛhatī* R645x1,1
Prabhākara-vijaya by Nandīśvara R645xK50,1
Prabhā-vali by Śambhu Bhaṭṭa R641x91,1,1
Prabhṛta-sāra R693x2,5
Prabhu-liṅgalīla Q234xK50,1
Pradīpa by Govinda Ṭhakkūra O15:gx8,1,7
— by Yaśodā-nandan Sarkār LBx3,1,M90
Pradīpa-prabhā by Vaidya-nātha O15:gx8,1,7,1
Pradīpoddyota by Nāgesa Bhaṭṭa O15:gx8,1,7,2
Pradīpikā by Utpala II Q233:2395,3
Pradyotana Bhaṭṭa: *Candrāloka-prakāśa-śaradāgama* O15:gxH10,1,1
Prajñāpana-upānga Q31:21214
Prajñā-pāramita-sūtra-śāstra R6947x1,6
Prajñā-pāramitopadeśa-śāstra by Maitreya-nātha R6946x1,1
Prajñā-pradīpa by Bhāva-viveka R6947x1,1,3
Prajñāpti-mata R6945x1,1
Prakaraṇa-ārya-vācā by Asaṅga R6946x2,2
Prakaraṇa-pañcikā by Sālika-nātha R645x5
Prakāśa by Mahā-deva and Dina-kara R625x7,1,1,1
— by Nāgeśa Bhaṭṭa O15:gxH50,2,2
— by Vardha-mānopādhyāya R625x6,1,1
Prakāśātman: *Pañca-pādikā-vivaraṇa* R66,5x1,1,1,1
—— *Sabda-nirṇaya* R66xD95,1
Prakāśikā by Nīla-kāṇṭha R625x8,1,1,1
Prakaṭārtha-vivaraṇa R66,5x1,1,3
Prakriyā-kaumudī by Rāma-candrācārya P15,Cx1,1,7
Prakriyā-kaumudī-prasāda by Viṭṭhalācārya P15,Cx1,1,7,1
Prakriyā-saṅgraha by Abhaya-candrācārya P15,Cx:4,1,3,5
Prākṛta-prakāśa by Bhāmaha P151x2,1,1
Prākṛta-sūtras by Vara-ruci P151x2,1
Pramāṇa-candrika by Calāri Seṣācārya R68xI20,1
Pramāṇa-mālā by Ānanda-bodha R66x6,2
Pramāṇa-mālā-vyākhyā R66x6,3,1
Pramāṇa-mañjarī by Sarva-deva Sūri R621xJ70,1
Pramāṇa-samkhyā by Diṅnāga R6947x4,2
Pramitākṣara Q2:4x2,1,2,2

Puruṣa-sūkta Q21:21x1
Puruṣottama: *Vedāntā-dhikaraṇa-mālā* R6893,5x1,1,4
Puruṣottama Dīkṣita: *Subodhinī* R66x5,1,2
Puruṣottama Miśra: *See* Puruṣottama Dīkṣita
Puruṣottama Deva: *Bhāṣā-vṛtti* P15,Cx1,1,F90
Puruṣottamjee (Go-svāmi) *See* Go-svāmi Srī Puruṣottamjee
Puṣpa-chūda-upānga Q31:21223
Puṣpa-sūtra P15,30Ax2,1
Puṣpika-upānga Q31:21222

Rādhāmohana-Bhaṭṭācārya: *Nyāya-sūtra-vivaraṇa* R625x1,1,M10
Rāga-vibodha by Somanātha NR441,KxK09,1
Rāghavānanda Śarasvatī: *Pātañjala-bhāṣya* R635x1,1,3
—— *Vidyānanda-varṣinī* R66x5,1,4
Rāghavendra: *Comm. Manu-dharma-śāstra* Q2:4x1,1,7
Raghavendra-tīrtha: *Nyāya-sudhā-parimaḷa* R68,5x2,1,1,1
—— *Tātparya-candrikā-prakāśa* R68,5x1,1,1,1,1
—— *Tattva-prakāśikā-bhāva* R68,5x1,1,1,2
—— *Vivṛti* R68,6x3,1
Raghu-deva: *Nyāyālaṅkāra* R625xJ40,1,1,1
Raghu-nātha: *Commentary* on *Khaṇḍana-khaṇḍa-khādya* R66x7,1,5
—— *Laghu-bhāṣya* P15,Cx7,1,5
—— *Padārṭha-mālā* R625xJ40,2
—— *Padārṭha-tattva-nirūpaṇa* R625xJ40,1
—— *Smṛti-tattva* Q2:4y8xJ20,1
Raghu-nātha Śiromaṇi Bhaṭṭācārya: *Dīdhiti* R625x6,1,5
—— *Kiraṇāvali-prakāśa-dīdhiti* R621x1,1,1,5,1,2
—— *Nyāya-līlāvatī-dīdhiti* R621x2,1,2
Raghunātha Śūri: *Śaṅkara-pāda-bhūṣana* R66,5xM50,1
Rahasyagāna Q131:218
Rāja-cūḍāmaṇi Dīkṣita: *Kāvya-darpaṇa* O15:gxK36,1
—— *See* also Rāja-cūdāmaṇi Makhin
Rāja-cūdāmaṇi Makhin: *Maṇi-darpaṇa* R625x6,1,K36
—— *See* also Rāja-cūdāmaṇi Dīkṣita
Rāja-mārttāṇḍa by Bhoja-deva R635x2,1
Rājānaka Tilaka: *Vivṛti* O15:gx4,1,3

Rāmānuja: *Śrī-bhāṣya* R672,5x2,1

— *Vedānta-dīpa* R672x2,2

— *Vedānta-sāra* R672x2,1

— *Vedārtha-saṅgraha* R672x2,3

Rāmānujācārya: *Tantra-rahasya* R645xL00,1

Rāmānuja-dāsa *See* Mahācārya

Rāma-rudra: *Mañjūṣā* R625x7,1,1,3

— *Prabhā* R625x7,1,12

— *Rāmarudrīya* R625x7,1,1,1,1

Rāma Sāstry: *Uddyotinī* P35,Ex1,1,8

Rāmāśrami by Bhānuji Dīkṣita P15, C:4x1,1,5

Rāma-tarka-vāgīśa: *Commentary* on *Mugdha-bodha* P15,CxF60,1,5

Rāma-tīrtha: *Anvayārtha-prakāśikā* R66x5,1,1

—— *Vidvan-mano-rañjanī* R66xJ25,1,1,3

Rāma Vārier: *Ārogya-kalpa-druma* LB:4:91xM90,1

Rāmeśwara Śūri: *Subodhinī* R641xM50,1

Ram-Yast Q8451:2527

Raṇaka by Bhaṭṭa Someswara R641x2,1,1

Raṅga-rājādhvarin: *Advaita-mukura* R66xJ10,1

Raṅga-rāmānuja: *Mūla-bhāva-prakāśikā* R672,5x2,1,6

—— *Nyaya-siddhāñjana-vyākhyā* R672xG68,4,1

—— *Para-pakṣa-nirākṛta* R672xL40,1

—— *Śārīraka-sāstrārtha-dīpikā* R672,5x3,1

Raṅgoji-bhaṭṭa: *Advaita-cintāmaṇi* R66xK50,1

Rasādhyāya LB:68x2,1

Rasa-gaṅgādhara by Jagan-nātha O15:gxK75,1

Rasa-mañjarī by Bhānu-datta O15:gxH50,2

Rasa-pradīpa by Prabhā-kara Bhaṭṭa O15:gxJ64,1

Rasa-ratna-samuccaya by Vāg-bhaṭṭa (son of Simha Gupta) LB:68x1,1

Rasarṇava-sudhākara by Śiṅga-bhūpāla O15:gxH30,1

Rasa-sāra by Bhaṭṭa-vādīndra R621x1,1,1,5,3

Rasa-taraṅgiṇī by Bhānu-datta O15:gxH50,1

Rasa-vaiśeṣika-sūtra by Nāgārjuna LBxD40,1

Rushm-Yast Q8451:2524

Rasika-rañjanī by Draviḍa Gopāla Bhaṭṭa O15:gxH50,2,5

—— by Gaṅgā-dharādhvarin O15:gxJ53,1,3

Śabdānuśāsana by Hema-candra P15,C*x*5,1
Śabdānuśāsana by Śākaṭāyana P15,C*x*4,1
Śabdānuśāsana-bṛhad-vṛtti by Hema-candra P15,C*x*5,1,1
Śabda-ratna by Hari Dīkṣita P15,C*x*1,1,6,1,1
Śabdārṇava-candrikā by Soma-deva P15,C*x*3,1,2
Śabdārtha-candrikā by Haṁsa-vijaya-gaṇi P15,C*x*7,1,1,K50
Śabda-śakti-prakāśa by Jagadīśa R625.13*x*3,1
Śabda-siddhi by Mahādeva P15,C*x*6,1,1,3
Śabda-vyāpāra-vicāra by Mammaṭa O15:*gx*E60,1
Śabdendu-śekhara by Nāgeśa Bhaṭṭa P15,C*x*1,1,6,3
Śadānanda: *Subodhini* P15,C*x*7,1,2,2
—— *Vedānta-sāra* R66*x*J25,1
Sadānanda Vyāsa: *Advaita-siddhi-saṅgraha* R66*x*94
Sadānanda Yogi (Kāśmīraka) *See* Kāśmīraka Sadānanda Yogi
Sadāśivendra Sarasvatī: *Brahma-sūtra-vṛtti* R66,5*x*6
—— *Siddhānta-kalpa-vallī* R66*x*L50,1
—— *Yoga-sūtra-vṛtti* or *Yoga-sudhākara* R635*x*1,L50
Sad-dar Q8451*x*92
Sad-dhammappaj-jotikā Q41:22523:*gx*7
Sad-dharma-puṇḍarīka Q42*x*5
Sādhana-mālā △42:87*x*8
Ṣaḍ-darśana-samuccaya by Hari-bhadra R6*x*1,1
Ṣaḍ-prabhṛta by Kunda-kunda R693*x*2,1
Ṣadavimsa Q131:222
Sad-vidyā-vijaya by Mahācārya R672*x*K90,4
Sāgara-nandin: *Nāṭaka-lakṣaṇa-ratnakośa* O15,2:*gx*G43,1
Sahaja-kīrti: *Sārasvata-prakriyā-vārtika* P15,C*x*7,1,1,K20
Sahasraka-āgama Q232:2318
Sahasra-kiraṇi by Śrīnivāsa R672*x*G68,6,3
Sāhitya-cūḍāmaṇi by Bhaṭṭa Gopāla O15:*gx*8,1,8
Sāhitya-darpaṇa by Viśva-nātha O15:*gx*H35,1
Sāhitya-mīmāṁsā by Ruyyaka O15:*gx*F20,2
Sāhitya-sāra by Acyuta-rāya O15:*gx*M31,1
Saint John Q6:234
— Luke Q6:233
— Mark Q6:232

Sārṅga-dhara: *Śarṅga-dhara-samhitā* LBx5,1
Śārṅga-dhara-dīpikā by Adhamalla LBx5,1,1
Śārṅga-dhara-samhitā by Śārṅga-dhara LBx5,1
Sārva-bhauma Bhaṭṭācārya (Gaurī-kānta) *See* Gaurī-kānta Sārva-bhauma Bhaṭṭācārya
Sarva-darśana-saṅgraha by Mādhavācārya R6x2,1
Sarva-deva-sūri: *Pramāṇa-mañjarī* R621xJ70,1
Sarvajñā-nārāyaṇa Q2:4x1,1,5
Sarvajñātman: *Samkṣepa-sarīraka* R66x5,1
Sarva-lakṣaṇa-sāra-saṅgrahamu by Timmaya P35,Ex5,1
Sarva-mata-saṅgraha R6x5,1
Sarvānanda Vandyaghatiya: *Tīkā-sarvasva* P15,C:4x1,1,2
Sarvāṅga-sundara by Aruṇa-datta LBx3,1,1
Sarvārtha-siddhi by Pūjya-pāda R693x1,1,3
Sarva-siddhānta-saṅgraha by Śaṅkarācārya R6x3,1
Sarva-varman: *Kātantra-sūtra-pāṭha* P15,Cx6,1
Sarvokta-āgama Q232:2347
Sarvottara-āgama Q232:2347
Sāsana-vamsa Q41:6xM20,1
Śastra-dīpikā by Pārtha-sārathi Miśra R641x7,1
Śāśvata: *Anekārthc-samuccaya* P15,C:4x4,1
Sata-dūṣaṇi by Vedānta Deśika R672xG68,6
Śata-dūṣaṇi-vyākhyā by Nṛsimharāja R672xG68,6,2
Satapatha Q127:22
Śaṭhakopa-muni: *Brahma-lakṣaṇa-vākyārtha* R672xL50,1
Śaṭhakopa-yati: *Commentary* on *Nyāya-pariśuddhi* R672xG68,3,1
Śaṭhamarṣa Śrīnivāsa Tātācārya: *Ānanda-tāratamya-khaṇḍana* R672xK50,1
Saṭoka-nāthar △28x42
Sattiya-nāthar △28x41
Sāttvata-śamhita Q222:232
Satya-jñānandā: *Veda-prakāśa* R64xL40,1
Śaunaka: *Ṛgveda-prātiśākhyā* P15,10Ax1,1
Saundarya-laharī by Saṅkara Q25x1,1
Saura-purāṇa Q23:228
Secret of golden flower △841xD77,1

Śisu-bodhinī by Bhairavendra R621xD95,1,4
Śiva-dāsa: *Caraka-tattva-pradīpikā* LBx1,1,4
Śivâditya: *Sapta-padārthi* R621xD95,1
Śiva-dṛṣṭi by Somānanda R663x1,1
Śiva-gīta Q22:2211
Śiva-jñāna-bodham by Mey-kaṇḍar R673x2,1
Śiva-jñāna-siddhi by Aruṇandi-śivācārya R673x2,1,1
Śiva-jñāña-yogi: *Drāviḍa-mahābhāṣya* R673x2,1,7,1
—— *Laghu-ṭikā* R673x2,1,7,2
—— *Tattuvak-kaṭṭalai* R673x91,1,1
—— *Tattuva-prakāśa* R673x91,1
Śiva-prakāśa by Umā-pati-śivācārya R673x2,1,6
Śiva-purāṇa Q23:2291
Śivārkamaṇi-dīpikā by Appaya Dīkṣita R673,5x1,1,1
Śiva-sūtra-āgama Q233:238
Śiva-śūtra-vārttika by Bhāskara R663x2,1,4
Skanda-purāṇa Q23:226
Skanda-svāmin: *Commentary* on *Nirukta* P15,10A3:28x1,1,4
Śloka-vārttika by Kumārila Bhaṭṭa R641x1,1
Śloka-vārttika-vyākhyā by Umbeka R641x1,1,1
Smṛti-candrika by Devana Bhaṭṭa Q2:4y8xF50,1
Smṛti-muktāphala by Vaidya-nātha Dīkṣita Q2:41y8xK30,1
Smṛti-prakāśa by Vāsu-deva Raṭha Q2:43y8xL50,1
Smṛti-sārodhāra by Viśvambhara Tripāṭhi Q2:4y8xJ30,1
Smṛti-tattva by Raghu-nātha Q2:4y8xJ20,1
Smṛtyārtha-sāra by Śrīdharācārya Q2:42y8xE55,1
Sneha-pūrti by Rāmā-miśra R672xE20,2,1,1
Śol-ladhikāram P31,Dx1,13
Soma-deva: *Śabdārṇava-candrikā* P15,Cx3,1,2
Somānanda: *Śiva-dṛṣṭi* R663x1,1
Somanātha: *Mayūkha-mālikā* R641x7,1,2
—— *Rāga-vibodha* NR441,KxK09,1
Someśwara (Bhaṭṭa) *See* Bhaṭṭa Someśwara
Spanda-kārika Q233:2395
Spanda-sarvasva by Kallata Q233:2951,1
Spanda-sūtra Q233:2395

Sruta-kīrti: *Pañca-vastu* P15,Cx3,1,4
Śrutānupālinī by Vādi-jaṅghāla O15:gx3,1,3
Śruta-pradīpikā by Sudarśana R672,5x2,1,2
Śruta-prakāśa by Sudarśana R672,5x2,1,1
Śruta-prakāśa-vyākhyā, *Bhāva-prakāśikā* by Varada-viṣṇu
    R672,5x2,1,1,1
Sruta-śāgara: *Commentary* on *Ṣaḍ-prabhṛta* R693x2,1,1,1
Śruti-kalpa-latā by Vāmana R68,7xK20,1
Śruti-sāra-samuddharaṇa by Totakācārya R66xD70,1
Stana-anga Q31:21113
Sthira-mayī R6947x3,1
Stobha Q131:214
Subha-vijaya-gaṇi: *Praśna-ratnākara* Q31y5x1,1
Subodhinī R66xJ25,1,1,2
Subhūti-candra: *Kāma-dhenu* P15,C:4x1,1,3
Subodhikā by Amṛta-bhārati P15,Cx/,1,1,2
Subodhinī Q2:4x2,1,2,1
— by Jayakṛṣṇa P15,Cx1,1,6,4
— by Puruṣottama Miśra R66x5,1,2
— by Sadānanda P15,Cx7,1,2,2
Subrahmaṇya Dīkṣitar: *Prayoga-vivekam* P31,Jx1,1,3
Subrahmaṇya Sāstri (A): *Kāvyā-darśamu* O35,1:g(P)x91,1
Sucarita Miśra: *Kāśikā* R641x1,1,2
Sudarśana: *Śrī-bhāṣya-vyākhyā-śruta-prakāśa* R672,5x2,1,1
— *Śruta-pradīpikā* R672,5x2,1,2
— *Tātparya-dīpikā* R672xE20,2,1
Sudarśanācārya: *Vyutpatti-vāda-vyākhyā* R625,13x4,1,3
Sudhā by Viśveśvara O15:gxH10,1,2
Sukha-prakāśa R66xG70,1
Sūkṣma-āgama Q232:2317
Sulakṣaṇa-sāramu by Tāṭam-bhaṭṭa Manunlakṣaṇa-kavi:
    O35,1:g(P)x13,1
Sūla-pāṇi Q2:4x2,1,4
Sulocana by Abinava-gupta R663x1,1,3
Sumaṅgala-vilāsinī by Buddha-ghoṣa Q41:221:gx5
Sundara-bhaṭṭa: *Dvaitādvaita-siddhānta-setuka* R6892,5x2,1,1

Tattva-saṃgraha by Śānta-rakṣita R6946x4,1
Tattva-saṅkhyāna by Ānanda-tīrtha R68x1,1
Tattva-saṅkhyāna-vivaraṇa by Jaya-tīrtha R68x1,1,1
Tattva-sāra by Rākhāldās R625xM30,1
Tattva-śekhara by Piḷḷāi-lokācārya R672xG80,2
Tattva-tīka by Vedānta Deśika R672,5x2,1,3
Tattva-traya by Piḷḷai-lokācārya R672xG80,1
Tattva-vaiśāradī R635x1,1,1,1
Tāyumānavar △25xK00,1
Tevāram Q23:417x1,1
Ṭhakkūra (Govinda) *See* Govinda Ṭhakkūra
Thana-aṅga Q31:21113
Thera-gāthā Q41:22518
Theri-gāthā Q41:22521
Tīkā-sarvasva by Sarvānanda Vandya-ghaṭīya P15,C:4x1,1,2
Timmaya: *Sarva-lakṣaṇa-sāra-saṅgrahamu* P35,Ex5,1
Tiṇai-mālai-nūṟṟaimpatu O31,1C44
Tiṇai-mozhi-aiṃpatu O31,1C43
Tīrtha-cintāmaṇi by Vācaspati Miśra Q2:4198y8xH30,1
Tiruc-canda-viruttam by Tirumazhiśaī Āzhwār Q22:417x1,16
Tirukkaliṟṟup-pādīyār by Uyya-vanda-devar II R673x1,1,1
Tiru-katukam O31,1C61
Tiruk-kural O31C5
Tiruk-kurun-tāṅḍagam by Tirumaṅgai Āzhwar Q22:417x1,22
Tiru-mālai by Toṇḍaraḍip-podiyāzhwār Q22:417x1,17
Tiru-mandiram by Tiru-mūlar Q23:417x8
Tirumangai Āzhwār: *Periya-tiru-mozhi* Q22:417x1,21
—— *Periya-tiru-maḍal* Q22:417x1,392
—— *Siriya-tiru-maḍal* Q22:417x1,391
—— *Tiruk-kurun-tāṇḍagam* Q22:417x1,22
—— *Tiru-neḍun-tāṇḍagam* Q22:417x1,23
—— *Tiru-vezhu-kūṟ-ṟirukkai* Q22:417x1,38
—— *Nān-mugan-tiru-vandādi* Q22:417x1,34
—— *Tiruc-canda-viruttam* Q22:417x1,16
Tiru-mozhi by Periyāzhwār Q22:417x1,12
Tiru-mūlar: *Tiru-mandiram* Q23:417x8

Vājasaneya-prātiśākhyā by Kātyāyana P15.26Ax1,1
Vākrokti-jīvita by Kuntala O15:*gx*E50,1
Vākya-pradīpa by Bhartṛ-hari P15,C:3x4,1
Vākya-sudhā by Saṅkara R66x1,17
Valaiyāpati O31,1C94
Vallabhācārya: *Aṇu-bhāṣya* R6893,5x1,1
—— *Bhāgavata-tīkā-subodhinī* R6893,7x1,1
—— *Nyāya-līlāvatī* R621x2,1
—— *Tattvārtha-dīpikā* R6893x1,1
Vālmīki △28x16
Vāmana: *Kāvyālaṃkāra-sūtra-vṛtti* O15:*gx*5,1
— *Liṅgānu-śāsana* P15,C22x1,1,3
— *Sruti-kalpa-latā* R68,7xK20,1
Vāmanācārya: *Commentary* on *Kāvya-prakāśa* O15:*gx*8,1,8
Vāmana Jayāditya: *Kāśikā-vṛtti* P15,Cx1,1,3
Vāmana-purāṇa Q21:224
Vamśīdhara Miśra: *Sāṅkhya-tatva-kaumudī-vibhākara* R631x2,1,3,8
Vana-mālī Miśra: *Mādhva-mukhālamkāra* R68xJ20,1
Vanant Q8451:2534
Vāncheśvara Yajvan: *Bhāṭṭa-cintāmaṇi* R641x91,1,L80
Vandya-ghatīya (Sarvānanda) *See* Sarvānanda Vandya-ghatīya
Vanhi-dasao-upānga Q31:21224
Varada-nātha: *Adhikaraṇa-cintāmaṇī* R672xG68,1,1
Varada-rāja: *Bodhinī* R625x3,1,1
—— *Commentary* on *Khaṇḍana-khaṇḍa-khādya* R66x7,1,2
—— *Sāra-saṅgraha* R625x4,1,1
—— *Tārkika-rakṣā* R625x4,1
Varada-viṣṇu: *Śruta-prakāśa-vyākhyā*, *Bhāva-prakāśikā* R672,5x2,1,1,1
Varāha Q124:4x3,1
Varāha-purāṇa Q22:226
Vara-ruci: *Liṅga-viśeṣa-vṛtti* P15,C:22x1,1,1
— *Prākṛta-sūtra* P151x2,1
— *Vṛtti* P15,Cx1,1,1
Vardhamāna: *Gaṇa-ratna-mahodadhi* P15 C302x1,1,3
Vardhamāna: *Kātantra-vistāra* P15,Cx6,1,1,1
—— *Nyāya-kusumañjali-prakāśa* R625x3,1,2

Vedānta Deśika: *Adhikaraṇa-sārāvali* R672xG68,1
—— *Brahmānanda-giri* R66,6x6,1
—— *Gītārtha-saṅgraha-rakṣa* R672,6x1,1,1
—— *Nyāya-pariśuddhi* R672xG68,3
—— *Nyāya-siddhāñjana* R672xG68,4
—— *Śata-dūṣaṇī* R672xG68,6
—— *Tātparya-candrikā* R672,6x2,1,1
—— *Tattva-muktā-kalāpa* R672xG68,2
—— *Tattva-tīkā* R672,5x2,1,3
—— *Vādi-traya-khaṇḍana* R672xG68,5
Vedāntādhikaraṇa-mālā by Gosvāmi Sri Puruṣottamjee R6893,5x1,1,4
Veda-prakāśa by Satya-gñānānanda R64xL40,1
Vedārtha-saṅgraha by Rāmānuja R672x2,3
Vemula-vāḍa Bhīmakavi: *Kavi-janāśrayamu* O35,1:g(P)x1,1
Veṇdidad Q8451:22
Veṇidatta: *Padārtha-maṇḍana* R621xL50,1
Veṇī-dattācārya: *Bheda-jaya-śrī* R68xL50,1
Venkanna (Koṭi): *Āndhra-bhāṣārṇavamu* P35,E:4x3,1
Venkaṭācārya: *Siddhānta-ratnā-vali* R672xK20,1
Venkaṭa-makhin: *Catur-daṇḍi-prakāśikā* NR441,Kx6,1
Venkaṭa-nātha *See* Vedānta Deśika
Venkaṭa-rāma Śāstri (Kallūri) and Saṅkara Raṅgayya: *Bāla-vyākaraṇa-guptārtha-prakāśikā* P35,ExM60,1,1
Veyagāna Q131:215
Vibhaktyartha-nirṇaya by Giri-dhara R625,13x2,1
Vibhanga Q41:232
Vidhāna-pārijāta by Ananta-bhaṭṭa Q2:4y8xL25,1
Vidhi-rasāyana by Appaya Dīkṣita R641xJ50,1
Vidhi-viveka by Maṇḍana Miśra R641x4,1
Vidvan-mano-rañjanī by Rāma-tīrtha R66xJ25,1,3
Vidvat-prabodhinī by Rāma-bhaṭṭa P15,Cx7,1,1,K80
Vidyā-bhūṣaṇa (Rāmacandra) *See* Rāma-candra Vidyā-bhūṣaṇa
Vidyā-cakravartin: *Bṛhaṭ-ṭīkā* or *Sampradāya-prakāśinī* O15:gx8,1,6
—— *Sañjīvanī* O15:gxF20,1,3
Vidyā-dhara: *Ekāvalī* O15:gxH15,1
Vidyā-kara Vājapeyi: *Nityācāra-paddhati* Q2:4xH80,1

Yāmuna: *Gītārtha-saṅgraha* R67,6x1,1

— *Siddhi-traya* R672x1,1

Yāska: *Nirukta* P15,10A3:28x1,1

Yaśodānandan Sarkār: *Pradīpa* LBx3,1,M90

Yasts Q8451:25

Yatīndra-mata-dīpikā by Śrīnivāsa R672xK80,9

Yi Ching Q8412·211

Yogācāra-bhūmiśāstra by Maitreya-nātha R6946x1,2

Yogāja-āgama Q232:2312

Yogānanda-nātha: *Āyur-veda-sūtra* LBx8,1

Yoga-rāja: *Commentary* on *Paramārtha-sāra* R663x3,3,1

Yoga-sāra-saṅgraha by Vijñāna Bhikṣu R635x3,1

Yoga-siddhānta-candrikā by Nārāyaṇa Tīrtha R635x1,1,M20

Yoga-sudhākara by Sadāśivendra Sarasvatī R635x1,1,L50

Yoga-sūtras by Patañjali R635x1,1

Yoga-sūtra-vṛtti by Sadāśivendra Sarasvatī R635x1,1,L50

Yogāvacāra: *Manual* △41:3x1,1

Yoga-vārttika by Vijñāna Bhikṣu R635x1,1,2

Yogāvataropadeśa by Dharmendra △42:3x2,1

Yogindu-deva: *Paramātma-prakāśa* △3xD50,1

Yogopaniṣad △2x4

Yukti-dīpikā R631x2,1,8

Yukti-ṣaṣṭikā by Nāgārjuna R6947x1,2

Yukti-sneha-prapūraṇi by Rāma-kṛṣṇa Miśra R641x7,1,1

Yoga-vāśiṣṭha-Rāmāyaṇa Q21:226

Zad sparam Q8451x2

Zamyad Q8451:2533

Zend fragments Q8451:232

Zōhar △5:8x1